A Constitutional Culture

Exploring neglected aspects of our colonial, revolutionary, and early national history and culture, Early American Studies reinterprets familiar themes and events in fresh ways. Interdisciplinary in character, and with a special emphasis on the period from about 1600 to 1850, the series is published in partnership with the McNeil Center for Early American Studies.

A complete list of books in the series is available from the publisher.

A CONSTITUTIONAL CULTURE

New England and the Struggle Against Arbitrary Rule in the Restoration Empire

Adrian Chastain Weimer

PENN

UNIVERSITY OF PENNSYLVANIA PRESS

PHILADELPHIA

Research in this volume was funded by the Society of Colonial Wars Fellowship in Memory of Kenneth R. LaVoy Jr.

Published by
University of Pennsylvania Press
Philadelphia, Pennsylvania 19104-4112
www.upenn.edu/pennpress

Printed in the United States of America on acid-free paper
10 9 8 7 6 5 4 3 2 1

Hardcover ISBN: 978-1-5128-2397-4
eBook ISBN: 978-1-5128-2398-1

Library of Congress Cataloging-in-Publication Data
Names: Weimer, Adrian Chastain, author.
Title: A constitutional culture : New England and the struggle against arbitrary rule in the Restoration empire / Adrian Chastain Weimer.
Other titles: Early American studies.
Description: 1st edition. | Philadelphia : University of Pennsylvania Press, [2023] | Series: Early American studies | Includes bibliographical references and index.
Identifiers: LCCN 2022034826 | ISBN 9781512823974 (hardcover)
Subjects: LCSH: Constitutional history—New England. | New England—History—Colonial period, ca. 1600-1775. | New England—Politics and government—To 1775. | Great Britain—History—Charles II, 1660-1685. | Great Britain—Colonies—America—History—17th century.
Classification: LCC F7 .W45 2023 | DDC 974/.02—dc23/eng/20220817
LC record available at https://lccn.loc.gov/2022034826

For David D. Hall

CONTENTS

ABBREVIATIONS

AAS	American Antiquarian Society, Worcester, Massachusetts.
ANB	American National Biography Online.
BL	British Library.
CO	Records of the Colonial Office. The National Archives, London. Accessed in part from Colonial State Papers Online, Gale.
ConnRecs	J. H. Trumbull, ed. *Public Records of the Colony of Connecticut*. Vols. 1–3. Hartford, 1850.
DCHNY	John R. Brodhead, ed. *Documents Relative to the Colonial History of the State of New-York*. Vols. 1–10 Albany, 1853.
MaineRecs	Charles Libby, ed. *Province and Court Records of Maine*. Portland, 1931.
MassArch	Massachusetts Archives, Boston.
MassRecs	Nathaniel Shurtleff, ed. *Records of the Governor and Company of Massachusetts Bay*. 5 vols. Boston, 1854.
MHS	Massachusetts Historical Society, Boston.
MsCP	Manuscript Clarendon Papers. John Carter Brown Library, Providence, Rhode Island.
MsWP	Manuscript Winthrop Papers [transcripts]. Massachusetts Historical Society, Boston.
NEHGR	*New England Historical and Genealogical Register.*
NEQ	*New England Quarterly.*
NHRecs	Charles Hoadly, ed. *Records of the colony or Jurisdiction of New Haven*. Hartford, 1858.
ODNB	Oxford Dictionary of National Biography Online.
PlymRecs	Nathaniel Shurtleff, ed. *Records of the Colony of New Plymouth in New England*. Vols. 3–4. Boston, 1855. David Pulsifer, ed. *Records of the Colony of New Plymouth in New England: Acts of the Commissioners of the United Colonies in New England*. Vols. 9–11. Boston, 1859.

RIRecs	John Russell Bartlett, ed. *Records of the Colony of Rhode Island.* Vols. 1–10. Providence, 1856.
SP	State Papers Domestic. The National Archives, London. Accessed in part from State Papers Online, Gale.
WMQ	*William and Mary Quarterly.*

Editorial note: In the text I have silently modernized “u” to “v”, “i” to “j”, and the thorn/y to “th” to facilitate reading. Instead of using double dating for days prior to March 25 (the first day of the “Old Style” year), the year is modernized, so 1 January 1665/66 becomes 1 January 1666.

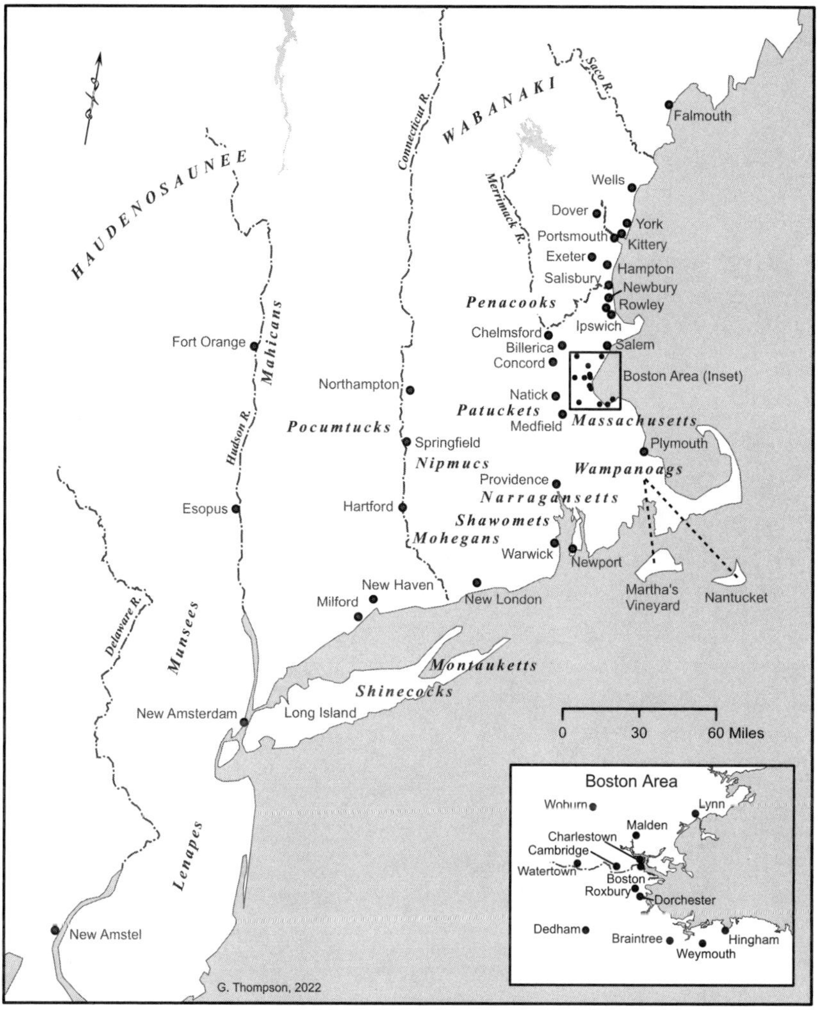

Figure 1. Map of Northeast region in 1664, emphasizing places mentioned in the text.

A Constitutional Culture

INTRODUCTION

On a cold Saturday night in January 1667, at the Ships Tavern in Boston, royal commissioner Sir Robert Carr was drinking with friends. It was the Sabbath, but he showed scant sign of knowing it. As he relaxed with a fellow commissioner and a local merchant in bald-faced indifference to local laws reserving the day for pious, charitable, or necessary ends, his behavior drew attention. Richard Bennett, a Boston constable pledged to uphold those laws, approached the men, ordering Carr and his crew to call it a night. Carr refused, at first with words and then with fists, "asayleing beating & wounding" the enforcing officer. An intoxicated Carr and company departed the tavern and made their way to the home of another merchant to continue drinking. Before long, however, a second constable, Arthur Mason, found the men and asked for Carr's version of events. Given the chance, Carr bragged drunkenly, he "would do it again."[1] Like Bennett, Mason did not suffer the haughtiness gladly. He told Carr that Charles II himself would risk arrest for breaking the Sabbath like this. The party, in turn, called Mason's words treasonous.[2]

Nursing his wounds, the original constable did not let it go. Early the following week, he appeared before Massachusetts magistrate and Major General John Leverett to issue a complaint. A veteran of the English civil wars of the 1640s, Leverett had a long history with the culprit. He had faced off against Carr on the battlefields of England and now, under very different circumstances, he faced his old opponent again. Leverett dissented vigorously from Carr's view of law and sovereignty. Insisting that Carr must obey local laws, he rebuked his "rietous & abusive Carriage to his majestys officer," thereby invoking the royal authority vested in constable Bennett through the colony charter. As he informed Carr about his scheduled court hearing, Leverett did try to muster some deferential language, stating that Carr would be treated "with the greatest respect to your selfe the case wil admit of."[3] Carr spent the evening weighing his options. Would he submit to local justice, risking a Boston jail stay or a hefty fine? Or would he refuse to acknowledge colonial authority?

Carr could have shown up and denied the charges, but there were too many witnesses who had seen exactly what he had done. He could not risk a trial. The next day he pulled rank: "As I am Sir Robert Carr I would have complyed with yor desyers but as I am Clad with the Kyngs Comission I shal not grant yor requests both in respect of his Majestyes honor & my owne duty."[4] Those with a royal commission, Carr claimed, were beyond the law.

Leverett was incensed. He knew what absolutism looked like, and would have none of it in Boston. He issued a warrant for Carr's arrest. But the royal commissioner did not back down, instead threatening Leverett personally and warning him in the king's name to make sure Carr and his servant were "not molested." For reply, Leverett—together with Massachusetts governor Richard Bellingham—ordered Carr apprehended, with special instructions not to inflict any harm. His offenses now included not only abusing Bennett but also "swearing divers oathes" and "Contempt of authority." By this point, Carr had taken refuge in the home of another wealthy royalist, Edmund Downes. Two constables found him there and, standing outside the door, read him the arrest warrant. But Carr refused to go with them, saying "he Could not answer it to the Kings Majesty." When one of the constables ordered Downes to open the locked door, Downes told him Carr had stolen and hidden the key.[5]

A royal commissioner holing up in Boston with a group of known royalists, flagrantly defying arrest? Governor Bellingham thought the incident so serious he called an emergency meeting of the Massachusetts Council. Weather led to delays, however; and Carr decided that now was an excellent time to head back to England.[6] He never did face any consequences to his actions at the Ships Tavern.

Carr's tale might seem minor or even humorous in hindsight, but it offers a microcosm of seventeenth-century constitutional issues: Were kings, or their commissioners, accountable under the law? Where was the line between constitutional defiance and sedition? Although the manuscript records of this particular episode have long been tucked away in an autograph collection, they point to a much larger contest over law and royal power in the early Restoration. Carr's behavior reaffirmed many colonists' fears about an expanding royal prerogative and deepened their commitment to local constitutional ideals.

The regional constitutional culture that emerged in defiance of the Restoration monarchy marks one of New England's major contributions to Anglo-American political history. In the face of royal demands and well-funded royal commissioners, colonists gathered to plan, enact, and justify certain lines the crown should not cross. This mobilizing happened across the social spectrum, from the General Court to taverns, markets, and homes. In a relatively short time frame, from 1660 to 1667, under extraordinary pressure to compromise with the crown, New Englanders developed a cohesive, broad-based constitutional culture.

The category of "constitutional culture" includes much more than laws, charters, or official documents. It also comprises the many forms of local mobilizing that undergirded the colonists' stance on the "transatlantic constitution," or the organic, negotiated, tenuous arrangement of authority between colonies and crown. A constitutional culture includes documents, commentary on those documents, arguments, policies, and "practical conventions," as well as laws and institutions. Involving more than just magistrates, this culture encompasses many kinds of so-called "meddlers" in affairs of state.[7] The constitutional culture forged in New England during the 1660s relied on traditional political forms such as position papers and debates, but it also took shape in more creative ways, including folklore, stories, prayers, and other cultural expressions that helped men and women imagine a limit to royal power. Upholding a strong vision of local authority, and enriched by a wide range of political, artistic, religious, and historical forms, this constitutional culture would define the region for decades to come. Its long-term implications can still be felt in some places.

The constitutional culture of those New Englanders who defied Charles II was marked by a wariness of metropolitan ambition, a defensiveness about civil and religious liberties, and a conviction that self-government was divinely sanctioned. It found expression through a set of well-rehearsed mobilizing practices, including fast days, debates, committee work, and petitions. Equipped with a ready vocabulary for criticizing arbitrary rule, with a providentially informed capacity for risk-taking, and with a set of intellectual frameworks for divided sovereignty, New Englanders forged a potent regional constitutional culture that would not easily succumb to an imperial metropolis intent on consolidating its power.

This work did not appear in a vacuum. Colonists had already undertaken a great deal of constitutional work between 1620 and 1660, building institutions that they saw as pushing the vanguard of reform. Freemen annually voted for deputies representing their towns (the lower house) and nominated and elected a governor, deputy governor, and magistrates (the upper house), who all together met at least biannually as a General Court or Assembly. In 1660, around fifty-five towns sent elected deputies to five General Courts (Massachusetts, Connecticut, New Haven, Plymouth, and Rhode Island), which together served a population of at least 33,000, a number that included freemen, non-freemen, women, children, indentured servants, and enslaved laborers. The Connecticut laws had a provision that the General Court could call itself if denied by the governor. Except Rhode Island, the New England colonies in 1643 formed an innovative confederation, the United Colonies, to regulate expansion, defense, and regional disputes.[8] The architects of these institutions were not radicals like Levellers or Fifth Monarchists. But as major recent studies of the region have shown, puritan colonists enacted legal and economic reforms that supported middling people rather than elites—and they did so in ways that progressives in England had long planned but struggled to implement in the face of entrenched landed interests.[9] Although neither modern nor liberal, these colonial institutions existed to benefit ordinary people.

What's more, these institutions offered benefits few Europeans at the time could claim. It is crucial to acknowledge the significant limitations of these benefits for Native Americans and Africans, free and enslaved, a topic on which historians are doing immensely important work.[10] Yet in general, New England legal systems were marked by simple and accessible law codes and low if any fees for court services, remarkable departures from European precedent. English inhabitants from Stamford to Casco Bay had accomplished an extraordinary amount of work on both the town and colony level, serving on juries, repairing roads, and arbitrating disputes. Towns observed a "near-universal practice" of giving all heads of households a say in local government and its distribution of resources, a practice that resulted in "the economic independence of the great majority of households."[11] Fighting-age men generally elected their own town militia captains. Almost every town had a church: university-trained ministers oversaw theological literacy and spiritual shepherding, but final authority rested with laypeople.

It is important to note that these towns were not designed to be inclusive. Most interviewed people prior to settlement to be sure that prospective residents could support themselves and aligned with the community's religious and civic ideals. Once men and women joined a town, however, if they fell into poverty or struggled with physical or mental disability, a combination of church and government aid—usually in the form of grants, employment help, or boarding (living with another household)—was almost always granted. And while residents sometimes disagreed with town precepts, and while some people, after long debates, either left or were forced out, overall this puritan-influenced social ethic fostered a strong sense of community, at both the town and regional level.[12] In adopting these flexible, highly participatory local institutions, New Englanders drew on the practice of sixteenth-century English towns and boroughs, whose traditions of active self-governance had, by the seventeenth century, drifted toward oligarchy.[13] In New England, however, these practices developed freely and effectively much of the time.

The constitutional landscape appeared quite differently back in England during this same era. Stuart officials at the highest positions in London saw the enforcement of regular parliaments as derogating from the king's inherent rights. Valorizing imperial Rome, post-Restoration officials and many Church of England divines "dwelt upon the sacredness of majesty, the damnableness of rebellion and the duty of obedience" with or without consent or representation. Even "constitutional royalists" who emphasized the king's obligations often still understood his power to be indivisible. While viewing themselves as protectors of liberty, Stuart elites saw the main threat to liberty as nonconformists who by their political intrusions would tear down both church and state. Intent on mitigating the threat of urban corporations and university intellectuals, royal officials set about limiting political access, imposing oaths of nonresistance, and condemning texts that saw rulership as contractual or accountable to the people. Those nonconformists and others who, prizing "electoral choice and consent," tried to maintain the constitutional reforms of the 1640s in England were, in effect, excluded from the conversation—even in powerful corporations such as London. And although they granted a role to laws and parliaments, over time Restoration-era political theorists would come to see these and other liberties as royal concessions, rather than belonging inherently to the people. Crown sovereignty was the "sole guarantor of the liberty of the subject." And only God, not the people, held rulers accountable.[14]

It is well known that after the failure of the Cromwellian regime, the political strength of nonconformists in England rapidly deteriorated. By the 1660s, ideals about broad-based, consensual self-governance and strong constitutional accountability for rulers were collapsing in England and endangered on the European continent. Puritan colonists and their allies saw themselves as one of the last remaining outposts of the spirit of the "good old nonconformists." They understood themselves to be acting within a long tradition of reformers who honored the king but insisted on limits to his power—limits based in religious, civil, and natural law.[15]

In New England, the constitutional narrative grows increasingly tense with the Restoration in 1660—and most strongly with the arrival of royal commissioners on warships in 1664. New Englanders faced an aggressive imperial metropole trying to impose greater leverage over its colonies. Charles II's government might not have understood the puritan-led colonies well, and perhaps royal officials lacked a clear sense of how these odd and—to them—potentially dangerous people fit within the larger imperial picture. But the royal government nonetheless insisted that New Englanders redesign their civic and ecclesiastical institutions to conform to the priorities of the new regime. At first glance, this time-consuming and expensive royal attention toward New England makes little sense. In the early Restoration, the crown tended to focus on sugar colonies such as Jamaica that would directly bolster its investment in the Royal African Company and the slave trade, or on protecting shipping routes from Dutch rivals, or on its new colonies by royal marriage such as Tangier. New England's forests were exploitable resources, and its potential customs duties were significant. But the Stuart government's rationale seems to have been as much political as economic. Pressuring New Englanders into obedience would help establish the new regime's legitimacy, and with it a culture of hereditary privilege.[16]

Crown officials focused especially on Massachusetts Bay, the largest colony and the only one starting the Restoration era with a verified royal charter. How would colonists be able to maintain their nonconformist churches and locally elected, semi-autonomous, puritan-led governments? Tracing the contours of this multifaceted contest requires attention to a broad range of print and manuscript sources: petitions, fast day records, committee notes, position statements of those who served as legal and political counselors; letters filled with providential anecdotes; and court records that highlight the role of Quakers, Gortonists, and Native sachems in shaping political debates. Together these sources reveal, in precise and surprising ways, the formation—despite the odds—of a robust constitutional culture.

While colonists did not agree on everything, most disliked the idea of a royal governor, or the crown overturning the decisions of local courts, or the enforcement of prayer book worship, or the loss of the charter. They wanted to maintain their civil and ecclesiastical liberties. To follow their specific efforts to defend these liberties does not mean subscribing to an older Whiggish history that linked puritanism to modern liberal ideals. Colonists' categories were often more medieval than modern. Importantly, most of these men and women saw liberty not in terms of individual freedom but rather as embedded in social obligations. They longed for the liberty to fulfill those obligations in accordance with biblical conscience and to live free from any kind of "unconstrained authority" in either church or state.[17] Some colonists took the opportunity of the Restoration to raise long-held grievances against local leadership, but their numbers were small. The most vocal of these critics, an alliance of mostly Boston and North Shore merchants, still generally agreed with colony leaders' larger goals, but they made tactical arguments to the effect that calculated concessions to the crown now might prevent further encroachments later.

The constitutional story of early Restoration New England invites us to observe, almost in slow motion, the coalescence of a set of ideas and practices for defending local liberties and fending off arbitrary rule—rule without limits or accountability. Through informal gatherings and formal courts, through prayer meetings, committees, town meetings, fireside conversations, and multiple drafts of letters, statements, petitions, and treatises, inhabitants debated the wisest and most effective course. For the most part, their defiance involved carefully planned political action rather than violence or threats of violence, although they did not rule out lawful rebellion under certain narrow conditions. On a spectrum from words to swords, they stayed well on the side of words. Thousands of people from dozens of towns mobilized with care and deliberation, drawing on lessons from the first charter crisis of 1634–1638, from the English civil wars, from transatlantic Reformed traditions, from natural law, and from the Bible. Both elites and ordinary people discussed the political, economic, theological, and moral dimensions of the contest between local liberties and royal prerogative. Then, following these deliberations, most colonists decided to stand firm behind their elected leaders and defy the king's demands.

As they negotiated the "transatlantic constitution," colonists took part in a century-and-a-half-long contest over how English laws or the king's decrees applied in far-flung colonies, a contest over authority that was in part "unwritten, located in the history and purpose of the English empire in America."[18] Were the colonies simply extensions of England, a geographically distinct but constitutionally uniform part of the king's realm? To this question many New Englanders voiced a resounding "no." Pointing to their charter, they said, in effect: we are under a different constitutional arrangement; we are loyal to the king but we operate as a self-governing enclave, with liberty to uphold local inhabitants' welfare over and above a distant ruler's current priorities.

In the chapters that follow I explore Restoration-era New Englanders' contributions to long-standing debates about the nature of constitutionalism and sovereignty, or what rulers and subjects owe to each other. While relying on archives primarily for one region, I do not aim to reinscribe an older model of stark New England exceptionalism. Related debates had been taking place in the three kingdoms of England, Scotland, and Ireland for centuries. Similar debates were simultaneously occurring in Virginia, where religion remained central to many discussions, and in places like Jamaica and New York, where the policies of royal governors were also met with forms of defiance. Indeed, the consolidating program of the restored Stuart government provoked alarm across the English Atlantic. To middling Protestants generally, Stuart actions seemed "part of a general scheme to deprive them of local control of their own affairs and subordinate them to a new hierarchy of great men claiming neo-feudal privileges." New Englanders were by no means alone in their opposition to a system based on hereditary obligations, politicized bishoprics, and wealthy landed elites. Even so, their local institutions, as John Locke himself noted, were among the most deeply antithetical to a program of consolidated royal authority.[19] This book describes how and why in the early Restoration New Englanders were able to defy what they saw as arbitrary rule, imposed by the crown.

In Chapter 1, I examine the colonists' relationship to the 1649 regicide of Charles I, first as an unthinkable prospect, then, for a few, as somehow justifiable, and finally as both a persistent accusation in anti-puritan tracts and a personal reality for two escaped regicides who arrived in Boston in mid-1660. In Chapter 2, the correspondence that flew back and forth across the ocean and among colonial towns reveals how colonists and their supporters gained access to information, the stories and figures that mattered to them, and the personal and cosmic stakes of the political crisis. In and around the Boston Town House, the setting for Chapter 3, magistrates, deputies, and other community leaders considered how best to honor the king and protect the people's welfare, engaging in the painstaking work of collaborative decision making, doggedly pursuing a rough, working consensus. During these years, men and women gathered frequently for public and private fast days, the subject of the fourth chapter. These were the occasions when most people learned about the political crisis, asked for divine wisdom, participated in communal discernment, and made resolutions about their own contributions. In Chapter 5, I describe the Privy Council's New England goals and instructions, introducing the four royal commissioners who arrived on royal frigates in 1664 and provoked scenes of awkwardness and alarm. Chapter 6 explores the story of the petition campaign of 1664–1665 in Massachusetts Bay, in which at least one-quarter of adult Anglo-American men, including hundreds of non-freemen and even joined by one woman, signed petitions advocating resistance to the royal commissioners' agenda and declaring that they prized their liberties—their right to self-government and congregational worship—more than wealth or life.

In early 1665, the royal commissioners set off on a tour of New England, the topic of Chapter 7. Their negotiations in Plymouth, Rhode Island, Narragansett, and Connecticut demonstrate the reach of royalist ambition. Along the way, their interactions with Gortonists, Quakers, and Narragansett and Shawomet sachems reveal the active role these groups took in shaping constitutional sensibilities. Chapter 8 narrates the climactic showdown in Boston over Charles II's demands and the Massachusetts Bay charter, culminating in a trumpet blast by which colonists declared their defiance of the king. The royal commissioners might have failed in the Bay, but they were not chastened: as we will see in Chapter 9, they traveled further out to the borderlands, attempting to annex multiple regions for the king (or for themselves). In Chapter 10, I follow Bay colonists as they enter an intense season of constitutional debate about the possibility of divided sovereignty—and as they face the most difficult test of their ability to reach consensus: the king's demand for named agents to be sent to London. And finally in Chapter 11, I argue that the Restoration-era culture of constitutional defiance would directly inform the armed men who overthrew royal governor Edmund Andros in 1689 and that it would continue, as one strand among many, to inform New Englanders' rapid organizing in eighteenth-century crises.

Organic and flexible, this constitutional culture refused to be tied down to any single charter or document. It consisted of a well-tuned radar for absolutist encroachment; a set of nimble practices such as petitions, committees, and fast days; and a repertoire of intellectual resources for defending civil and ecclesiastical liberties. Notions of liberty and constitutional boundaries remained central to these New Englanders' sense of themselves as a people, and they took steps to keep that understanding primed and readily available for any new threat to local governance.

Watching the 1660s unfold in New England means entering into a remarkable era of widespread mobilizing, when colonists articulated the grounds of their legal privileges and resolved to hold onto them. Although dwarfed by the revolution of the 1640s in England and less dramatic than the

1689 rebellion in North America, the slow, deliberate constitutional action of the early Restoration marks a crucial and understudied chapter in Anglo-American history. In response to pressures from the Stuart government, colonists creatively and determinedly rallied behind local authority while fending off accusations that they posed a danger to monarchy. They thereby articulated a powerful—and pointed—threshold for deference, limiting their obligations to the crown by summoning their obligations to each other, to God, and to their descendants. In doing so, they formed a resilient, popular constitutional culture.

CHAPTER 1

Shadows

The Memory of Regicide

New Englanders' struggle with Charles II's regime played out in the shadow of regicide. Like other English nonconformists, colonial puritans wrestled with the psychological weight of the 1649 execution of Charles I and their coreligionists' role in that event. The burden they experienced was rooted less in the fall of a despotic ruler than in the violent rupture of the link between divine authority and the body politic that the king embodied. This "deepe wound," as many referred to it, reopened after the Restoration, when high church royalists scathingly satirized puritans as irrational, regicidal fanatics.[1] When a colonist uttered seditious-sounding words about Charles II, the colonial courts took notice, balancing local priorities against the need to distance themselves from the 1649 event. Tensions escalated when Edward Whalley and William Goffe, two judges on the court that condemned Charles I to death, sought refuge in New England in mid-1660. When Charles II demanded their capture, colonists had to think in immediate ways about their constitutional obligations and the ethics of Christian resistance. For critics, Whalley and Goffe's presence in New England constituted overwhelming evidence of what they had assumed all along: puritans could never be truly loyal subjects. For colonists in general, regardless of their political leanings, the two men represented a living link to the constitutional struggles of the 1640s, and an agonizing choice between religious and imperial loyalties.

New Englanders felt the weight of regicide in part because post-Restoration crown-sanctioned historians rubbed nonconformists' faces in it. The Stuart regime favored histories that blamed "puritan-inspired resistance" along with "popular politics" for all the "calamitous violence, religious chaos, social disorder and tyranny" of the previous two decades. Some royalist historians embraced a narrative of conspiracy that placed duplicitous and power-hungry puritan zealots at the center of an international plot to undermine England's government and even its Protestant Reformation. Puritan "culpability" for civil war and king-killing justified purging nonconformists from the new post-Restoration religious and political establishment.[2] Even more darkly, unsanctioned works such as Peter Heylyn's targeted Calvinism generally as motivating "the Tumults, Murthers, and Seditions; the horrid Treasons and Rebellions," whether on the continent or in England.[3] Puritan theology itself was unsafe, on this reading.

Modern historians are working to untangle this narrative, uncovering the range of groups whose members chose the parliamentary side in the English civil wars and noting that some of these groups appeared much more concerned about constitutional or legal issues than religion. We now know how essential it is to separate out how a person thought about Charles I from how he or she viewed regicide or monarchical rule.[4] Puritans stood at the forefront of those protesting Charles I's absolutist policies in the 1630s and 1640s, but few supported the king's execution or envisioned an end to the monarchy. They did, however, help create the conditions under which regicide first became thinkable and then, somehow, doable.

Making matters even more knotty is the fact that four puritans with close New England ties played outsize roles in the events of 1649: the civil war veterans Goffe and Whalley; the prominent Independent minister John Owen, who in 1664 would be invited to the pastorate of Boston's most prominent church; and Hugh Peter, the former pastor of Salem, Massachusetts, whose 1660 execution for his role in the regicide would send shock waves through New England. A brief look at their civil war–era pasts will help bring into focus the regicidal shadows overlaying the post-Restoration constitutional struggle in New England.

We can take our beginnings with William Goffe. A devout puritan layman and a quick-minded, tough-bodied soldier, Goffe helped lead the New Model Army to victory over Charles I's troops in 1645. He then wrestled, as did most army leaders, with the king's decision to abandon negotiations and instead recruit new allies among the Irish and Scots. He and other Independents expressed alarm when the Presbyterian-dominated parliament attempted to disband some army regiments and send others to Ireland without promising that they would pay the soldiers' wages. Goffe often led prayer meetings with the army's leadership. He continually urged them to humility and self-examination as they sought the Lord's will over these seeming betrayals by both king and parliament.[5] Fluent in apocalyptic tropes, Goffe saw the royal supremacy, or the king's role as head of the church as well as the state, as "a mistery of iniquity," an evil to which no Christian should give "life or strength." When kings started acting like popes and setting up idolatry, great changes might have to occur, he mused, perhaps even "great alterations of states." Although not explicitly calling for regicide, Goffe did think further negotiations with the king would be fruitless: Charles I should be brought to trial. Goffe's spiritual insights earned him the respect of army leaders; high-ranking officer Henry Ireton said that Goffe "hath never spoke butt he hath touched my heart."[6] Yet many puritans in the army urged caution, still hoping for an inclusive Church of England, a broader franchise, and a parliament that firmly limited monarchical powers. These arguments became harder to propound after the king escaped house arrest in November 1647 and, forging an alliance with a faction of the Scots, launched a second civil war. The king's perfidy in the negotiation process, together with the shattering effects of the second civil war, stripped Charles I of public support. Puritans' appetite for restoring him personally to power waned. Goffe's desire for a trial increased, and more puritan army leaders joined him in calling for one.

During the same months, another devout layman and regiment commander, Edward Whalley, advanced the possibility of regicide in conversations with Elizabeth Poole, a prophetess invited to mediate New Model Army discussions. Poole presented a vision of the army healing the land; the king was "due to bee judged," she said, but the army was "for the Lords sake to honour his person." The king must not be executed. Whalley protested her reluctance to seek the death penalty: what if Charles I, he asked, was convicted of "very filthy thinges," such as murder or other "great crimes . . . then must hee nott die?"[7] In imagining the death of the king, Whalley went further than most of his fellow puritans. After the New Model Army again defeated royalist troops in 1648, Goffe and Whalley watched, dumbfounded, as parliament renewed the attempt for a personal treaty with the king that ensured a Presbyterian establishment and, possibly, the criminalization of Independency.[8] Army leaders feared a settlement that could open the way to their own arrest, or a third civil war. Many wanted a constitutional convention, a new way of doing things. And they insisted that the king had to be held accountable, though very few at this point contemplated his death.

Hugh Peter, former pastor of Salem, Massachusetts, spent a good deal of time with the New Model Army during these months. He preached and helped organize days of prayer and fasting among the leadership. For most of this period, Peter struck a tone of moderation and compromise. He vocally defended the army, however, when soldiers marched on Whitehall in December 1648 and either arrested or intimidated those members of parliament who had opposed them, an event that became known as "Pride's Purge" (after its leader, Colonel Thomas Pride). Immediately afterward, Peter delivered a fast day sermon justifying these actions. Negotiations continued to stall. By the end of December, army leaders agreed to a trial, although they remained undecided about what the king's fate would be if he was pronounced guilty. They were not unified behind regicide. Lieutenant General Oliver Cromwell had been secretly trying to negotiate Charles I's abdication, with the monarchy passing to another royal heir.[9] The House of Commons's announcement of the king's trial met public outcry. As the possibility of a royal execution became clear, both royalists and many parliamentarians, including most puritans, expressed opposition. Peter was not among them. As one of a handful of prominent puritan clergy who steadfastly supported the army, he personally escorted Charles I to London for the trial and oversaw his imprisonment at St. James Palace. He also repeatedly tried to persuade the king of his guilt, although he supported Charles's request to see his own chaplains. Present through the trial, Peter exhorted the judges—including Whalley and Goffe—to courage; he urged the soldiers to chant "Justice," and he preached the legitimate role of the people "to bind their kings with chains."[10] His actions would brand him as one of the most formidable proponents of the king's execution, a legacy that would haunt New England.

A fourth important voice in these events, puritan minister John Owen, supported Pride's Purge, the trial, and even the regicide. Like Goffe, Owen believed the "Mysterie of Iniquity" was promoted through the royal supremacy—or through any arrangement that intertwined civil and religious authority too closely.[11] As with most of the men involved, he probably expected the trial to force the king into lasting constitutional concessions. When Goffe, Whalley, and fifty-eight other men agreed to serve as judges at the trial, they did not have to agree to the possibility of regicide to do so. But as the proceedings launched in a packed, tense Westminster Hall, the king refused to cooperate, denying the authority of the court altogether. The judges' options were dwindling. Historians still debate whether the judges introduced the possibility of regicide as a real option or only as a reluctant, desperate attempt to compel Charles to negotiate. Even after all the king's trespasses, his subjects had not formed any widespread or popular movement agitating for his death. Most puritans looked on with horror, in fact, as the judges' verdict, guilty of treason, came in and as, on 30 January 1649, the king faced the executioner.

Whether fairly or not, Owen and Peter emerged from the fray as two leading defenders of the regicide. They did not seem to mind their newfound reputation. After the verdict but prior to the execution, Peter preached the king's funeral sermon, reflecting on the biblical "terrible denunciation to the King of Babilon."[12] The day after the king's death, Owen preached for a House of Commons fast day. He did not frame the regicide as a positive event but rather as an outpouring of divine judgment on the English people. Still, the judges were right, he implied, to avoid the model of King Saul, who, out of covetousness, had refrained from killing King Agag. Owen argued that subjects possessed a "retained sovereignty" that made them ultimately responsible for the monarch's unrighteous actions, and so legitimately empowered them, when necessary, to restrain and even destroy a king.[13]

Not everyone shared this bold opinion. Former New Englander Nathaniel Ward strongly condemned the regicide both before and after the king's beheading, delivering his opposition through sermons and in print.[14] Most puritans sided with Ward. Indeed, "most of the godly never forgave the army and its friends for killing the king rather than making the best deal they could with him." Even for those who might have sympathized with the judges, the king's death was dreadful, a judgment foreboding only ill things to come.[15] At the same time, trenchant proverbs such as "Presbyterians held him by the hair, till Independents cut off his head," gained popularity, retaining their long life span probably because they had a grain of truth to them.[16] And the prominent roles of puritans such as Whalley, Goffe, Peter, and Owen, men with strong ties to New England, ensured that the specter of regicide would overshadow the transatlantic constitutional contest during and after the Restoration.

* * *

Keenly attuned to all these events in England, Bay colony ministers had hinted at the legitimacy of regicide as early as 1635. In a jointly authored treatise on the nature of church and state, they had allowed church members who held civil authority to "suppresse by force the violence of Usurpers, as Jehoiada did Athaliah."[17] In this line of thinking, they followed John Calvin—himself indebted to Lutheran and medieval thought—who insisted that "where the glory of God is not the end of government there is no legitimate sovereignty, but usurpation." Therefore lesser magistrates (not individuals) could resist tyrannical rulers. Englishman Thomas Cartwright further developed this Calvinist resistance theory, arguing as early as 1575 that obedience to magistrates "owght to be squared owt first by the love off God then off men / our brethren especially." Submission to a ruler's decrees, in other words, should go only as far as their injunctions agreed with God's glory and the people's good.[18]

These ideas about legitimate resistance to authority no doubt influenced Bay colonists' decision in the 1630s to defy an attempted royal takeover. The Commission for Foreign Plantations, headed by the anti-puritan Archbishop William Laud, had issued a *quo warranto* (legal challenge) against the Massachusetts charter, with plans to revoke it and impose a crown-appointed governor. Faced with the possible loss of the colony's self-governance, John Winthrop and other magistrates asked local ministers for advice. These clergymen responded that the colony "ought not to accept" a royal governor, and if one were sent to American shores, the colonists should "defende our lawfull possessions (if we were able) otherwise to avoide, or . . . protracte." Winthrop and other leaders insisted that their property and privileges were their own, and "not subject to illegal seizure by the king's servants or his courts." The Stuart government dismissed these arguments, readying a warship to convey a royal governor to Boston. The colonists prepared to defend their territory by force. In what seemed to many a clear providential reversal, the warship proved unseaworthy.[19] When the Stuart government finally did revoke the Massachusetts charter in 1637, colonial magistrates refused to send it back to England, saying if they did the people would consider themselves "freed from their allegiance and subjection" and therefore independent from the crown.[20]

Prominent first-generation ministers such as Thomas Shepard emboldened colonists in these actions (in sermons later printed for the Restoration-era crisis). Shepard preached in the 1630s: "Being come hither for publick helps, and means, and all Ordinances; Oh do not betray your Liberties! but lose your Bloud before you lose them, and the Lord in them." From Laud, whom he distrusted, Shepard feared "as deep [a] mischief plotting against New-England as ever the Sun saw. Enemies will first deal subtilly before cruelly, but subtilly that they may deal cruelly." He went on to declare that God's presence, stirring up prayer and faith, would grant protection to New Englanders. Viewing an elected magistracy as crucial to the preservation of their churches, Shepard urged his listeners: if Charles I's government "make Laws, deride them; if they execute Laws, appeal from them."[21]

Similar ideas would receive formal support in the Scottish National Covenant of 1638, which qualified a pledge to defend the king with the stipulation that he preserve "true religion," and which implied that "were a king to introduce corruption, the people were empowered to purge church and state on their own." In England, related concepts appeared in parliament's Protestation of 1641, which separated loyalty to the monarch from the defense of "true reformed protestant religion."[22] Colonists followed these proclamations closely. Boston minister John Cotton's sermons on the Book of Revelation in the early 1640s justified the Scottish rebellion against Charles I, advocated curtailing the powers of monarchy, and argued for strong limits on all earthly power, whether in church or state.[23]

Colonial leaders would later declare their neutrality in the English civil wars, a claim belied by the number who served as soldiers or chaplains for the parliamentary army, by Massachusetts's 1644 law prohibiting local royalist recruitment, and by prayerful fasts for England's "Godly Parliament" and its "Victorious Army."[24] Even so, the war itself seemed a dreadful scourge even across the Atlantic. As Harvard student and Rowley schoolteacher John Brock wrote of the events of 1647 in England, "The Rod is shaken over the Country. Many a Time are we delivered. The King is above all: The Parliament looks upon us. God will not, as yet, be at Peace with England." Although mourning news of colonists' deaths in the war, Brock noted that "God is with the English Army." And when the New Model Army gained ground in late 1647, he expressed hope that "Our Church Way [congregationalist] may be in England."[25] Many New Englanders joined Brock in celebrating parliamentary victories.

When news of the regicide reached Brock, however, he did not celebrate. Instead, with awe he wrote: "King is beheaded! O dreadful Judgment! The Beginning of Sorrows!"[26] Rather than justice on a tyrant, Brock saw in the regicide a judgment on all. Similarly, the Boston merchant John Hull called the king's beheading "a very solemn and strange act; and God alone can work good by so great a change, both to the nation and to the posterity of the king."[27] Like most English puritans, New Englanders reacted with grim shock to the beheading of their king.

There were a few exceptions. Harvard president Henry Dunster saw Charles I getting what he deserved. He defended the New Model Army's "principle of reforming verity" in a letter to his former parishioners in Bury (Lancashire) who had asked how he and other New Englanders "relish the proceedings" in England. Although reform came through "popular men and means," Dunster wrote, the changes underway were like a "fullers soap purifying the sonns of Levi."[28] "Truely," he declared, "wee are all one heart (I mean the body of the Godly) with the parliament and Army." Directly justifying the regicide as a clear and obvious "Act of glorious justice," Dunster reflected: "If they had ever found Charles pliable to Termes of piety or righteousness in sincerity, & not still doubling with them he had bin King unto this day. But whoever eyther reads Mayes story [Thomas May's 1650 *A Breviary of the History of the Parliament of England*] or Heeds the Kings words and Declaracions with his Contradictory Actions, shall be forced (yea though he weer the kings owne sonne) to say he deserved to Die by the Lords appointment."[29] Dunster then cited Proverbs: "A man that doeth violence against the blood of a person, shall flee unto the grave, and they shall not stay him."[30] For Dunster, God was at work in these righteous actions, even in the regicide.

In the same letter, Dunster alluded to a colony-wide thanksgiving day in Massachusetts, organized by clergy in late 1650 and celebrated in January 1651, close to the anniversary of the king's execution. No New England court records in 1650 or 1651 acknowledge Charles I's death, so this thanksgiving day can be seen as the first official response. The day was set apart for gratitude for "for gods exceeding mercyes towards old England in the prosperous good successe of the armie there under the conduct of Coronall Crumwell." Thanks was due especially for victories against Irish and Scots.[31] Cotton preached an extraordinary sermon for this occasion that drew on decades of political reflection and, like Dunster, defended Pride's Purge and even the regicide.[32]

Cotton's sermon is worth a careful reading. Taking a position similar to John Owen's, he did not outright reject monarchy, but his words make clear he was not fond of it. He had alluded to this opinion much earlier: in the ca. 1641 debate on his proposed law code, "Moses His Judicials," Cotton had argued that David's monarchy was "fit" because it led to Christ, but "hereditary government by succession" was, in ordinary circumstances, "not safe for any kingdom, or very seldom fit for any nation."[33] In his 1651 thanksgiving sermon, Cotton returned to these ideas as he responded to those colonists who "Scruple the Lawfulness" of recent events in England. It is tempting to see Cotton as representative of Bostonians' opinions, but it is more likely the case that his anticipated objections reflect his audience's typical views. These objections suggest colonists were deeply troubled by the regicide. Colonial puritans knew that they shared in the opprobrium directed against "Sectaries in Religion & Such as are usurpers & traitors against the state of the kingdome."[34] At issue were not only long-standing legal, ethical, and spiritual principles but also the fury and ire now being directed at puritans for their role in the king's death.

Cotton took on both difficulties. He first acknowledged that "it is a matter of Great thoughts of Heart: the putting to Death the Late king," and men's spirits, he knew, were "much exasperated" in trying to understand it. He offered a version of Calvinist resistance theory in which lesser magistrates could legitimately rise up against tyrants, distinguishing between a "Disloyall & a wicked Conspiracy" and "A Lawfull & Loyall Conspiracy." Cotton knew, however, that his audience would find this line difficult to toe, particularly when one added into the mix the oath previously taken by many nonconformists in the Solemn League and Covenant, a 1643 agreement by Scots and English parliamentarians for a unified state under Charles I with a Presbyterian national church. This oath included a pledge to maintain the king's "Life & honour." What were they to do now with that abandoned promise? Cotton cleverly argued that the covenant was conditional and that its most important provisions involved providing "for the worship of god" and preserving "the Liberty & safety of the people against tyrany."[35] Put simply, the king's safety was not above religion or the people's well-being.

But what about Pride's Purge? Cotton knew this event to be a point of profound "Contention," especially because "Religion itselfe is Said to Suffer A deepe wound in the eyes of all christendome upon this Cariage." Indeed, a majority of ministers in both England and Scotland (including Ipswich's own Nathaniel Ward) had preached against the army's use of the sword on parliament.[36] To address these concerns, Cotton relayed his understanding of the events leading to the purge: the failed negotiations with the king and parliament's irregular elections in late 1648. He evoked a hypothetical parallel in Massachusetts that hearkened back to the *quo warranto* of the 1630s and Charles I's plan to send over a royal governor. What if the General Court then had voted that it was "Unsafe to the state of church & Commonwealth" to receive a royal governor, but then "A Sudeine Confluence of Deputies & Some magistrates shall Reverse that act"? In that circumstance, he asked, would it be right for the major general of the militia, "with the Consent of his trained Bands (which are through god the strength of the Countrey)," to take action? Could this major general not "Seclude Such of the magistrates or Deputies as were Redy to Betray the Safety of church & Common wealth, which they had Bought & maintained with theire Blood"?[37] Given this kind of revolutionary preaching, it is not surprising that even years later, in 1663, high church royalists such as Maine's Robert Jordan were still cursing John Cotton as a "lyar . . . gone to hell with a packe of lyes" and accusing Massachusetts colonists of being "Trators & Rebells aganst the King."[38]

In London in the days immediately following the regicide, confusion reigned. It was not at all clear that the monarchy would go the way of Charles I. Although the Rump Parliament moved quickly to abolish the monarchy, for most people in and around parliament, such a decision remained a fraught undertaking, far riskier than simply discontinuing the Stuart succession. Even those who viewed monarchy as "elective"—a choice of the people, rather than divine right—were not sure they wanted to let the institution go away entirely. It is quite possible that if there had been a viable alternative heir, "there would have been no republic."[39] After deliberations in which avoiding a third civil war became paramount, the Rump decided to invest the powers of the monarchy in a Council of State rather than in another Stuart king. Following the Rump's lead, English writers such as John Milton used Hebraic and classical sources to elaborate on the dangers of monarchy and the blessings of a sovereign parliament.[40]

Roxbury's John Eliot was one of the few colonial ministers who joined Milton in the theological project of delegitimizing monarchy. In the summer of 1649, hearing news of the regicide, Eliot saw "that Antichristian principle for man to be above God, whether the Pope in the Church, or Monarches in the Common-wealth, is thrown to the ground." It was a bright moment, he exclaimed: the Lord had "put into the hands of this renowned Parliament and Army" the "glorious work of . . . setting up the glorious kingdome of Christ."[41] As Eliot contemplated events in England and studied the ideal form of government for Native American praying towns, he searched the scriptures and found commonwealth, not monarchy, as the Christian ideal. Revisiting these ideas in the early 1650s in a treatise, *The Christian Commonwealth*, Eliot decried the English monarchy as a human invention, rightly "cast down" along with human inventions in the church. Once these old forms had been struck down, he argued, "the Lord Jesus will bring down all people, to be ruled by the Institutions, Laws, and Directions of the Word of God," not only in churches but also in civil government. Where Calvin, Owen, and Dunster had found the word of God flexible on the preferred form of human government, Eliot took a firmer line: he claimed that "there is undoubtedly a forme of Civil Government instituted by God himself in the holy Scriptures." Implicit in Eliot's vision was an obligation to resist a government that failed to operate according to the Word. The people should make the "Word of God . . .

their only Magna Charta," he maintained.[42] Eliot's version of godly rule was distinct in its open anti-monarchicalism and in the extent of its dependence on the Hebrew scriptures, although it bore affinities with the tradition of Calvinist resistance that included Shepard and Cotton, among others.[43] Significantly, Eliot insisted that if grounded in proper authority, a text itself, rather than the accumulated decisions of persons, could become the ultimate law.

Eliot's writings also serve as a reminder that colonists in the 1650s experienced a remarkable freedom of thought and action. They solidified and refined the constitutional work of the previous two decades, adding towns, negotiating disputes among magistrates and deputies about their respective powers, and continuing to develop the United Colonies confederation. They used this freedom to develop commercially, ignoring parliament's 1651 Navigation Act, and to expand territorially, convincing townspeople in Piscataqua and Maine that it was in their best interest to submit to the Bay and its protection. Many towns submitted because they liked functioning courts, ready defense, and legal security for their freehold lands. Colonists understood themselves as English and would have expected help from London if in real distress. Yet Massachusetts negotiated its own commercial and political alliances, declared its own wars, and coined its own money—actions that, in theory, only sovereign powers should carry out. In the Bay, coins bore only the inscription "Massachusetts in New England," and freemen swore oaths only to the colony. When parliament requested that members of the Massachusetts General Court sign writs in the name of the "Keepers of the Liberties of England" and initiate charter renewal, they politely declined.[44] No warships came to enforce Cromwellian rule over the Northeast as they did in the Chesapeake. On occasion, colonists in the 1650s sharply criticized Cromwell, especially when he tried to rule with the aid of the army rather than parliament. But in general, the Lord Protector shielded New Englanders from their enemies even when they declined to participate in his wars, letting the entire region develop with remarkable freedom into a distinctive constitutional polity.

* * *

When the experiment of puritan rule in England failed in 1660, nonconformists on both sides of the Atlantic had to reimagine their lives in the aftermath of a crushing political defeat. Working with limited and confusing information, New Englanders struggled to come to terms with the chaotic end of the Cromwellian regime. To them it seemed that a political hailstorm was hovering, one that might pummel the tender shoots of godly government, "threatning the utter frustrating of those hopefull beginnings" on both shores.[45] For most of their history, colonists could proudly say that "we in this poor Country have had an open door."[46] Now that door appeared to be closing. As Dorchester pastor Richard Mather wrestled to interpret the upheavals in England, he chose to preach from the Book of Ezekiel: "I will overturn, overturn, overturn, it: and it shall be no more, until he come whose right it is; and I will give it him." Mather might have had a hand in writing the Bay's colony-wide fast day proclamation in June 1660, "imploring of the Lords favorable presence yet to be continewed" among the people. If God was present, then even these recent "unsetlements & overturnings in church and state" in "our dear native countrie" could be seen as somehow advancing God's kingdom.[47] Put another way, for many puritans, political crises could signal a hopeful work of God. The continuity of a regime ultimately mattered less than the advancement of Christ's rule, and if the Stuart monarchy did return, who knew if it would be permanent? Nonetheless, as they worried about the lives and livelihoods of friends and relatives in England, the same colonists who grasped for signs of hope also grieved the end of the Cromwellian era.

Charles Stuart's return from exile in May 1660, enacted in a triumphant hours-long procession through the London streets, brought with it not just a resumption of royal ceremony but also new uncertainties. Surely he would not embrace those who had orchestrated or allowed his father's death and engineered his own exile—but would he exact revenge on them? The new king's religious convictions became a topic of speculation. Some thought he harbored "papist" leanings: his mother, Henrietta Maria, was Catholic; he had asked Pope Innocent X for help regaining the throne; and at various points he had forged alliances with Catholics in Ireland, France, and Spain. Others pointed out his tendency to show mercy to nonconformists. In negotiations with Presbyterians prior to the Restoration, Charles II had signed the Declaration of Breda, a document drawn up by Edward Hyde (soon to be Earl of Clarendon) and others that promised "free and general pardon" to nonconformists except for the regicides. He initially offered Presbyterians such as Richard Baxter high appointments, acknowledging the group's role in restoring his throne.[48] Colonial Presbyterians like Thomas Parker, minister of Newbury, Massachusetts, expressed genuine hopes for the new king's "noble achievements" in promoting godly churches and learning.[49]

In the months that followed the royal return to power, Charles II, the Privy Council, and various committee members in London debated how to deal with the puritan-led colonies now. Should they repeat Charles I's attempt to impose a royal governor? Would a Church of England bishop more effectively promote royal interests?[50] Answering these questions proved difficult, in no small part because the new Stuart government lacked the most basic information about New England, possessing not even a map or a copy of the Massachusetts charter, much less any details about New Englanders' courts, laws, trade, or militias.

Those who rushed to provide this information often came bearing an agenda. Most prominent was the Bostonian Samuel Maverick. Although Maverick was the only non–church member in Massachusetts granted freemanship (a political status with the franchise), he had long nursed grudges, loudly proclaiming that only a strong show of force—including revoking the charter—would reduce the colony to obedience. The wealthy royalist Thomas Breedon also offered his services to the crown as an informant, blasting the Bay for viewing itself as a "free State" and insisting that the colonial population was groaning under an oppressive General Court.[51] Old claimants to northern New England territory such as Robert Mason castigated Massachusetts leaders as utterly disloyal. If not checked, Mason said, the New England colonies would become the "invincible States of America." Colonial coins, writs, oaths, and disdain for higher judicial appeal told a silent tale of disloyalty. Even worse, some New Englanders "did resolve to oppose him" if the king sent a royal governor, or claimed they "would sell their Collony to the King of Spaine" if the king undermined their local courts by hearing appeals. Few critics really believed that puritan-led colonies would submit to Catholic Spain, but was the Netherlands a possibility?[52] Detractors often listed Hugh Peter and other undesirables with New England connections as proof that the colonists were "fanatics" who needed to be quickly and forcibly reduced. So Edward Godfrey could say that Maine under Massachusetts's control was "mad[e] a receptacle of those of Heugh Peeter, [Henry] Vane: [Thomas] Venner: Baker: [Vincent] Potter," all either regicides or men branded as dangerous seditionists.[53]

The newly appointed Lord Chancellor Clarendon listened carefully to these concerns. He took a personal interest in New England and made it a priority for the recently formed Council for Foreign Plantations. Although other colonies such as Jamaica and Virginia were more lucrative, for Clarendon, New England held strategic importance. He weighed the options, eventually coming up with a plan both more comprehensive and more careful than efforts in the 1630s to bring New England in line with the priorities of the crown. As he did so, Clarendon gathered information about the colonists' responses to the Restoration. He paid special attention to their reception of Edward Whalley and William Goffe, who, fearful for their lives, fled to Boston in July 1660.

The tale of this flight and its aftermath is worthy of consideration. It reveals even more fully how the shadow of regicide, now tangibly present in the persons of the two judges, raised the stakes of the Restoration-era contest. Should Whalley and Goffe receive shelter? As the crown demanded the men's capture, answering that question meant bringing more fundamental constitutional dilemmas, or what precisely colonists still owed to the king, into open debate within the colonies.

* * *

What might have been going through Cambridge minister Jonathan Mitchell's mind as he learned that his parishioner Daniel Gookin had sailed to Boston in the company of William Goffe and Edward Whalley? A gifted second-generation intellectual, Mitchell had been mentored during his Harvard years by Thomas Shepard and had received the honor of succeeding Shepard in the Cambridge pulpit in 1650. Though young, Mitchell was a seasoned diplomat. He had orchestrated Henry Dunster's removal from the Harvard presidency (for heterodoxy, unrelated to his political views) without losing the latter's trust or friendship. Mitchell would have known that Whalley and Goffe were among the signers of Charles I's 1649 death warrant and that they had gone on in the 1650s to serve in Oliver Cromwell's government. He was not sure what he thought about the regicide. Later in life, he would say that after the two men's arrival in Boston, he took time "by reading and discourse, to look a little into that action for which these men suffer"—the king's execution—and "I could never see that it was justifiable."[54] Yet the arrival of two distinguished civil war veterans, men known for their godly piety, had to have stoked Mitchell's curiosity, even if he sensed the danger that accompanied their presence.

Why Whalley and Goffe chose New England as their safe harbor is not entirely clear. By birth, marriage, or friendship, the two men were related to families with New England ties, although they did not enjoy direct acquaintance with many colonists.[55] The strongest connection came through Whalley's sister Jane Hooke. Her husband, William Hooke, had served for a decade with John Davenport as a teacher in the New Haven church before the Hookes returned in the mid-1650s to England, where William served as chaplain to Oliver Cromwell (nephew to Jane and Edward Whalley's mother, Frances Cromwell). William Goffe had married Edward Whalley's daughter Frances (Jane Hooke's niece) and the Hookes were already sheltering Frances and three daughters. When the regicides left for Boston, they might still have hoped for amnesty from the new Stuart government, but a quick departure seemed wise to be on the safe side. If convicted of treason, their intestines would be ripped out before their severed heads and limbs were displayed as a warning to all who would "compass or imagine the death" of a king.[56]

Whalley and Goffe surely hoped that godly New Englanders would take them in. During the ocean journey, the men "kept Sabbath abord," probably joined by Gookin in their worship. As they rode the swells and prayed, the two regicides must have thought about their wives and children back in England, about the rapid and baffling turn of political events, and about what kind of welcome they might receive on new shores.[57]

On arrival they lodged in Daniel and Mary Gookin's Cambridge home, meeting Mitchell and attending his church. Goffe gave Mitchell "testimonials" from two English ministers regarding his faithfulness and orthodoxy. Whalley may have presented a testimonial as well; he had belonged to the London church led by the distinguished puritan Thomas Goodwin. Although few details of this initial meeting remain, the encounter was warm enough to inspire Goffe to present Mitchell a handwritten paper, a kind of condensed relation of faith. Goffe explained that he wrote it to remind himself "hereafter of my present purposes to cleave to the Lord" as the spirit enabled him. He desired his words to be read aloud to the Cambridge congregation and thus to serve as his introduction to the godly community—as well as offering a public testimony of God's deliverance:

> Having received much mercy from the Lord, at his Leaving his Native country, and in his passage thro: the great deeps; as also in this Land; wherein he is a Stranger: Now before the Lord in the congregation of his people, doth humbly desire that the praises due unto God, -may be rendred on his behalfe. And that the Lord may be Entreated yet to follow his poor Unworthy Servant with goodness & mercy; that he may walk as becometh the Gospel, & forever cleave to the Lord; & Love him, and Serve him, in all conditions.[58]

In this public narrative Goffe used a vocabulary colonial puritans recognized and revered: praise for divine mercy, acknowledgment of personal unworthiness, and submission to the discipline of the Christian community. Personally unknown to most congregants, he requested and received a place within the spiritual body. Without delay, Whalley and Goffe were welcomed into the church—including both ministerial and lay gatherings—as kindred spirits to the colonists.

Following a visit from Mitchell and others, Goffe praised the vibrant communal discussion, writing that "our discourse tended to provoke to give up our selves wholly to Jesus Christ & make him the whole delight of our Souls." In Cambridge, the two men attended "occasional lectures, fasts, and thanksgivings," as well as "private meetings for devotion."[59] They also led meetings in the Gookin home, "where they preached & prayed" and "were in exceeding great esteem for their piety & parts."[60] Fascinated with John Eliot's evangelizing mission, Goffe attended an "Indian lecture," taking detailed notes on Native Americans' questions about human agency in salvation, the sword of the spirit and conscience, Judas's free will, and access to baptism.[61] Goffe noted in his diary that Harvard president Charles Chauncy, "expressing much affection," said that "he was perswaded that the Lord had brought us to this Country for good both to them and our Selves." Whalley and Goffe engaged in pastoral visits to the sick and received "blessed entertainment" from a broad spectrum of colonists.[62] Shared piety accelerated their entry into the community.

Not everyone approved. As tight a community as Boston could seem to outsiders, the seaport hosted a variety of perspectives. Seeing Whalley and Goffe walking in the street with a group of clergy, a royalist stopped them and said that if they had not been in such company, "he would have had us by the hair of our heads." Goffe responded with a biblical quip: his hairs were "numbred by the Lord." But he was driven to more somber meditation later that evening when shown a newly arrived warrant that declared the regicides would have no pardon. The warrant further warned that if they did not turn themselves in, they would forfeit their lives and estates. The two men knew their lives were at risk, but forfeiting their estates was an added blow for their families. Goffe turned to a passage in Hebrews 13 exhorting contentment rather than covetousness; taking comfort in God's presence, he knew the godly could say, "The Lord is my helper, and I will not fear what man shall do unto me."[63]

While Whalley and Goffe were coping with the possible loss of their estates, other colonists were probably taking in the final provision on the warrant: those who would "harbor or conceal" any of the named regicides would themselves be "under pain of Misprision of high Treason."[64] The decision about harboring the regicides would be one of the most difficult colonial puritans faced. After all, Whalley and Goffe were more than army veterans or Cromwellian officials; they were leaders in the cause of Christ, individuals whose powerful spiritual gifts helped usher in God's presence. For many puritans, turning these men in to the English authorities to face trial and execution would mean betraying Christ's own. Yet continuing to shelter them would make any protestations of loyalty to the crown ring hollow in London.

On 22 February 1661, Governor John Endicott gathered the magistrates in the Town House to discuss their options. After an intense exchange, no decision emerged. A ship had just arrived with the ghastly news that Hugh Peter, along with ten others, had been "hanged dra[w]n and quartered."[65] The Boston-area ministers suggested a colony-wide fast day to hear the Lord's will and to ask for "the Continuance of our peace & libertys in Church & Common wealth." As John Hull recorded, "it was the serious desire of many" as they fasted and prayed "that the Lord would direct the country concerning these two gentlemen, Mr. Whally and Goffe." The colonists had to decide whether to obey the king and arrest them or—at great risk—"to suffer them, if they see cause, to go whither they please." Colonists knew that wrapped up in this decision was the royalists' persistent accusatory question, whether "our religion doth not teach us to be disloyal."[66]

For a core group of colonists, protecting Whalley and Goffe became an act of faith and a sign of puritan solidarity in the face of an aggressive high church ascendancy. When royalist merchant Thomas Breedon all but ordered Governor Endicott to arrest the two men, Endicott countered that "without a commission from England none should meddle with them." Breedon was then, by his own account, "abused by many" who called him "malignant." Even more audaciously, Marshal General Edward Michelson, "grinning in his face," taunted the crown-supporting Breedon: "Speak against Whalley and Goffe, if you dare, if you dare, if you dare."[67] That a man like Breedon, who had a record of open disdain for local institutions, insisted on arresting the regicides probably further deepened others' desire to protect them.

Whalley and Goffe did not wait around to hear how the Boston debates would play out. Just prior to the February fast, they decided either that their presence was putting the Bay at too much risk or that they were too vulnerable in the Boston area—or perhaps both factors played a role. They secretly set out under cover of darkness for New Haven, where minister John Davenport was arranging for their concealment.[68] The Boston colonists must have breathed a sigh of relief, especially when they heard, through sources in Barbados, that the king himself knew Whalley and Goffe were in New England and was expecting colonists to apprehend them. Aware of the regicides' safe escape, on 8 March 1661, Endicott and the Council finally issued a warrant for the two men's arrest. They issued it, however, to Marshal General Michelson, the same man who had spoken the "if you dare" comment to Breedon. Largely a symbolic action, the warrant was nonetheless meticulously copied and sent to London.[69]

Receiving a stern official letter from the king regarding the regicides in late April or early May, Endicott made a unilateral decision that puzzled many. He engaged two recently arrived royalists, Thomas Kellond and Thomas Kirke, to find and arrest the fugitives.[70] According to Thomas Temple, Endicott made this move "after a serious consultation" with Temple and "others of approved integrity and fidelity to his Majestie." Although a relative of the puritan nobleman Lord Saye and Sele, Temple had his priorities elsewhere: his main goal was to shore up his control over Nova Scotia; without Endicott's knowledge, Temple also arranged a "secrett designe" with merchants John Pynchon and Richard Lord to capture the regicides, a sure way to curry favor with the crown. John Hull later reported that "many very honestly minded of the deputies, and some among the magistrates, could not consent to own the governor's acting without the council" in sending Kellond and Kirke to apprehend the two men, resulting in a prolonged and frustrated court meeting.[71] New Englanders' local constitutional arrangement, built and refined over three decades, involved broad-based, representative, largely consensual deliberations. Why would Endicott have made such a momentous spiritual and political decision on his own?

More than anyone, Endicott knew that the longer the regicides resided freely in the Bay, the more opportunity would arise for detractors to accuse the entire population of sedition and call for a royal governor to be installed. A former Harvard student who had boarded with the Boston minister John Norton, now an aspiring playwright back in London, John Crown told royal officials that Endicott had personally "embraced" Whalley and Goffe and "wished more such good men as they would come over."[72] "Penitence for the horrid murther for which they fled," Crown sneered, "did not appear to be any part of that piety which sainted them in their esteem." Probably embellishing the truth, Crown claimed that "Whaley said frequently & openly . . . that if what he had done against The King were to be done he would do it again." Breedon similarly reported that "the two Hectors [braggarts] Whally and Goffe" were "dayly bussing [buzzing] in their Ears a change of Government in England." Samuel Maverick saw a conspiracy between the regicides and the Dutch, with New Englanders' collusion.[73] Still other detractors in London would go so far as to report that "Whalley and Goffe were in the head of an army in New England," provoking Lord Saye and Sele, the colonists' main advocate on the Privy Council, to call these detractors "rogues" who "belyyed the Country."[74] Endicott realized it would be almost impossible to claim allegiance to the crown without making some effort to capture the two men. Perhaps, given the tension within the General Court, he could not foresee a consensual decision; or perhaps he wanted to take the guilt of the action onto himself. In any case, Endicott hired Kellond and Kirke to hunt down the regicides, although without local cooperation they were unlikely to succeed in their mission.

While these events were unfolding, the Massachusetts General Court undertook another symbolic pledge of loyalty, making the painful decision to approach John Eliot about his *Christian Commonwealth*, which had just come to print in 1659, probably sponsored by those hoping to forestall the return of the crown. Eliot's specific targeting of monarchy as antichristian was now live ammunition for the Bay's critics, and as much as colonists admired the Roxbury pastor, they now felt compelled to take action. In May 1661 the court asked Eliot to disown the book. By this point word had reached the colony of former New Englander and Fifth Monarchist Thomas Venner's violent revolt against the king, an uprising that rapidly hardened the regime against nonconformists.[75] Eliot did what fellow colonists needed him to do, acknowledging "such expressions" in his book "as doe too manifestly scandalize the government of England, by King, Lords, & Commons, as anti Christian, & justify the late innovators." He also testified that monarchy was "not only a lawfull, but an eminent forme of government," although he added an interesting qualifying postscript: "All forms of civil government deduced from Scripture" are "of God, & to be subjected unto for conscience sake." In effect, Eliot disowned only those parts of his argument that were inconsistent with the Bible. Bay leaders did not quibble with the statement, for it still helped them accomplish their larger goal. Suppressing *Christian Commonwealth*, they hoped, would be seen as an expression of true allegiance. They posted

Eliot's statement in five major towns along with an order recalling copies of the book.[76] Whether people obeyed the order or the court destroyed the copies remains unknown; it is not, however, difficult today to find extant volumes. In his 1663 correspondence with Richard Baxter, an unchastened Eliot still hoped for "the Lord to direct his People into a Divine Form of Civil Government, of such a Constitution, as that the Godly, Learned in all Places, may be in all Places of Power and Rule."[77] Whalley and Goffe certainly must have hoped that the Lord would empower godly New Englanders to frustrate Kellond and Kirke's search.

* * *

In New Haven, John Davenport was bolstering men and women for the kind of public-spirited self-sacrifice the regicides' presence would require of them. A royal commissioner would later ask Connecticut governor John Winthrop to investigate Davenport's sermons, which were immensely popular. As the people of Israel understood, Davenport explained, "the Saints could not be satisfied with their own private welfare, if the Church of God was in affliction and danger, or under reproach." The work of God took precedence over private needs. Davenport's lesson was timely: colonists knew that a £100 reward from Whitehall was being offered for assistance with the capture of Whalley and Goffe. Davenport reminded his flock to hold fast. Although it might seem like the welfare of churches depended on the state, in fact it was the other way around: "the welfare of all States and people, where Churches are, depends upon the welfare of the Church." The colonists should emulate the biblical figures Daniel and Eli, who "preferred the publick advantage before their own private interest." Queen Esther grasped this truth, as well, he argued, and "it prevailed mightily with her to run the utmost hazard of her own person when there might be hope of some good to the Church thereby."[78]

Davenport also cited biblical examples of those who failed to uphold the public good. One such case was the town of Meroz, "cursed by the Angel of the Lord" because its residents "came not to the help of the Lord against the mighty." Those towns or communities that did not offer help, Davenport implied, placed themselves at spiritual risk. Also drawing on early and medieval church history, he argued that colonists might be "called fools and fanaticks," but so had Bernard and Augustine been called before them. Only a true fool will "hazard the losse of his soul . . . to free himself from the mocks and scoffs" of the profane. Like the early Christians, Davenport concluded, "Let us . . . own the reproached and persecuted people and cause of Christ. . . . With-hold not countenance, entertainment, protection, from such, if they come to us, from . . . France or England." As had happened in the Bay, the cause of Whalley and Goffe here in New Haven became conflated with the cause of Christ. While it seemed self-destructive, "harbouring Christs witnesses" ushered in God's protection and true safety.[79] Along with legal declarations, these biblical and historical stories contributed to the region's constitutional culture, inspiring sacrifice in defense of godly people and institutions.

Davenport practiced what he preached. He personally hid Whalley and Goffe in his home for several weeks. His old friend Hooke, Whalley's brother-in-law, wrote approvingly: "I hope yet all will be well; though now I hear (as I am writing) of another order to be sent over, yet still I believe God will suffer no man to touch you."[80] Davenport may not have needed much encouragement. From correspondence, we know he believed that Jesuits and Quakers had forged an apocalyptic conspiracy to bring back the Stuart monarchy.[81] Some residents of New Haven felt so strongly about the incompatibility of their local institutions with the Stuart regime that, with Davenport's approval, they began negotiations for settlement in the Dutch territories, eventually founding Newark.[82]

New Haveners' decision to hide the regicides was perhaps hardest on their governor, William Leete, who experienced a tortuous crisis of conscience. Early historians painted Leete as a weak, vacillating figure; modern historians often depict him as weaselly and duplicitous. It is possible, however, to read his experience in its larger context as a genuine conflict of loyalties, one shared by many others. Caught between the constitutional culture of Davenport's sermons and the principles of the Stuart government, Leete agonized over lawful, godly action.[83]

On their arrival in New Haven, Kellond and Kirke knocked on Leete's door and asked him for aid in apprehending the regicides, including a warrant to search New Haven homes. The governor balked, first wanting to meet with the colony's magistrates and then with the entire body of freemen. Although scholars rightly have seen artful procrastination in his actions, a delay that allowed the regicides time to escape, Leete's impulse to include as many people as possible in a decision that affected the population is consistent with long-standing local tradition. Acting unilaterally had recently brought strong consternation to Endicott. Requesting time for broad-based meetings, Leete told the royalists that "hee could not, nor would not make us [Kellond and Kirke] magistrates," meaning he would not empower anyone not elected by the community.[84] In halting, hesitant terms, Leete drew and held the line against arbitrary rule.

Kellond and Kirke did little to hide their revulsion at these rural colonists' scruples. Recently arrived from London and operating within a very different culture, they railed against the delay, accusing Leete of trampling on the king's honor. They loudly warned "how ill his sacred Majestie would resent such horrid and detestable concealments and abettings of such traitors and regicides." Leete, they suggested, was signing his own death warrant. The governor, receiving this feedback, carefully replied, "wee honour his Majestie, but wee have tender consciences." He thus expressed in simple terms the constitutional struggle experienced by many puritan colonists who sought loyalty to the king without betraying their conscience or the public welfare. Leete also tried to appeal to Kellond and Kirke's human sympathy, taking their hands and saying he "wisht had been binn a plowman and had never binn in the office . . . since he found it soe weightie." The royalists would have none of it, brusquely pressing the governor and other New Haven leaders to declare "whether they would owne his Majestie or noe." Now defiant, the New Haveners replied that "they would first knowe whether his Majestie would o[w]ne them."[85] Their allegiance, in other words, was conditional. It was not a given.

As had happened in the Bay, not all New Haven inhabitants supported harboring Whalley and Goffe. At least two individuals were happy to tip off Kellond and Kirke as to the two men's whereabouts.[86] Even so, the fugitives escaped, first to a mill and then to a rocky outcrop in the woods.[87] With opportunity to reflect, Whalley and Goffe realized that they had put the entire colony of New Haven, which lacked a charter, in grave danger. They decided to turn themselves in, hoping that doing so would clear Leete and Davenport's names from charges of sedition. At the last minute, however, they either had second thoughts about this selfless act or were persuaded by local leaders to flee once again.

The hunt continued for months. In July 1661, a message from the Council for Foreign Plantations reached Leete, stating that "non attendance with diligence" to arrest Whalley and Goffe would "much hazard" the colonies, especially New Haven, and even harm Leete personally. The council possessed intelligence that Whalley and Goffe had been seen in New Haven, and it would use this information in its prosecution. Edward Rawson, the secretary to the Massachusetts Court who conveyed this message, added a personal plea to Leete: "Sir, Your owne welfare, the welfare of your neighbours, bespeake your unwearied paines to free yourselfe and neighbours" from these charges.[88] Distraught, Leete went to Davenport and the Boston minister John Norton "to disburden his heart." Since the regicides' latest flight, he had "been a Man depressed in his Spirit for the neglect wherewith he chargeth himself therein." On Leete's request, Norton wrote to Richard Baxter in September 1661, asking his aid to "avert trouble" toward Governor Leete and the New Haven colony.[89] Davenport wrote directly to Secretary of State William Morrice in London, claiming disingenuously that New Haven magistrates had "wanted neither will nor Industery . . . in apprehending the 2 Collonells."[90] These efforts, along with Leete's own "pitifull letter," might have done more harm than good. A friend in London wrote that without such reminders "the Bussines I thinke would have dyed," lamenting generally, "I am sorry to see that yow should be soe much surprized with feares of what men can or may doe unto yow."[91] This friend was right that colonists, and especially Leete, were fearful, Leete both for himself and for his colony. The following September, at a meeting of the commissioners of the United Colonies, Leete at last reversed course, signing a resolution "forwarn[ing]" all colonists "not to receive, harbour, conceal or succour" the regicides and to provide any intelligence regarding them to magistrates.[92]

Not everyone agreed with this decision. The other New Haven commissioner, Benjamin Fenn, cast a dissenting vote. Fenn's hometown of Milford had just taken in the regicides and would hide them until July 1664. There, sheltered by Micah and Mary Tompkins, they continued a lay ministry in which "each of them frequently prayed, and also exercised [preached] . . . at private meetings in their chamber."[93] Suspicion that New Haven residents had colluded to protect the regicides would contribute to the colony's failure to secure a charter, and to its subsequent absorption into Connecticut in 1665.[94] In the 1680s, however, Leete would have another chance to protect Goffe, who had by then moved to Hartford. When a disgruntled Hartford resident tipped off Governor Edmund Andros to the regicide's whereabouts, Leete, conquering his fears, would again help secure Goffe's safety before claiming a diligent search was underway.[95]

Some in London might have thought the £100 reward would suffice to ferret out the regicides. Those who held this opinion underestimated the religious solidarity many colonists felt with the two men. This solidarity even included more cosmopolitan puritans such as John Winthrop, who in 1661 had showed Kellond and Kirke great respect in Hartford before setting them on the wrong track toward New Netherland. Families such as the Saltonstalls would give generously for the two men's support.[96] Daniel Gookin successfully transferred their estates from England and invested them partly in cattle, which royal commissioners would later try to seize "for his Majesty's use." The royal commissioners would also attempt to search Gookin's home for evidence but, "standing upon the priviledge of their Charter," Gookin "refus[ed] to answer." There was little the royal commissioners could do. The youthful minister Increase Mather would send and receive letters for Whalley and Goffe, a task that required outsmarting the king's censors and spies. Jane Hooke's letters to Rebecca Russell, and Frances (Whalley) Goffe's to her husband, provide intriguing hints of a transatlantic female puritan network involved in the decades-long effort to provide for the fugitives.[97]

Native messengers, guides, and traders also lent assistance. Their involvement is difficult to pin down but was certainly present. New Haven colony leaders assigned an Indian to watch for Kellond and Kirke and give notice of their arrival. Aware of Native tracking skills, the two royalists "offered great rewards to English and Indians who should give information that they might be taken," but their efforts met with no success, even though the rocky outcrop where the two men hid was probably in a wooded section of Native hunting ground. While in Hadley, Whalley and Goffe engaged in trade with Indians, facilitated by local intermediaries. A number of these traders and others might have been in a position to alert royalists to Whalley and Goffe's location, and there is no evidence they did.[98]

The regicides' hosts—the Gookin, Davenport, Jones, Tompkins, Russell, and Bull families—bore the greatest risk and labor in protecting Whalley and Goffe. The Russell family served the longest, hosting the men from 1664 to 1676, and briefly a third regicide arriving in 1665, John Dixwell, building several rooms onto their house for the regicides' use. Hadley's church also met in the Russell home from the town's founding in 1660 until a church building was constructed in 1670.[99] It is certain that more locals knew about the regicides' location, and it is remarkable that not one person, Native or Anglo-American, stepped forward to claim the king's reward.[100] Most New Englanders chose to defy the king's command for their capture.

The regicides' presence in New England inflamed tensions with the Stuart regime. In a letter to London in late 1661 reporting on efforts to secure Whalley and Goffe, Endicott tried to preempt censure, pleading for "an oportunitie to vindicate our innocencyes & still enjoy the liberties . . . grant[ed] unto us."[101] Yet few royalists were convinced that the colonists were searching energetically. Detractors such as Samuel Maverick used the opportunity to redouble their efforts to link puritan colonists to the regicide. Maverick would publicize a narrative in which the colonists' regicidal impulses went all the way back to the *quo warranto* crisis of the 1630s, when they were "Bringinge theire forces in armes and declaringe it was to resist the landinge of a generall Governor sent by the Kinge." Ministers then recruited for the parliamentary army in the 1640s, he pointed out; and when hearing of the 1649 regicide while at a meal together, "one [Bay magistrate] asked if it were good newes, another answered the best that ever came and no contradiction." From forbidding trade with royalist ports to expressions of "affection" to Cromwell, their stance was clear, Maverick concluded. And now, by their "Courteous Intertaynement of Goffe and Whaley, many monethes, after they knew they were proclaymed traytors," all could see just "how loyall" these colonists really were.[102] In a moment when colonists needed more than ever to dispel the shadow of the regicide, the presence of the two judges made it easy for enemies such as Maverick to darken it.

Despite their critics' accusations, the colonists' refusal to arrest Whalley and Goffe does not mean that they had come to terms with Charles I's execution or that they were generally anti-monarchical. I would argue that New Englanders' actions had more to do with the two men's piety in the present than any approval for their past actions. As we saw earlier, Jonathan Mitchell's research and conversations in the 1660s led him to condemn the lawfulness of the regicide. We do not know what Mitchell was reading, but his Charlestown colleague Thomas Shepard (his mentor's son) had recently acquired copies of Francis Osborne's *A Plea for a Free State Compared with Monarchy* and Philip Hunton's *A Vindication of the Treatise of Monarchy*. Osborne drew on both Hebraic and classical republican models, along with that of the United Provinces, to argue that the nature of monarchy "is to decline into Tyranny." Hunton defended subjects' "right of resistance" when kings tried to claim absolute power, drawing on reason, Calvin, and scripture, although expressly rejecting any effort to touch the king's person.[103] All of these ideas were available to colonists as they contemplated Charles I's death, encountered his son's regime, and made decisions about Whalley and Goffe. With few exceptions, however, the colonists did not justify the regicide or reject Charles II's legitimacy. Although reading inflammatory books, Shepard went in a different direction, urging colonists to be like the "old nonconformists" under King James, exemplary subjects "to the government god hath sett over us 1st to the kinge as supreame," and then "subordinately" to local magistrates.[104]

The "nostalgic" phrase "old nonconformists" or "good old nonconformists" referred to a time before 1640 when the puritan movement was more invested in spreading the gospel than restructuring the state.[105] It expressed a hope that a constitutional balance could indeed be reached that allowed puritans to continue their project of reform while maintaining steady allegiance to the king. The conundrum of Whalley and Goffe proved so difficult precisely because colonists badly wanted to show themselves as loyal to the monarchy, thereby proving their accusers wrong. Yet in stumbling increments, the decisions they made about the regicides provoked men and women to commit to a constitutional arrangement that allowed for "tender consciences," one that prioritized the welfare of the godly before the interest of the king. These decisions would, as we will see, have long-term implications for New Englanders' constitutional sensibilities.

CHAPTER 2

News

Correspondence and Flying Speech

It is one thing to trace the formation of a constitutional culture through dramatic decisions aimed at thwarting regicide-hunters. It is quite another—and just as important—to find it in the everyday, diffuse flow of news and rumors. Ephemeral letters and recorded speeches capture colonists' fears and desires for their community as they faced the restored monarchy. Who in the colonies had access to political information? How did they obtain it? And what kinds of topics and stories mattered to colonists as they weighed constitutional questions? News and rumors flew across the Atlantic in the early Restoration. In this era, epistolary communication mattered as much as printed newssheets, which in any case were scarce and generally government run. Most often, colonists heard about the rapid changes in post-Restoration England through letters, scribbled-ink words in tight lines on linen- or cotton-fiber paper. The contents of their correspondence, however, can strike modern eyes as strange. If we delve into the hundreds of letters sent and received by New England colonists in the early Restoration, we might come away surprised by how many include stories of prodigies and supernatural news of divine action in the world—right alongside reports of the parliament or Privy Council. These letters also often include news of the condition, both bodily and spiritual, of English nonconformists. The fate of one New England founder, Hugh Peter, as he tried to elude London constables claims outsized space on the transatlantic airwaves. Overall, colonial Restoration-era correspondence underscores the deeply religious and personal nature of the news that informed many colonists' deliberations. Paying attention to the variety of accounts that circulated and the wide spectrum of colonists who read or heard these narratives provides us with a deeper, if refracted, view of the formation of a constitutional culture in this era. More specifically, it clarifies how, for many colonists, rallying behind civil and religious liberties fit within broader narratives of providential guidance over the transatlantic godly community.

When travelers entered a town, they could expect to meet the query, "What news?" In contrast to our own glutted newsfeeds, colonists "greedily hoarded whatever stray words happened their way." This desire for news was not unique to Europeans. Native Americans were "as eager for fresh news as were the English, and . . . more efficient at spreading it." And as in other regions such as the early South, the content of information was impossible to separate from the people and networks who made its acquisition possible.[1] News was a valuable resource, copied or summarized, passed along from home to home, sometimes arriving fourth or fifth hand. Colonists expected friends and business partners to fulfill the role of "intelligencer" whenever possible, and the absence of news usually came with an excuse. Men and women read aloud their letters, sharing what they had received with groups large and small.[2] Collecting and interpreting information about transatlantic events formed an intensely communal endeavor.

Rather than hoarding news, ministers and magistrates played a vital role in shaping and empowering access to it.[3] Those who have studied puritanism in early Stuart England will not be surprised to hear of this involvement. Laudians tended to keep political information and access from ordinary people, whereas puritan communities typically nurtured men's and women's informed and critical judgment. Letters, diaries, and court records reveal that many kinds of people in the colonies gathered information and expressed an array of knowledgeable opinions, at times so much so that leaders felt overwhelmed by their input. Although a proponent of broad access to information, one Cambridge minister felt the need to remind people to let those at the helm guide the ship and "justle not into their Places, nor refuse to acquiesce in their Conclusions." Even so, he encouraged people to keep communicating with their leaders: "if there be place for a modest Suggestion, tender it as becomes you."[4]

Those limiting access to the latest news and ideas were not colonial elites but rather the king's censors. One royalist official condemned newspapers that made "the Multitude too Familiar with the Actions, and Counsels of their Superiors," familiarity breeding "not only an Itch, but a . . . License, to be Meddling with the Government."[5] In England, more effective surveillance led to the interception of letters from nonconformists suspected of sedition. Some colonists wrote glowingly of their esteem for the king's piety in the expectation that their mail would come under such surveillance.[6] Nonconformists concerned about royal censors used a cipher for names, or sent letters to a third party rather than to the intended recipient, to throw them off. It was common practice to send letters inside packets of books or inside bookbindings. Colonists also gathered news about tactics for evading spies.[7]

Whether or not a given letter successfully arrived at its destination rather than meeting interception or the ocean's soggy depths was itself often understood to be providential. One observer noted that ships containing anti–New England reports were dangerously prone to storm damage. Six times, prodigious squalls or other obstacles had prevented one set of ungodly reports from reaching London; the sixth occurrence proved to be a Jonah-like scene, where "violent stormes" persisted until the messenger revealed the offending letters and cast them overboard![8] When news arrived from England or circulated within the colonies, it often seemed a divine gift.

Sifting through their updates, colonists labored to distinguish verified information from rumors. Calling some items "rumors" did not imply falsehood but merely quick conveyance—this was information that had not yet had time to be verified. An early modern synonym, "flying speech," captures the rapidity and ephemerality of such rumors.[9] When John Leverett wrote from London that "rumours" about the colony were flying, and that the "general vogue of people is, that a [royal] governor will be sent over," he considered this (dreaded) imposition a real possibility, although not yet confirmed.[10] Some rumors would prove false, of course. Still, in a culture of broad access, reining in errors remained difficult, to say the least. When pressed by royal officials to control rumors they disliked, Massachusetts leaders would point out the near impossibility of reining in the flow of information, simply because so many people contributed to it.[11]

As contradictory news came from multiple sources, arriving fresh or stale, true or fabricated, colonists tried to distinguish between reliable and unreliable accounts. Virginian and Quaker sources tended to be suspect. One premature March 1660 report from Virginia claiming that "the King of Scots is in London" provoked a colonist to say it was just as likely as a recent Quaker report that the radical Friend James Naylor was Bristol's new governor.[12] Yet who could know what was really going on? The same colonist went on to note that he hoped both reports, along "with many other rumours," would be "found not true" once more letters arrived.[13] The most trusted sources of information were English nonconformist ministers such as William Hooke, who took their role as intelligencers of colonial puritans very seriously, often writing at great personal risk.

In their letters, New Englanders often overlaid news with biblical or moral exhortations, sometimes interspersed with proverbs. John Hull encouraged his friend Leverett, daunted by events in London, to "put on the Armour of Righteousness . . . while you are in the place of danger you may stand like an Iron pillar," defending against "columniating tongues." He offered proverbs related to political reversal, such as "In the snare which Enemies lay is their own foot taken the snares broken & we are escaped." Hull also mentioned the frequently cited biblical story of Esther to evoke the power of a God who "soe offten brings his people into danger & in the nick delivereth them beyond all expectation."[14] As with Hull's, Leverett's letters included biblical and providential frameworks. Reporting in mid-February 1661 that "Episcopacy, common prayer, bowing at the name of Jesus, sign of the cross in baptism, the altar and organs are in use, and like to be more," he reflected, may "the Lord keep and preserve his churches, that there may not be fainting in a day of trial."[15] Many letters include prayers or promises to pray.

Letter recipients especially prized news of fellow nonconformists in England. Colonists passed along reports that although "divers godly ministers" had been imprisoned, these faithful men remained "full of Joy & Comfort," continuing to preach "to the greate good of many."[16] As the new Cavalier Parliament began its crackdown on nonconformity, some letters began hinting at a potential influx of unemployed and harassed puritans into New England, including such renowned preachers as Thomas Goodwin. Some merchants and ejected ministers did wind up coming to North America, while others expressed their hopes to do so in the future. Emigration was not, however, as easy or desirable as they might have wished. Before people could set sail, they had to swear an oath of loyalty to the new English king; and New Englanders learned that some would-be colonists "chose to die in prison rather than take it." Other potential migrants expressed concern that New England was not a place of lasting safety: they feared the colonies would experience "revolutions" if the crown imposed "a new forme of politie" on unwilling subjects. Thomas Goodwin's wife, Mary, simply refused to come.[17]

Dagmar Freist's conclusion about English towns is true for early America: "politics . . . cannot be understood fully without recognizing that it is centrally connected to communication, information, rumour, and gossip."[18] Although much news initially traveled along ministerial networks, abundant evidence suggests that laypeople, including women, also heard and discussed the heated issues of the day. Friends sent news reports to Elizabeth Winthrop, for example, expecting her perusal when her husband was away.[19] Diligently and energetically, colonists sorted and assessed the significance of prodigies and apostasies, declarations and arrests, as they weighed the constitutional balance between colony and king.

* * *

In letters and news reports, prodigies or wonder-tales emerge as one of the most common ways colonists expressed frustration with the monarchy, the Cavalier Parliament, or the Church of England without crossing over into disloyalty. Coupling piety with political wisdom, these reports of celestial signs or unusual events reflected a long-standing literary tradition, now increasingly politicized and subject to debate. Prodigy accounts were usually rumors, in the sense that people passed them along quickly. They were not, however, considered outside the realm of verifiable information. As with healing and miracles, later seventeenth-century Protestants invested significant effort in evaluating these wonder-tales.[20] Early Restoration prodigies "caused the government a great deal of anxiety" because they "did not specifically advise people to disobey civil authorities or call for the overthrow of monarchy, but they did criticize the restored church and implied that the government would soon be overturned."[21] Put another way, prodigies became prime methods for sounding the constitutional alarm.

These tales ignited the reader's or hearer's imagination. From correspondents in England, colonists heard stories of ghostly armies fighting in the sky and of infants suddenly uttering prophecies. They learned of dogs running mad till they died, acting out the madness of a changed political world.[22] "White horses very white" flew in the sky near Montgomery, provoking a frightened local jailer to free seventeen prisoners, presumably nonconformists. Interviews with the local population confirmed this equestrian sighting, and afterward, astrologers were asked "whence should the warr arise." Other signs confirmed for puritans that despite their suffering political defeat in England, "God's great affaires this day seeme to be placed upon our stage."[23] The precise interpretation of a prodigy often seemed secondary to the fact that the divine hand was still writing messages to them. Even those reluctant to interpret these signs acknowledged their importance to the godly. As one ejected minister, a recent migrant, mused, "what god meanes I know not, but sure I am it lyeth very heavy upon gods people."[24]

Prodigies required imagination, but they also invited the secret pleasure of seeing judgment fall against those who had failed the cause. Many accounts expressed divine judgment on people who had conformed to the Church of England under pressure, those about whom Edward Taylor penned the bitter lines, "Some wanted Courage: and some wanted Coine: / Which made them Daube, and Dodge, and so Purloine."[25] Northampton's Eleazer Mather reported "strange multiplied prodigies the yeare last past" indicating heaven's judgment on puritan apostates who were now "zealous for Ceremonies" and persecuting the faithful—prodigies linked, perhaps, to a king who "hates those that are against Common prayer, & service Ceremonies, with a perfect hatred."[26] Surely it was not coincidence that an English lawyer who jeered against "such as prayed with zeale" within two hours was killed in a lightning storm?[27] Or that the Harvard-trained minister Joseph Swinnock, who yielded "with reluctancy" to the surplice (high church vestments) and led a prayer-book liturgy, was, "with a disturbed spirit . . . so smitten in it, that he took his bed & died"? A Bay colonist passed along to a friend in Springfield the rumor that of nine nonconformist ministers newly ordained in the Church of England, seven "were immediately struck dead, the 8th struck blind, the 9th mad." This "Intelligence" eventually made its way to New Haven's personal information hub John Davenport, who esteemed it "a very remarkable hand of God."[28] Another minister supposedly did not even make it to the bishop for ordination before tripping and hitting his heart on a sharp rock or branch, dying shortly thereafter. This report was especially believable because a former New Englander participated in its investigation.

In addition to correspondence and oral reports, prodigies circulated by means of the great wonder-compilation of the early Restoration, *Mirabilis Annus.* Its authors alerted congregations to their desire to collect wonders, and stories flooded in. These accounts, like those circulating in letters, included sudden deaths and celestial events such as comets. The authors buttressed their tales with masses of classical, biblical, and historical evidence, especially citing Martin Luther to prove "the whole World being nothing else but Gods Book in Folio, and every Creature and Providence as a several page." Remarkable occurrences here included double suns and the strange inability of antipuritans to ignite a godly minister's effigy, despite using more than a hundred bundles of sticks. *Mirabilis Annus*'s industrious authors counted the prodigies, estimating their occurrence at more than twice a week.

Why such an outpouring? It must be the Lord's "mercy and compassion," they offered. Politically ostracized but "highly reluctant to accept the idea of permanent exclusion from social, religious, and political power," nonconformists "turned to providential explanations for consolation," as well as to express "implicit criticism of those who held the reins of power."[29] *Mirabilis Annus*'s printers and booksellers, including Giles and Elizabeth Calvert, faced great risk for their determination to see these tales in print. When Giles was imprisoned in London in mid-1661, Elizabeth printed the volume and faced subsequent arrest as well.[30] But the book escaped its publishers' confinement. Colonists eagerly read the volume and its sequel the following year, finding it "full of many strange and formidable stories" and expressing sympathy for the imprisoned booksellers.[31]

The sheer number of prodigies circulating among nonconformists would provoke scorn from royalists and, over time, alarm from moderate theologians who sought a Christianity more calmly aligned with the principles of Newton's universe. Yet hearing and reading such reports must have transformed and invigorated many. Surely it made sense for colonists to take a deep breath and wonder, "Did ever God speake soe loud, & shew soe cleerely, by multiplied signes, in heaven, earth, & sea, & in the Bodyes of men . . . to speake, & foretell calamities approaching, as he hath done to England since the late change of government?"[32] The natural order cried out that the story of reform would continue. To ignore the divine voice in prodigies, for many, seemed pure folly, as they evaluated safety and risk in their own response to the crown.

* * *

In addition to hearing and reading these wonder-tales, colonists also saw local prodigies with their own eyes, taking time to record and relay astronomical events, sudden deaths, and other providential occurrences. Sometimes they simply noted them in writing, as did John Plumbe of "Seabrok," who saw a pike-shaped flashing star that seemed to write symbols in the sky, first a mysterious shape and then a half-circle: he sketched all of these figures out with exactitude.[33] Other times the witnesses sought an interpretation or meaning. In a letter to John Winthrop about the contested border between Connecticut and New York (an issue involving the king's brother, the Duke of York), John Davenport (the son) mentioned seeing a night rainbow, noting that it "seems to be prodigious," and praying "the Lord teach us by all these dispensaconns to enter into our own hearts."[34] When Davenport later reported a second night-rainbow, this time with "watergalls" (secondary rainbows), which he considered "a speaking dispensaconn," Winthrop wrote back requesting a more specific account.[35] If they had access to *Mirabilis Annus*, or to someone who had read it, these two colonists would have

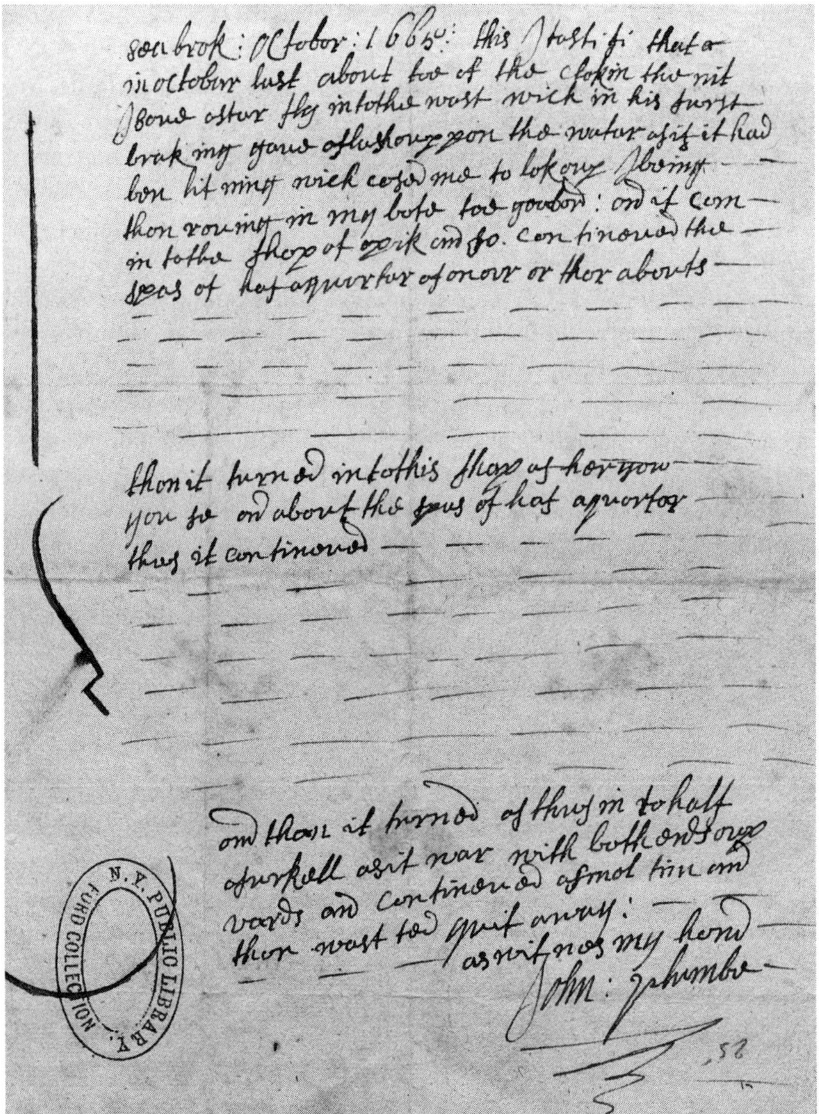
seabrok: October: 1665: this I testifi that a
in october last about too of the clok in the nit
I sone a star fly in to the west wich in his furst
braking gave a flashing upon the water as if it had
ben lit ning wich cosed me to lok up I being
then rouing in my bote too goword: and it com
in to the shape of a yoik and so continued the
speas of haf a quarter of an our or ther abouts

then it turned in to this shape of hor you
you se and about the spas of haf a quarter
thus it continued

and then it turned of thus in to half
a furkell as it war with both ends up
wards and continued a smol time and
thon wast too quit away:
as witnes my hand
John: plumbe

Figure 2. Letter from John Plumbe, October 1665, John Davenport Papers, Manuscripts and Archives Division. Courtesy of the New York Public Library, and the Astor, Lenox, and Tilden Foundations.

known that nighttime rainbows had recently been seen at least three times in England—and that sightings extended as far back as the days of Pliny and Aristotle. Some colonists probably would have agreed with *Mirabilis Annus*'s prayer that God would "in due time discover" its meaning and "turn [it] for good to all that tremble at his Word and Works."[36] Celestial news possessed universal reach. No censor could prevent the godly's access to these signs from God in the natural world.

Prodigies also managed to be uncannily transatlantic. John Allen of Dedham, Massachusetts, wrote with alarm to his son in London about strange noises of trumpets, horses, and a clattering like that of weapons. His son, astonished, replied that similar noises had been heard in England, adding that "we know not what god is doeing but prodigious signes are here & there frequent."[37] Boston merchant John Hull saw an apparition of "many companies of armed men in the air" similar to the armies reported in the sky over England. A meticulous recorder of celestial events, Hull also noted a double sun like that reported in *Mirabilis Annus*, seen for "half one hour, by sundry persons," for which he provided the precise time and point on the compass.[38]

Colonists did not hesitate to share stories about New England's enemies who met dark fates. Ipswich's William Hubbard recorded how a merchant named Stevens "informed much against the country" in England, and afterward "was suddenly and strangely smitten with an incurable malady at Boston." Another opponent of local interests, Capt. Isam or Isham, reported against colonists in England, and on returning to Piscataqua he "was seized with a loathsome disease, in which he rotted by piecemeal." Those who gave "sundry vaunting speeches against the country"—together with spies who relayed intelligence about colonial militias and harbors—also faced sudden catastrophe. In Hubbard's words, "it is not unworthy the observation of the reader, that the providence of the Almighty did, by solemn accidents, upon sundry persons bear witness against them."[39] Prodigies warned those who might betray New England that dire consequences could follow.

Catastrophes that struck down the godly were harder to interpret. In 1665, lightning hit the Boston Castle, killing Captain Richard Davenport and injuring others. What was the event meant to say? Struggling to find a message, the young minister Simon Bradstreet recalled that the 1664 comet had presaged England's plague, war with the Dutch, and the London fire; and another "Blaze or Beam" in the sky had forewarned the deaths of several beloved local clergy. The meaning of the more recent death by lightning in his own backyard, however, evaded interpretation. Bradstreet commented only that "the terrible effects of the same storm was seen in diverse places," and if the Lord had judged the captain, he was not alone.[40] Responding more pointedly to the same lightning strike, Charlestown minister Thomas Shepard offered a solemn call to repentance as necessary for colonists to preserve their liberty. We should "consider our wayes," he said, seeing as how "the Late awfull stroke by Lightening from Heaven . . . at our only Castle" had killed a faithful, "valiant Captaine," "the very porter of the Country." Through this sign, God was knocking. Colonists could either "open the Door to all oppressing mischeifs" or "open the Door to His tender mercies by a zealous Repentance," a door they had "so long enjoyed to preceous Liberty & deare bought enjoyments." In light of this thundering, catastrophic knock, Shepard pleaded, "Oh New-England Awake, awak!" if they did not want to lose their liberties.[41] The Boston merchant John Saffin came to a similar conclusion. Reflecting on God's "late Sore Stroakes" in drought, mildew on the crops, and deaths by lightning "to the great Amazement and Terror of many," he argued that colonists needed to "search and Try our wayes," turning from their sins, "whether in Church or State in famelies or in persons."[42] Sudden disasters elicited calls to repentance and renewed vigilance, both individually and as a body politic.

Prodigies and celestial events gave colonists a way to place crises in cosmic perspective or to express growing alarm. Malden pastor and avid prodigy-recorder Michael Wigglesworth noted in his 1662 poem "God's Controversy with New England" that "The Heavens more began to lowre, / The welkin Blacker grew: / And all things seemed to forebode Sad changes to ensew."[43] Roxbury minister and almanac-writer Samuel Danforth took notes on earthquakes, droughts, sicknesses, and deaths of eminent men in the early 1660s, alongside governmental and ecclesiastical events. In the winter of 1664, he turned his full attention to tracking "a Comet in the Heavens"—the same comet noted by Bradstreet.[44] As he studied the night sky, Danforth, perhaps drawing on *Mirabilis Annus*, wrote a widely circulated treatise on the biblical and historical significance of comets. Although not always associated with disaster, Danforth said, comets often portended calamities such as the death of a revered minister, plague, war, or "the Supremacy of the Bishop of Rome"—or sometimes they pointed to regime change.[45] Reading Danforth but also drawing on their own observations, multiple colonists similarly contemplated the "signes of heaven by the blazeing starr."[46]

Some colonists exchanged information about the 1664 comet as far as Virginia to Hamburg and back again, praying, "the Lord continue truth and peace in our dayes as in our Fathers if it be his blessed will."[47] Winthrop sent a tract about the comet—perhaps Danforth's—along with news of its New England and Dutch sightings to the prominent scientist (and New England Company governor) Robert Boyle in London and to the royal commissioner Richard Nicolls, who served as governor of New York. In his letter to Nicolls, Winthrop recorded how Native peoples (unspecified) remembered seeing the comet two hours before dawn around the time of the corn harvest and that multiple Indians confirmed these accounts, "most to be credited amongst them." Winthrop must have conversed at length with these Native American astronomers, paying special attention to elderly Indians' memories of a comet forty-six years earlier, followed by a time of "great mortality amongst the Indians," and their apprehensions of the 1664 comet "portending some ill consequences." Winthrop ended, however, by belittling these Native intelligences, referring to them as "impertinencies [irrelevancies] of the Indians observations."[48] Yet news of prodigies marked a site of cultural encounter, even if not of cultural agreement, heightening a shared sense that celestial events might guide men and women through future upheavals.

* * *

Not every nonconformist approved of collecting prodigies. Richard Baxter thought these wonder-tales did more harm than good. Under intense surveillance, he chose instead to write his own life story, and with it the story of English nonconformity, as his own act of literary resistance.[49] Often those concerned about the overabundance of these fantastical tales, or their increasing politicization, simply omitted them from letters rather than taking the time to openly criticize the genre. Yet puritans of many kinds felt the sting when royalists turned against prodigies, or certain prodigies, as a way of discrediting nonconformists and labeling them foolish or worse. One royalist wrote with urgency in a 1661 newssheet, "We must now tell the reader, for we can hold out no longer, how strangely impudent the lying faction have been in forging prodigies and monstrous accidents."[50] Over time, Charles II's government came to see nonconformists' accounts of prodigies as a threat to the regime, although royalists were not above composing a few of their own.

Stuart officials worked in multiple directions to undermine nonconformist wonder-tales, whether confiscating books and arresting authors, printers, and booksellers or promoting works that compiled countertestimonies to discredit specific prodigies—one example being Robert Clarke's *The Lying*

Wonders.[51] Official newssheets, now firmly under royalist control, ridiculed *Mirabilis Annus*'s tales of those "strook dumb, blind, dead, as they were reading Divine service" as "bottomless fictions," a claim backed up by local magistrates' signatures.[52] Royalists did not shy away from faith in supernatural action: they too could believe in prodigies and miracles, such as the king's healing touch. William Berkeley in Virginia would see the London fire as a punishment for the regicide and the rebel Nathaniel Bacon's death as divine judgment.[53] For royalists generally, however, nonconformist prodigies were too profligate, underevidenced, misinterpreted, and above all alarmingly critical of the established church and state.

Colonists heard about these criticisms; they learned, too, about another line of attack on their prodigies, a play perhaps titled *The Play of the Puritan*, based on Ben Johnson's *Bartholomew Fair* and performed in 1661 before the royal court, including the Earl of Manchester and three bishops. In it, a mock-puritan placed in the stocks for theft finds them unlocked, "admires" this "wonderfull providence," asks God whether to flee, and on escaping prays in an exaggerated puritan-style, "lifting up his eyes to heaven." News of the play reached the colonies with reports from eyewitnesses who "were afrayde the house would have tumbled downe" and who described the play's author as saying "if he were damn'd, it would be for those 2 playes." At a later performance in 1670, the galleries actually did collapse, confirming these providential beliefs.[54] News that their king had hosted such a mocking play may have resounded more loudly with New Englanders than his professions of love and care for the colonies.

Royalists might label puritans "Foolish Fanatick, silly Scismatick, / Round-headed Fury, Crack-brain'd Lunatick," in Edward Taylor's pithy summary, but puritans nonetheless continued to share their prodigy tales in letters, viewing them as essential information for the constitutional crisis.[55] The anti-puritan bishop Samuel Parker was scandalized that nonconformist "leaders should so confidently affirm" prodigy tales and that "the deluded populace should so eagerly swallow them!" Amazed that early Restoration books of prodigies were "consulted and perused with no less diligence than the Scriptures themselves," Parker observed that of all their "innumerable libels . . . those were most pregnant with sedition which they publish'd concerning prodigies."[56] Some royalists were so concerned that they recruited the Cambridge biblical scholar John Spencer to provide an official response. Pulling out all the stops, Spencer argued that nonconformists' prodigy tales were low class, feminine, and more African than English.[57] These accusations probably only encouraged puritans to keep scribbling their wonder stories alongside their family updates, the Cavalier Parliament's latest maneuvers, and the suffering of English nonconformists.

* * *

One of these beleaguered nonconformists, Hugh Peter, appears in an unusually high number of early Restoration letters. His frequent presence at first seems as strange as the number of prodigy tales in circulation at the time: although he had helped build institutions in multiple colonies while serving as Salem's pastor, Peter had not lived in New England since 1641.[58] Often incapacitated and temperamental, he had abandoned his Salem congregation and now lived apart from his wife, Deliverance Sheffield Peter, who suffered from mental illness. A successful preacher for the parliamentary cause, he enjoyed a close if tempestuous relationship with Oliver Cromwell, a connection he used to protect colonists from military conscription even if he did not always see eye to eye with colonial leaders.[59] He was far from a perfect spokesperson for the godly community. Yet the number of lines mentioning Peter makes sense when we remember that his prominence in rousing parliamentary troops and in justifying the regicide made him a prime target for royalist pamphleteers. Assaults on Peter, whether in person or in print, formed assaults on puritanism and the puritan colonies.

Colonists sought out news about Peter especially after learning in mid-1660 that he was being accused of playing a role in Charles I's execution.[60] They were shocked when, at his trial, royalist judges accused New Englanders themselves of a role in these events, claiming that colonists had deliberately sent Peter to England to foment civil war. For better or for worse, his reputation had become intertwined with New England's reputation. Decades after Peter's death, royal official Edward Randolph would still angrily label offending Massachusetts leaders as Peter's "disciples."[61] News of Peter's fate mattered to colonists as they discerned for themselves how far to comply with the Stuart regime.

A brief look at anti-puritan satire targeting Peter leads us into the raucous literary culture of Stuart England. A 1649 royalist parody depicts Peter giving a thanksgiving day sermon for the regicide. In the mock-sermon, a drunk, lascivious, meddling Peter preaches in a raunchy vernacular: "Now (Sirs) I conceive a belly-full is a belly-full; and if a man have not his belly-full, it is no Thanksgiving. . . . Pox o' your Dutch Ordinaries, I think they will become English, and give us all a belly-full; but in another kind (I fear) then I gave my Dutch Land-Lady and her Daughter." The parody took aim at the supposed gluttony of puritan holidays, dangerous alliances with Dutch Calvinists (or Peter's father's Dutch heritage), and hypocritical standards of sexual conduct. The classic promiscuous-puritan trope then extends to the colonies, as the Peter-character continues: "Then I went to New-England, and there I saw a blessed sight, a world of wild Women and Men lying round a fire, in a ring stark naked. If this custom should come up in London (as I see no reason but it may, if the State will vote it) then every woman may have her belly full, and it would be a certain cure for cuckolds and jealousie, and so the City would lose nothing by this Thanksgiving."[62] Hypocritical puritans taking their cues from "wild" Native Americans and turning their excesses into state legislation: these were potent mockeries.[63] When satirists lampooned Peter, they simultaneously skewered the puritan movement and New England.

Even if these royalist works did not make their way directly into the homes of colonial New England, news of them certainly did.[64] Colonists heard about fictionalized parodies of Peter as often as they heard about the actual man. Roxbury pastor John Eliot wrote to Peter pastorally, "You are indeed much envied, evil spoken of, smitten with the tongue, no matter!" Those who spoke evil were themselves blind, Eliot reminded him, assuring Peter of divine favor, of his "great use and service" in England for "the cause of God," and of Eliot's own love and esteem.[65]

In early Restoration letters that circulated in the colonies, reports of Peter show up more frequently than news about a potential royal governor or a Church of England bishop, or speculations about groups of new migrants. One rumor arrived via Newfoundland, for example, that Peter had been "in sore horror of spirit crying out of himself as damned, and confessing strange activities of which he is guilty."[66] Peter's own medical issues and family history of mental illness may have increased the rumor's credibility. At the same time, the trope of guilty madness was often directed against puritans, whose spontaneous, emotional style and emphasis on thorough repentance seemed almost to invite caricature.[67]

By August 1660, colonists knew that Peter still had a chance of regaining his confiscated English lands, thanks to the intervention of a kinsman of the Presbyterian general George Monck who "sometimes dineth with him."[68] Although Peter tried to curry Monck's favor and was allowed to preach before him, it quickly turned out that Monck distrusted Peter, suspecting him of helping to plot a revolt.[69] When John Davenport (the father) finally heard more concrete news of Peter's situation, he interrupted his sermon preparation to pass along the details. A letter had arrived reporting that Peter and two other prominent nonconformist ministers, Thomas Goodwin and Philip Nye, had been imprisoned and were "likely to lose theyre lives."[70] Davenport saw the fate of these three leaders, along with the ascendency of bishops and presbyters, as indicative of dark times for godliness. "That good men are under some sufferings," he preached, "many being turned out of theyre places: but greater things feared: Spaine like to make peace: France like to differ. The good Lord prepare his people, in Old England, and New, for what they and we may expect!"[71] The fall of these godly men formed part of a larger assault on international godliness that could soon reach across the ocean, he feared.

Colonial grief and anxiety formed a stark contrast to the comical rhyming ballad about these same imprisonments that hit the London press: *England's Object, Or, Good and true Newes to all True-hearted Subjects, for the . . . apprehending of that horrid deluding Sower of Sedition Hugh Peters*, set to the tune of "Come hither my own sweet Duck." The ballad played off rumors that while evading capture in London's Southwark neighborhood, Peter hid in the bed of a woman who had given birth several days before. When finally discovered by a constable, he persistently lied about his identity.[72] Another ballad began, "Sing hey ho my honey, / My heart shall never rue, Twenty four Traytors now for a penny, / And into the bargain Hugh."[73] A third portrayed the devil as possessing Peter while he wrote his will, in which "Unto his Sisters he gave his Bable [Bible/babble/bobble, with sexual connotation] / Which stood in their service as long as 'twas able, And unto the Kirk his brains and eyes, And unto the Queen of Morocco his thighs."[74] Hearing about these mocking ballads while in a state of distress for the actual person, and forced to move forward without verified information, would have been galling for colonial friends.

While most puritans would have discounted the ballad's salacious lines, they paid close attention to stories of Peter's spiritual struggles. Did Peter, under pressure, recant his faith or his role in the parliamentary cause? Colonists had to wait, with thinning patience, for news on his inner well-being. When reliable information detailing Peter's October 1660 execution finally crossed the ocean the following February, colonists across the social spectrum registered their shock. Bostonian Elizabeth Richardson first heard the account from her brother, who had just arrived from Virginia. In her retelling, "ther is many put to death 10 in one da[y] hanged dra[w]n and quartered general Hareson and mr. Peters 50 in all so to be served." The details of this report would turn out to be exaggerated, but the terror accompanying the executions comes through clearly. All three men endured disembowelment—and at least one, the parliamentary army officer Thomas Harrison, was still alive when it happened. Elizabeth's husband, Amos, was so overwhelmed by the news that he could not put quill to paper: "it is so bad that I cannot tell how to speake of it in regard of Mr. Peters and divers others." Elizabeth had to pass along the gruesome story herself.[75]

When sixty-year-old Hannah Waterhouse of New London heard the news of Peter's death, she expressed taut anger to a neighbor. The king, she said, "was a traitor, and if . . . she was a man and was in England . . . she would be his death or he should be hir death."[76] In her view, Charles II was England's betrayer, not Peter. The royalists' treatment of Peter precluded her acceptance of the new king. Like many women, Waterus was informed and had strong opinions about politics.

Boston militia captain Edward Hutchinson took the time to confirm the executions of John Cook, Harrison, and Peter with more than one set of recently arrived ship passengers, noting that Peter had been both "hanged and quartered." This grisly detail was true for all three men: after they had been hanged, their bodies were cut up into four parts, then draped along the city gates, with their heads mounted—Peter's prominently displayed on London Bridge. New Englanders would have recognized the ritual pageantry of statecraft in these actions, in which the corporeal humiliation of the regicides was required as expiation for the dishonor and death of the old king, thus helping usher in the return of the new king. For Hutchinson, as for Davenport, all this news came with foreboding of worse to come. Seven more men had been condemned, "and it is thought that many more wil dye."[77]

However distressing these updates, many colonists understood that bad news was better than no news at all. In early March 1661, John Winthrop (husband to Elizabeth Reade Winthrop, Peter's stepdaughter by his first marriage) finally received "books of newes and trialls" about those executed. He thanked his news bearers effusively for not keeping him in the dark: "your loveing care in so speedy transmitting them must be acknowledge[d] a singular respect to your friends here, who were tingling after the true information abord those reports, which had beene rumored amongst us." The books included three "Inteligences" or official newssheets and a volume of the "speeches of them thatt are executed," probably a more sober account such as *An exact . . . accompt of the indictment . . . of nine and twenty regicides* or the anonymously authored *Speeches and Prayers of Some of the Late King's Judges*.[78] While grief at Peter's death would remain raw for some time, these and other printed accounts at least consoled colonial readers regarding his integrity and spiritual state. They also removed the sense of dread that came with not knowing.

Colonial readers would not have been comforted, however, when learning about the royalists' efforts to link New England and rebellion during Peter's October 1660 trial. During the proceedings, prosecutors accused Peter of using his ministerial authority "to make himself a Trumpeter of war, of Treason and Sedition in the Kingdome."[79] Peter's tendency to become delusional when ill was used against him; his physician testified that Peter in his sickness had railed and scoffed against the king, the royal family, and "Monarchical Government" itself.[80] Worse, Peter had supposedly confided his real reason for leaving Salem in 1641: "for the driving on of this interest of this Reformation, he was imployed out of New-England for the stirring up of this war and driving of it on." Versions of this anti-puritan rumor—namely, that New Englanders had sent Peter to foment civil war—spread quickly. Pamphlets elaborated that Peter, after supposedly betraying his spouse, "went himselfe to New-England . . . till the very Natives were faine to give him Money to be rid of him." He then returned to England "just as the Warr's was broke out in Flames: this Atheist came again to lay more Fuell to the fire."[81] On hearing this account, Samuel Maverick quickly fed it to Lord Chancellor Clarendon. Many colonists, he said, "came over and served against the King . . . others were sent to sow sedition, as Peeters and Weld." A version of this tale would later appear in notes circulating in Whitehall committees.[82] How could New Englanders counter such a damaging rumor?

Peter did his best to clear himself and the colonies during his trial. He argued that the physician spoke falsely, was not a competent witness, and had a personal grudge. In a closing statement, he carefully laid out the chronology of his role in the civil wars: "I was not here in the beginning of it, but was a stranger to the carriage of it." Even so, the final list of evidence against Peter included "proof that he hath been in action in New England, that he came from it with that [rebellious] intent," alongside his seditious prayers and sermons.[83]

The trial account also included a kind of political confession before the court: Peter supposedly said, "I am very sorry to hear of my carriage towards the King, it is my great trouble, I beg pardon for my own folly and weaknesse, I thought God had a great controversie with the Nation. . . . I went into the

Army." Yet he defended his orthodoxy and spiritual integrity. He had called out corruptions in his own camp as well as among royalists. It was not political, he tried to argue. He asked the jury to consider whether revenge was motivating his trial, and he ended with a reflection on intentionality and an appeal to prodigies: with "neither malice nor mischief in my heart against the King," he said, he had entered the civil wars because "invited . . . and there I found very strange and several kinds of providences, as this day hath been seen." Though he admitted to stirring up opposition against the king, he had done so, he claimed, in an honorable way.

Peter's confession and defense would have relieved the Winthrops and other colonial readers. This was a puritan voice, repentant and attuned to the supernatural. Peter did not veer into the hypocrisy or madness his enemies predicted and assumed. On a practical level, of course, none of these arguments mattered; the trial's conclusion was foregone. The Solicitor General lambasted Peter as a "carnal Prophet," asking, "what man could more contrive the death of the King then this miserable Priest hath done?"[84] Colonists reading the news may have asked themselves: can we count on the justice of a royalist court?

Detractors in London might call Peter "A State Juggler drest in Divinity; a meer Proteus [shape-shifter], and yet a Regicide . . . belching from an Impure Throat the loathsome Vapours of Sedition."[85] New Englanders' enemies might continue to lambaste the colonists as "those of Heugh Peter" who could never be loyal to the king.[86] But in puritan letters and reports, Peter's legacy was not mocked. An English merchant traveling in Boston around 1661, conversing with local merchants about Peter's execution, heard them say "that there were many Godly in New England that durst not condemne what Hugh Peter had done."[87] Despite his faults, many colonists continued to express solidarity with Peter, whose devotional writings enjoyed an extended life in the colonies.[88] Their fascination with Peter embodied the confusion and determination that characterized the colonial response to the Restoration as a whole. And his horrific death would long inform popular colonial distrust of Charles II's government.

Although colonists rarely mention the 1662 execution of Sir Henry Vane, the onetime pro-"Antinomian" Massachusetts governor and long-time puritan member of parliament, this event, too, must have heightened their distrust, despite Vane's heterodox past. Charles II had promised to spare the former parliamentarian if he abjured officeholding, a promise the king subsequently broke under pressure. Just before his execution, Vane said, "I value my Life less in a good Cause" than Charles II had valued "his Promise." His biographer contrasted Vane's faithfulness with royalists' "groundless aspersions" and "causeless hatred."[89] Such news must have rankled hearers whether in London or Boston.

It seems important to note that in Restoration correspondence, tales of executions and narratives of prodigies frequently show up in the same letter or even the very same paragraph, often appearing right alongside specific accounts of the king's words or parliamentary legislation. All these types of news formed part of a larger whole: while its ecclesiological boundaries were permeable, puritanism was, above all, a network of people linked by a common language of devotional practices and affectionate relationships. It is not surprising, therefore, that people saw prodigies around Peter and others' executions. God was present in all these happenings.

An example might prove useful. In one account, as Peter was suffering at the gallows, a poultry dealer was "rayling most bitterly" against the dying man, saying, "Now the Rogue Peters was gone to be hanged, and would Preach no more." All of a sudden, a friend's gentle, friendly dog violently attacked the naysayer, ripping at least eighteen "dangerous holes in his body."[90] Later versions of this story would depict the unfortunate royalist "inveighing against Peters" to his face, only to be "torn and almost kill'd by his own tame favourite dog."[91] For puritan readers and storytellers, the natural world expressed its own justice when human courts did not.

Just after the regicides' executions, a man reported seeing "the appearance of Five naked Men exceeding bright and glorious, moving very swiftly." If angels graced the men's exit, prodigies also sanctified their mutilated limbs: After their bodies had been quartered and their limbs draped along the London city gates, "a bright Star" shone above Aldgate for upwards of two hours. This bright afternoon star reappeared for the next four days, which "many hundreds in the City" witnessed. At Bishopsgate, the dead men's limbs were adorned with seven sky-high "Pillars of smoke."[92] Nonconformists expressed the righteousness of those executed—and of their cause—when they recorded and passed along the news of these celestial signs.

One royalist polemicist went so far as to link the degradation of the regicides to the degradation of prodigies: "Look as (sometimes) Persons once Sacred, found guilty of capital crimes, are solemnly degraded, before they are executed: so things once reputed Sacred, should be first degraded (by a well inform'd judgment) from that Opinion and degree of respect they held in mens mind."[93] The dismissal and eradication of nonconformist prodigies paralleled the judgment and eradication of the regicide's physical bodies, and by extension their place in the political body. There was one problem with such assumptions, however: these tales never disappeared entirely. Puritans continued to gather portentous news and, through the written word, send it flying back and forth across the Atlantic. In myriad ways, they proclaimed that judges, executioners, bishops, and ballad writers did not wield all the power. An eclectic correspondence fueled colonial puritans' commitment to a political settlement that kept arbitrary power at bay—and that opened the door to their own project of ongoing reform.

CHAPTER 3

Courts

Articulating Sedition and Loyalty

From poring over letters about Charles Stuart's return in 1660 to watching royal commissioners sail, flags proudly waving, on a frigate into Boston harbor in 1664, Bay colonists struggled to articulate their constitutional commitments. Many of their discussions occurred in or around the courts, both legislative and judicial. Whether in seditious speech trials, patent-study committees, formal debates, or informal gatherings to offer (solicited or unsolicited) advice, colonists worked out their obligations to the new king, to God, and to each other. Knowing the impossibility of perfect unity, they nonetheless put tremendous, prolonged effort into forging a working consensus.

As they rode or walked to the Boston Town House in the brisk fall of 1660, the representatives charged with this task must have anticipated the constitutional dilemmas awaiting them. Their numbers included thirteen magistrates (the higher court, elected by all freemen) and thirty-five deputies (the lower court, chosen by each town). Multiple trustworthy sources had confirmed for them the rumors about the new king. They could no longer avoid asking the questions: How should puritans acknowledge a restored Stuart monarch? Should they apologize for the past two decades or pretend no connection to Cromwell's administration? Was it safer to hold firm to their distinct governmental and economic practices, or should they compromise in deference to the new regime? There were no easy answers.

The deputies came from twenty-seven towns, some more than a hundred miles away. Most heralded from towns of a few hundred households; only two came from Boston, with its burgeoning population of three thousand. Some arrived with written or spoken instructions from their town meetings back home—and surely felt obligated to represent these concerns. Even so, political norms discouraged inhabitants from voting based on a candidate's stance on a particular issue: what mattered most was that candidate's wisdom or integrity.[1] The deputies would be expected to weigh each decision and obey their consciences accordingly.

As they approached the Town House from multiple directions, the travelers would have gained sight of the striking new building that served as an economic as well as legal center for Boston. The Town House sat in a prime location on the busiest road in the city, with steady horse and carriage traffic back and forth from Long Wharf. Built in 1658 and resembling an English town hall, the structure's ground level boasted an airy, open pillared space where merchants transacted business, and its upper level consisted of larger chambers for meetings.[2] A balcony served well for delivering official speeches and proclamations as well as for taking in a breath of fresh air.

This group already had experience working together, for members had met as the General Court after the May 1660 election. But as they walked up the Town House steps now, most of them probably sensed this October meeting was different. A king had returned to the throne. They would spend the next few weeks formulating motions and deliberating over their potential outcomes. The weeks when the General Court met were busy ones for Boston, with dinner parties, tavern gatherings, and long walks by the court members in pairs or groups. Often these discussions expanded to include many more people than those formally serving on the General Court.

The first task at hand involved taking care of regular business. The October court began with a discussion of ordinary issues—the new lawbook, the mint, capital punishment, territorial boundaries, militias, poor relief, juries, and diplomacy with New Netherland. All of these would have seemed routine issues for this group, although they were, in fact, aspects of a singular constitutional arrangement developed over years with little concern for divided sovereignty. Next, a court member identified a more freighted issue: should they send a formal address to Charles II? At first, many of the deputies seemed in favor. But then a rumor arrived from Barbados that the English government "was in a very unsettled state" because Lord Fairfax, the former commander of the New Model Army, had raised an army. So much had happened in the previous few months—was it possible a letter expressing submission to Charles II could backfire, winding up before a new "committee of safety, council of state, or a junto with some other title"? Heated and extended discussion ensued, and the motion to address the king at this point failed.[3] The magistrates and deputies traveled home, no doubt still worrying about their decisions.

By late November, however, more accurate and authenticated information had arrived at the Bay colony. Charles II was indeed securely on the throne. Reading this new "intelligence," Governor John Endicott, along with magistrate Simon Bradstreet and Major General Humphrey Atherton, decided the Council (consisting of available magistrates) should be called. The new letters indicated, alarmingly, that ill-wishers were "petitioning his Majesty parliament & privy councill against us." Should an address to the king now be sent "for the prevention of such <evill>"? Hesitant to act on their own, the members of this Council decided to rapidly assemble the full General Court. Interestingly, they also ordered the town constables to "assemble the freemen" in each town to "choose & send their deputy or deputies" to "Consult" on these "weighty & important occasions of the Country."[4] In light of Leete's decision to involve all New Haven freemen in responding to Kellond and Kirke's demands, as well as the Bay's 1664–1665 efforts to involve as many inhabitants as possible in decisions regarding the royal commission, this impulse toward wide participation marks a significant aspect of the region's constitutional culture.

Probably assisted by the Council, Endicott and Deputy Governor Richard Bellingham then quickly drafted letters to sympathetic noblemen in England, prominent nonconformists to whom Charles II, in a short-lived effort to prevent insurgency, had granted high appointments in his government: Lord Saye and Sele, now Privy Councillor, and the Earl of Manchester, now Lord Chamberlain.[5] Endicott and Bellingham's language in the letter to Lord Saye and Sele indicates their strong commitment to maintaining their current constitutional arrangement, perhaps reflecting some of the discussion at the October court. They asked Lord Saye and Sele to convince the new king that their worship and "Civill Government" were set up "as was necessary to our well being here" and were "fully graunted to us in our Pattent." Aware that Quakers and royalist claimants to New England territory were complaining of injustices, the two men acknowledged they were not perfect—noting that they remained ever "subject to humane frailtie & infirmitie"—but insisted that they had governed "impartially" according to their best judgment. And as for being disaffected regarding Charles II or, worse, monarchy in general, as was rumored, Endicott and Bellingham asked Lord Saye and Sele to please tell the king they "detest such accusation as false & scandalous" and freely submitted to the new regime. Notably, they undertook this submission conditionally, "with Reservation of our rights, priviledges Liberties & Immunities graunted to us by his Late Royall Majestie & possessed by us many yeares." They hoped the king in his wisdom would ignore their naysayers and make no changes in the patent (the colony's charter) or "in our Government in church and Commonwealth from what wee have so Long Enjoyed." This carefully chosen language of "many years" and "so long" served to remind the king that current legal norms discouraged overturning longstanding arrangements.[6] If he did make such alterations, the result would be drastic: it "would in all probabilitie subvert this Plantation, & frustrate the hopefull worke among the natives." Overall, the letter indicates that even at this early stage, some Massachusetts leaders wanted to assert their long-established liberties—and to do so boldly—as constitutional limits on their submission.

Reconvening in December 1660, the full General Court quickly voted to formally address the king and parliament. Finding the right language for this statement, however, proved challenging. As they sat in Town House chambers during the day and gathered in homes or taverns in the evenings, court members tried many times to draft a letter. Each draft, however, proved unsatisfactory to the larger group. They finally turned to the ministers for advice.

Among the most well-educated men in the colonies, clergy often sat in on General Court sessions and were expected to make themselves available for prayer or counsel. On this occasion, a group of ten mostly Boston-area ministers gathered to help. They probably met either at the Boston minister John Wilson's home, where their regular lecture-day gatherings occurred, or in the second large chamber of the Town House.

The ministers' first impulse was to affirm the magistrates' competence and godliness, specifically "Gods singular presence" with those who drafted the earlier letters to puritan noblemen.[7] This deferential language reflected the Reformation-era theory of two kingdoms, civil and spiritual, often noted when New England ministers gave advice to local courts. It meant, in essence, that the ministers were willing to offer counsel, as clergy had been doing for centuries in Europe when they helped magistrates rule according to divine law, but that they would not overstep from the spiritual into the civil kingdom by wielding direct political authority. A blurring of civil and spiritual powers had characterized Laudian-era bishops who sat on the Privy Council and the Star Chamber, a royal prerogative court that had prosecuted puritans in the 1630s; the bishops' "theocracy" was seen by many puritans as a dreaded mark of antichristian tyranny, dangerous to both church and state.

Non-authoritative, carefully prescribed advice, however, Bay clergy would give willingly.

After endorsing the earlier letters, the ministers offered more specific counsel. Yes, they said, colonists should acknowledge "our allegiance and subjection" through an address to the king and/or parliament. The early settlers had acknowledged subjection to Charles I, the ministers reasoned, so subjection in itself did not threaten their liberties. There was no need, however, to delve too deeply into the history of the last two decades—"the confusions by past however grievous"—nor to explain the colony's specific support for Cromwell. And they should not go overboard in their praise as they crafted this statement. Acknowledging the king's return, the clergy said, was important, of course: "yet how high the congratulations should be, considering things present and the sequels thereof (to God only known) we cannot apprehend." The stability of the Restoration government remained an open question. In short, the ministers called for a real but tempered acknowledgment, one that honored the king without evoking the tumultuous past or forestalling an alternative future. One had to keep the options open.

Norton then drafted a letter to the king, endorsed with few exceptions by the other ministers, for the court's evaluation. We can imagine the scene: multiple drafts circulating, papers being brandished, voices calling out across the room, then finally the ministers thanking everyone for their efforts. Norton, a senior and beloved minister, would generally advocate a high level of compliance with the Restoration government; indeed, his election sermon the following May would proclaim "Gods Out-casts are not Fanaticks," urging quick obedience to the king as both a Christian and rational duty. In his mind, colonists should not "betray liberty, under the pretence of liberty," nor risk the charter out of prejudice "against the present, and ancient Government of our Nation."[8] Norton's draft letter probably leaned too hard toward submission for most. Court members eventually sidestepped it, choosing again to try to compose their own address.[9]

The first lines of the court's final letter capture the difficulty of their situation: "Wee at present owne such impotency as renders us unable to excuse our impotency of speaking unto our lord the king." Avoiding effusive rhetoric, the letter creatively invokes a shared experience of exile, representing the emigrants of the 1630s as free from "any dissattisfaction as to the constitution of the civil state." It rejects the ministers' advice to avoid talking about the Cromwellian past, instead claiming that Bay colonists had only a "passive part through out these late vicissitudes & successive overturnings of state," a statement perhaps technically true but that masks the high number of colonists who had fought or served as chaplains for the parliamentary cause.[10]

Court members did highlight the mission to Native Americans, following Endicott and Bellingham's lead. Established by John Eliot and the Native preachers he trained, this mission had long helped counter negative images of the colonists circulating in England. For example, on a trip to England one colonist observed that "the conversion of the Indians with you mak[e]s New England very Famous."[11] Protestant and Catholic empires competed for the moral high ground in spreading the gospel, supposedly the purpose of any colonial enterprise. Charles II might see Native missions as valuable to his regime's moral legitimacy. This hope undergirded Eliot's decision to dedicate one edition of a new Algonquian-language Bible to the king. Charles II would in fact soon renew the charter for the New England Company, the mission's administrative and fundraising body.[12] Perhaps, Massachusetts Court members reasoned, the mission would also serve to bolster colonists' standing with the king.

The letter went on to offer conditional allegiance, in line with the earlier letters to those English nonconformists holding appointments in the king's new government. Colonists, the court members assured the king, were "fearers of God and the king . . . zealous of government & order," neither "seditious" nor "schismaticks." But their ability to set up biblical worship was non-negotiable: it formed the very lifeblood of their plantation, they argued, without which "wee could not live." Certain lines could not be crossed. The court had finally reached a working consensus over how to address the king: offer submission *and* plead for, in John Hull's summary, "gracious confirmation of our patent, and therein of our liberties, civil and ecclesiastical."[13] After a scribe carefully made a fair copy of the marked-up draft, the letter was signed, sealed with wax, and put on a ship to London.

* * *

As they waited for the king's response, colonists continued to process the regime change. Some exploded with grief and anger in ways that pressured the General Court to regulate seditious speech. One such case involved Joseph Jenks, an iron worker prone to argue about politics on the job and not afraid to express his blunt opposition to the monarchy. Back in August 1660 a coworker had told Jenks that "he heard that the king was now Crouned." Jenks denied it. The coworker held his ground, and Jenks blurted out, "but what is the king[?] is he better then another man[?] for ought as he knew he was as Good a man as he."[14] Shortly thereafter, on a business trip to fetch molds and plates for "cinder holes," Jenks crossed the line from republican to regicidal, saying, "if he should meete the kinge between thir and Concord he would cutt of his head and mak a foot ball of it." Later, at a friend's home, he asked, "what newes doe [you] heer from England"? When the friend mentioned Charles Stuart's return, Jenks said, "I should rather that his head weare as his fathers Rather then hee should Come to England to set up popery."[15] Jenks's concerns about "popery" were widely shared by his fellow New Englanders. In this context "popery" could mean Catholicism, but more often meant a Catholic-leaning Church of England, or absolutism in either church or state. But for most colonists, evoking a second regicide as Jenks had done would have been unthinkable.[16]

Could Bay leaders overlook this kind of speech? The stakes could not be higher: seditious speech was a capital crime. As we saw in Chapter 1, the colony needed to shed its associations with regicide, not confirm them. And although Jenks's language was exceptionally violent and radical, he was not alone in his sense of anger at the Restoration. His case went all the way to the General Court, which functioned as a court of judicial appeal as well as a legislative body.

At his May 1661 trial, Jenks admitted he had said most of these words, although he argued that he had been interpreted incorrectly. He sent in a petition defending himself, ironically, with the king's "act of Indempnity" in the Declaration of Breda. He also, however, expressed some awareness of the pressure his case was putting on the General Court. He asked that the magistrates and deputies would "extend their Charity" toward him, but only "soe far as may bee without hurt to themselves." Jenks had come to realize his words might be a gift to the colony's enemies. Almost as an afterthought, he added that the judges' mercy should be offered only if it did no "Iniury to my Sovereigne Lord the king."[17] His toeing the line worked: the court acquitted him. By contrast, in a seditious speech trial in York County, Virginia, the following month, Thomas Cheney, who spoke "dangerous and unlawfull words" about the king's restoration, received a sentence of thirty lashes "well layd on till the blood come."[18]

* * *

The General Court may have given Jenks's seditious speech a pass, but members knew it was imperative that they hammer out their constitutional relationship to the new regime. Arriving by ship in late spring 1661, Charles II's response to their address began with praise: surprisingly, he called New England "one of the chiefest" of his colonies, with a "long and orderly establishment." (Royal letters frequently confused "New England" with "Massachusetts.") The king had found the General Court's letter "very acceptable" and vowed to exceed "his Royal predecessors in a just encouragement and protection of all his subjects there." The colonists, he wrote, would be "equal partakers of those promises of liberty and moderation to tender consciences" that had been declared the previous year at Breda, promises he was sure they would "make a right use of."[19] In the wake of this letter, pressure mounted among the population to organize a public ceremonial proclamation of the king.

During the June 1661 court meeting, Endicott took the helm of debate and initially struggled to guide the magistrates and deputies to "be unanimous in voting" on this official proclamation, as well as on the capture of the two regicides hiding out in New England. Searching for a way to "begett unity amongst ourselves," the court undertook what might be a familiar move for many of us today: it called for a committee. Appointing four ministers, four magistrates, and four deputies "seriously to discusse & rightly to understand our liberty & duty" by studying the patent or charter, the court deployed a basic strategy for building consensus: letting a smaller set of representative voices work out an agreement that they could bring back to the larger group.[20] Their actions paralleled those of the Corporation of London, which also created a (much larger) committee for studying the city charter and its privileges in 1661. In the Bay, the twelve men cleared their calendars, unrolled the dusty patent, and set to work.[21]

The committee's thorough study of the patent was supposed to locate a constitutional balance between "the due observance of obedienc & fidelity unto the authority of England & our oune just priviledges."[22] The General Court instructed them to "consider . . . our pattent, lawes, priviledges, & duty to his majesty" and to discern how the people "may speake & act the same thing, becoming prudent, honest, conscientious, & faithfull men."[23] The committee thus had as its charge the tackling of core questions surrounding seventeenth-century constitutionalism: What kinds of authority did local government wield? Which types of royal decrees and warrants did colonists have to obey? What was the meaning of allegiance—and the role of conscience?

The statement the committee produced provided an exceptionally clear articulation of many colonists' constitutional assumptions. First, it enumerated the people's liberties, beginning with their belief that the patent was, "under God," the "first & maine foundacion of our civil politye here." Their "Governor & Company" were a "body politicke," one with the "power to make freemen." Those freemen had the power to elect their own leaders, who in turn could set up new officers, growing and expanding government to meet the needs of the population. And this elected leadership enjoyed "full power & authoritie, both legislative & executive," over the colony. This power included both "eclesiasticks & in civils, without appeale," as long as laws were not repugnant to those of England (a clause in the charter). By power over "eclesiasticks" the committee did not mean authority over forms of worship but rather power to approve and protect biblical churches. Lastly, the government could defend itself, by arms if need be. Any "imposicion prejudiciall to the country," one that undermined their laws (as long as not repugnant to England's), amounted to "an infringement of our right."[24] This bold reading of the colonists' semi-autonomous privileges of self-government was backed with the power of their militias.

What was left in terms of allegiance to the king? The people of the Bay should acknowledge that they held the colony like "his majesties mannor of East Greenwich," and so could not submit to Spain, the Netherlands, or any other "forreigne prince." They had to work to preserve the king's "person, realmes, & dominions," report any plots against him, and punish anyone who committed a crime against his peace. Committee members also placed missionary work in the category of allegiance, given the king's title of "defender of the faith." And they supported Endicott's recent actions to apprehend the regicides, adding that the colony must declare that no other fugitives should "expect shelter"—although as we have seen, at least one member of the committee, Daniel Gookin, was at that very moment helping maintain Edward Whalley and William Goffe in hiding.[25]

Immediately preceding the regicide section, the patent-study committee inserted a pointed sentence which, framed in monarchical language, outlined a potential basis for constitutional heel-digging: "The premisses considered, it may well stand with the loyalty & obedience of such subjects as are thus priviledged by theire rightfull soveraigne . . . as cause shall require, to pleade with theire prince against all such as shall at any time endeavor the violation of theire priviledges."[26] True obedience, in their understanding, did not mean immediate submission in all cases but rather involved a conversation. Colonists had a role to play in defining their charter privileges. Their duties included not only honoring the king but also defending their liberties, enshrined in the patent, against anyone—surely not the king himself—who would violate them.

The General Court approved the committee's work, but some colonists found this language foolhardy. As the June 1661 court meeting drew to a close, several towns engaged in petition campaigns to criticize the committee's reading of the patent and to express frustration with the court's delay in proclaiming the king. A number of royalist-leaning English colonies, including Barbados and Virginia, had, as might be expected, rapidly organized their own official proclamations. Other colonies such as Rhode Island that were "especially dependent on the favor of the central government" also hurried to proclaim the king. The independently minded Connecticut had just done so in March.[27] As the days ground on, some colonists began to sound the alarm about Massachusetts's delayed response. Would the king see their letters as empty words without further demonstrations of allegiance? A small but vocal group of colonists, viewing the patent-study committee as overly reckless, petitioned the court to make further signs of submission. We will explore the history and practice of petitioning more fully later, but it is worth noting here how these petitions illustrate the range of opinion that existed in mid-1661.

Take Sudbury as one example. Fourteen Sudbury inhabitants, including the minister Edmund Browne, in their petition drew on Proverbs to argue that on the king's favor depended "much of our Externall Happinesse," so "obtaining" that "Favour should bee our studious, & Conscientious Endeavour." This was especially the case for "so dependent, & poor a people." If demonstrations of loyalty were neglected, surely those in London would think them "Children of Beliall, not sons of obedience." As a Christian duty, honoring the king might bring divine rewards, such as "Enemyes to bee at peace" and favor among men. Citing the court's recent letter to the king, the Sudbury petitioners argued that backing down from those expressions of allegiance could make the colony seem like "a Deceiver, & bring a Curse upon us." Indeed, they were already experiencing that curse in part through "the Quakers aspersing [falsely accusing] . . . us in print." Heal and remove "dissatisfactions in many Considerable setled Inhabitants," they urged, by quickly and thoroughly honoring the crown.

Aware they stood in the minority, the Sudbury petitioners then presented a series of queries for the court's "Judicious debate." First, had not the patent-study committee "assume[d] too much Liberty unto our[selves]" and "take[n] too much of Royalty from His Maiesty"? Would it not be safer to interpret the patent "Candidly & warily"? And who had "cheife power [of e]xpounding" the patent in the first place—king or colonists? The petitioners here raised a contentious and live point of constitutionalism: who had the authority to interpret charters?

The petitioners' second query urged discussion of "some seasonable use & owning" of Charles II's authority, an official proclamation and inclusion of his name in writs, or legal documents. Their third called attention to the "aspersions Cast upon us" and "the Dishonour thereby cast on Religion" by the lack of support for Endicott's warrant for arresting the regicides. Fourth, was it not time for the court to review the laws, and if some frequently used statutes were not in line with England's possibly "to seeke for Royall assent, or concession"?[28] Other charters included the crown's review of laws, but the Bay's did not.[29] Granting this power would have been a major constitutional compromise—and the Sudbury petitioners knew it.

Next, they turned to the linked issues of baptism and the franchise. Here they advocated not only for an expansion of baptism to the grandchildren of full church members, a change already gaining momentum in the colony, but also for wider admission to full church membership, which in the Bay colony was the gateway to the franchise. The petitioners also came at the franchise issue from another direction, asking the court to discuss detaching it from church membership altogether in certain cases. Could freemanship be offered also to "men of approved Probity of life, & wisedome & fidelity testifyed to satisfaction," wealthy enough to be paying high taxes? And perhaps a "trusty Agent" sent to London might convince the king not only to confirm but also to expand "our Pattent priviledges," especially with regard to "our Chiefe desire, the House of God"? As they wrapped up their plea, the Sudbury petitioners asserted their places within, rather than outside of, the people of God, declaring "your servants are true men, & not spyes. . . . If we erre, we erre in Love." They promised "Earnest Prayer" for court members' "serpentine" wisdom and "Columbine" (dove-like) innocence, that the Lord's "Glory may still dwell in our Land."[30] As puritans loyal to the colony, these men thought selective compromise would guarantee the future of both the Bay government and its churches.

Along with Sudbury, the inhabitants of Ipswich and Newbury also sent in petitions, now lost, regarding how to express allegiance to the king. Belatedly, thirty-six Boston inhabitants, including the revered minister John Wilson, drew up their own petition, still extant.[31] More formal and sharply worded than Sudbury's, the Boston petition professed unwillingness to speak out but pleaded "conscience of our duty to god, to you, to our Selves, to our All." In their view, the king had been most gracious, and if the colony lost its liberties, the fault would be its own. "Any plea for Independancy" was futile and unwise. Amid dangerous enemies, the General Court's "Steering the vessel wherein we are all imbarqued" would either lead to safe haven "or hazard our Ruine uppon the Sands." Back words with "Real Actions," the Bostonians urged, enacting "a Loyall, and Religious compliance with our Royall King in all Lawfull Commands," and thereby establishing anew "our Aincient Libertyes." In particular, the Boston petitioners, like Sudbury, urged sending an agent (or two), supporting the warrant for the regicides, and quickly proclaiming the king. Despite their "Candor," they concluded, they hoped for continued "affection," pledged themselves "sincerly faithfull" to Christ's "Interest" in their churches and "Civil priviledges . . . Equall with others that may not be like minded with us," and ended with a prayer.[32]

The Sudbury and Boston petitioners evoked a shared commitment to activist and biblical public-spiritedness, one that encouraged lively debate without succumbing to factionalism or rancor. As William Ames, John Wilson's Cambridge mentor, had described it, the godly possessed a right or even a duty to evaluate their leaders' actions and decrees, offering informed consideration of what was "lawfull, convenient and binding."[33] Robust political participation, including the ability to give and receive scriptural and rational critique, had long been nurtured within puritan culture, drawing more broadly on humanist and classical models.[34]

Back at the General Court, the deputies shouldered the responsibility of drafting a response to these town petitions. Although declining to immediately translate the various suggestions they had received into policy, they affirmed the petitioners' goodwill and role in the political process: "Wee cannot but acknowledge theire care, & approve of theire good intencions in most things." They also reminded the petitioners, a bit defensively, that "this Court hath not binn altogether negligent to provide for theire & our oune safety, and to manifest our duty & alleagiance." The king had, after all, just sent a "favorable" message, and the colony's leaders would continue working diligently to promote their peace.[35] The June court adjourned without further action. Eager to return to their homes and farms, court members were inclined to wait for more complete "intelligence . . . from England" before taking any additional action. The court did, however, appoint a smaller committee, composed of ministers, magistrates, and deputies of notably diverse political leanings, to draft new letters to the king and sympathetic advocates and to strategize on raising the funds that the next stage of diplomacy would surely require.[36]

* * *

If information at the General Court was lacking in June 1661, it flowed abundantly with the mid-July return from London of the Bay colony's agent John Leverett. Colonists learned firsthand about the anti-puritan backlash taking hold in England, spurred on by the Fifth Monarchist and former New Englander Thomas Venner's uprising. Venner had initiated an armed revolt against the new regime in January, his fifty followers, including at least one woman, crying out "King Jesus, and the heads upon the gates," a reference to the regicides' mutilated bodies. Although quickly crushed, the revolt had profoundly altered the political calculus in England. Many more royalists now openly argued that nonconformists could never be truly loyal subjects. Repulsed by the "horrid act" committed by Venner and his "companions in evil," John Hull understood the necessity for "all that do indeed fear God" to redouble their efforts to distance themselves from such disloyal and un-Christian "principles and companies."[37] English congregationalists had already raced to distance themselves from Venner's "daring madness," disavowing religious violence and affirming earlier commitments "to pray for Magistrates, to honor their persons, to pay them Tribute . . . to obey their lawful commands . . . for conscience sake."[38] Although the qualifier "lawful" left the door open—albeit just barely—for resistance, after Venner's revolt the priority for nonconformists became controlling their own radical fringe and bending over backward to demonstrate unwavering loyalty.

Leverett also probably shared details about the Privy Council's new attention toward New England. Listening to informants with grudges against the colonies or old competing land claims, in May 1661 the King in Council had formed a "Committee touching the settlement of the Government of New-England." Colonists would be relieved to discover that their friend Lord Saye and Sele had managed to find a place on the committee but disconcerted when they considered the bigger picture: New England had become a problem that required the Stuart government's critical oversight. The committee had called in Leverett to "demaund some answer" regarding complaints. Fearful of arrest or being forced to renegotiate the charter, Leverett had declined the invitation, saying his commission as agent had expired.[39]

Some additional context might help round out the picture. Leverett had been in London for the spring 1661 parliamentary elections, which ushered in a cohort of high church, anti-puritan royalists. Mobilized in part by the Bishop of London Gilbert Sheldon, a protégé of the executed Archbishop William Laud, this "Cavalier" Parliament would work quickly to bypass the king's promises of amnesty at Breda, suppressing nonconformists as dangerous to the state. One former New Englander reported that in Restoration England, all could see "the Crowne & the Miter are ingaged."[40] From people arriving by ships in August, colonists probably learned about the Corporation Act, legislation introduced by the House of Commons in mid-June that would prohibit anyone from holding office in a corporation (the governing body in many cities) who refused to take the Eucharist in the Church of England. This law, which became effective in December 1661 and was sporadically enforced by the removal of nonconformists from local political power, "created and artificially sustained an Anglican governing elite." Further, it required all corporation officers to swear that "it is not lawfull upon any pretence whatsoever to take Arms against the King." In London, the Stuart government deliberately worked to "subordinate" local authority so as "better to harvest its wealth for state purposes."[41] Whether Massachusetts Bay was a corporation like London—and whether parliament could legislate for the colonies at all—would be debated in the years to come. It seemed clear, however, that a new, high church political orthodoxy had demoted nonconformists to second-class citizens and regarded them as potential dangers to the state.[42]

With all this information in hand, Bay colony leaders hastily organized a ceremonial proclamation of Charles II as king in August 1661. They scrambled to figure out the proper protocol; it had been a long time since the 1625 coronation of Charles I. The deputies wanted to follow the old tradition of pardoning criminals on the ceremonial day, but the magistrates thought this act of goodwill unnecessary. All agreed, however, to forbid "drinking of healths." The crossed-out phrases and insertions made to drafts of the manuscript proclamation reveal multiple editors messily at work, trying to find words of congratulation that were, as the ministers had advised the previous October, high but not too high.[43]

In the end, the colony's leaders decided that the grand occasion should take place on 8 August 1661, immediately following the Boston Thursday lecture, a weekly topical sermon that often drew wide attendance. The entire membership of the court attended this outdoor event, the magistrates ringing the crowd on horseback. Also gathered were the "elders, & multitudes of people," four armed militia companies, a troop of horse, and the "masters of ships" currently in the Boston harbor. Those assembled removed their hats, and the court's secretary Edward Rawson read the final version of the proclamation: "as Charles the Second is undoubted King of Great Brittayne . . . wee therefore doe, as in duty wee are bound, oune & acknouledge him to be our soveraigne lord & king." Together the crowd responded, "God save the king!" followed with a "shout." The militias then sent up "sundry volleys of shot," joined by "all the guns in the castle and fort and town and ships." The event concluded with a feast for officers on the colony's tab.[44]

It is difficult to know how colonists experienced this ceremony. There were no wild parties as had supposedly taken place in London when the king had returned the previous year. One of the few to record the event in detail, John Hull was probably relieved that the ceremony had finally taken place. A member of John Wilson and John Norton's church, Hull had signed the Boston petition asking for further demonstrations of allegiance. Yet others most likely had mixed feelings, not so much because a king had returned but because he was a Stuart king, tainted with his father's reputation for absolutist-leaning, anti-puritan policies. Still, many probably felt some hope. They had no way of knowing that the Act of Uniformity, legislation ejecting nonconformists from the Church of England, would be issued the following year. At the moment, they still had reason to hope that Charles II's regime would diverge from that of his father.

Following this August proclamation, the magistrates, or perhaps only Endicott, drafted a letter to the king responding to Venner's revolt and stridently, if awkwardly, rearticulating New England's loyalty. A strange letter, it described the colonists' "eucharisticall approach" to a god-like ruler who had not "abhorred the affliction of the aflicted." It denounced "Disabollical Venner" who "went out from us, because he was not of us," and claimed Charles II's "just title to the crowne enthronizeth you in our consciences." If colonists had made an error in matters of "subscription & conformity" back in the 1630s, they hoped their "voluntary quitting of our native and dearest country" was "sufficient to expiate so innocent a mistake." Self-exile was surely adequate punishment. The letter then compared Charles II to David, the biblical king who had also undergone long and difficult troubles, praying the Lord would make Charles II's reign "both greater & better" than David's or that of any of his English predecessors. Before they made a fair copy, the deputies reviewing the letter cut a lengthy and even more convoluted central section on the feelings evoked by the king's last letter and the colonists' "Desert condition," which made them "fitter to magnifie princly radiature . . . [as] Croesus's dumbe son speaks to prevent miseries, and Zechariah's tongue breakes loose to acknowledge mercie."[45]

This unusual letter demonstrates how hard it was to find words to express the colonists' relationship to the king. Virginia's Governor Berkeley, by contrast, penned eloquent superlatives that seemed to flow without any need for editing or revising: "god is my witness as farr as I am able to know my own heart I alwayes in all Conditions had more feare of your Majesties Frownes then the Swords or tortures of your enemies." In the Bay, the August court also took several preliminary steps toward enforcing the Navigation Acts, helping boost royal customs revenues, perhaps sending a clearer message than any they had written for the king's eyes directly.[46]

* * *

During this same season, Bay colonists grew alarmed at the extent to which Quakers, also called Friends, had the king's ear. To their shock, Charles II had sent a letter demanding the colonies cease executing Quakers and send them to England for trial instead.[47] By this point the Bay was no longer even enforcing its banishment on pain of death law on these intrepid missionaries who cursed magistrates and interrupted court and church services; Bay authorities had just released the Friend Wenlock Christiansen, although he had been declared guilty of returning after banishment. Those crafting New England's law codes generally worked to reduce capital offenses; the anti-Quaker law itself had been a "desperate move" that they had not really anticipated having to enforce.[48] In the conflict between crown and colony over Quakers, neither a principle of toleration nor the fate of Quakers themselves was as central as it might seem: if sent back to England, Quakers would likely end up in disease-ridden prisons.[49] The more salient issue, at least from the colonial perspective, was that the king, favoring London Quaker lobbyists, was limiting colonists' ability to regulate migration and keep the peace. Further, Charles II sought to deprive them of a traditional mark of sovereignty: capital punishment. His letter shifted the constitutional balance.

With the court's consent, Endicott had already solicited advice on this very issue from Richard Baxter, a supporter of New England though a Presbyterian. Colonists were distressed, Endicott explained to Baxter, about reports of "high Complaints" against them, especially those from "our bitter and restless Enemies" the Quakers. At stake was nothing less than the colonists' "Liberty to serve God according to the Scriptures," a right that did not entail "Liberty unto Errour and Sin, or to set up another Rule besides the Scriptures." Endicott hoped his fellow New Englanders did not err in "any Fundamental Matter," and in "inferiour" matters were willing to be instructed. But they had for "many years enjoyed" this liberty, "advantaged and encouraged by the Constitution of our Civil Government"—established by royal patent, he reminded his reader. The colonists, he added, eschewed Machiavellian strategy—"nothing that is unjust, or not honest, both in the sight of the Lord, and also of Men"—and hoped to "continue as faithful Subjects to his Majesty (according to our Duty) and be every way as beneficial to the Interest of our Nation, under an Elective Government as under an Imposed."[50] Enacting capital laws in accordance with scriptural principles formed a constitutional line whose upholding Endicott found imperative. Baxter surely responded with pointed advice, sadly not extant.

Quickly regathering in November 1661, the court asked the ministers for counsel on five specific questions, three regarding Quakers and two concerning the possibility of sending agents to London. That Quakers had the ear of Charles II was a strong argument for sending agents: someone had to make sure the king and Privy Council heard the other side. Sending agents, however, required a hefty financial investment. The colony's government operated on a shoestring budget, with much volunteer labor, some repaid later in land. Agents would need London-scale funds for lodging, dinners, and legal fees, to start. And who would leave their families, churches, and farms to face possible imprisonment for the colony's offenses, or to endure the godly's scorn if forced to renegotiate the charter on weaker terms?

After much debate and prayer, the ministers soft-pedaled—at least for the moment. They recommended temporary suspension of the anti-Quaker capital laws, replacing them with other methods "for the restraint of Turbulencies in church or state." In their view, the king's letter did not discourage but actually encouraged them to promote order, though not by executions.[51] (They turned out to be right; the king soon clarified he never meant for colonial leaders to give "indulgence" to Quakers, whose disruptive presence was, he realized, "inconsistent with any kind of government.") Send the imprisoned Quakers to England along with letters explaining their concerns to the king and well-funded agents to plead their case, the ministers advised.[52]

The magistrates and deputies agreed with some of this advice. Regarding agents, however, the deputies needed assurances that whoever was nominated would not compromise the colonists' liberties. After a near-stalemate and an extraordinary series of backroom negotiations involving smaller groups of magistrates, deputies, and elders (church leaders), the court finally voted to send minister John Norton and magistrate Simon Bradstreet to London "in behalf of the churches and Commonwealth."[53] But neither wanted to go, citing concerns about compensation, clarity of the mission, and the burden of shouldering responsibility for its outcome. Norton also needed his church's permission.

The next few months of patient, ground-level mobilizing to address the concerns voiced by the would-be travelers demonstrates just how committed many colonists were to helping the court follow through on its hard-won consensus. A range of colonists negotiated with the Boston church, potential financiers, and ships' captains to provide Norton and Bradstreet what they had asked for. Others gathered old manuscripts the agents might need to defend their constitutional arrangement. Bradstreet traveled home to Ipswich to discuss the matter with his wife, the poet Anne Bradstreet, returning with much greater clarity regarding his own terms. He and Norton both wanted financial and legal protections, as well as a say in the wording of the court's letter to Charles II.[54]

The obstacles seemed overwhelming. At one point, some colonists asked why, when prayerfully using "all lawfull means," should "so many clouds" be "darkning our pathes"? Even so, they remained committed to "our owne peace and safety," to "the honor of the Lords name, church and wayes," and to a decision made "upon mature councills in sundry debates." Dangers could accompany inaction as well: the Lord's "servants grieved . . . friends in England offended, the Kings Majestie incenced, our adversaries animated . . . our God dishonoured and displeased."[55] With Norton and Bradstreet's input, the court revised its letter in a more formal, precise, and submissive direction. Court members also devised a method of "secret conveyance" for their correspondence to bypass royal surveillance. Governor Endicott's reluctance almost doomed the larger mission. The jolting sign of a mild earthquake, coupled with further prayerful negotiations, got things back on track, and provisions were finally loaded shipboard. Shortly thereafter, however, Norton fell seriously ill; and colonists waited and prayed for his recovery. Less patient than the prayerful, the delayed shipmaster cornered the magistrates at a church lecture, pressing them for "liberty to depart."[56] Powerless before Norton's illness, the magistrates made plans to release the ship, return bills of exchange, and write explanatory letters to London concerning the change of plans. They even went so far as to unload the provisions, although storing them close by "with a secret hope" for divine intervention. Another tense day passed. The following dawn "the Lord so encouraged and strengthened" Norton that he decided to board the ship.[57] Provisions were retrieved, letters reassembled, money reorganized, and Norton and Bradstreet sailed forth to meet the king.

* * *

On the occasion of her husband Simon's departure, Anne Bradstreet wrote: "At Thy command, O Lord, he went, / Nor nought could keep him back. / Then let Thy promise joy his heart, / O help and be not slack." Asking God to give their address favor in Charles II's eyes, she prayed, "Remember, Lord, Thy Folk whom Thou / To Wilderness hast brought; / Let not Thine own inheritance / Be sold away for nought."[58] As we will see later on in the fast day records, many colonists joined the poet in praying for their agents. They heard fearful rumors that the two men "were detained in England" and "that Mr Norton was in the tower." These rumors proved unfounded; the visit went off without incident. In London, prominent nonconformists, including Richard Baxter, came to Norton and Bradstreet's assistance, offering money, friendship, and introductions.[59] The wealthy Boston-based merchant Thomas Temple was also on hand, supposedly telling the king that the tree imprinted on Massachusetts coins was actually "the emblem of the oak which preserved his majesty's life," his hideout while fleeing Cromwell's army in 1651.[60] Samuel Maverick, by contrast, actively undermined the agents, reminding Lord Chancellor Clarendon that they represented a colony which did not own "his majesties Soveraigntie" until "there was no avoydinge of it," and "frequently bragged they were the elder Commonwealth." Maverick went so far as to say that Norton and Bradstreet themselves had long "spoake[n] & acted vyolently against his Majesties interest." Favoring the agents would mean a "shattered" New England, he argued; much better to require the full "Oath of Allegiance" and, in time, to outlaw nonconformity and impose Church of England ceremonies on the region.[61]

Norton and Bradstreet's personal meeting with Clarendon in spring 1662 went well. Envisioning New England's strategic potential, Clarendon was willing to be patient with these odd nonconformists—he kept the bigger picture in mind. The previous year, when the new Council for Foreign Plantations had recommended sending a threatening letter from England to the region demanding agents, Clarendon had overruled this hard-line approach. He had a keen sense for the rule of law; in the early 1640s he had opposed Charles I's absolutist-leaning policies. A pragmatist, Clarendon also believed threats of this sort could backfire. In his view, New Englanders were "a very humerous People, and must be handled with greate dexterity" within the Restoration empire. Acutely aware that the use of force would signify failure of authority, and that England's resources were limited, he chose instead to delay and send the matter to a newly formed Committee for New England.[62] Probably pleased that the Bay had finally sent agents of their own accord,

Clarendon now responded to Norton and Bradstreet's request for reconfirmation of their liberties with "fair promises of a full grant to their whole desire in the country's behalf." No one, however, was willing to put a signature to these promises.

In June 1662, Charles II finally issued a letter directly expressing his expectations. The Bay colony "may have swerved" from the terms and scope of the charter, but the king imputed it to the "iniquity of the times" rather than to "evil intentions." He went ahead and confirmed the charter with its liberties and privileges, and "declare[d] our free and gracious pardon" to all colonists except the regicides, whose capture he expected. There were conditions, however: colonists must change their laws, writs, and oaths, as well as allowing prayer-book worship and significantly expanding baptism and the franchise. These demands, which we will discuss in more detail momentarily, would allow high church ceremonialists and royalists much greater access to political power.[63] And they would spark some of the Massachusetts General Court's most intense debates over the following two years.

While in London, Norton and Bradstreet engaged in long conversations with Baxter, who had accepted appointment as royal chaplain in June 1660 in hopes of rebuilding an inclusive Church of England. In later writings on Norton and Bradstreet's mission, Baxter worried they had been deceived by his appointment, which the king made so "the People might think that such Men as we were favoured and advanced, and . . . might think their Condition happy." With the bitter clarity of hindsight, Baxter remembered suspecting it was a short-term appeasement and "that afterward we should be silenced with rest in time, yet . . . especially those in France and in New-England . . . were far more deceived by these Appearances, and the more ready to bless us in our present State, and almost wish it were their own." In Baxter's view, enticed by this deception, New Englanders quickly "grew . . . a great Inclination to Episcopal Government."[64] In other words, some colonists in the early 1660s, including Norton and Bradstreet, thought the restored Church of England might be broad enough to include them. Faced with being forced underground or reconfiguring their relationship to the church hierarchy, the latter seemed more appealing. Like other post-Restoration nonconformists, such colonists assumed their estrangement "was provisional, malleable, susceptible of substantial renegotiation, within the confines of monarchy and a national church." They may have hoped for a place within, or at least in communion with, an elastic Church of England.[65] Baxter worried they were being set up for disappointment.

What was to be done? According to Baxter, he and another supporter had tried to "disswade" the two agents from this "inclining to our English Episcopacy." But Norton and Bradstreet had been "deeply . . . afraid" of their supply of godly ministers being cut off unless rapprochement with the Church of England could be found.[66] Over the course of their stay in London, however, it became clear—even to the optimistic nonconformist—that the Cavalier Parliament and the new crop of bishops intended to enforce full conformity, even on minor issues; their informers constantly sat in on the sermons of Baxter himself, accusing the popular preacher of sedition.[67] Baxter recalled that Norton and Bradstreet "at last . . . saw how things went, and those in New-England heard at last how we were all silenced and cast out." The agents witnessed "Black Bartholomew's Day," 24 August 1662, when under the Act of Uniformity nine hundred nonconformist clergy were ejected from the Church of England. According to Baxter, as they bore witness to these events, the colonists "began to remember again, that there is something beside Schism to be feared, and that there lyeth as perilous an Extreme on the other side."[68] Was it only a matter of time, Norton and Bradstreet must have wondered, before prayer-book worship, which to many puritans seemed full of unbiblical and idolatrous human inventions, was also imposed across the sea?

Returning to Boston in time for the fall 1662 court meeting, the two agents relayed the king's June letter demanding major ecclesiastical and civil changes. The colonists should repeal laws "derogatory to our authority," take the oath of allegiance, allow prayer-book liturgy, and extend sacraments to everyone "of good and honest lives and conversations." Further, in elections they should overlook candidates' religious "opinions and outward professions" and include in the franchise "freeholders of competent estates, not vicious in conversation, and orthodox in religion."[69] These changes would open the door for wealthy high church royalists unsympathetic to the founders' vision to acquire political control. Many colonists expressed alarm; few seemed to think Norton and Bradstreet's mission a success. At the meeting, the prominent royalist-leaning merchant Thomas Breedon tried to command the magistrates and deputies to obey the king, receiving a whopping £200 fine (later remitted) for "his Contemptuous Carriage."[70]

No doubt Norton hated being found on the same side as someone like Breedon. The new political reality in London, however, had convinced him of the wisdom of submission. The colony's political liberties were not as closely linked to gospel liberty as others assumed. Present before the court, Norton argued passionately that if the magistrates and deputies "complied not with the King's Letter, the Blood that should be spilt would lye at their dores, or upon thiere heades."[71] Childless himself, Norton had a twelve-year-old nephew and namesake whom he was preparing for Harvard. He could not bear letting his nephew's generation die futilely before the firepower of English warships.

The magistrates and deputies respectfully heard Norton's arguments and then began a heated discussion. A wealthy puritan-leaning merchant who had emigrated to Boston following the Restoration, Humphrey Davie reported that after reading the king's latest letter, the court "had large debate what should be don. . . . They have great strugling." Most of the colony's leaders feared the king's demands were the prelude to a royalist takeover of both church and state. In Davie's words, "truely the eyes of most begin to be opened, & to see plainely the designe to exterpate the profession and professors of the pure & right waies of the Lord, out of this Collony, if not out of the Country" or region.[72] Obeying the king in full might forestall violence, but it could spell disaster for the colonists' ideals of godly reform.

A compromise of some kind seemed essential. The court finally agreed that changing their writs to be in the king's name was reasonable. They could not, however, justify or approve the king's demands to change their franchise, baptism, and oaths.[73] Above all, the deputies wanted to build consensus, pushing for delay "so all persons Concerned may have time [and] oppertunitie to Consider of what is Necessary to be donne."[74] Any constitutional defiance of the king's demands required broad input leading to a thoughtful, strategic, consensual response.

The royal letter had come with an appended instruction that it be published (read or disseminated) in the towns, so Charles II's expectations would be clearly understood by all. But colonists disliked being told when or how to transmit the royal agenda. They took measures to guard the press, saying that the only colony printers would be in Cambridge and temporarily appointing censors.[75] After much discussion, the magistrates and deputies had agreed that the letter could be published but differed on whether transcriptions should be sent to each town for public proclamation, the deputies finally agreeing on this mode of dissemination.

At the town level, however, whether to read the king's letter publicly became a fraught decision. Ipswich leaders decided to read it on the November public thanksgiving day, the occasion implying their support for compromise with the king. When their minister William Hubbard read the letter and tried to defend the possibility of expanding the sacraments, however, some Ipswich inhabitants shouted him down.[76] After all, other towns on this same thanksgiving day heard about how God could move kings, even great kings, out of his people's way.

Woburn inhabitants took their disagreement a step further. They declined to read the king's letter in the first place. In doing so, they opened themselves up to charges of sedition. Their constable further refused to put writs in the king's name, the demand to which the General Court had already agreed. Rebuffed, the General Court's messengers took the letter to Woburn selectmen, but they too declined, protesting that such matters remained the purview of the constable. Another town official confronted the messengers, asking them "would you have the book of Common prayer?" One messenger retorted, "we desire the booke of Common prayer no more then you doe." The disagreement grew heated. According to one deposition, countered by others, the official then said that the "two brought Popery into the Towne," and a messenger shot back, "be it what it will wee did not send for it into the Countrey."[77] Neither side of this debate was eager for prayer-book conformity to be imposed on New England. In this case, however, for the constable and selectmen, the king's very letter crossed a constitutional line.

Because the situation at Woburn involved seditious speech, the case came to trial at the next General Court. As with Jenks, the court members did not punish the Woburn selectmen, citing conflicting evidence. Divided over the constable's role in the matter, they ended up saying they would deal with the case later. They never did.[78] There was clear sympathy within the court for the men's defiant actions.

Despite the court's decision to delay an official response to the king's demands and seek broad input from the population, something had to be communicated immediately to Charles II. Meeting in November 1662, the Council (governor, deputy governor, and available magistrates) drafted a letter thanking the king for confirming their charter, for assuring protection, and for "passing by whatsoever during the late Changes might have beene offencive." They reported that the king's letter had been read in court and then "published," omitting precisely where, and that writs were now being issued in the king's name. On laws derogatory to king or monarchy, the magistrates said, "we are not conscious of any of that tendency." On the king's demands regarding worship, they claimed that "none as yet among us have appeared to desire" the Book of Common Prayer, a statement that perhaps held true on the level of formal petitions but was not wholly accurate, especially for inhabitants of Maine. They also defended their censure of Breedon, who they knew was on his way to England "& possibly may Complaine." To neglect fining Breedon for his "high contempt" would be, they argued, to "prostrate our Governmen[t] derived from his majesty & by us so long & orderly enjoyed," an outcome they knew the king would not desire.[79]

On the baptism issue, interestingly, the Council members mentioned a synod, or formal gathering of ministers, that had met in March 1662 and endorsed expanding baptism to the grandchildren of full church members. The momentum behind baptismal reform, an emotionally charged issue that we will explore further later, predated the Restoration.[80] Council members were not, however, the only ones linking the expansion of baptism, sometimes called the halfway covenant, to the Restoration political settlement. The June 1661 Sudbury petition had advised more "Latitude of the subjects of Baptisme" as a path toward political safety.[81] And the preface to a multiauthored letter to the Scottish ecumenist John Dury also claimed that the synod diffused critics' "Asperson" of New England congregationalists "as too much favouring the way of the Separation," better facilitating communion with the Restoration Church of England.[82] The synod was not primarily politically motivated; its conclusions, however, could usefully demonstrate movement on one of the king's demands, without full submission. They would cite their compliance where they could find it.

On elections, the Council drew a firm constitutional line. They had always taken "great care" that men of virtue were elected, they stated, and that those who voted were orthodox. They would not, however, separate the franchise from church membership. Men vetted at the local level were admitted to freemanship "according to the orders & Customes of this Colony here established agreeable to <the liberty of> our charter." Although they alluded to ongoing consideration of the issue, with these words the Council nonetheless defied the king's direct command.[83]

* * *

The Council's letter, and especially its firmness on the franchise, set off mobilizing efforts among multiple groups in the Bay colony. Witnessing his fellow magistrates' lackluster response to "his Majesty[s] Gracious Returne," Massachusetts secretary Rawson wrote, "brings me to shame & sorrow." According to Rawson, another set of petitions in late 1662 objected to the Council's letter, asking for another meeting of the full court "to Consult &

Conclude of the best & fitting[e]st Remedy" prior to the ship's departure.[84] There is no record, however, that the Council pulled its letter off the ship or responded to these petitions if they were sent. Support for constitutional defiance of the king's demands ran high. "Such has been the Jealous Disposition of our New-Englanders about their Dearly bought Privileges," wrote Cotton Mather in a later comment on the situation, that "there were many, who would not stick to say, that [Norton] had laid the Foundation of Ruine to all our Liberties."[85] Indeed, more towns would send petitions in support of constitutional defiance than in support of concessions. And on the franchise they would not budge far: Bay colonists linked the franchise with full church membership as a way of guarding their society from leaders who placed personal gain over the common good. Church membership meant moral accountability; at stake for many was protecting the body politic from forces of corruption.

Some who supported the current franchise decided to inform inhabitants about its history by printing a ca. 1635 treatise defending this link between the franchise and church membership. *A discourse about civil government in a new plantation whose design is religion* was printed in early 1663, ostensibly for New Haveners who, fearful of Restoration changes, had begun contemplating migration to the territory later called Newark. In reality, however, the treatise was printed for a Massachusetts audience considering the king's demands. Some colonists thought the publication "would Rather Increase the flame then quench it." Personally incensed over its contents, Rawson "labored not a litle to have procured their stifling," but, he lamented, "out they Come." Describing the treatise as a providential trial, its words would, he feared, hasten the colony's "Ruine . . . Unless the Lord Miraculo[usl]y [comes] to our reliefe" to thwart opponents' "designes."[86] This tension spilled over into the May 1663 elections, when a group of non-freemen, identified as "Sundry young merchants and others," took the bold step of nominating magistrates. Hearing the king's June 1662 letter, they pushed for access to freemanship, possibly even sending a formal petition to the court.[87]

The magistrates and deputies who were finally elected that year thus faced a formidable task. They needed to find a way "to Answer his Majesties expectaccion, sattisfy those that are differently minded among our selves, [and] secure the Religious interest of this Collony." At stake were no less than "the Honor of God, & weale of this Country."[88] To shore up these men, Salem minister John Higginson preached an election sermon that reminded leaders of the colony's rights and liberties: like ancient Israel, the colony had a "right from God, and liberty from God, to keep Gods Commandments in matters of Religion." These rights did not belong to individuals but rather to the Gospel itself, which possessed "a Divine & Supream right to be received in every nation," one no "power upon earth . . . can lawfully hinder."[89] Drawing on a Geneva Bible note on 1 Kings 8:45 that translates "cause" as "right," Higginson explained that true worship was a divine right even more fundamental than the right to property. If the Stuart regime tried to curtail these rights, whether through bishops, "imposed Liturgies," forcing admission of "Scandalous Persons to the Lords Table," or toleration of "any false Religion," then in those moments of extreme stress "we must obey God rather than men," he argued, and decline "to serve the times." Quoting one of Jonathan Mitchell's sermons from the previous year, Higginson clarified that "for our Civil Government to put forth any act of consent" to these impositions "would be a thing to be trembled at." Even so, he reminded colonists that whether they liked it or not, their "Supream Civill Governour under God" was the king, and the colony's government was "subordinate." Colonists should somehow find "a narrow way" to be "faithfull to the cause of Religion according to our duty to God: faithful to the King according to the oath of Allegiance, and faithfull to the Government here according to the Oath of fidelity." In these "shaking times, and trying times," he realized, such faithfulness was no easy task.[90]

Tellingly, Higginson ended his sermon with an anecdote from 1628, when he heard a minister—probably his father, Frances Higginson—preaching to a crowd of thousands in Leicester about his rationale for emigrating to New England. One reason he gave was "the mercy . . . and the largeness of the Patent," allowing "the people here to chuse their own Magistrates and to admit unto freedom such as they should think meet." Another was "that Religion was the Principall end of this Plantation in his Majesties Royal intention and the adventurers free possession." God had blessed the colonists under their charter government. "Therefore," Higginson concluded, "as in the matter of Religion we are to keep to the Word of God, so in the matter of the Civil Government keep to the Patent." Although stern on the local government's subordinate status, and amenable to several of the king's demands, this May 1663 election sermon gave colonists plenty of material from which to work toward constitutional defiance.[91]

Higginson did not rest his case with the sermon. He also spoke in the court meeting itself, offering a fresh case for limited compromise. Remarkably, the manuscript notes of his speech survive.[92] On biblical and practical grounds he argued generally for enlarging the franchise, a position with which the majority of Salem's freemen agreed.[93] He began by affirming the court: to each member, he knew "the cause of God & his people is most deare," and all desired "the narrow way of well doing" like the biblical Daniel.[94] No Machiavellian "reason of state" policy here.[95] Turning to the *Discourse*, he said it failed to see the colony's situation realistically. Some people might have freedom to set up governments from scratch, but the Bay colony did not. Using specific evidence from the 1648 Cambridge Platform and the propositions of the Synod of 1662, Higginson further argued that baptized but non-communicant colonists still served as "members of the militant visible church" and "believers & saints," so they could have the franchise.[96] The king's demand in this regard agreed with the "ende & minde" of the 1631 "Law for freedom" (the franchise law). Less confidently, Higginson offered a model for, in the last resort, stomaching the Book of Common Prayer. Maybe it could be allowed as a kind of "abstracted . . . witnyss to the truth" like Paul used "testimonies from heathen Poets"? He was sure, however, that the court should send a present to the king, as in 2 Chronicles when "all Judah brought presents to Jehoshaphat."[97] Tribute sweetened diplomacy.

Many others gave speeches at the same May 1663 court meeting, and magistrates and deputies reread aloud all the correspondence between the colony and London. After "long & serious debate" on the franchise, however, no consensus emerged. In an internal vote, a majority of magistrates "resolved on the negative"; the deputies again wanted further deliberations and broader input.[98] A tired court sent the matter to another committee, this one composed of four magistrates, five deputies, and four ministers, to reconsider the franchise and law code.[99] Having declined thus far to formally request ministerial counsel, the May court now asked the "reverend elders" to send their advice to this committee, an invitation they extended, as well, to any "other of the freemen" who desired to share their opinions. Later, the court expanded this clause to include "other the inhabitants": non-freemen, too, were now encouraged to send in advice. All knew that a successful constitutional defiance of the Stuart regime would require a broad coalition. A range of "apprehensions" and "arguments," they hoped, would lead to policies both "satisfactory and safe, as best conducing to his glory and this peoples felicity."[100] Court members gathered their belongings and traveled home, continuing to discuss these vexing issues with their families and local communities.

With all the uncertainty during these days, colonial leaders became anxious about the possibility of election disruptions. Some merchants, citing the king's 1662 letter, had pushed for the franchise and were unhappy with the response they had received.[101] Gathering again in October 1663, the court's first order of business was declared: they must "better regulat[e]" voting. Each town constable, they decided, would send in the freemen's votes in a sealed package by proxy, rather than having the freemen come in person. This experiment proved short-lived. The court learned the change was "not so sattisfactory of the freemen as was expected." The next year, elections would be "runne in the ordinary course, as formerly."[102] Court members had underestimated the extent to which the freemen prized the election day ritual of casting their votes in person. Over time, however, the magistrates and deputies also continued to keep an eye on malcontents. Verdicts would be tougher on those who spoke disrespectfully against local "laws & Law makers" than those who spoke against the king.[103]

In response to a strong letter from the Privy Council, sent also to Virginia, Maryland, Surinam, and multiple Caribbean islands, the fall General Court also took concrete steps toward compliance with the Navigation Acts. For the previous several decades, the Bay, like most colonies, had ignored English restrictions on trade, regularly doing business with the French or Dutch, but no longer.[104] Royalists too resented the newly formulated restrictions on trade. Governor Berkeley had pleaded for the king to see Virginia as a commonwealth to be nurtured rather than simply as a source of commercial income, even traveling to London to try to negotiate a reprieve. Beset by hurricanes, Dutch attacks, and scarcity, Caribbean merchant-planters had also pushed back against the Navigation Acts, affirming loyalty but insisting on "liberty" in trade.[105] Maryland's proprietor Lord Baltimore had turned impeding royal customs collectors into an art form. Aware of constitutional precedent, the October 1663 Boston court passed its own law on trade. Enforcing parliament's Navigation Acts, the court appointed colonial officers to require bonds and seize violators—and reported all this good behavior to England. Although they might have to rein in trade, colonists still controlled the harbor. The ever-vigilant court also attended to military readiness and cracked down on celebratory gun-firing on visiting ships.[106]

One final point about the October court warrants attention: its letter to the distinguished English nonconformist leader John Owen. John Norton had passed away not long after his return from London, and his Boston church decided to invite Owen to fill the pulpit. The deputies and magistrates made the risky decision to write a letter reinforcing the Boston church's invitation.[107] As we saw earlier, Owen had emerged as a prominent spokesperson for the parliamentary cause, a defender of the regicide, and a close advisor to

Oliver Cromwell. In the late 1650s he served as pastor to a number of notable Cromwellian army officers, including William Goffe. After the Restoration, he came under suspicion of sedition. In January 1661, a militia raided his home and discovered several cases of pistols.[108] The court's 1663 letter to Owen assured him that "it will be very acceptable" both to them "& wee hope to the whole country" if the Lord led him to Boston. Acknowledging the hardships of colonial life and the imperfections of the people, the court's letter claimed the colony's purpose to be "the faith & testimony of Jesus," through whose favor they still enjoyed "peace & liberty."[109] Recruiting godly leadership outweighed disarming the colony's critics.

* * *

Back in London, the Cavalier Parliament was as busy as its counterparts in Boston—but to quite different ends. Parliamentary members were working to "prevent and suppress seditious Conventicles," whether participating nonconformists contributed to the realm's prosperity or not. Those who supported the Conventicles Act, introduced in the House of Commons in May 1663, heard in nonconformist worship itself the sound of disloyalty. The bill stalled that summer in the House of Lords when the king expressed disapproval and put forward an alternate plan that would allow indulgence for both Catholics and some nonconformists.[110] The king's moderate declarations might have had a chance of success; however, in late 1663 a group of northern England Presbyterians were discovered in another plot to overthrow Charles II. Mercy went out the window: in subsequent days, the Cavalier Parliament's brutal suppression of nonconformists went virtually unopposed. After July 1664, it was no longer legal for puritans or Baptists to gather for worship in England.[111] As this news reached the colonists, their concern was amplified by additional reports that the king was sending four royal commissioners to New England to gather information and encourage full submission.

In their initial responses to the Restoration, the General Court and those who advised or aided it scrambled to articulate their liberties and duties under charter, God, and king. Watching them work out their stance reveals a messy but surprisingly collaborative process, one marked by a willingness to hear opposing views, to sit through long debates, and to weigh the concerns of multiple constituencies. Tensions over the boundaries of appropriate speech persisted and would increase in the years to come. Yet within these sometimes loud and passionate meetings, the colony's elected leaders determinedly hashed out a wide range of difficult and high-stakes constitutional issues, in most cases reaching hard-won, if rough, consensus.

They did so, in part, because many colonists understood respectful, rational debate as both a political and religious imperative. Pressure from the bottom up, as well as from the crown and Privy Council, contributed to the shared constitutional culture that found expression in and around the Town House. Many believed it was essential to respect the goodwill and piety of those who disagreed with their own opinions. For example, one colonist warned against "uncharitable censures": no one should say another group was "disaffected to the Cause of God and his People, because they see not in some things as others do." Another reminded his community that those on the opposing side are also "lovers of the welfare of this plantation." These admonitions indicate that uncharitableness and party-spirit could sometimes be present and were deeply concerning to those who witnessed such behavior. Although condoning loose alliances, men and women frowned on factions, those who "engaged unto parties" rather than identifying with "all the People of God."[112] Inhabitants expected "an Universall, & Rationall concurrence" among leaders as they fulfilled their primary obligation to "salus Populi," the people's well-being. For most, then, the ideal was not majority rule but rather to diligently keep up arguments, drafts, and committee-work until they could "be unanimous in voting."[113] Rather than "agree . . . to Disagree," leaders should use their "best Endeavours" to discern the right path for "the public Welfare." And even if full agreement proved elusive, disagreements should not be allowed to produce intransigent divisions. "Let not them that Unite in the main, be dis-united by lesser Differences," was how one colonist put it.[114] A heated conversation was far better than no conversation at all, as colonists worked toward a unified response to the crown.

CHAPTER 4

Churches

Fast Days as Communal Discernment

Fast days imparted a strange calm within a week's busy, dusty labor in home, farm, and market. Preparing and eating a meal would wait until sundown. Physical exertion, however, for many gave way to spiritual and emotional labor. After minimal care for farm animals, a household might gather in front of the fire and take from the shelf a worn devotional manual, reading a passage aloud. Then they might begin a spontaneous prayer, asking forgiveness for shortcomings and entreating the Lord's presence. Walking to the meetinghouse was a social affair, with nodded greetings to friends and neighbors. Taking a seat, fast day participants might feel a keen sense of anticipation, wondering what the minister would share about the king's latest letters, or their enemies' complaints. Would fervent prayers disarm faraway schemers and incline the hearts of the powerful toward godly reform?

Fast days were the occasions when most New Englanders would have contemplated the upheavals of the Restoration. Moving fast days—rarely studied outside religious history—to the forefront of political history does not make these events any less spiritual. Rather, it acknowledges that for many seventeenth-century men and women, communal prayer informed political decision making and consensus building. Wise statecraft and even the king's favor were understood to be divine gifts, most often given to communities rather than individuals—particularly to communities whose members had purged their hearts of selfishness. As we have seen, colonists faced a series of extraordinarily difficult decisions in the early Restoration, such as whether to protect the puritan regicides who had fled to New England, how and when to send agents to London, and how to respond to each of Charles II's demands. During these moments of crisis, they organized days of fasting.

The rituals of a fast day asked auditors to relate current events to their own patterns of conduct and desire, putting the agency of ordinary people at the center of the crisis, both its origin and its resolution. The proclamations, sermons, and narrative accounts of Restoration-era fast days reveal how colonists immersed themselves in biblical frameworks where immediate divine action undergirded any lasting political safety, even as they resolved on their own certain contributions to the colony's welfare. Fasts helped shape a constitutional culture as men and women discerned their obligations to local institutions and to the crown.

From the Reformation onward, English Protestants had organized fasts that drew on medieval rituals of communal penitence, reformulated along Old Testament lines. Foundational passages included stories of David fasting when his enemies had surrounded him and of Esther organizing three days of "fastynge and prayinge" when King Ahasuerus threatened the Jews.[1] Protestant fasts were supposed to be undertaken voluntarily, cheerfully, and in moderation, "so farre as health will permit." Subduing the flesh should enhance other faculties, such as memory and understanding, to better internalize the Word. Further, fasting could nurture patience and humility, teaching the soul "to hunger more eagerly after spirituall and heavenly food." On the Church of England calendar, days of fasting, along with feast days, appeared within a fixed annual cycle. The 1571 book of homilies offered a biblical rationale for a "publique fast" observed by "a whole countrey," advising that true fasts must be "inwarde in heart, and not in outward shewe onlye." Protestant monarchs proclaimed fasts in times of danger, such as plagues or invasions.[2]

As tension with the earlier Stuart king mounted in the 1620s, parliament added fast days to its opening sessions. In February 1642, Charles I tried to harness this tradition, inaugurating monthly Wednesday fasts throughout the realm for an embattled Ireland. Puritan parliamentary leaders such as John Pym saw in these monthly fasts an extraordinary opportunity. To Charles I's consternation, they brought in gifted, reform-minded preachers (including, as seen earlier, Hugh Peter, Nathaniel Ward, and John Owen) to deliver parliamentary fast day sermons. Parliament's fast days "functioned also as a means of displaying the unity of the parliamentary cause and as a vehicle for rendering the cause coherent." In other words, they symbolically communicated a coordinated and principled resistance to Charles I's (or his evil advisors') absolutist tendencies. When the king tried to abolish these Wednesday fasts, parliament ignored him.[3] Concern about those who were trying to "reverse the Reformation," a criticism advanced subtly and not so subtly within the parliamentary fast day sermons, fueled the petition campaigns of the early 1640s, when many more people began expressing concerns about the king, bishops, and church.[4]

Liturgically minded Protestants usually fasted according to an annual calendar, but puritan churches generally rejected this model as unbiblical. Spontaneous communal fasting became "a sign of puritan difference" that set their practice apart from the cyclical high church year.[5] Fasts might be held weekly or monthly for a season, but they were rarely annual or indefinite. The minister Thomas Cobbet summarized the logic of puritan fast days: "Publick wants call for publick Petitions; Publick sins for publick confessions. The plaister [bandage] must bee as large as the sore." When a crisis affected the entire community, everyone should come together to seek repentance and wisdom. On these gatherings could depend the rise or fall of states. Cobbet later reflected on the many times communal prayers had ushered in "divine protection and deliverance" for the colonists' churches and "civil state; and that from enemies forreign or domestick, pagan, or in pretence christian." The practice thus affirmed and reinforced an intensely providential view of the world, one in which supernatural power was accessed through prayer. That puritans appointed their own fasts proved an ongoing bone of contention with the crown and a reminder that even a shared practice did not always mean shared beliefs.[6] The Massachusetts Laws and Liberties guaranteed churches' "freedom to celebrate dayes of fasting & prayer and of thanksgiving, according to the word of God."[7] It was a prized freedom.

In New England, fast days might be private—organized by families, churches, or groups of churches—or they might be public, organized by the magistrates of a colony or sometimes coordinated across multiple colonies. During particularly fraught times, a General Court might hold its own fast, led by clergy, a direct borrowing from the parliamentary fast tradition. For the general population, the spiritual disciplines of puritan fast days revolved around family devotions, two prayer-and-sermon-filled church services, a collection for the poor, and discussions over a shared post-sundown meal. Like other occasional sermons, fast day sermons were "grounded in immediate, memorable circumstances . . . the Word made palpable" for a large and varied audience.[8] No doubt some people slept through fast day sermons or heard only their grumbling stomachs. For many, however, the messages alerted them to larger political or environmental crises and involved them in their resolution.

Historians are still uncovering the politics of public fast day proclamations, which listed specific items for prayer and involved a collaboration among magistrates, deputies, and ministers. Ministers might suggest a fast, but the General Court issued the formal proclamations. This formal role did not, however, mean that civil officials controlled the events. As with election day sermons or series such as the parliamentary fast day sermons, civic leaders could invite ministers to participate but would have had much difficulty prescribing what was said. From the specific issues listed on a public fast day proclamation, preachers could choose which ones they wanted to emphasize or highlight. Ministers also individually chose biblical passages to provide supernatural and ethical context for their congregants. They enjoyed considerable freedom to tailor the scope or emphasis of these messages for particular communities.

Although older histories sometimes describe fasts as a means of social control, more recent scholarship has revealed the highly participatory nature of these rituals, which operated according to an ethic of "assertive humility" for both laypeople and clergy. The days included lengthy extemporaneous prayers and sermons with strong attention to lay response. Far from comprising passive opportunities for indoctrination, "the bodily customs, reading practices, and sermonic form" on fast days came together "to emphasize the devout subject's active participation. . . . requir[ing] quick and authentic responsiveness."[9] Articulating a heartfelt prayer or biblical analogy could help the community diagnose a given problem and formulate a desired outcome. While led by ministers, fasts often operated as flexible times for communal discernment. Magistrates' attendance alongside shopkeepers and day laborers probably helped leaders hear the concerns of broader constituencies, as well as influence them. Magistrate Thomas Danforth later reflected on God's remarkable gift to New England in the early 1660s of "a spirit of prayer and mourneing . . . stirred up among us, & that He is uniteing his peoples Hearts more close to Himselfe, & one to another" through fast days and other gatherings; the people seemed "in some measure awakened, to a sence of the worth of those mercies, that before were as this light food," he observed.[10]

Manuscript fast day sermon notes give even more specific examples of the spaces for lay participation. Preachers might pose open-ended questions or offer opportunities for reflection to the congregation, encouraging men and women to take a certain passage and "apply it in good earnest." In January 1662, Charlestown inhabitants seated in their wooden pews heard a sermon about the Lord's ability to quicken, revive, and repair even those for whom "evills & sufferings felt or feared were ready to sink their spirits." The biblical passage could apply, according to the preacher, to people's souls, to their outward estates, to the church, and to the commonwealth. On the latter, the preacher said, "in regard of the commonwealth, as I might inlarge but at present rather desire to leave it to yourselves to inlarge upon in your own private meditation."[11] Rather than imposing a single message, fast days provided dynamic space for biblical reflection on current events.

Prayer is sometimes understood to be an alternative to political action, but in the case of puritan fast days, town-wide prayer meetings could serve as a forum for political mobilizing.[12] Fast day sermons frequently urged colonists not only to pray but also to make resolutions regarding future action. As one colonial minister said, "a Day of Fastinge as we call it, is & should be a day as of Humiliation in regard of sin past or present, soe also a day of solemn Resolution <for time to come>."[13] On fast days, colonists focused their attention on political dilemmas, drew wisdom from biblical models, pleaded for divine power to intervene, and imagined their own contribution to the colony's welfare. Practices of communal fasting helped build a constitutional culture.

* * *

As we have already observed, the restoration of the Stuart monarchy took many colonists by surprise. They knew about "sad distractions in England, such as threatened the frustration of all the hopes of the reformation begun." And they worried about the possibility of violence, harboring "great fears of troubles breaking forth there" in another civil war.[14] Colonists could still hope, however, that the turmoil might bear good fruit. In a June 1660 fast day across Massachusetts and Connecticut for "the present sad & deplorable condition of our deere native countrie," colonists prayed optimistically that "all thiere unsetlements & overturnings in church & state" might result in "the advancement of the kingdome of the Lord Jesus, & setting up of his throane in that land whose right it is."[15] Few anticipated the news that would arrive, piecemeal and inconclusive, over the next several months that Charles I's son had claimed the English throne. When news of the Restoration was finally confirmed, Bay ministers gathered to pray. They felt God calling them to organize an all-church fast to "intreat the lord for the Continuance of our peace & libertys in Church & common wealth."[16] Most likely, this late February fast marked the occasion when many colonists first came to terms with the Restoration and what it meant—or might mean—for their own lives and communities.

A month or two earlier, in December and January, Richard Mather's Dorchester church and John Eliot's Roxbury church had spent days fasting for these same concerns. Mather and Eliot were recognized leaders within the broader community, and the multichurch February fast that followed probably had its impetus in their earlier fasts. Dorchester had set apart the time, as the church record puts it, to "repent of our sinne which may provoke the lord to take away or to deny us those Libertys & priveledges which we have injoyed thes many years in Church & Common wealth." Although grateful that the king had been restored "in pease without the effusion of blod," the Dorchester congregation desired to pray for the continuation of that peace. They also prayed for all those "in place of rull[e] & goverment" in England, that "the lord would rull[e] & sway ther harts that they may favour the Cause of Christ & promote the gosple."[17] Hopefully, the new Stuart king would follow through on his promises of liberty of conscience for nonconformists, allowing godly churches to keep thriving. Eliot and others involved in the Native mission also probably hoped for royal favor on the New England Company.

For his morning sermon, Mather chose as his text 1 Timothy 2:1–2, an exhortation to pray for all men, and especially "for Kings . . . that we may lead a quiet and a peaceable life, in all godliness, and honesty." We can imagine Mather and his congregation huddled close in their small wood-frame meetinghouse, shivering against the winter cold, praying fervently for Charles II's heart—and for his stance toward nonconformists in England and the colonies. Eliot, the guest preacher for the afternoon sermon in Dorchester, chose a darker text from the Book of Job: "For the thing I feared, is come upon me, and the thing that I was afraid of, is come unto me."[18] For Eliot, grappling with the Restoration was an intensely theological problem. As we discussed earlier, his study of scripture had led him to see monarchy as an anti-Christian form of government, a view he expressed in a book, *The Christian Commonwealth*, which he would have to publicly renounce just a few months after this fast day sermon. The Restoration was indeed a thing to be feared.

The February 1661 multichurch fast, like the earlier fasts, focused on asking God for peace and liberty in both civil and ecclesiastical realms. When colonists prayed for religious liberty, they were most often asking for ongoing freedom to set up churches that aligned with New Testament practice—congregations with godly preaching, mutual accountability, and a high bar for the Lord's Supper. While separatists and some congregationalists in England had started to refer to religious liberty on an individual level—that is, the liberty to "err on the path to truth"—in New England, the main concern was liberty to continue their reformation, a utopian liberty "to be as good as men would be and as they should be."[19] Royalists, too, invoked religious liberty but meant something different by it: they focused on liberty as freedom from inquiry into people's thoughts or "internal conviction[s]," as long as they conformed to "the external worship and observances of the Church of England."[20] Many New Englanders wanted liberty from what they saw as unscriptural human inventions contained in the Church of England liturgy, or from rituals such as making the sign of the cross, or from (crown-appointed) bishops. They sought liberty of the ordinances, liberty to reform their churches in line with biblical ideals. Praying for civil liberties in New England usually meant asking for the continuance of their distinctive modes of self-governance under an exceptionally generous charter. Many believed their laws and constitutional arrangement aligned most closely with biblical and rational principles, marking the cutting edge of Protestant reform.

The February fast also included prayers for "the ginerall sickneses," elsewhere called an "Epidem[ical] Cold," and "thos addresses which have been latly made," letters from the Massachusetts Bay General Court to the king, parliament, and sympathetic noblemen.[21] According to the merchant John Hull, laypeople in their prayers went well beyond the ministerial template. The proclamation did not mention the decision about whether to protect the puritan regicides, but it was definitely on colonists' minds. Bostonians directed prayers, as well, toward "the great question about the right and privilege of the children in our churches, and the duty of each church toward them." Expanding baptism to the grandchildren of full church members, a volatile issue even in good times, would soon become the topic of a synod. Here it is important to note that laypeople brought the issue to the forefront of the Boston fast. They prayed also for the new Stuart government to "see our religion doth not teach us to be disloyal to our native land, the parliament, or our sovereign."[22] The ways men and women articulated these prayers would carry over into their broader constitutional debates and discussions.

As colonists in Braintree prepared for the February fast, they witnessed a remarkable event that seemed to be a divine sign. Their pastor, William Tompson, had long suffered from a debilitating depression that had kept him even from leading "family worship," much less emerging to preach, and that left him reproaching himself as a "reprobate." The week of the February fast, however, the Braintree teaching elder, Henry Flint, fell ill, and so congregants approached their suffering pastor. Tompson, "being solicited earnestly by the people . . . to preach, did hearken; though before this, through deep melancholy, had wholly neglected all public exercises." He rallied for the first time in years to lead the fast day service.[23] At least one colonist's notes of this event survive, so we know that Tompson's sermon from Ezra 9 acknowledged the current moment to be a time of "grat afflictions" for God's people. Yet, he preached, "the presenc of god in the mids[t] of his people is matter of security and stability both of ther harts and ther outward estate."[24] This message would emerge as a central theme of Restoration-era piety: only God's presence brought true safety, whether spiritual or political. News of Tompson's fast day recovery spread quickly throughout the colonies.

Connecticut inhabitants were also praying and fasting as they heard about the new king. Connecticut did not possess a written charter, so the colony's situation at first seemed more precarious than the Bay's. In March 1661, Connecticut magistrates invited the churches to fast the following month. They wanted to seek God's favor, asking God to "direct us in those waies that may conduce to our settlement in peace and privilidges, and that peace and truth may be setled in England." Connecticut's sense of crisis was augmented by grueling divisions within the Hartford church over minister Samuel Stone's Presbyterian leanings. The inhabitants' political fears, however, were assuaged when Governor John Winthrop traveled to England and personally negotiated a charter for Connecticut. In October 1662, the colony celebrated a day of thanksgiving for the previous year's "mercies," especially for Winthrop's "good success . . . obteining our Charter . . . and for the hopes we have of settlement in the waies of peace and righteousness."[25] The New Haven colony also held a public thanksgiving day that month for the year's mercies, but they added on a fast day for God's "guidance . . . in this weighty busines about joineing with Connecticutt colony, &c." Connecticut's new charter absorbed New Haven into its jurisdiction, although John Davenport and other leaders protested the act as illegal and unchristian.[26] New Haveners had good reason to continue fasting.

* * *

When they heard about the Cavalier Parliament's move to suppress English nonconformists in late 1661, Bay ministers wasted no time organizing another colony-wide fast, acting with new urgency. As they planned the event during a regular lecture-day gathering, they thought the topics should include local sickness, "the fears of the looseing our libertys in Church & Common wealth," and blessing on "our Native country . . . & that sup[er]stition & popery & prophannes may not t[o]o far[r]e abound in that land."[27] For despite Charles II's former promises to uphold liberty of conscience, the Corporation Act meant that access to many political offices now required taking sacraments in the Church of England, as well as swearing an oath of total nonresistance, even to a tyrant. These Stuart political orthodoxies would soon make their way into the liturgy of the Church of England through an annual fast day remembering the regicide and a thanksgiving day commemorating the Restoration, during which worshippers vowed obedience to the king and his heirs as God's anointed rulers.[28] Recognizing the power of fast days, crown officials were now busily harnessing them to their own ends. Their determination did not sit well with the colonists. Many men and women in the colonies fasted for their persecuted brethren overseas as well as for themselves. Despite some disapproval for magistrates who conducted business on the fast day (sometimes the work of governance took priority), men and women prayed too for their "Generall Court" which, they knew, was "exercised this wintertime with many difficulties."[29]

On the next major public fast, in January 1662, the colonists' mood was darker. Prayer was needed, the proclamation said, for "Gods suffering many ennemies & underminers to multiply complaints against us to our soveraigne lord the king; the impetuous & restless intrusions of haereticks & ennemies to the wayes, worship, & ordinances of God; the cursed combination of Antichrist & his adherents to ruine & trample upon all the sincere servants of God the world throughout." For many puritans, an apocalyptic framework permitted them to link heretical intrusions (Quakers who cursed ministers and magistrates) with London detractors (mostly those with competing claims to northern New England land) and also with the suppression of the godly in England and elsewhere: they ran these challenges together, seeing them as coordinated attacks against the true church. Yet repentance comprised a powerful engine of change. As the proclamation continued, it was "obvious to all pious & serious persons amongst us that we are called of God deepely to humble ourselves for the many & great sinns & evill of the country." Such spiritual honesty might jump-start a reversal of their political fortunes, "diverting such calamities as are coming upon us & the people of God the Christian world throughout."[30]

For some puritans, slowing down to fast during a crisis seemed counterintuitive. During the January 1662 fast in Charlestown, Thomas Shepard began his sermon by stating the obvious: yes, they had held a fast less than a month before; and yes, the colonists were doing a lot of fasting lately. Yet Shepard determinedly argued that the situation required it. As he had said at the prior fast, "the present miseries & calamities of the church" in their

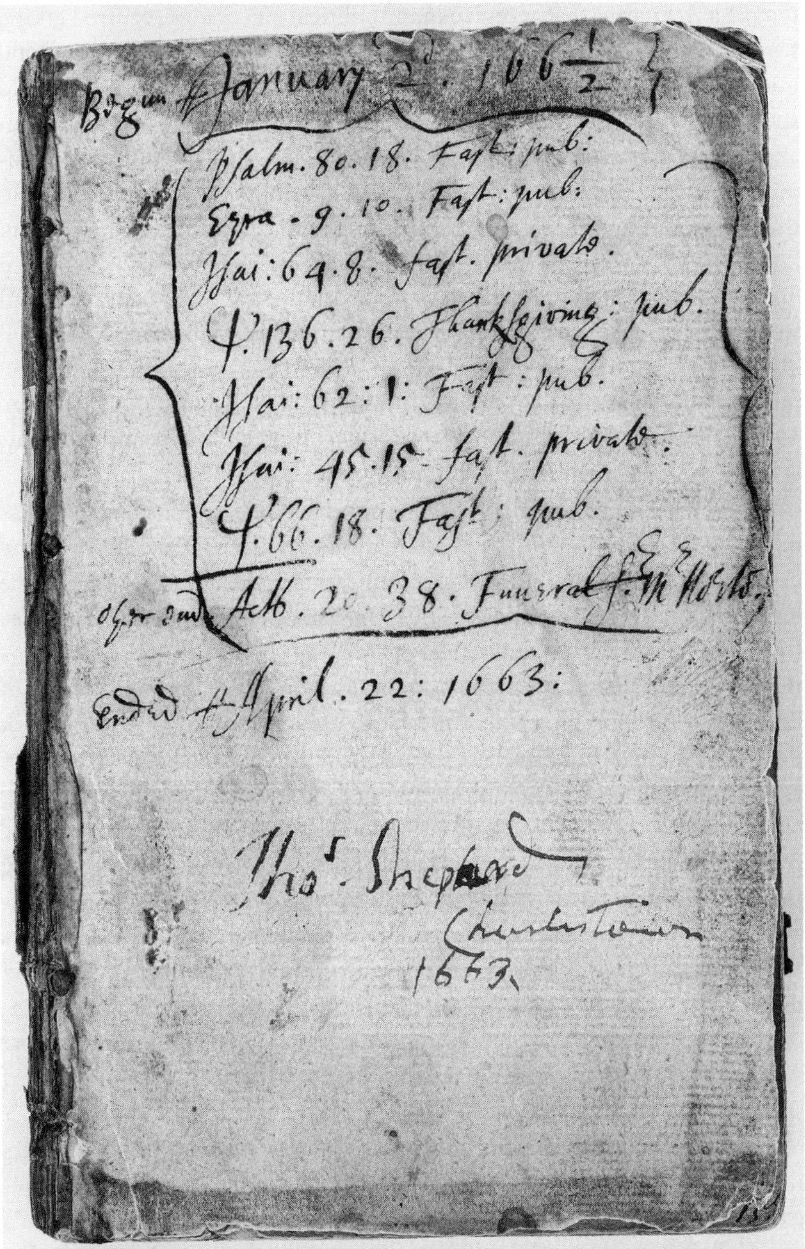

Figure 3. First page of Thomas Shepard notebook, 1662–1663, Octavo 5, Shepard Family Papers, 1636–1681. Courtesy of the American Antiquarian Society.

own time were comparable to the situation of ancient Israel, a "vine devoured & wasted by the boare & the wild beast." Shepard reminded his hearers that the Lord had planted them, "& would he now leave his owne plantation" or "after all suffer them to be destroyed?" He urged "the holy Resolution of the church not to goe back from God." Going back meant "to be careless of, & neglect, & dispize, & cast off any ordinance . . . any command of his whatever." To do so was to "cast off God himself." They should instead stand firm, although not in "their owne strength" but rather as "god quickens them" through prayer. If asked, the Lord would engage in the "cheeringe & refreshinge of their hearts & spirits . . . in their cause & work & way." Shepard then invited inhabitants to reflect on how God might "repaire and revive" the commonwealth. Prayers on this topic, he assured his flock, were "exceedinge pleasinge unto God."[31]

When Shepard proceeded to elaborate on each item in the General Court's fast day proclamation, he highlighted "insensibleness of evil occurences." Keeping informed about public events that threatened the church constituted a duty for people of faith, and being unaware or detached from such events marked a deficiency. Reflecting on those "enemies & underminers" who complained to the king, Shepard noted an excessive "Athenian spirit" in London: obsessed with novelty, people would entertain "fals reports raised & carried about for most credible news." As a counterweight, he hoped to encourage "that spirit of Nehemiah 1" among colonists, who, like King Artaxerxes's cupbearer, would speak a timely word for the godly community. Far from a radical, Shepard also urged personal accountability, asking colonists if, even amid such changes, they would behave so "none may have cause to say we are those who cast off our subjection" to Charles II. Perhaps alluding to the Jenks sedition case, Shepard reminded his congregation that speaking carelessly about the new regime only gave the colony's detractors ammunition, further imperiling English nonconformists. Remember your forebears, he exhorted, especially those good puritan subjects under King James who focused on evangelism rather than on overhauling governments.[32] Shepard thus used the fast day to remind colonists of a long-standing ideal of puritan monarchism as both pious and loyal, and to urge them to take care for the colony's reputation.

By May 1662 the General Court, recognizing the magnitude of challenges the colonies faced, wanted to call for another public fast day but struggled to find the right wording. The manuscript proclamation that survives is full of revisions and last-minute edits. Both magistrates and deputies finally agreed on a version that identified the current moment as a turning point in God's dealings with the Bay. Colonists had experienced "many years of his Fatherly Tendernesse," they wrote, in which they seemed "a people singularly exempted from his sharpned stroakes" even as Protestants in Europe had suffered. But now the Lord, in all righteousness, had chosen "In respect of himselfe and us to chainge his way . . ."

> Turning our healthynesse Into sicklynesse
> our sweet union to much disunion.
> our fruitfull seasons, to seasons somtymes threatninge overflowing scorgue
> somtymes threatning to withhould the rayne
> soe that the Earth and Creatures seemes mournfull.[33]

Although the colonists had had their ups and downs in the previous two decades, until now they had not faced the critical eyes of an unsympathetic regime or confusion over sacramental access on top of an "epidemical cold," poor harvests, and the regular hardships of colonial life. It was a trying time: "our spirrits many wayes exercised as to events <&> unsetled as to trueths of great Consequence." The fast proclamation's authors hoped "that wee may Injoy and feele more of his gracious presence In recovering our primative [apostolic-era] beautie in his ways." They yearned for assurance of God's presence in both civil and ecclesiastical realms, particularly his blessings on "the synod now shortly againe to be assembled" regarding baptism, as well as divine "assistance with our Agents abrod," John Norton and Simon Bradstreet in London.[34]

When the June fast day arrived, colonists got to work praying. The people of Dorchester considered the Lord's promise in 2 Chronicles 7 that if they "humbled themselves . . . and seek my face, and turn from their wicked ways; then will I . . . heal their land."[35] Charlestown inhabitants meditated on the "great opposition" Jews faced from a Persian king when trying to build the temple, reminded that in all worthy "Temple work" adversaries attempted opposition, but their efforts did not discount the legitimacy of "the Temple of god that is abuilding." Likewise, in colonists' endeavors to build a godly "ecclesiastical & civil state," men and women should not falter or put "private gaine before the publiq welfare." Current events might seem like such a daunting "reddle of providence that we knoweth not what to say," but colonists could still, like Ezra, confess their sins, remember the Lord's mercies, and continue with the work of reform, each making his or her own contribution.[36]

* * *

Providential winds, however, continued to blow in confusing directions. At their October 1662 meeting, the Massachusetts General Court announced a November thanksgiving day for "the libertyes of the gospell which we doe yet injoy," as well as for a good harvest despite the drought, and "the safe & speedy returne of our publicke messengers" Norton and Bradstreet.[37] This thanksgiving day, however, was announced in tandem with a December fast. Two factors likely prompted the calling of this latest fast day: colonists were taking in parliament's act to eject nonconformists from the Church of England and from universities; they were also struggling to make sense of Charles II's June 1662 letter, which, while confirming the Massachusetts charter, had demanded major alterations to the colony's institutions, including their churches.[38]

As we have seen, the king had requested that his letter be published throughout the colony. Some ministers chose to read this letter aloud at the November thanksgiving day, with volatile results. After reading the king's statement, William Hubbard of Ipswich decided "to help the vulgar [less educated] to Understand his Majesty[s] Grace in the Interp[reting] that part that speakes to Comon praier," the passage that said that high Church of England worship must be allowed and that ministers must follow the Book of Common Prayer by inviting "all persons of good and honest lives and conversations" to participate in the sacrament of the Lord's Supper, along with baptizing their children.[39] Hubbard tried to argue that by opening up church membership more broadly, as the king had commanded, New Englanders would be bringing their churches into line with the mainstream of Protestant traditions. But Ipswich inhabitants interrupted him: Hubbard's words were "much Cryed out . . . against" with the chant, "no more!" The "vulgar," it seems, knew enough to protest the king's order. Even Ipswich non-freemen joined the protest, so much so that one colonist who wanted quick obedience to the king puzzled over why the non-freemen would care more about forms of worship than the broader franchise.[40]

From church records, we can identify palpable fear that the king's letter presaged worse things to come. On the morning of the thanksgiving day, the Dorchester congregation heard a message from the biblical prophet Isaiah: even if the Lord sent "adversity" and "affliction," the people's teachers would not "be removed into a corner any more, but thine eyes shall see thy teachers." In other words, although godly ministers were being ejected from the Church of England, God could still protect colonial pulpits. Discern the

Lord's voice, Richard Mather urged congregants: "And thine ears shall hear a word behind thee, saying, This is the way, walk ye in it." Colonists should focus not on the strength of the English navy but on keeping to the Lord's path. William Stoughton, a Harvard and Oxford graduate recently ejected from his English parish, preached to similar effect in Dorchester that afternoon: the Lord, he argued, "delighteth not in the strength of the horse: he taketh not pleasure in the legs of a man" but rejoiced "in those that hope in his mercy."[41] Do not amass an arsenal, these clergy cautioned; rather, look to the Lord for deliverance.

For their part of the thanksgiving day, Charlestown residents got a full lesson in biblical and providential history. Remember, Shepard said, how the Lord had shown mercy to the Israelites, caring for them "in the wilderness & removing great Kings out of the way"? So also had God shown mercy to England facing the Spanish Armada in 1588, as well as during "the gunpowder treason" of 1605. And in New England, just the previous summer the Lord had removed a great drought the day after ministers and others had gathered to pray and fast. Their God had done these things, Shepard reminded listeners; this same God was also the one who "turne's the hearts of Kings about as the ripls of waters: & when the great ones of the earth rage & combine together against Christ & his church yet . . . he that sitts in heaven shall laugh at them."[42] God laughed at great men who conspired against his own. Why should colonists fear a Stuart king?

Yet colonists *were* fearful. Reeling over the king's demands, the confusion over baptism, and stories from England about the personal costs of ministers' ejections, apprehensions across the colonies mounted. Late in 1662, the General Court asked men and women to pray about "the afflictive & lowe estate of the cause & people of God universally, with the prevayling power of Antichrist over the Reformed churches beyond the seas, together with some publicke rebukes of God among ourselves." This time the court asked for prayers not only on the fast day but also continually, day in and day out, asking that people "be instant in season & out of season." The times demanded it.[43]

The crisis prompted reflection on New England's overarching purpose and vision. Although the idea of setting up Christ's kingly office in a civil polity "be now distasted as a Fanatic Notion," Cambridge's Jonathan Mitchell declared in December 1662, it was still the primary cause of settlement. And it is still "Christ's Design," he added, "in these Latter Days; to set up His Kingdom, in a public and Openly prevailing manner" in every part of either "churches or commonwealth." Building God's kingdom on earth was a cause for which "God will Overturn, Overturn, Overturn, until it be Erected in it's Glory." Mitchell was not speaking metaphorically. Not just "Inward and Personal," the Kingdom of Christ also had a visible manifestation, "Outward and Publick," in human "societies." He acknowledged that there were "those among us, that desire to set up in this Country . . . Prelacy, stinted Liturgies, Human Ceremonies in Worship." It was the magistrates' job to push back against these encroachments, protecting the "Purity and Liberty" of the ways of God. Moving backward, rather than forward, in the way of reform was wickedness, "& Hence for our Civil Government to put forth any act of consent unto wd be a Thing to be Trembled at." In the commonwealth, what did it look like to set up Christ's kingdom? All "laws and Civil Administrations" would "most fitly and effectually tend to advance, promote, and maintain Religion and Reformation." As they pursued this cause, colonists should not fear their detractors. God could overturn the power structures of the world, making faithful colonists "a Burdensome Stone to all Opposers, as He has done hitherto." Their job, accordingly, was to "faithfully cleave to the whole interest and kingdom of Christ," in both "church and commonwealth." In this "Hour of Temptation," the task of New Englanders was to stand firm.[44] In this language, Mitchell's sermon suggests the ideas of the Scottish Covenanters, one of whom had told James VI in the 1590s that he was merely a subject in an ecclesiastical kingdom of which Christ was king.[45] For Cambridge inhabitant Daniel Gookin, hearing his pastor Mitchell preach on "Ch[ris]ts Kingly Gover[n]ment upon a civill Acco[un]t" helped him understand in a new way how local laws and government were gifts from Christ and encouraged him to question how letting the king "destroy our selves in our greatest Concernes" could ever be a wise course.[46]

Ipswich inhabitants heard two different kinds of sermons on the December 1662 fast day. In the morning, Thomas Cobbet preached hopefully that though the people had been "brought very low," even labeled "Fanatiques" or "Traytors," yet God would deliver them. Remembering Christ's own humility in suffering, colonists should "be meek . . . be righteous . . . be humble" and "love the lord actively." The godly across the sea were asking for prayer, and so Ipswich should "be earnest with God in prayer & plead for the Churches abroad." Whether in England or New England, Cobbet said optimistically, all should know that "Extremityes . . . are Gods opportunityes." The afternoon sermon offered a less positive tone. William Hubbard preached a dark warning against political activism that might cross the line into unlawful behavior. The colonists' role, he said, was not to scheme or lobby but to prepare to suffer persecution by an apocalyptic beast of such magnitude that only those with "divine assistanc" could endure. Even the godly reformer Thomas Cranmer had recanted before his martyrdom, Hubbard reminded; colonists would need extraordinary faith and patience to "endure to the end." And above all, "Let us not by unlawful means cast of[f] the yoake," which would only "bring evil on ourselves." Instead, colonial believers should imitate David, who "would not put forth his hand against the Lords anointed" and who waited for a God who "wil in time deliver."[47] Hubbard acknowledged the temptation to forceful resistance and worked to prevent any foray into Machiavellian scheming.

Hubbard's evocation of martyrdom would find its reinforcement in a local 1664 printing of martyrs' letters, *Divine Consolations for Mourners in Sion*. In early modern England the martyrs' correspondence, compiled by John Foxe and others, had become a staple of devotional encouragement for sufferers and non-sufferers alike. The preface to this colonial edition expressed hope that the volume would be a resource "in this hour of darkness and temptation" in New England, and especially for fast days. God had inspired their leaders "to call for seeking God by Fasting and Prayer," a divinely appointed method for "obtaining mercy in the day of thy distress." Lamenting the suffering of nonconformists and European Protestants, "our Brethren [who] lay bleeding," the authors urged colonists to use the martyrs' letters as guides to repentance. Like Hubbard, however, they also urged caution: "this time is a time for the Prudent to keep silence" and to "seek good and not evil."[48]

By contrast, on the same December public fast Thomas Shepard urged not silence but outspoken activism. Holding up the prophet Isaiah's words, "For Sion's sake will I not hold my peace," Shepard offered a powerful definition of a "true citizen of Sion." True citizens should be as restless in prayer as the waves of a stormy sea. They should pray with "holy impudence," as did the poor widow in Luke's parable or Deborah in Judges 5. Prayer did not, however, substitute for "suitable indeavors & actions." It should be accompanied by "the laying out of our selves & what we have & can doe for the good of Sion." Words mattered, but "words alone will never doe, there must be deeds." In Shepard's model, "the spirit of a true citizen of sion a sinceer Christian 'twill be in motion" like "the waters of a living spring" on behalf of the church and people of God. Those with "a publiq spirit for Sions sake" would experience restlessness in each faculty: thought, memory, will, affection, words, and especially "behaviors, & indeavors, & constant labours."[49] The fast day for some was about prayerful mobilizing for action. Bay colonists may have heeded Hubbard's warnings, but they embraced Shepard's public-spirited restlessness.

New England puritans' freedom to act on these restless impulses contrasted starkly with the situation of their brethren overseas. Those nonconformists who suffered repression in England—or who had fled to the continent—struggled with feeling useless, tangential to the larger drama playing out elsewhere. Milton's conquered, imprisoned Samson figure in *Samson Agonistes* captured this emotion: "Now blind, disheartn'd, sham'd, dishonour'd, quell'd, / To what can I be useful, wherein serve / My Nation"? In private correspondence, Milton, who had escaped the fate of Hugh Peter but remained, like most English nonconformists, in "straitened and difficult circumstances," prayed that God would not leave him "useless, whatever remains for me in this life." Other dissenters escaped to the continent, those on the extreme end seeking alliance with the Dutch or French in an effort to oust Charles II, a radicalism for which there is almost no evidence among the colonists. Many more English nonconformists stayed home and turned their energy into an outpouring of print, prose, and poetry. Yet they continued to struggle with a sense of political irrelevance.[50] Nothing could have been further from the case among their counterparts in New England, where men and women leaped into public action, determined to maintain their nonconformist outposts within an increasingly inhospitable Restoration empire.

* * *

In the months that followed, colonial men and women embarked on an extraordinary season of mobilizing and fasting in individual churches, in homes, and in two colony-wide series of fast days. During these same days, the Massachusetts Court continued to use fast proclamations to communicate dangers to the body politic. If we look only at public fasts, however, we would miss other, more informal fast days—those exhibiting a more organic feel and perhaps marking even more influential occasions.

Large or small, private meetings for prayer and fasting proliferated as spaces for communal reflection. Men and women in Charlestown, fasting at Francis Willoughby's house, imagined the Lord as "the great potter of heaven & earth" who had "framed us out of the clay," not only as individuals "but in respect of our {civil [and] {ecclesiastical state." God's people were worrying about "wicked men" who desired to "spoile the fashion of his own workmanship if they could." But were these foes "stronger then the potter"? No, the preacher Thomas Shepard declared. Rather, "the enemies of the church" are themselves "poor potsherds & he can break them in peices." Rather than fearing wicked men, men and women should fear the Lord, who "frames kingdomes & commonwealths according to his pleasure infinitely with more ease then ever any potter did." Participants in this private fast then took time to "wait upon god as the answer of all our good." Shepard recorded the name of the fast's host in shorthand, along with the group's specific prayer "that God should divert that general letter . . . the king sent us" through the work of the General Court sitting "next week."[51] Fasting offered a time to analyze the political situation, as well as an antidote to worry.

The Boston church fasted to mourn the death of John Norton and discern whether the benefit from inviting the great English nonconformist preacher John Owen to lead them would outweigh the risk.[52] Afterward, following a trip to England, Boston church member John Hull hosted a "day of humiliation" in May 1663 for multiple families in his home, probably to share and pray for what he had witnessed abroad. In the months that followed, Hull twice went to the home of Braintree pastor Henry Flint "to join in fasting and praises." A week after the second visit, Hull kept his own personal fast day, recording in shorthand that he was "confessing my own sins, and my family's, and the country's, and my native country's, desiring mercy . . . For the country, submission to God's ordinance. . . . Of the country . . . from s[in]s. Gulling us by fomenting jealousy, with no cause . . . of God's mercy, and peace and preservation of . . . the Commonwealth . . . in the church to the generation[s]."[53] Although partial and somewhat cryptic, Hull's notes make clear he was using a personal ritual of fasting to wrestle with the political crisis. Laypeople rarely kept notes on personal fasts but they were surely a time for contemplating what risks were worth taking.

The young Increase Mather also recorded attending a private fast at "Mr Collicotts where. . . . I spent an hour with them in prayr."[54] Mather also inscribed his name on a book printed around this time, *A Compleat Collection of Farewel Sermons* (1663), although precisely when he acquired the volume remains unknown. These Bartholomew's Day sermons, final words preached by English ministers just prior to their ejection from the Church of England, were gradually making their way into colonial libraries. While "invariably deferential" to Charles II, Bartholomew's Day sermons generally placed "religious fidelity above earthly loyalties." They could have easily formed a resource for Mather and others as they prayed for suffering nonconformists in England and for the future of the puritan-led colonies.[55]

Two series of multichurch fasts in 1663 and early 1664 deliberately emulated the fast days of the English civil wars. Several magistrates in August 1663 informally expressed a need for "more than ordinary seeking to god by fasting & prayer," and the ministers proposed "to turne the lectures of thes severall towns into days of humilliation as the like was donne about the begining of the trouble in England about the year 42 & 43." Drawing on the last struggle against a Stuart king, the movement to turn lecture days into fast days spread from Boston to the surrounding towns, so that many congregations "kept a weekly fast" from mid-August through late October 1663.[56]

That first fast series must have been successful, for several months later Boston-area ministers organized another one, this time monthly. They wanted to direct prayers "in [an] Especiall maner for England" as well as toward the colonists' own predicament. People would gather to seek the Lord's "mercy with respect unto that great affliction and reproach" experienced by "so many thousands of Ministers and Christians . . . by means of Episcopall usurpation, and human impositions" in worship, as well as "the dangers threatning ourselves." According to Salem church records for one of these early 1664 fast days, people "chearfully consented" to fast and pray for the preservation of their liberties. The Salem congregation culminated this period of intense fasting with a covenant renewal ceremony, a ritual for bringing more inhabitants into the fold of the church.[57]

The second series of fasts saw tensions over baptismal reforms erupting alongside political concerns. Baptism had long been a contentious topic, one in which laypeople as well as ministers were highly invested. In most Bay churches, the threshold to full church membership was a convincing profession of faith or spiritual relation, and only the children of full church members could be baptized. If full church members' children did not eventually step forward to give their own relation and fully join the church, then their grandchildren might be denied baptism. Laypeople tended to prize this high bar to church membership, seeing it as a mark of authenticity and spiritual power. Many were appalled by the corruptions in the Church of England when dishonest traders or those who mocked the Lord were given free access to the sacrament. Those opposing baptismal expansion resonated with an ideal of the church composed of "visible saints, visible believers . . . escaping the pollutions of idolatry and the world" and committed to an ethic of mutual love and holiness. On the other side, those who wanted to welcome more into baptism thought it essential for these children, as well as unchurched adults, to be taken "under the Wings of the Lord Jesus Christ in his ordinances" and receive the benefits of "Church Care," rather than being left out in the spiritual cold.[58] Emotions churned on both sides. Back in 1661, the General Court had asked for a ministerial synod to address the issue, although many acknowledged that the timing was not ideal: given the political upheavals, it was "unseasonable" to begin digging into "controversies, especially about Religion." At the spring 1662 synod, a majority of Bay ministers agreed that baptism should be expanded, although individual congregations continued to contest the issue. Fast day records reveal that a number of colonists understood these political and sacramental crises as interrelated.[59]

The second fast series had launched in the two Boston churches before moving to Charlestown and other towns. Boston minister Increase Mather recorded how his "spirit" was "troubled" at the Charlestown fast because its leaders brought up controversy when they should have promoted unity. In the morning sermon, Charlestown pastor Zechariah Symmes "exhort[ed] people to read mr Shepards discourse about church worship," referring to the late Thomas Shepard's *The Church-Membership of Children*, just printed in 1663. In the preface, the author's son (and Symmes's co-minister) Thomas Shepard offered a rationale for expanding baptism in opposition to both Catholic and Baptist theologies.[60] In the afternoon sermon, according to Mather, Shepard went so far as to say "that God was provoked because there were such multitudes unbaptized."[61] Although Shepard's sermon is not extant, a later manuscript treatise gives us a sense of his strong rhetoric: "Alas, are we com into the wildernes to leave the Little ones behind us no part of the worshipping congregation?" If we would keep "that open Door which we have so long enjoyed to preceous Liberty & deare bought enjoyments," he wrote, we should "awake & turne, consider & Repent" of our sins.[62] As he later prayed over the Charlestown fast sermons and his own frustration with them, Mather privately noted that God "quieted my spirit, again resolving that if they did amisse in preaching upon such controversies, I [did] not in doing contrary."[63] Mather thought fast days should keep prayers for colonists' liberties separate from the divisive issue of baptismal reform, which he at this point opposed.[64]

He was not alone in this impulse to keep baptism separate from other hot-button issues of the day. Another opponent of the baptismal reforms, Nicholas Street thought the 1662 synod over baptism was a terrible diversion aimed at "hinder[ing]" the great work God was doing through the fast days, "calling alloud to his people every where . . . for extraordinary mourning & humiliation, in the behalfe of his afflicted churches & faithfull dissenters of his word."[65] John Davenport of New Haven saw political and religious issues as indeed connected, but in reverse fashion from Symmes and Shepard. He argued that God's protection of the charter might be linked to the colonists' "returne to the first waies of reformation here begun," ways that the "last synods conclusions" about expanding baptism had clearly abandoned.[66] Yet for some colonists, Shepard and Symmes's pro-expansion exhortations made sense. Discerning communal sin as a part of self-examination and repentance, two traditional fast day practices, some men and women zeroed in on the colonies' failure to incorporate the younger generation into the church, a glaring omission that might, they believed, be provoking divine judgment upon them—in the form of political instability and tense relations with England. Perhaps baptismal reform would restore the Lord's favor on colonists' liberties.

When the fast day rotation made its way to Dorchester in late March 1664, Richard Mather invited his son Increase to preach the second sermon. Although father and son stood on different sides of the baptism controversy (Richard was for expansion), they avoided conflict by focusing on repentance and the power of God to purge lips and hearts of iniquity. They shared a meal together afterward. In his diary, Increase noted that he had spent a long time preparing for that afternoon's fast day sermon. Choosing as his text Zephaniah 2:3, he urged colonists to "seek righteousness, seek lowliness," so they might "be hid in the day of the Lord's wrath." As he prepared for this message, Increase read older commentaries on Revelation, trying to place current events within the longer framework of Christian history. He was personally struggling with finances, with his calling to the Boston church, and with doubts about his place in New England. His diary, like Hull's, reveals how a fast day could allow an individual to attend to both transatlantic politics and individual needs.[67] Yet he had other reasons for wanting to seek lowliness and hiddenness during this "sweet fast." While ministering in England in 1660, Increase had experienced the political upheaval of the Restoration firsthand, refusing to take a loyalty oath before retreating to the relative safety of home. If he was not already doing so, he soon would be operating as the primary conduit of information between the regicides and their friends and families in England, hiding their letters within his own books and packets. He tended to see helping the regicides and defying the king's commands as part of a larger apocalyptic battle between the true church and its enemies. His concern about the overreach of royal and episcopal power in England was such that he wondered if "I must fly for it ere long again heere, as in England I have beene faine to doe."[68] For Increase, it was imperative that the fast day series focus on the immediate political crisis.

Increase had his work cut out for him; so too did the General Court as it considered royal demands and local churches' relationship to the Church of England. For magistrates and deputies, the 1662 synod's decision to expand baptism proved politically useful. It became a way to claim movement back toward the Church of England and its king.[69] Expanding baptism brought congregational churches closer to a parish model, one in which the church served the entire community rather than the gathered few. As such, it perhaps smoothed the way to greater acceptance within the new religious and political establishment in England. At the fast day gatherings, however, a providential framework predominated, as colonists linked right action on baptism to divine favor on their future.

The crisis played out differently in Connecticut and New Haven, as we can see in the language of their spring 1664 fast day proclamations. The people of New Haven fasted for "the aflicted state of the people of God in our native countrey" and elsewhere, along with "our owne present distractions" and "publike concernments." Some New Haveners still attempted to maintain their status as a colony, but as more towns supported Connecticut, the chances of these holdouts grew slim. The people of Connecticut, on the other hand, fasted so "that health may be continued amongst us, that peace and truth may be establisht amongst ourselves and throughout his Majesties Dominions." No doubt Connecticut colonists were relieved that the patent Winthrop had managed to acquire had not been recalled when various boundary conflicts with Rhode Island came to light. Even as Connecticut leaders were adjusting to language such as "his Majesties Dominions," however, they would continue to prayerfully defy the Privy Council's requests for maps and other information about New England's resources.[70] Not everything could be smoothed over easily.

How colonial royalists experienced fast days remains a difficult question. One can imagine that if you were looking for incriminating information regarding the colonists' political views, a fast day might be a good event to attend—although you might have to do some biblical decoding. We do know that at least some royalists decried the politics of sermons that delivered immoderate exhortations to prepare for persecution and suffering. Royalist-leaning men and women might also chafe at the political tone of fast day sermons. One Bay colonist would later rage that "the General Court was guilty of rebellion, & that the ministers hereabouts were the Authors of the rebellion."[71] Further, modes of prayer could easily be mapped onto political affinities. Even on a regular Sabbath day service in Boston, one royalist observed that "their tongues faulterd as not being well accustomd to pray for the King."[72] Those drawn to more liturgical worship tended to hear spontaneous puritan prayers as incoherent babble, as the royalist Abraham Corbett would grumble regarding the Portsmouth minister John Reyner. Royalists sometimes recoiled from the ethos cultivated on colonial fast days, finding it distasteful and lending cause for mockery. Some called the puritans' worship "rude" and complained that they had "miscontrued all the King's letters" while "pray[ing] constantly for their persecuted bretheren in England."[73]

Yet these royalists were right to identify community-wide prayer meetings as one forum in which inhabitants interpreted royal decrees. A consistent theme of the fast days held that God ultimately controlled the fate of kings, and so faithfulness in religion translated to political safety.[74] Colonists took away multiple messages from these events, but they at least had time and space to reflect in a sustained way on their colonies' relationship to England and on each person's contribution to the common good. As one among several opportunities for the difficult work of forging consensus, communal prayer helped colonists evaluate which risks were worth taking and which liberties were worth protecting. In early Restoration England, nonconformists enjoyed very few opportunities for public political reflection. New Englanders, they might have felt, should count their blessings. Even as the colonists grappled with threats to civil and religious liberties, and however much they disagreed over what to do, New Englanders tilled a rich soil in which a distinct, regional constitutional culture firmly took root.

CHAPTER 5

Frigates

The Arrival of Royal Commissioners

Charles II and his councillors realized over the year 1663 that however many pointed letters they sent, Massachusetts was unlikely to offer full compliance. In July the king gave the Quaker and Baptist stronghold of Rhode Island a generous charter, in part because he viewed it as a potential royalist base to check the Bay's power. But stronger action now appeared necessary, especially to enforce the Navigation Acts. New Netherland was drawing in New England colonists and attracting their trade. This Dutch interruption of a solid English Atlantic coastline seemed an affront to the English crown. It was probably Samuel Maverick, in London advising the Council for Foreign Plantations, who strategically linked the New England problem to the New Netherland problem, demonstrating "with what facilitie . . . the Dutch Plantations may be regained & the English reduced." An unofficial naval war with the Netherlands over control of the slave trade in West Africa was already underway. Royal frigates sent to conquer New Netherland might score another victory against a powerful maritime rival and serve also to "overawe" difficult New Englanders.[1]

The problem of the Dutch and the problem of nonconformists overlapped in other ways as well. While most English religious dissenters stayed in place, trying to avoid the worst of the new penal code, others fled to the continent, often to the Netherlands. The Stuart government sent spies and assassins after them. One of these spies, for example, would discover that "Fanaticke" army men (nonconformist civil war veterans) had begun sending arms in "small parcells to London," coordinating with "the honest party in <Scotland>" and hoping Dutch-English differences might provide them with an opportunity. This spy would also hear that the regicide Edward Ludlow was "in the holland plantation in new England." Although the information about Ludlow's location proved to be mistaken, the larger intelligence would prove accurate. In 1665, the exiled republican Algernon Sidney would approach first the Dutch and then their French allies for support with a potential coup, which despite French aid never materialized.[2] Accusing the regicides Edward Whalley and William Goffe of assisting with "the strengthninge the New Netherlands," Maverick commented, "I wish some in New England be not also involved."[3] These insinuations lacked corroborating evidence. But on hearing a rumor that Charles II planned to forcibly impose episcopacy on New England, Dutch officials themselves wondered hopefully if New Englanders, instead of harassing New Netherland, might "prefer to live free under us at peace with their consciences."[4] Although it existed only as rumor, an alliance between English nonconformists and the Dutch was an unsettling thought for Stuart officials in 1663, a potential union that—in their wary view—perhaps confirmed the wisdom of royal intervention in both New Netherland and New England.

A more moderate advisor with colonial experience argued "that the shipps desired by Mr Maverick are too many . . . [and] maye afright [New Englanders] and awaken Jelousyes and stir up resolves not yet thought upon."[5] Yet militant voices prevailed. Linking the New England and the Dutch missions appealed to some high-ranking Englishmen. Hawkish Privy Councillors and the Duke of York, who also served as Lord High Admiral, liked the idea. They set to work convincing the king to approve an enormous subsidy for this as yet undeclared war.[6] The non-hawkish Clarendon, however, urged caution. He did not oppose the Dutch conquest, but regarding New England he wanted to take things slowly, ferreting out various loyalties and then governing them "by divideing" them. Clarendon was especially interested in identifying troublemakers—those "whose venom and Contagion infects the rest"—so he might bring them to England for questioning. He could not imagine that colonists would refuse a direct summons, even if it were for "the Governor himselfe" (they would prove him wrong). He also wanted royal commissioners to identify clergy "of a good Temper and discreccion" who might promote the king's interest in the colonies. This task would not prove easy, even in newly chartered Rhode Island.[7]

An unspoken but pressing additional motivation behind the royal commission was Charles II's and the Duke of York's rising debt and serious need for increased revenue. In 1663, the Council for Foreign Plantations endorsed the effort to assign "customs farmers" to enforce colonial tax collection, but the plan failed when no one could figure out how the farmers were actually to obtain the cooperation of New England magistrates.[8] In the last decade, the colonial Northeast had unexpectedly risen as an economic power; the royal family was set on obtaining a percentage of that revenue, if not through direct taxation then through land and resources. The Duke's patent, which would include land from Maine to Pennsylvania and the strategically located islands of Martha's Vineyard and Nantucket, "assumed the land was vacant," ignoring Native sovereignty.[9]

The king approved sending a royal commission on four armed frigates to subjugate New Netherland and to pressure New England into submission. The Duke of York and a committee for New England then faced the tricky task of selecting commissioners. In an era before a trained civil service or permanent officer corps, talented diplomats were few and far between, and not many would desire such a distant and thankless post as the colonial Northeast. The committee had originally considered including "some principal persons" from the region itself, but who were such people? Committee members did not know many names, much less any colonial leaders well enough to trust them. They ended up choosing, instead, "persons well knowne to us," hoping these appointed men might at least be loyal to the crown and have a chance of seeming impartial.[10] Three of the chosen commissioners were civil war veterans close to York. The most obviously qualified was the commission's leader, Richard Nicolls. Although he had little colonial experience, Nicolls had served as a royalist troop commander and then became a long-time groom to the Duke. It seems likely that the second commissioner, Sir Robert Carr, a baronet and civil war colonel imprisoned by Parliament in 1644, was chosen for his long service and loyalty. The third, George Cartwright, had also served as a royalist civil war colonel; little else about his background or connections is known today.[11]

The fourth choice, a name likely added at the last minute, continues to puzzle historians: Samuel Maverick, whose antagonism toward Bay leaders was well-known in London. Maverick had spent the previous several years decrying Bay colonists as congenitally disloyal, long overdue for a royal governor and a show of royal force. Even so, he had extensive New England experience. In acknowledgment of his 1624 migration, Bay leaders had given him the freemanship despite his disdain for puritan worship. He was also an early and notoriously brutal enslaver, and over the years had repeatedly challenged Massachusetts's laws and legitimacy.[12] Aware of his animosity toward the Bay, Clarendon would later warn Maverick not to use his position to avenge old grievances. The official royal commission also stipulated that decisions among two or three of the commissioners would require Richard Nicolls, who also had the deciding vote; at list initially, Maverick and the other two could not act alone.[13]

Probably authored by Clarendon, the instructions for the royal commission came in three sets, one public for the Bay, the second also public but primarily intended for Connecticut, and the third private, secret instructions for the royal commissioners' eyes only, regarding all of New England. The first set of instructions told the commissioners, in brief, that they must convince Bay leaders of the king's high regard—he viewed them as "an example of sobriety & industry"—and set them at ease about the charter. Charles II had no thought of "abridging or restraineing them from any priviledges or liberties" given by his father but on the contrary stood ready to expand these. The commissioners should gather information about the colonists' loyalty and communicate the king's affection, thwarting those troublemakers who wanted to sow animosity. Acknowledging ignorance of the "climate . . . disposicion of the people and . . . constitucion of affaires," they should rely more on the colonists' "information . . . & advise" than their "owne observacion" when making decisions (a generous thought that would remain on paper). Local advice, too, was essential for "reducing the Dutch," along with material supplies such as troops and a regional map.[14]

Regarding Native Americans, the instructions were clear: royal commissioners should investigate and enforce existing treaties with Native inhabitants, for violations of these agreements would "obstruct our great end of the conversion of infidells in those parts." Harvard College and other schools serving both Anglo-Americans and Natives should also be inspected. The public instructions for Connecticut repeated some of the Bay's directives but primarily focused on a complicated mishap regarding the region's recently granted charter. Commissioners were additionally called to investigate the 1644 document by which Narragansett sachems had "transferre[d] that their Countrey to our Royall Father." If the document transferring Narragansett land was authentic, then royal commissioners should "seize upon the same in our Name," calling it "the King's Province" and requiring annual quitrents. The king also authorized the royal commissioners to make further treaties with Native sachems, a mark of sovereignty that both Connecticut and Massachusetts, usually through the United Colonies, had earlier claimed for themselves.[15]

Both sets of public instructions kept the focus on colony revenue and resources. The four commissioners had their marching orders: they were to gather information about shipping, making sure the Navigation Acts were "punctually observed." They should find out about the ironworks, especially whether the quality of iron and steel "bee of good temper for shipps," and they should look into "timber," whether it was suitable for masts and if it "growes neare the sea." Any gold or silver mines should be noted, as well, and a "fifth part" recovered for the crown, as stipulated in the charters. Further, when investigating "the whole frame & constitucion of the government there, both civill and ecclesiasticall," the royal commissioners must especially keep an eye on annual tax revenue, on militias, and on forts.[16]

The instructions' author—probably Clarendon—made sure to limit the royal commissioners' powers. They could authorize boundary decisions only if the lines by charter were clear and uncontested, or "by consent of parties." Every colony had its share of "discontented" men who would readily complain of its governors. The four royal commissioners should discourage complaints about local leadership *unless* these claims were "seconded & owned by men of equal condicion" or rank to the magistrates, or involved complaints regarding colonial magistrates' own direct violations of the charter. The royal commissioners should get to know colony leaders on friendly terms before bringing up the king's demands in his June 1662 letter (of which only changing the writs had really been obeyed). And at this point they should investigate the regicide issue, finding out who hosted them and orchestrating the fugitives' capture.[17] The public instructions' author tried to prevent overreach and guide the royal commissioners in the subtle arts of diplomacy, aware of the difficulty of their task.

The private or secret instructions, which applied to the commissioners' work in all New England, are more candid, revealing significantly more details about the Stuart government's assumptions and goals. By using "all kind and dextrous carriage" to insinuate themselves "into the good opinion of the principall persons there," the royal commissioners should "lead and dispose them to renew their Charters and to make such alterations as will appeare necessary for their own benefit." These changes included increasing the king's "dignity and authority" by having colonists nominate, rather than freely elect, their own governors, who would then serve three to five years rather than one. The proposed modifications also included putting the colonial militias "under an officer nominated or recommended" by the king. It would be especially favorable if the Bay colonists would choose "Coll. Nicolls . . . for their present Governour and Collonell Cartwright for their Major Generall," the author of the private instructions added. The message was clear: the commissioners should influence local elections, clandestinely working to "gett men of the best reputation and most peaceably inclined, to be chosen into that Assembly." Once royalist-leaning colonists had won election, the four men could then "give them all advice and encouragement to promote our [the king's] service." These new leaders should know of the king's "great affection" for them, and further that his "fatherly care" or patronage would extend to them as to those who advanced royal interests in London or Edinburgh. The commissioners were also to investigate colonial law codes.[18] If the public instructions promised to affirm the charter, the private instructions outlined significant constitutional changes, fulfilling some of the colonists' worst fears.

Regarding religion, the commissioners should take great care not to incite suspicion that the king meant to impose another "forme of worshipp among them." Although the monarch would love for God to "reduce all our subjects in all our dominions to one faith and one way of worship with us," puritan colonists were probably not yet ready, the instructions acknowledged. Beware of supposedly high church colonists who might be spies. Be wary too, the message continued, of those presenting investment opportunities for the crown, most likely "ayrey imaginations," or schemes that could be implemented only by the king's "immediate power and authority" and that would likely incite local opposition. The commissioners needed to keep an eye on local resources, however, and if by chance colony leaders made "proposicions" to sweeten their negotiations with the crown, that was a different matter. It would be highly appropriate, for example, for the royal commissioners "to settle some annuall tribute of the growth of that country, as masts, corne, and fish" for the king, as Norton and Bradstreet had supposedly hinted.[19] Fulfilling these instructions would have been an arduous task for the most talented and conscientious of diplomats. For men inexperienced with or antagonistic to New Englanders' culture, it would prove nearly impossible.

* * *

The work of commissioners for the 1661 Corporation Act in England probably helped shape the new royal commissioners' expectations for their own charter negotiations. As we saw earlier, the Corporation Act required all corporation officers, who included many town officials, to swear royalist oaths and within a year take the Eucharist in the Church of England.[20] The commissioners sent in 1662–1663 to enforce the Corporation Act throughout England generally followed a conciliatory policy. Trying to avoid the appearance of bias or harsh dealings, for the most part they let the oaths do the purging for them, as nonconformists wrestled with their consciences over whether to say the words. Priding themselves on "moderate exercise of their discretionary authority," these English commissioners encouraged people to keep their offices and gave some towns more thorough attention than others. And a well-thought-out appeal to the king sometimes meant a nonconformist could maintain his civil post.[21]

Once corporation officers had been vetted—either by the commissioners or prior to their visit—English towns could renegotiate their charters, with plenty of fees and presents to grease the wheels. Often local groups initiated this process themselves, concerned about their shaky legal standing post-Restoration or hoping to oust nonconformists and gain influence. In most cases, the crown reserved the right to approve corporation officers, although prior to 1680 none were denied. While most towns lost some autonomy, they gained in other ways, such as increased allowance for landownership. The glaring exception, of course, was Ireland, in which towns tended to lose autonomy, although the policy was still inconsistent no matter the territory.[22]

The Corporation Act did not apply to the colonies. If it had, the royal commissioners would have needed to gut New England's General Courts. Based on the accomplishments of the Corporation Act commissioners, however, the royal commissioners in the limelight now probably expected colonial charters that were not already reconfirmed to be freely offered up for renegotiation. They almost certainly anticipated a give-and-take process facilitated by generous gifts. One estimate for their expenses boldly anticipated remuneration through "Rents, Fines, Customes or other profitts" from the region.[23] Sailing over on armed royal frigates in mid-1664, Nicolls, Cartwright, Carr, and Maverick may have looked forward to their mission's perks. Their enthusiasm likely dwindled, however, as the voyage stretched to a long ten weeks at sea, with rising swells, few entertainments, and dwindling water supply.[24]

* * *

News that royal commissioners on four warships were sailing across the Atlantic provoked "great feare of changes both in . . . church, & civill state" among many colonists.[25] Colonial leaders sprang into action, first to settle boundary disputes among themselves. Generally, mutually agreed-upon arbiters—sometimes officials of the United Colonies—decided colony lines. In late May 1664, Plymouth and Bay magistrates turned their attention to their long-contested boundary, much preferring to settle things among themselves than to cede those powers to a royal commission.[26] Plymouth and Rhode Island, however, failed to reach an agreement, and Rhode Islanders decided it might be to their advantage to let the royal commissioners weigh in.[27]

In the Bay colony, the General Court took the extraordinary measure of hiding the patent or charter in preparation for the royal commissioners' arrival. It is telling that in the court's June 1664 handwritten records, the order regarding the patent is scribbled right alongside a new colony-wide fast proclamation for the country's "many dishonors & troubles." The juxtaposition of these two matters on the manuscript page reveals the dual impulses at work during this time of crisis: safeguard the patent and pray.[28]

The patent order acknowledged that keeping the patent secret remained of "great concernment to this commonwealth" and argued that the document should stay out of reach of any royal agents who might abscond with it and whisk it back to London. Some General Court members would have vividly recalled the senior John Winthrop's 1630 decision to bring the patent with him across the ocean and his later reflection declaring "that which the King is pleased to bestow upon us and we have accepted, is truly our owne."[29] The June 1664 court unanimously ordered the original and all copies of the patent to be brought in to their Town House chamber; afterward, the deputies and magistrates each appointed two or three people to hide them in multiple places. Some names of those chosen appear on the original manuscript draft, but a clever scribe crossed them off. In a solemn political ritual, acting secretary Thomas Danforth then brought forward the "Grand Pattent" and delivered it to Richard Bellingham, who presented it to those appointed to "dispose there of as may be most Safe: for our Country." Concealing the patent comprised an act of faith in—as the fast proclamation put it—the "lords mercy" and "gracious returne to his people."[30]

What about the royal warships? Those could not be hidden away. The gentlemen onboard would need appropriate greeting and hospitality. Many colonists likely found the prospect of English soldiers traipsing around Boston disconcerting. The court decided that when the ships arrived, after presenting "respects" to the gentlemen, two militia captains should make sure that lower-ranking English officers and soldiers only came onshore in limited numbers. What was more, these visitors must be unarmed and "behave themselves peaseably & orderly . . . Carefull of Giving offence to the people & lawes of this place." Messengers running around the colony to deliver these instructions stayed busy: on the reverse side of the manuscript order regarding the warships, the secretary provided a list of towns needing copies of the fast day proclamation, with each checked off in turn.[31]

Some inhabitants evidently grumbled about holding a fast day at this precarious moment, calling it "needless" or even "dangerous." What if royalist spies took note of people's prayers? One minister compared the colonists' situation to that of Daniel, cast into the lion's den for declining to pray to the king. Another reminded people that in a time of "publique calamity threatned & feared & in parte com," fasting remained crucial: all should repent, embrace humility, sacrifice, and "fellowfeeling," and continue the work of reform. Drawing on the popular civil war passage, the curse of Meroz, this same minister also warned, "To bee at ease in Zyon at such times & dayes is to bee under a woe of god." And responsibility did not rest only with men: as the biblical figure Jael had impaled an enemy warrior with a tent peg, so the congregation heard the message, "rise up yee women"![32]

Before the commissioners' arrival, no royal warships had entered New England's ports, and no royal agents had stepped onto the region's shores. One can imagine men and women starting to gather near Boston's harbor on the warm and sunny day of July 1664 as the royal frigates became visible on the horizon, wondering what their future might hold. Two militia captains quickly took a small wooden shallop or rowboat toward one of the frigates, probably eyeing closely its guns. The royal vessel first arriving carried Richard Nicolls and George Cartwright. On the captains' embarking on his ship, Nicolls took the opportunity to give a speech about the providentially guided and "pretious opportunity" that their arrival had afforded the colonists to defend "his Majesties Just Right" against "Usurpers of his Dominions"—here meaning the Dutch. Realizing the General Court had dispersed two weeks earlier, Nicolls also expressed steely confidence that Governor Endicott "would give us a speedy and satisfactory answer to our first demand," most likely an immediate meeting of the General Court to receive the king's letter. Nicolls's impatience probably stemmed both from weariness after what he admitted had been a "tedious" journey and from the impending assault on New Netherland. Approaching Boston on the captains' shallop, Nicolls and Cartwright received a thirteen-gun salute from the Boston castle (in Nicolls's estimation, a "small fort") and another salute from fourteen merchant ships. By this point, a crowd had gathered along shore, as "great numbers of people flockt to see the sight." Yet another loud salute rang out as the two men stepped onto colonial land and received greetings from civil war veteran and major general John Leverett.[33] If the power of the new regime had seemed distant before, it was now tangibly present in Boston.

Nicolls and Cartwright wasted no time getting to work. Although it was six o'clock on Saturday evening, just before the puritan Sabbath, they demanded an immediate meeting with the governor. Leverett told them Endicott was unavailable due to his age and illness. Although tempted to go find the governor in his home, the two royal commissioners finally decided against such an action, thinking it "ill manners." They asked, instead, to be taken to the local Sabbath service. Escorted to the Boston meetinghouse, the two men tried to decline the colonists' efforts to seat them in Governor Endicott's place, but their demurrals went nowhere. So they sat in the designated pew—and, as the frail governor entered, the royalists stood up and bowed formally. According to Nicolls, whether Endicott "was blinded with devotion, or otherwise I cannot say, but hee tooke soe little Notice of us at his Entry"—or through the rest of the three-hour service—that the commissioners eventually departed with Endicott still seated behind them. The service itself, Nicolls thought, "for contrivance is no bad Theatre." Although he deemed it entertaining, the preaching, in his view, focused oddly on "patience in affliction and persecution," and the prayers for the king seemed faltering and unpracticed.[34]

The two men rested at Leverett's home on Sunday evening. On Monday morning, they asked again to visit Endicott but were informed of his "sudden Infirmity." A planned meeting was abruptly canceled when a messenger announced that Endicott "was fallen ill againe." The royal commissioners had indicated their plans to leave for New Netherland as soon as the other two ships had arrived from their current docking at Portsmouth harbor; delay might prevent a meeting altogether. Frustrated, Nicolls tried a cajoling approach. He "Jestingly told" Leverett and others that it seemed as if Governor Endicott and Deputy Governor Bellingham "did keepe us of[f] at Push a Pike," that is, they were keeping the commissioners at just enough of a distance that a weapon could not reach them. According to Nicolls, colonists continued to protest "the Age and weaknesse of their Governour" and Bellingham's hearing difficulties, "even to a stupidity." By now angry, Nicolls retorted that those who had elected such infirm leaders were themselves "more blameable." At this moment, he pulled the regicide card, saying he knew some Bay leaders "had showd much more Civility to Common strangers even to such as ought rather to have beene apprehended and to have sufferd death as Traitours." His words carried significant weight. "Imediatly the seales turnd," Nicolls later reported; and two magistrates came to arrange a time for "a decent reception of his Majesties Letters and Commission" by the governor and Council. "I hope," Nicolls mused with satisfaction, "they are better Instructed, for the future."[35]

When they finally met with Endicott and several magistrates, Nicolls and Cartwright presented an April 1664 letter from the king. Later, Nicolls would have a copy "privately communicated" in order "to prevent lyes" spreading about its contents, probably giving it to Thomas Breedon or another royalist-leaning Bostonian. In language similar to his public instructions, the king here praised New England and disavowed any intention of "violating or in the least Degree infringing the Charter," which he claimed to be "very willing to confirm or renew" or even "enlarge." He complained, however, that the Bay colonists' response to his June 1662 letter had disappointed him. That letter "did not answer our Expectations, nor Professions made by your said Messengers," Norton and Bradstreet. The king therefore expected "satisfaction" in the current conferences with his royal commissioners, to whom he knew great respect would be accorded.[36]

All of this must have sounded reasonably promising to colonial ears, but then Nicolls and Cartwright presented their actual commission, which granted them "full power & authoritie to heare, & receive, & examine, & determine all complaints & appeales in all causes & matters, as well military as criminall & civil, & proceed in all things for the . . . peace & security" of the colony according to the four men's "discretions" and the king's most recent instructions.[37] Hearing these words as they probably sat crowded together in the Town House upper chamber, Endicott and his Council must have struggled to maintain their composure. This was not the constitutional arrangement they thought the charter had secured. While some colony charters included a provision for appeals or review of laws, Massachusetts Bay's did not. The senior John Winthrop had fought much the same battle before English commissioners for foreign plantations back in 1646–1647, during the debate over Robert Child's petition and appeal. Although the ruling back then held some ambiguity, it essentially favored the colonists, acknowledging appeals to London were impracticable and would undermine local government.[38] To hear a royal commission now granted such extensive powers undoubtedly filled the colony's leaders with dismay.

Nicolls and Cartwright pressed ahead to their most urgent item of business, the Bay's assistance in New Netherland. They expected immediate support, noting that raising troops would "be a signall testimony" of the colony's "compliance with his majesties affaires, & of great honor to this colony." The governor and Council, however, replied that while they were "very desirous to testify their loyalty," they first needed to meet with the General Court. A decision as weighty as war recruitment required the entire representative assembly. Nicolls and Cartwright "manifested themselves not well sattisfied." Departing briskly, they told the Council to focus on the king's 1662 demands, which had yet to be fulfilled.[39]

Immediately prior to Nicolls and Cartwright's departure for New Netherland in late July, fourteen non-freemen, all merchants and probably wealthy, paid the royal commissioners a visit. Having heard that the king "requird an obedience" to his June 1662 letter, the merchants wanted to inform the two men that they had "petitiond . . . for their Liberty as freemen" and "were refusd." According to these non-freemen, "some have beane punisht others discounteanct ever since" (these cases are difficult to find). On these words, Nicolls reflected, "I never saw people kept under such a slavery as many are under this Government." Nicolls and Cartwright instructed the merchants to petition the General Court again, and if refused a second time, "to appeale to us."[40]

A few days later, the frigates carrying the royal commissioners left for New Netherland. Bostonians must have had many questions as they watched the ships glide off from the harbor. In one historian's estimation, "all that was known was that the colony had been subjected to the veiled threat of armed intervention and had been treated as though its government no longer existed."[41] As they watched those sailing vessels shrink to pinpricks on the horizon, colonists must have been especially troubled that the royal commissioners had claimed such broad authority without leaving a full copy of the king's instructions behind. They were also alarmed by reports of Maverick and Carr's arrival on the two other ships in Portsmouth. Maverick had supposedly acted so "menacing" toward the local constable that onlookers had asked Carr whether the royal commissioners intended to take over the government. Carr had deescalated the situation, telling Portsmouth inhabitants that "they ought to continue in their obedience to the present government, till they had further orders." Overall, the royal commissioners' "words and carriages . . . occasioned in the hearts and minds of the people a deep sense of the sad events threatening this colony."[42] Everyone knew the frigates could sail back to Boston in short order.

* * *

Energized by these fears, the General Court that met in early August 1664 gathered all resources at their disposal. Early on, magistrates and deputies asked the ministers for their "best advice" on the "weighty affaires now before them in refference to his majesties letter, commission, & propposition" for military assistance. Probably already gathered for their usual post-Thursday lecture meeting at John Wilson's spacious—by colonial standards—wooden home, the ministers received the General Court's request along with a set of papers, most likely copies of those few the royal commissioners had left behind. Increase Mather found his "heart serious" as he joined with sixteen other ministers in "consulting what answere to return unto the General Court" regarding these ethical, diplomatic, and constitutional issues.[43]

The ministers gave extended attention to the conditions for just war.[44] Ethically, they argued, the colonists could only join in armed conflict against the Dutch if, first, the latter were "Intruders and injurious possessors of that place," had committed "atrocious wrongs," and "due meanes" had already been used to encourage repair of those wrongs; second, if English colonies' "wellfare and safety" were at risk; and third, if they had the resources to sustain the conflict. The ministers also addressed the broader relationship between warfare and sovereignty, contending that if the court did send soldiers, such a move should be framed as a gift rather than as a charter duty, thereby not obligating them to provide future military aid. As usual, the clergy also reaffirmed the line between civil and spiritual realms, deferring to the court's authority in such matters.[45]

On the king's demands, the ministers advised standing by the patent; the colonists had the power to write their own laws and oversee their own churches. They urged the court to quickly write a "humble and affectionate Petition" to Charles II asking "for his Favor in the Continuance of our Patent Priviledges." The king, they reminded the court, had repeatedly offered "Gracious expressions" of "encouradgement" toward them and their charter. They saw no reason to cave in to the royal commissioners' attempted encroachment on local authority.[46] In effect, the ministers advised holding the constitutional line.

Brushing past the ministers' just war considerations in favor of pragmatic details, the court ordered that the royal commissioners could recruit a maximum of two hundred volunteers and arranged to finance the effort temporarily. (It would turn out that young men did not jump at this volunteer opportunity.) The clergy's advice to write a strong but affectionate letter to the king, on the other hand, court members readily took, even borrowing some of the ministers' wording. The magistrates and deputies would go even further, however, when they directly asked the king to block or withdraw the royal commission. They appointed a magistrate, Francis Willoughby, a deputy, Major General John Leverett, and a minister, Jonathan Mitchell, to draft such a letter, "filled with such rationall arguments they can finde." Mitchell ended up as primary author. At the same time, the court symbolically renewed the official search for the regicides, who at this point retreated back to the woods before moving on to Hadley.[47]

Court members also followed the ministers' advice to stand by the patent. In fact, they took the remarkable step of making a solemn constitutional resolution on the matter: "God asisting, to beare faith & true alleagiance to his majestie" and "to adhere to their pattent, (the duties & priviledges thereof,) so dearely obteyned & so long enjoyed by undoubted right in the sight of God & men."[48] This August Resolution amounted to an incredibly bold pledge to preserve their long-standing constitutional arrangement. The king would not be pleased, and the court well knew it.

In line with this resolution, the magistrates and deputies refused to change their oath or baptism policy.[49] They did minimally expand the franchise, a move probably advised by a large committee of magistrates, deputies, and ministers who had worked since May 1663 to solicit broad input from freemen and non-freemen.[50] At stake in this debate was nothing less than godly rule, or the ability to elect leaders who would protect churches and continue the work of reform, rather than allowing anti-puritan royalists access to authority. The August 1664 General Court repealed the law that limited freemanship to full church members. Voting privileges would now extend to those wealthy, long-time householders who could provide a local minister's letter vouching for their uprightness and orthodoxy; even then, however, their freemanship would be subject to a majority vote of the General Court "according to the rules of our patent."[51] To many colonists, this expansion of the franchise beyond full church members seemed a real, sacrificial effort to demonstrate loyalty to the crown, although to the royal commissioners it would appear a negligible concession.

The court also took measures to encourage greater cooperation among the militias of Boston, Charlestown, Salem, and Ipswich. In their statement, court members ordered their officers to "take into your care & chardge the souldiery, great artillery, & fortiffications within your toune, and precinct, & harbor." Any attack "upon the shoare or water" should be "represse[d] by force of armes," as militiamen responded to orders from either the General Court, the Council, or Major General Leverett.[52] Whether they had in mind assaults by Dutch or English frigates is unknown.

Unsurprisingly, after taking such momentous action, the General Court declared another fast day. Resembling a mini-sermon, this poignant fast proclamation declared that from poor harvests to the warships' arrival, multiple "tokens" of God's "displeasure" had saddened the godly, who worried that their sins would provoke God to "withdrawe his shepheardly care . . . the greatest of all miseries that can befall us." They must pray for themselves and the "hower of sad triall" elsewhere, humbling themselves and trusting in Christ's "blood & merits." Believers hoped, then, for God's continued presence and "special blessing accompanying his oune ordinances & providences." Even amid these "difficulties," they hoped God would "give his people one heart & one way." This unity would be for God's honor, the people's good, and the good of their descendants. Dorchester congregants linked the fast with the court's being "called together upon the Coming of the Commissioners from England," and added to the proclamation's prayer list an additional plea that, in spite of "troubles feared; yet god [w]ould grant us our libertys in Church and state."[53] They had used all the means they could think of and now waited pensively—if not anxiously—for the royal commission's return.

* * *

By the time Bay representatives traveled south to deliver to Nicolls the August General Court's resolution to contribute soldiers to the New Netherland conflict, most of the larger-scale action was over, and Nicolls declined the offer. He did commit to "speedily" report their "ready complyance" to Charles II while also reminding them that they still needed to address the king's other demands.[54] Connecticut, however, had played a significant role in the armed struggle, contributing troops as Winthrop mediated between Nicolls and Dutch governor Pieter Stuyvesant. Through Plymouth magistrate and trader Thomas Willett, Stuyvesant had long known the royal frigates were coming, though some "intelligence" had informed him that their mission was to bring all of Charles II's "kingdoms under one form of government, both in church and state," installing bishops over New England rather than threatening the Dutch. Still, the Dutch governor had already faced uprisings from English towns on Long Island in 1663. Taking no chances, he had asked for help—and was promptly turned down. The Dutch

West India Company refused to send arms, believing the English frigates were intended only for New England.[55] In his August 1664 attack, Nicolls, aided by Long Island militiamen, first cut off Dutch supply routes. Stuyvesant tried to rally his band of 150 soldiers against Nicolls's 1,500 troops, but civilians petitioned "in bitterness of heart" for "an honorable and reasonable capitulation": "you know, in your own consciences," they pleaded, that the dilapidated Dutch fortress "is incapable of making head three days against so powerful an enemy." After multiple letters back and forth, Stuyvesant finally signed Nicolls's terms of surrender.[56]

Nicolls then sent Cartwright to take Fort Orange and its surrounding settlements and Carr to take the villages on the Delaware. At Fort Orange (renamed Fort Albany), Cartwright and Dutch leaders' negotiations ended on relatively generous terms that included a Dutch-held monopoly on the fur trade. The Dutch in the upper Hudson were more willing to surrender because they were caught in the middle of a yearlong conflict between Haudenosaunee Mohawks and a coalition of Sokoki Abenakis, Pocumtucks, Mahicans, and others. Cartwright also negotiated a treaty with seven spokesmen from Mohawk and other groups, agreeing to continue the fur trade, to supply "wares and Commodities" (presumably including weapons), and to provide justice for injuries and mutual aid if attacked. Left unspoken was the extent of the Duke of York's patent and its glaring disregard for Haudenosaunee or Abenaki sovereignty.[57]

Carr's mission to the Delaware was a disaster. He was supposed to deal respectfully with the inhabitants of New Amstel, assuring them of their property and privileges and inflicting minimal damage. When local governor Alexander D'Hinoyossa refused his terms, Carr quickly ordered his 130 men on two frigates to a full-on assault. After overpowering D'Hinoyossa's thirty soldiers in a bloody battle, Carr allowed his troops to plunder Dutch estates and to sell Dutch soldiers into "slavery" (probably servitude) in Virginia. He then destroyed the nearby fledgling utopian colony of Swanendael.[58] In the aftermath, he started seizing Dutch estates for himself, for his son, and as patronage for another officer.

Hearing about the Delaware fiasco, a furious Nicolls put Cartwright in charge of New York and rushed down to see for himself. "I found Sr Robert Carre," he said, "determind to sett up his rest with the booty in his hands . . . presuming that his majestie had Employd him onely to make his owne fortune." Nicolls tried to convince Carr to direct the seized goods to "the support of our poore souldiers this winter," but Carr refused, claiming "hee had wonn it by the sword and could part with his Life rather than suffer so high an affront." In the time Nicolls gave him to reconsider, Carr busily and unsuccessfully tried to hide the booty, though "with terrible oathes of a Gentleman & Christian he flatly denied" any subterfuge. Not fooled, Nicolls discovered the goods in back rooms and even under a mattress, delivering them up to an ensign for both the soldiers' and local planters' provisions.[59] It would take Nicolls many months to undo the damage from Carr's actions in the Delaware, delaying his ability to attend to the second mission of New England.

Things went from bad to worse. Returning to New York, Nicolls discovered that under Cartwright's overly brutal command—involving "cursed Gallowes, Horse and Strapadoe to make us ridiculous to the Dutch"—the soldiers had mutinied.[60] The conquest of New Netherland was not turning out to be as quick or simple as he had hoped. Nicolls had to delay sending one of the frigates back to England so that he could restore order. Looking around at his chaotic surroundings, including the ill-maintained fort, and sensing the potential need for Winthrop's aid, Nicolls negotiated a generous boundary line with Connecticut, although it was later contested.[61] Even so, he designed the new government of New York in a manner that sent a clear message to Winthrop and other New Englanders about the Stuart penchant for consolidated top-down authority.

Under "The Duke's Laws," the royal governor appointed an advisory council of ten men, mostly "recent emigrants" who "retained commercial and political ties to England" and who usually served for life. Although he consulted with local inhabitants, Nicolls declined their requests for an elected assembly. New York's Council would be by appointment only.[62] The Duke of York would later comment on the tendency of such "dangerous" assemblies—meaning those by election—"to assume to themselves many priviledges which prove destructive to, or very oft disturbe, the peace of the government." Nicolls also appointed justices of the peace and, turning back the clock a few centuries, created four medieval-style "manors," the lords of which remained beholden to the governor. And while parish overseers (nominated by householders but chosen by town officers) could select a Protestant minister (subject to governor approval), they had little room for creative maneuvering when it came to church governance: they must baptize all children of Christian families, perform marriage rites, and offer yearly communion to those not "of scandalous or vicious life." This requirement excluded most puritans, Quakers, and Baptists. The governor had power to adjudicate church doctrine—no line between civil and spiritual kingdoms here. Unsurprisingly,

Nicolls's efforts to recruit New Englanders to New York would be unsuccessful.[63] When notifying Long Islanders of the agreement with Winthrop that placed Long Island within New York, Nicolls promised residents "equall (if not greater freedomes & imunityes) then any of his majesties Colonyes in new England." Long Island inhabitants, many of whom were puritan-leaning and strongly preferred Connecticut's government, likely doubted his words. They experienced intense disappointment as they watched New York's constitutional arrangement take shape. For years to come, they would petition for a more representative government—and would be continually denied.[64] The royal commissioners had succeeded in ousting the Dutch from power and creating a new royalist base in the Northeast.

* * *

Back in Massachusetts, rumors and high feelings erupted as colonists struggled to come to terms with the royal commissioners' show of force. News filtered in of Carr's plunder, Cartwright's abuse of soldiers, and Nicolls's absolutist-leaning powers as governor. Militia training days became one forum for expressing outrage. Before the Salem militia, gathered with muskets in hand on the grassy commons, the deputy William Hathorne supposedly questioned the validity of the royal commission itself, saying it was likely "made under an old hedge" and "sealed with yellow wax," not the official red wax of the crown. Calling Nicolls and Cartwright "unmannerly," and offended that they "would not put off their hats to the authority of the country," Hathorne (according to one account) gave his men an ultimatum: "You that are for the king's commissioners stand, and you that are for the country, follow me."[65] At the Boston meetinghouse, the frail Endicott, too, supposedly rose up before the people to deliver a ringing speech urging constitutional defiance.[66]

Men and women throughout the Bay colony expressed consternation at the great "charge" to the colony of hosting the royal gentlemen and speculated on the commissioners' plans to "exact 12d for every acre of land, and £3000 a year besides." Many worried about the imposition of prayer-book worship and the royal intent "to abridge them of their greatest priviledges, liberty of their consciences." Others expressed concern that the men would "infringe the discipline of the Church by compelling children to be baptized" whose parents were not full members. Many were furious that the commission would try to "interrupt their form of government by . . . admitting of appeales." In "whispering" tones, colonists even placed "wagers" that the four men "shall never sit here as Commissioners."[67]

* * *

More had to be done. In September 1664, the Bay Council decided that the best way to aid the towns in mobilizing against royal imposition was to articulate their government's foundation and publish it as widely as possible. Implementing the General Court's August Resolution to "adhere to their pattent," they retrieved a copy from hiding and again studied it closely, with an eye toward protecting "Lands, government, & many precious priviledges." Probably also drawing on the 1661 patent-study committee's work, the Council then made a declaration of "the summe of certayne particulars" in the patent "for publique use & benefitt."[68]

In what I will call the September Declaration, the magistrates assured people they did indeed possess the power to make and enforce their own laws. If the royal commissioners tried to rewrite the law code—as they would do in 1665—such an attempt would directly violate the patent.[69] And if any local royalists tried to defame or discredit the colony's courts, they could be punished. The patent or charter also gave the colony power to defend itself on land or sea, with "all fitting meanes (and if neede be) by force of armes." Anyone who attempted to invade, destroy, or even annoy the colony or its inhabitants could be repelled by local militias. Further, if any group of royalists (presumably encouraged by the royal commission) tried to mount an armed insurrection "or perfidiously Attempt the alteracion & subversion of our frame of Polity or government," they could be executed. For good reason, the September Declaration has been called "virtually a declaration of independence."[70] Colonists were drawing a line that the king and his royal commissioners should not cross, and they were willing to defend it.

Bay leaders also worked to shore up cooperation among the United Colonies, the confederation of Plymouth, Massachusetts, Connecticut, and New Haven. At their September 1664 meeting, United Colonies commissioners (two representatives from each colony) discussed the royal commissioners' arrival at length. Without full knowledge of the king's instructions, they found it difficult to know how to prepare. The United Colonies commissioners decided that whenever any colony learned of the royalists' actual proposals, that colony should alert the others. Further, any decisions "of Comon Concernment to the whole" should be made through the United Colonies.

In this way, the local commissioners declared, "wee may approve our selves faithfull and Loyall to his Majesties Just Interest and the best good and welfare of these Plantations."[71] It will not come as a surprise that the royal commissioners would try to eliminate the United Colonies, which they viewed as an illegal usurpation of sovereignty: only kings, not colonies, had authority to form confederations.

The frigates' arrival on New England shores had brought home to many colonists the seriousness of the threat to their constitutional arrangement and had elicited a widespread commitment to defending it. The royal commissioners' words and high-handed behavior had not spurred obedience; it had incited defiance. Colonists began to mobilize in earnest. Subsequent town petitions, drawing on both the Massachusetts Court's August Resolution and the searing September Declaration, would mark a season of heightened activism at the town level. Fearful of losing their charter and the liberties they believed it to guarantee, townspeople across the colonial region would rally behind a principled constitutional resistance.

CHAPTER 6

Towns

The Resistance Petitions of 1664–1665

The door of the General Court's chamber in the Town House opened again and again in October 1664 when representatives from eleven towns knocked and requested entrance. They had come carrying petitions. The emissaries from Cambridge went first: Edward Jackson, his older relative Richard Jackson (a non-freeman), Edward Oakes, and Deacon Gregory Stone. These men had served in local offices, helping build the highly participatory institutions for which the New England colonies were now known. Entering the court's chamber, the four Cambridge men unrolled their petition, a large manuscript sheet formally addressed to the court. The petition urged the magistrates and deputies to defy the new king's demands. The inhabitants of Cambridge pleaded that they did not wish to be "subjected to the arbitrary power of any who are not chosen by this people according to theire patent."[1] They had signed their names in two lists, some making only a single mark, their full name added by another. One hundred and seven freemen and heads of household, and one woman, Rebeccah Daniell, had signed the first list. Thirty-five members of "the traine band [militia] and singell men" had signed the second.[2] Court members, impressed that the petition "was subscribed by very many hands," took the manuscript from its bearers and studied the contents carefully, debating anew the constitutional balance between colony and crown.

The Cambridge petitioners, along with those from ten other towns, responded to the crown's demands by rallying around their local institutions. As their liberties in church and state appeared threatened, many colonists responded by participating in town-wide petition campaigns and expressing their own understandings of long-standing legal privileges and just limitations on imperial authority.[3] Although not radicals, these men and women were willing, most of them claimed, to risk their lives and livelihoods rather than submit to the king's demands that they change their oaths and baptismal practices or expand the franchise in such a way that wealthy anti-puritan royalists could gain access to power.[4] The petition campaigns of this period in New England's history demonstrate the extent and texture of local constitutional sensibilities coalescing in response to imperial pressures.

These sensibilities were hard won and hard argued. As they grappled with a confusing set of directives and rumors, colonists struggled to articulate the foundations of their liberties and to explain why the Stuart king or his newly arrived royal commissioners could not weaken them. Their strategies and arguments were more ad hoc than systematic, drawing on a wide array of religious and legal traditions—some from the time of the English civil wars, some going back to the Magna Carta, and others rooted in the Protestant Reformation on the continent. Even as the General Court continued to debate how far to submit to the crown, the petitions of 1664–1665 reveal a remarkable moment of constitutional mobilizing at the town level. This movement centered on protecting the charter, and especially the colonists' charter-granted privileges of electing their own magistrates and writing their own laws, laws that allowed for the freedom of churches from state control.

Deeply protective of local decision making, many colonists feared a scenario in which wealthy, self-interested Englishmen with court connections might show up in the colonies with royal warrants and tell colonists how to run their affairs, or charge them fees to do so. Or worse, they feared a bishop arriving to eject puritan ministers from their pulpits. As we saw earlier, although Charles II had signed the Declaration of Breda, the Cavalier Parliament was not similarly inclined toward leniency; and the suppression of nonconformists in England in the 1660s took a more brutal tone than even the 1630s.[5] Why would anyone in line with the crown allow nonconformists to continue to administer their own colonies? Many colonists could remember the 1634–1638 attempt by Charles I's government and Archbishop William Laud to revoke their charter and impose a royal governor, an attempt John Winthrop and others had chosen to resist.[6] More recently, a royal governor named Francis Willoughby had been reinstated in Barbados, where he used a heavy hand to suppress nonconformists.[7] Fearing that royal commissioners would "improve their power" with complete disregard for local courts and elected officials, townspeople in the Bay expressed a "general solicitude for the preserving of their enjoyments, according to their present constitution."[8]

As we have seen, they had designed their modes of political and religious affiliation in light of the inequities they or their fellow nonconformists had experienced in England and according to sustained biblical and legal reflection. Fearing the life span of their innovative modes of governance might be short, these townspeople stepped forward to take action.

A major catalyst for the 1664–1665 petition campaigns involved anger over misrepresentation of Bay colonists in London. Detractors were filling the king's chamber with reports of dissatisfaction and antagonism among them. While the colony had its problems, inhabitants preferred that their reputations not be defined by their least happy constituencies, especially Quakers, wealthy royalist merchants who maligned them as disloyal or incompetent, and disgruntled neighbors such as the Rhode Islanders currently contesting a piece of land in Southertown: these men had taken their case over local magistrates' heads directly to the king. Individual "malcontents" were one thing, but when dissidents in London started to portray Massachusetts Bay as catastrophically divided and therefore in need of royal intervention, colony inhabitants bristled.[9] Such harsh characterizations of disunity and unrest, when they reached colonial ears, seemed an affront to decades of painstakingly constructed and for the most part functional local government. Thus one reason to sign a petition was to set the record straight.

Bay magistrates realized they would need an informed and mobilized citizenry to have even a chance of preserving local institutions against imperial infringement. They were still wary of democratic forms of government, which they tended to associate with anarchy. But they began actively fostering popular opinion to assist them in dealing with the crisis of the Restoration.[10] As we discussed earlier, the May 1663 General Court had issued an invitation to both freemen and non-freemen, or those without the franchise, "to send in their apprehencions . . . with such arguments as are prevalent to their oune understandings." "The matters in question," the court said, "are of great concernment, both ecclesiasticall and civil," and as such, a range of people should be asked for their opinions. A committee of magistrates, deputies, and ministers would then give all this input "serious consideration" and decide on a course of action to promote God's glory and the people's happiness.[11] Town meetings were one, but far from the only, forum for inhabitants to discuss the constitutional crisis. Some towns sent their deputies back to the General Court with written instructions first drafted by a committee and then put to a vote. Debates over these instructions could include how best to respond to the king. For example, the question of enlarging the franchise was raised for a general discussion among inhabitants of Salem. The residents voted that including "som that are not members of particular Churches" would be acceptable. Both freemen and non-freemen spoke at crowded town meetings, which, if sometimes rowdy, aimed at consensus or at least compromise.[12] Taverns and church meetings were also likely places for discussions. In one or another of these varied forums, the notion of large-scale petitions started to circulate. It was an idea whose time had come.

* * *

By early 1664, a group of colonists whose ranks included Edward Johnson had initiated a colony-wide petition they suggested sending from the freemen directly to the king. The draft they wrote for the General Court's consideration has received scant attention, but its language is noteworthy for what it reveals about the concerns of one active constituency.[13] Johnson heralded from Woburn, an opinionated town where local officials refused even to "publish" the king's 1662 demands.[14] The petition highlights the dependence of religious on civil liberties: losing patent privileges meant opening the door to episcopacy. The petition also pushes back against those who would see the colony as a mere appendage of England, describing Massachusetts Bay's patent, laws, and form of government as a holistic and distinctive polity.

We can look at this argument in a little more detail to appreciate its significance. According to these freemen, the Bay government, a "Comly Structure" and "Rare Edifice," had flourished for more than thirty years despite its remote location and lack of "fresh inteligence" regarding English governance.[15] Their "Civel policy" had been "organized in Europe Naturall to our English Nation," and residents chose "the most learned lawyers," trained at the Inns of Court, for magistrates. The "Freemen" still saw their polity as fully English, and certainly not divergent from English law (grounds for revoking the charter).[16] Yet their "Ecclesiastique & Civel policy" remained distinct and cherished, and so they hoped rumors of "your Majesteys intention to Alter our present Government in the Least" would prove false.[17] This language of a distinct polity or commonwealth hearkened back to a Christian humanist tradition that informed much early colonization. It contrasted with newer Hobbesian theories envisioning the colonies and England as a unified state, existing for the benefit of the metropole.[18] These freemen drew on older humanist models when describing their distinct polity.

The "Petition from all the Freemen" also borrowed vocabulary from the English civil war period, describing colonists as "a more Honest intrest" for the king than any European prince could claim. During the early 1640s, as resistance to Charles I's rule had mounted, the language of an "honest party" or "honest men" had served to define godly citizens who, in a self-reflective, informed way, contributed to the good of the state—doing so in contrast to subjects who seemed loyal but in fact floated with the tides and betrayed the public trust.[19] It made sense that the petition's authors would tap into this older political rhetoric as they tried to prove their loyalty without compromising their liberties.

Additionally, the era of the civil war informed the "Petition from all the Freemen" in the assumption that an attack on civil liberty was part and parcel of an attack on religious liberty. Prominent nonconformist John Owen had preached at a post-regicide parliamentary fast day that every age had its own "work" and "light," and theirs was discovering the "mystery of Civill and Ecclesiasticall Tyranny" as "interwoven, and coupled together." Accordingly, the great work of God in this age was "untwining of this close combination against himself." Earlier Protestants might have said that Christian liberty, or liberty from sin and the devil, existed independently of civil liberties such as freedom from arbitrary taxation. In many puritans' memories, the civil wars had been fought precisely to uphold Christian liberty in the sense of pushing back against the tyranny of kings who tried to control the church and royally appointed bishops who taught unqualified obedience to kings as a religious duty.[20] The Bay colony's flourishing, petitioners argued, could be directly attributed to the freedom of its churches from governmental control, churches "furnished with fit persons men of Knowledg in the mystery of godlyness & skeild in the wisdom of winning soules." But this freedom appeared now to be in danger: petitioners feared the crown imposing prayer-book worship or suppressing nonconformist preachers. "As for Cerymoneys to re[a]gitate the peoples Devotion wel may they be spared," the petitioners pleaded; what turned the "wilderness (with indefatigable Labor) into Townes" was not ceremonies but rather "zelous affection to worship the Lord."[21] If the king deprived them of godly preachers, the towns would wither.

The "Petition from all the Freemen" also sought to recover colonial reputations from the damage inflicted by detractors in London. Those who complained of the colony's "Arbytrary power or Tyranous Lawes" were simply ambitious men who thirsted after rulership themselves or those who, through "Contempt of authority," had "felt the force of Justice[s] Sworrd," probably a reference to Quakers. Broadening the franchise, far from strengthening the government, "would but Enervate" it. Worse, it would "put your majesties Leige people upon a 2d perregrenation," a not-so-veiled threat to join forces with the Dutch or another Protestant empire. If anyone persuaded the king to withdraw the colonists' liberty of freely electing their local leaders, the colony would likely be overtaken or dispersed. For New Englanders a royal governor was not a mild change in policy, it was a "first-order threat."[22]

At the same time as they claimed poverty and weakness, the petitioners implied their potential for military resistance. They not-so-subtly dropped big numbers for the population of the colony—eighty thousand—and for the amount spent on the Boston castle—£40,000. While couched in the language of "your Majesties Lands" and "your Majesties Subjects," the message was pointedly clear: colonists could repel any infringement upon their prized local institutions. On the flip side, if the king let them continue flourishing, it would redound to his benefit, especially in the shipping arena—both "Building And vytaleing," or finishing off the essential parts of a vessel.[23]

As they made a concluding plea that the king "suffer us not to be yoked againe with the Highrarchy" (a bishop), the petition's authors drew on the story of Esther. "We expect," they declared, "With honest ould Mordachy to find place in your Majesties Chronicle." In the biblical account, when Haman, the Persian king's highest official, plotted to hang Mordecai, a Jew, the sleepless king called his servants to read to him from "the booke of the Records, and the Chronicles." From those records, the stunned king learned that Mordecai had thwarted a plot on his life, and he decided to reward him, albeit belatedly.[24] The colonists' use of this biblical tradition reveals more clearly their view of the political landscape. Rather than emphasizing English lineage or English citizenship, the petition authors linked themselves with the Jews and the king with the Persians. Charles II's advisors, who would have read the petition (if sent) first, were by inference the duplicitous, murderous Haman. The General Court may have chosen wisely in not endorsing or forwarding such a petition. But the supplied biblical context suggests a widening cultural chasm that some colonists perceived between themselves and the Stuart government.

Esther, however, was also a classic tale of political reversal, of subjects who, on first glance threatening, later turned out to be the most loyal. The heading in the Geneva Bible teased out this larger significance: "The king turneth over the Chronicles, and findeth the fidelitie of Mordecai, and commandeth Haman to cause Mordecae to be had in honour."[25] Maybe the English king, too, would find puritan colonists to be his most faithful supporters, and in the end honor them?

When they presented their draft petition, the authors who stood before the magistrates asked them to consider it before acquiescing to "the least" of the king's demands. The petition was meant for the eyes of the king; but its postscript implied it was also meant for God: if the Lord were "ownd in his providences," perhaps he would sustain the colony's government. Holding fast to their local institutions might, like Esther's actions, bring a divine intervention; and through that intervention, the king would find colonists "true to him" while they courageously remained true to their "principles." The petitioners hoped the outcome would be "Gods people incouraged & our Consciences quietted."[26] If they were to join their English brethren as a repressed minority, they would not succumb without a struggle.

* * *

The colonial petition campaigns fit well within the longer history of puritan petitioning. In the 1640s, the last time they had perceived an overwhelming threat to church and state, the parishes and counties of England had flooded the English parliament with petitions. Some decried episcopacy; others opposed clerical corruptions; still others targeted the power of the monarchy, especially arbitrary taxation. Petitioning tended to snowball. Once one town heard of another's petition, townspeople grew inspired to write one of their own. By 1642, "petitioning had become the most potent weapon in the provincial armoury."[27] Charles I had strongly opposed this kind of activism: his "government had always insisted that it was illegal and seditious to arouse popular support in this way." Royalist critics saw petitioning as a contagious disease and treated petitioners to blistering satire. Even so, people on both sides of England's civil wars turned to petitions as a way of inserting popular opinion into the political realm.[28]

It seems likely that at least a few of those now involved in the colonial petitions had been active in the earlier efforts of the civil war period, perhaps signing a 1640s petition—some of these included as many as ten thousand hands. English puritan Nehemiah Wallington remembered the earlier petition campaigns as a spiritual movement. He wrote an account of them so that "generations to come" might "behold what our God hath done in the stirring up the people of all counties, and of all sorts, high and low, rich and poor, of both sexes, men and women, old and young, bond and free, both in the cities and counties, for to go up to Westminster . . . with their petitions for the removing of those great obstacles" to "that blessed Reformation both of Church and Commonwealth."[29] And although some earlier historians viewed these English petitions, especially ones similar in language, as the work only of elite organizers, more recently scholars have seen them as "genuine attempts at representing a consensus" and as communicating "deeply felt local opinion."[30] Involving people of many sects, the petition campaigns were nonetheless consistent with the puritans' tendency to encourage men and women to measure their leaders' actions against the benchmark of scripture.[31]

Some colonists had petitioning experience from events closer to home. Over the previous two decades, local petition campaigns in New England had touched on a range of issues, from the attempt to subdivide an overflowing town to the effort to resolve a difficulty over a land boundary, a militia captain, or a minister's recruitment. The 1641 Body of Liberties gave all people, whether "Inhabitant or Forreiner, free or not free," the liberty to present petitions "to any publique Court, Councel, or Towne meeting" as long as they did so in an orderly and respectful manner. Colonists retained this right to petition even after Robert Child and Samuel Maverick led a small but potent petition campaign in 1646 that fiercely criticized the charter, the government, and the churches—especially the link between church membership and the franchise. When called in by the General Court, the Child and Maverick group was not "questioned for petitioning" but rather held accountable "for such miscarriages . . . as appeared in their petition." In this instance, the leading petitioners, who claimed Massachusetts's laws were repugnant to the laws of England—a politically dangerous claim that could serve as grounds for the king revoking their charter—were declared seditious and fined.[32] Yet the free practice of petitioning continued.

In most cases, colonial petitions involved routine requests for the General Court to grant land or poverty relief or services of arbitration, which it usually did provide. The tone, popularity, and content of the 1660s petitions proved to be a dramatic change from most of what had come before, an intense outpouring of local opinion directed toward shaping the colony's imperial politics. Although "persistent tensions about popular participation and popular politics" continued, the colonists, as much as their English counterparts, thus helped usher in an important seventeenth-century movement that, over time, granted a significant role for broad-scale political opinion.[33]

The petitions of 1664 and 1665 probably originated with a small group of townspeople, possibly aided by selectmen, deputies, or a minister. Most likely these petitioners received input from several different constituencies. The process probably took some time, as it did with a 1641 petition in Kent, England, where the townspeople drafted a very long petition and a local representative helped shorten and refine it. At least nine colonial ministers signed resistance petitions.[34] While Bay clergy were not really the kind to add a petition-signing ritual to their church services, as had happened in England, church meetings or fast days offered prime opportunities to gather signatures informally.[35] Townspeople across the colony decided to organize; they wanted to make sure the General Court heard their concerns. At least one-quarter of adult Anglo-American males in the Bay colony signed these 1664–1665 petitions, advocating firm constitutional limits to the king's power. Historians have noted the existence of these petitions, especially in the acrimonious academic debates of the 1960s and 1970s over whether Massachusetts had been an oligarchy or a democracy; but they have paid little attention to the petitions' motivations or contents.[36] None of the town petitions comes solely from freemen; all come either from the "Inhabitants" of a town or from its "people," or even from "freemen and others." Two petitions—Dedham's and Boston's—are signed entirely by non-freemen, and a third, from Cambridge, has a section of non-freeman signers. Cambridge's is the only petition signed by a woman. That their language is religious is not surprising. Politics at this time was not yet fully a discursive field; rather, it borrowed its vocabulary from law and religion.[37] Overall, New Englanders joined these petition campaigns to articulate their deeply felt concerns and to bolster the resolve of the General Court in resisting compromise with the king.

* * *

Cambridge inhabitants likely had a role in launching this petition movement. Theirs is the earliest to show up, with a date of 17 August 1664. As noted before, Cambridge inhabitants were the first to knock at the Town House chamber door and present their petition.[38] Cambridge minister Jonathan Mitchell had stood in the vanguard of popular activism, as well, preaching rousing sermons about how God's kingdom extended to the reform of civil government and how civil liberties themselves should be regarded as divine gifts. When Cambridge church member and magistrate Daniel Gookin reflected on whether or not the colony should obey the king's demands, he was moved by Mitchell's preaching to ask, "if this Gove[r]nment of ours bee of Ch[ris]ts establishing & gift & a fruit of his purchase <as I

judge it is>" would it not be wrong "for us to bee Active in parting with it"? If Cambridge residents saw Christ's kingship established when the franchise belonged to "godly persons" rather than to the wealthy or landed elites, and if they also saw those who tried to subvert the local government—royal commissioners possibly included here—as undermining Christ's work, then we should have little difficulty seeing them as also inaugurating a petition campaign.[39]

The Cambridge petition likely served as a model for other 1664 town petitions—there were eleven in all—and as such, its language is worth a careful look. Like the petition from all freemen, the Cambridge authors explained that they were writing because of disgruntled colonists' reports to the king about "divisions among us and dissatisfactions about the present goverment of this colonie." Although writing to the General Court, the authors clearly wanted to testify for a transatlantic audience that such grumblings did not represent Cambridge as a whole: they hastened to note their "satisfaction" with their local institutions and their "earnest desire of the continuance theirof." Their patent privileges had been given to them by both James I and Charles I (of "famous memory" rather than of "blessed memory," as would have been standard). Because of this "encouredgment and security," the Cambridge inhabitants went on, "we or our fathers ventered over the ocean into this wildernesse through great hazards, charges, and difficulties." Through many years of hard work, their families had come to trust in the security of their liberties of self-governance. The authors now pleaded with the General Court to ask the king "for his royall favour in the continuance of the present estableshment and of all the previleges theirof."[40] Cambridge inhabitants would have known that the court had already appointed a committee to write a letter to the king; Mitchell was a member. Protesting the royal commission, however, marked an incredibly risky move. The danger was worth it if it kept them from "Arbitrary power," such as royal governors or bishops.[41] Harvard president Charles Chauncy started the line of signatures, which included most of the adult men of the town and the widow Rebeccah Daniell, as well as a list of non-freemen that we will look at more closely momentarily.

Subsequent petitions from the towns of Concord, Billerica, and Medfield borrow language from the Cambridge petition. Their additions and substitutions, however, offer intriguing glimpses into how local communities mobilized. As we have seen, circulating templates for county petitions was common practice in England and did not necessarily mean that participants who relied on borrowed language were less personally engaged. Describing Charles I, Concord petitioners changed "famous memory" to "Blessed Memory," more careful than their Cambridge counterparts to avoid offense. Before we assume that such caution meant Concord inhabitants were somehow less invested in resistance, however, we should note that they replaced the section expressing concern about "Arbitrary power" with a more militant promise based on the court's September Declaration: "Seeing our rightful Soveraign hath priviledged you with power by force of arms to defend this place and people . . . we doe declare that we are readie to assist both with persons and estates, that soe by the goodness and mercy of God we may still enjoy our present priviledges." Concord authors also affirmed "it a mercie of God, that you so minde the good and preservation of this place, and people, according to oath."[42] In referring to the magistrates' previous declaration, adding a note of appreciation for their efforts and stating their readiness to assist, Concord petitioners were bringing their petitions more fully into line with English precedent. Many English petitions from 1642 began with thanks for parliament's work, whether their "unwearied labours . . . for the publike good" or their "wise and gracious Passages and Proceedings."[43] And they often ended with a promise of "humble tender of our service and devotion unto you" or claimed that the signers would "ever honour this honourable House, and to the utmost of their power defend the same."[44] The Concord petition, then, was both more customary and more militant than the Cambridge version.

Billerica gave a shortened version of the Cambridge petition, adding an original second half that, like Concord's, included expressions of thankfulness, along with a less militant promise to be "faithful, obedient, and serviceable (to our utmost power)." The authors primarily aimed to encourage the court's defiance of the king and to advocate for the preservation of their "civil and ecclisiastical" privileges, not only for their own good but also for their "posterity." Billerica inhabitants added a prayer: "wee comit you to him who is Able to direct you in all the weighty matters you have in hand."[45] While earlier English petitions frequently ended with a version of the formula "your Petitioners will be bound to pray," the colonial petitions often conclude with affectionate and original prayers. For the most part, the Medfield petition followed Cambridge's narrative, but like Billerica it added a prayer, and like Concord it voiced a promise: "earnestly begging the sweete presence and blessing of God on all your faithfull Endeavours," Medfield signers pledged "to support the present Government with our Persons and estates."[46] It is easy to gloss over these prayers, but it would not be surprising if local gatherings to compose the petitions actually involved spoken prayer for the welfare of the colony, or if some of the mobilizing took place on fast days.[47] The prayers might have been real prayers, in other words, spoken aloud by the faithful. They help reveal a bedrock cultural expectation among New England puritans that God would move in and through the political process and that pious faithfulness would be rewarded with political safety.

Of the 1664 petitions, Dorchester's went the furthest in pressing the General Court and sacralizing the patent. It comes to us in the handwriting of minister Richard Mather, the first of its 112 signers, although that does not mean other inhabitants had no involvement in its composition.[48] A member of the 1661 patent-study committee, Mather, as we have seen already, was known to preach edgy sermons.[49] He had endured the political crisis of the 1630s in England and had thought carefully about resistance and risk. Suspended from his Church of England ministry in 1633–1634, he had blessed God for being able to face the "threatning words" of Archbishop Richard Neile's "pursevants" without succumbing to terror. His ideas about religious purity and political stability had taken root in that moment of crisis. "No instance can be given to the contrary," he elsewhere declared, "when God ever suffered any people to perish that did purely observe his Ordinances, and execute Justice and Judgement, untill by their defection and sin they had . . . caused their Shield to depart from them."[50] For Mather, the supernatural element in politics meant that people who established godly institutions lived under divine protection, whatever mischief bishops or kings might attempt.

In their opening appreciation, Dorchester petitioners quoted directly from the General Court's August Resolution and September Declaration, which they saw as "a great mercy" and "favor from God." They also quoted from the patent, reminding the court that they owed only a percentage of gold and silver ore to the crown; otherwise, they would pay rates only to "such as doe here reside and dwell, and are by the country chosen to labor amongst us in this church and civill goverment."[51] More than other petitioners, Dorchester inhabitants pushed the court to stay the course, insisting that to change direction now would be both "uncomfortable & dishonorable." "We pray god," they wrote, "that such a thing may never bee." The king's letters had confirmed the patent, and, as the court had resolved, the magistrates and deputies should "adhere" to it.[52]

Dorchester petitioners were especially concerned about the imposition of prayer-book conformity. Since the patent gave the colony the power to make its own laws, the Dorchester petitioners argued, they had full power to uphold laws regarding their churches. Here they quoted the section from the 1641 Massachusetts Body of Liberties that touched on church liberties: "noe injustice shall bee put upon any church officer or member, In point of doctrine worship or Discipline, whether for substance or sircumstance besides the Institutions of the Lord." If they became forced to use Church of England ceremonies or baptize indiscriminately, "consciences truly tender would be trobled." It was "well knowne to the world," petitioners argued, that freedom from "human Inventions & impositions" constituted "one spetiall cause" behind the settling of New England. Their religious convictions were known and public at the time the patent was sealed, they argued; therefore, any laws based on those convictions existed within the realm of permissible divergence from English law. To be "burdened and encombred againe" with unwanted religious ceremonies might seem a slight thing to the king or his commissioners, but to the Dorchester petitioners it would violate their patent liberties in a "lamentable and greiveous" manner.[53]

Four more 1664 petitions, each dated later in that same October month of the General Court's meeting, departed from the earlier petitions in language but still advocated for resistance. The first was Roxbury's, probably penned in the hand of the minister John Eliot. It would make sense that Eliot was reluctant to submit a petition, for, as we have seen, the court had recently suppressed his anti-monarchical book.[54] Brief but original, the Roxbury petition asked the court to "stand fast" and pledged, "we doe desire not to cease to pray for you who are at the helme; that the Lord would please to guide, & assist you to steere right in these shakeing times." The other three October petitions originated in Boston and are markedly brief and subdued in tone. Written after discovering that other towns had mounted petition campaigns, the Boston petitioners said only that they wished "the present Government withall there Libertyes may in there Latittude be still Continued." They did not promise any specific support beyond prayer.[55] As we noted back in Chapter 3, Bostonians had sent in a petition alongside other towns in 1661 calling for compromise with the king's demands rather than defiance, so it is not surprising that these 1664 petitions appear a bit perfunctory and minimalistic. Less than a year later, in May 1665, Bostonians would send deputies to the General Court with instructions to promote a moderate course of "an amicable compliance" with the royal commissioners, although they still wanted to keep the patent.[56] As we will see, in 1666, Boston, cooperating with Salem, Ipswich, and Newbury, would send in yet more petitions arguing for moderation and even deference to the king's demands.[57] Clearly, there were divisions in the colony, and people mobilized around compromise as well as defiance. Yet even the moderate Bostonians found a way to participate, albeit coolly, in the 1664 demonstration of unity.

In his diary, Boston moderate John Hull mentioned that "some of the original authors" of the Cambridge and subsequent petitions were more radical than the Bay population as a whole. Some of the language in the petitions reflected the views of those who tended to see Massachusetts Bay as a "State independent," he worried. Hull wanted to emphasize that those who signed the petitions and those who did not were equally pious. Those "doubtful" about the petitions were just as much animated by love for the colony's welfare, and members of both sides of the colony-wide debate desired their liberties in church and state to continue. Each side, however, held a different view of the meaning of "duty of subjection to our sovereign."[58] Perhaps the Christian obligation was simply to obey the king, an action that might also prevent more serious royal impositions.

Colonists delivered their petitions in person to the October 1664 General Court. Over two days, petitions were presented from the towns mentioned above, as well as from Woburn, Reading, Chelmsford, and Dedham. Other towns may have discussed petitions but did not have the unity or leadership to follow through. The ritual of delivery would have been familiar to colonists who had heard about or participated in petition campaigns in pre-Restoration England. To process into the Town House chamber and present petitions before an imposing group of magistrates and deputies was an act of political theater that reinforced the urgent message of the petitions themselves. It is possible that those sitting on the court helped orchestrate the timing. Even so, in their personal delivery of the petitions, the men sent by their towns communicated that they expected their opinions to be taken seriously. Although court records do not mention the precise run of show, it would have been traditional for the magistrates to read the petitions aloud, then formally thank the petitioners who stood, waiting, before them.[59]

The royal commissioners would later say that those who signed these petitions had been cowed into doing so by the General Court itself through "underhand dealing."[60] Even a brief familiarity with the way Massachusetts politics worked, however, casts doubt on this view. As we observed earlier, when the magistrates tried to have the freemen vote by proxy rather in person, the freemen raised vocal concerns; and the magistrates quickly reversed the decision.[61] Although horizontal and vertical social influences no doubt played some hand in these petitions (as they would in almost any movement), the court's ability to coerce signers remained limited. It is much more likely that the petition campaigns, even if quietly encouraged by the magistrates, were motivated by local concern over rumors in London and by perceived threats from the royal commissioners and the Restoration regime.

Drafted by Mitchell, the 1664 official letter from the General Court asking the king to withdraw the royal commission shares key ideas and phrases with the town petitions. It also draws explicitly on expressions of support voiced within the petitions to affirm that the colony was indeed united, not divided, in its support for local institutions. After rehearsing the terms of the patent and the king's earlier encouragements, the letter turns to the colonists' "affliction of heart" over the damage done by "adversaries," who "by their misinformations, complaints, & solicitations" had managed "to precure a commission under the great seale." The royal commissioners, including "our knoune & proffessed ennemy" (Maverick), were trying to overpower the rule of the General Court, subjecting the colony to the "arbitrary power of strangers." In just a few months, the commissioners' behavior had been "enough to confirme us in our feares" that their actions would "end in the subvertion of our all." If the king did not act to recall the royal commission, the colonists would be forced to leave or "sinck & faint under burdens that will be to them intollerable."[62]

Like the earlier "Petition from all the Freemen," the court's letter situates the colonists within the biblical story of Esther: "Whatever become of us," the court declared, "wee are suer the adversary cannot countervaile the kings damage." Whether Charles II would have picked up on the reference is unknown. In the biblical story, when the Hebrew people were about to "perish" under the Persian king, Queen Esther argued for their preservation based on what the king's own loss would be if her people were destroyed. The Hebrews' enemies, she said, "cannot countervaile the kings damage." This reference supported the court's economic argument: the expense required to bring the Bay under tight imperial control through "Imposed rulers & officers" would be twice any possible return, especially because the king stood to lose much more "by the discouragement & diminution of mens endeavors in theire severall occupations," which would decrease customs. These economic arguments were crucial to the court's larger point. Although the approaches taken by Massachusetts and Connecticut to royal authority were strikingly different, in part because John Winthrop (the son) had the coaching and support of his Royal Society colleagues, in their letters to London both had downplayed the potential wealth to be made in New England—or at least had suggested that such wealth would not be possible apart from hardworking colonists. The rocky soil, weather, and other defects of the country should discourage the king from gifting New England land to great men. If the king did award parcels of the puritan-led colonies to royalist "gentlemen," the Massachusetts Court's letter continued, he should know that doing so would drive most inhabitants out, "for to a coalition therein they will never come."[63]

The General Court's letter also drew on the evidence of the town petitions to declare that "high representations of great divissions & discontents amongst us" were false and should not have led to the perceived "necessity of sending commissioners to relieve the agreived." "Abhorrent from change," the people of the Bay stood with the General Court. New England had its malcontents, but "through the favour of God" these naysayers were few and far between. The magistrates and deputies then made a concerted effort to state their aversion to plotting, voicing the hope that, if opportunity and righteousness allowed, they would be able to further "testify our dutifull affection." But they could not do so right now: what the king had requested as a testament of subjection was, in effect, self-destruction. In bold language that made loyalty contingent on semi-autonomy, the authors urged: "let our government live, our patent live, our magistrates live, our lawes & liberties live, our religious enjoyments live; so shall wee all have yet further cause to say from our heart, 'Let the king live forever.'" The colony would be loyal, but on biblical and constitutional terms. The king thus had two options: destroy the colony or recall the royal commission and let the Bay continue its quiet course, redounding to his material and spiritual benefit.[64]

* * *

Responding on behalf of Charles II, Secretary of State William Morrice liked neither of the General Court's options and expressed serious dissatisfaction with the "temper and spirit" of the request to recall the royal commission. He chose to believe that the court's letter did not represent the colony as a whole but only "a few persons who have had too long authority there."[65] The official response had barely made its way back to the other side of the Atlantic, however, when colonists launched another set of town petitions. Organized in early 1665, and cognizant of the intensifying disagreement, this next set of petitions takes a darker tone. They also include many more non-freemen. The royal commissioners and the colony's London detractors were building a case against the Bay based on the colonists' supposed oppression of non–church members who could not vote in provincial elections. In early 1665, the commissioners decided land claims for Rhode Island against the interests of the Bay, siding with anti-puritans such as Samuel Gorton and offering protection to an escaped felon, thereby undermining the authority of the Massachusetts Court.[66] The 1665 petitions were thus characterized by a more immediate sense of the crown's threat to local government and by a stronger display of support for the Bay colony's leaders, including from those who did not yet have full political rights. Every voice mattered when the stakes were this high.

The inhabitants of Northampton, represented by eighty-six signatures, both freemen and non-freemen, put great care into the religious and constitutional language of their petition. Claiming that they were "not insensible of the sad frowns of God upon us and threatenings toward us manifested both by signs from heaven & earth," the petitioners repented for having "forsaken our first love & forgotten to do our first works which wee came into this land to do," and looked to divine help for political deliverance. Echoing Mitchell, they averred that godly local institutions were and would always be a sacred gift: "wee have enjoyed much of the presence of God affording us his own ordinances both civil & ecclesiastical in his own way & according to his own institution." Thus they pleaded with the magistrates, as "fathers of our country under whose shadow wee look for protection under God," to think carefully about the "state of our country churches plantations familyes & persons" as well as to remember the reason for the colonists' migration. Was this reason "not a quiet & peaceable enjoyment of God in his ordinances & the advancement of the Kingdome of Jesus Christ without humane traditions or molestacon"? Northampton inhabitants saw reformation as central to their colony's purpose and their local institutions as divinely sanctioned. They asked the court to "Stand for confirme & maintayne our former & ancient rights libertyes & previleges both in Church and Common wealth," liberties grounded in the Word and "purchased" by Christ.[67]

The phrase "ancient rights libertyes & previleges" evoked England's ancient constitution, the traditional liberties of Englishmen based in reason and common law, as well as making a claim for the longevity of the Bay's system of governance.[68] The language of liberties "purchased" by Christ probably drew on the Geneva Bible's translation of Ephesians, a text long recognized as a resource for resisting tyrants.[69] While the King James Version used the word "possession" in Ephesians 1:13b–14, the Geneva Bible supplied "liberty":

"ye were sealed with the holy Spirit of promise, Which is the earnest of our inheritance, for the redemption of that liberty purchased unto the praise of his glory." Verses such as this one and Galatians 5:1, "Stand fast therefore in the liberty wherewith Christ hath made us free, and be not entangled again with the yoke of bondage," were traditionally interpreted to mean liberty from sin. These petitions, however, added a civil gloss.[70] Civil liberties, as well as religious liberties, were gifts purchased by Christ. English royalists despised and railed against such civil glosses on these texts. But these interpretations, also used by the poet and polemicist John Milton, would gain traction over the next century.[71]

Hadley petitioners, with regicides William Goffe and Edward Whalley living in their midst, expressed an even greater sense of the looming crisis: "If ever there were apperances of danger towards us we think now more." Hadley minister John Russell had taken in Whalley and Goffe a few months earlier, a feat he could not have pulled off without the cooperation of the townspeople. With "sad thoughts of heart," the people of Hadley were trying to "foresee the danger and hide ourselves." Made vulnerable by the regicides they had moved to protect, they sought a more solid shelter in the presence of God and the bulwark of godly rulers. Like the Northampton petition and Mitchell's sermons, Hadley petitioners saw their liberties in church and commonwealth as a gift from God, not only from the king: "Whatever royal grants of grace we have received either from the Lord in Heaven or kings on earth the accepting holding fast and maintaining of the same with due thankfulness is the true magnifying of that grace." And "to throw away or cowardly to suffer ourselves to be flattered or frightened from it is the despising and dishonoring thereof." The patent was a sacred gift, and honoring that gift meant holding on to it, even if the earthly giver (the king) asked for its modification.

Pressing their argument even further, the Hadley petitioners redefined the nature of kings and subjects in terms that allowed for constitutional resistance. True kings, godly kings, could handle being challenged if a fundamental right was at stake. "The king of heaven will give his poorest subject on earth leave to challenge resolutely his right and not to let it go for frowns or threats." Should not "just and gracious" earthly kings in the same way allow their subjects to protest for their rights? They concluded, "We have a right from God and man to chuse our own governors" and "make and live under our own laws."[72] The Hadley petition amounts to an exceptionally daring expression of local constitutional culture.

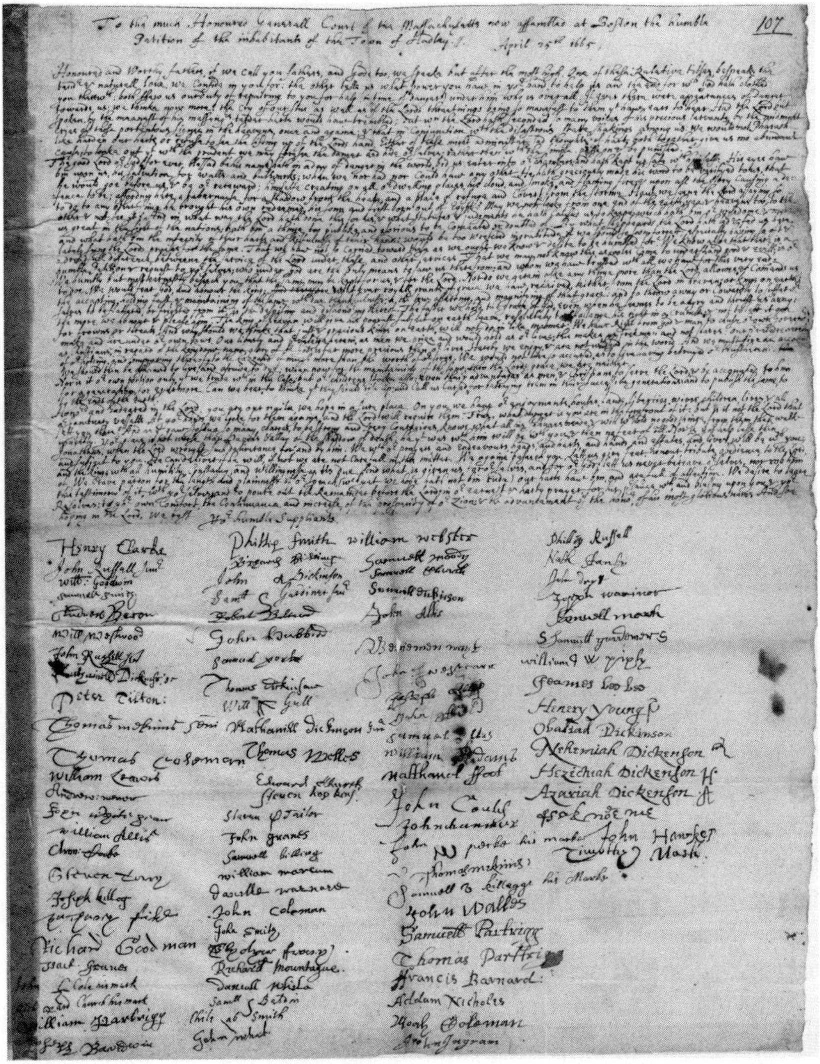

Figure 4. Petition from Inhabitants of the Town of Hadley to the Massachusetts General Court, 25 April 1665, vol. 106, fol. 107, Massachusetts Archives Collection. Courtesy of the Massachusetts Archives.

The final set of 1665 petitions, from non-freemen, are some of the most perplexing. Why would these men have signed to support a system that excluded them? We know some non-freemen felt they deserved the franchise, trying to nominate magistrates in 1663, perhaps sending a formal petition to the court, and meeting with the royal commissioners to complain in 1664.[73] Yet many more non-freemen than these signed resistance petitions. It is possible that the freemen or magistrates coerced them into signing. There were situations in England where the bishop or local gentry had cornered laborers into adding their names.[74] Still, there were non-freemen who did not sign, with no evident repercussions. The gulf between a freeman and an Anglo-American non-freeman in the Bay was not as cavernous as might first appear. Non-freemen voted in town elections after 1647, and evidence from multiple towns shows they were politically active before that date.[75] While the bar for the franchise in Massachusetts was high in terms of behavioral and spiritual performance, voting men did not have to be wealthy, guild members, or otherwise pedigreed. Very few people who persisted in seeking full church membership were denied. Some full church members chose not to become freemen, most likely because it entailed a hefty load of civic duties. That multiple non-freemen signed the town petitions of 1665 further demonstrates that the distinction between freemen and non-freemen, although important in provincial elections, did not prevent joint political action. In their petitions, the non-freemen state directly that they were motivated to act by the mistaken assumption, voiced frequently by the colony's detractors, that they disapproved of local government and would rather side with the king.

Dedham's non-freemen expressed their solidarity with other petitioners in countering any who "may possibly endeavour to make some disturbance in these our chiefest and dearest enjoyments." These men were incensed by reports of their disaffection with the government and by the actions of "enemyes to the cause of Jesus Christ"—here they linked Christ's cause with the actions of the General Court. They corrected those who would harbor suspicions about the petition's authorship: "and in this our request we entreat we may be beleeved to be very reall." Their primary message? They wanted the court to strongly uphold "our precious liberties and privilidges civil or ecclesiastical," so that these privileges would not "be enfrindged shaken or weakened." As they prodded the court to courage in the face of "feare favour threats or flatteryes," they simultaneously—and a bit awkwardly—affirmed those patent rights as "confeirmed to us that is to the Governor and

Company."[76] Put another way, the freemen here asked for the preservation of rights that were not fully theirs, although some probably expected that they or their children would gain freeman status over time.

Any analysis of the 1660s petition campaigns needs to deal with the deeply religious nature of Dedham's non-freemen petition. Parts of it read like a relation or testimony: "we may and (we hope) shall say our portions are faine amongst the godly by whome wee are Incouraged to breath after God and Christ." They knew that silence had political consequences and did not want to suffer a curse "for not coming out to helpe the Lord against the mighte"—a reference to the curse of Meroz from Judges 5, a common civil war–era passage also evoked in a recent Bay colony fast day sermon and heard in New Haven as well.[77] Dedham's non-freemen did not want to stay quiet or passive in a time of crisis. They became more positive and optimistic, however, when they expressed gratitude for "that great blessing we Injoy under the shaddow of yor wings in a Godly righteous and peaceable government." And, if anything, their pledge of assistance rang out with even more strength than the pledges offered by other petitioners: "we purpose and promise to the uttermost with our persons lives and estates when so ever need shall be."[78]

Boston non-freemen also petitioned. While the three petitions from Boston's "inhabitants" the previous October had opted for brevity and coolness of tone, the petition of the Boston non-freemen in May 1665 struck a different note altogether. Although some had lived in the colony longer and some shorter, the petitioners nonetheless wrote "most humbly & freely to declare our reall contentment in & with the present Government." They admitted they had not always "esteemed nor Prised" the government as they ought. They still, however, had "great cause to bless God for the hapines wee have had therein." Like Dedham's petitioners, the Boston non-freemen worried about how they were being perceived and described in London. They wrote to forestall "suspition of unfaithfulness," as well as to lift up "the honour & glory of God." "All of us," they declared, "have great cause to bless God for the hapiness wee have" in the Bay, "above other people else where both in Civell and Ecclesiasticall aspects." And, like other petitioners, they were deeply concerned that "the Solemne dispensation of God in his providences past & present seemed to threaten both Church & State."[79]

This group of Bostonians did not presume to speak for all non-freemen. They understood that just grievances might arise from "deffect or deficiency in Poynt of law" and hoped that, when such legal errors took place, they would be "rectified & prevented for the future." The current government, beneficial as it was, needed work. Even so, they feared that "sylence at such a time as this might be a discouragement unto mutuall proceeding of our honoured Magistrates & freemen." Pointedly, they expressed concern about dissension within the court itself. Despite differences of approach and imperfection of policy, these non-freemen wanted their leaders to stand as one. And they promised to help: "we shall as God shall inable us be faithful Assistant [to] yor selves for the utmost for the honour of God." They would lend this aid "with due respect & aleageance to our Lord the King," but they went even further than the other petitioners in specifying how their allegiance to the crown would be qualified: they would follow the king only "so farr [as he] may concurre with the word of God & the Patent."[80] Their true allegiance lay with the colony.

The relationship between inky petition signatures or signature marks and popular opinion is not a simple one. Those who chose not to sign have left little evidence of their concerns. Surely some people signed without full knowledge of the petitions' contents. The non-freemen's evocations of curses on those who stay silent point to another motivation for political engagement. Even within towns that joined the petition campaigns, some were more opposed to the threat of a bishop or prayer book than to a royal governor. There would have been social pressures to sign, as well, not to mention pressure from local elites, including ministers. Even so, it is unlikely that, in a small New England town governed by the norms of English common law and biblical conscience, signatures would have been anything but voluntary.[81] These petitions deserve to be taken seriously as evidence of how local inhabitants mobilized in defiance of the king's demands.

It may be that some non-freemen found Samuel Maverick's attempts to raise a royalist contingent distasteful. In early 1665, Maverick was traveling around the countryside trying to "undeceive" the population, running up an "unavoydably" high bill for expenses in the process.[82] He seems to have deliberately set up meetings "in the morning on the Lords day." Two brief examples will give a sense of these gatherings. On one occasion, when talking about "divers things, and persons in the Contry," Maverick took the opportunity to say that the royal commissioners "were the men, we were to obey." Startled, a man listening to his words asked, "suppose I was Comanded on[e] thing by them and another thing by our governors, which must I obey"? According to one account, Maverick responded, "I might obey them [local magistrates] till the next election, but no Longer," implying an overturning of the colony's leadership. Those present must have protested, for Maverick accused the colonists generally of being "rebels and traytors for minting of mony and printing which was treason," along with other language.[83] On a second occasion, Maverick initiated a tavern conversation about whether a certain fort lay within the patent bounds. Arguing with several colonists present, Maverick sneered that if that fort was indeed within the bounds, "so is Conectecut and Vergeenea & Maxego [Virginia and Mexico]." The men retorted with language from the patent, stating that their line ran three miles south of the Charles River. Maverick, noting the irregularity of the tides, said: "& who shall interpret The pattent Mr Belingham" (the governor)? Now inflated to take in "13 pattents," it "was A madd peece Of work to grant such A pattent it is that they are Ashamed of now." When colonists protested that towns to the east had voluntarily submitted to the Bay's jurisdiction, Maverick labeled Piscataqua and Maine inhabitants criminals and "Rogues" susceptible to bribery.[84] Ipswich's William Hubbard later observed that Maverick's "greater animosity than is usual against the country in general" and disdain for their churches "did his Majesty no little disservice."[85] Even a secretary to the Privy Council started to believe that Maverick did more harm than good.[86]

A few merchants were eager to listen to Maverick. There were dissatisfied parties in early Massachusetts, to be sure. From the days of Robert Child's petition for the franchise, a contingent of wealthy colonists, mostly Bostonians, had chafed at their exclusion from political power. And as we will explore a little later, Quakers were happy to mobilize, as well, although on very different grounds.[87] Overall, however, the non-freemen's petitions help us see why attempts to raise a royalist party in the Bay were for the most part unsuccessful. Pushed to take sides, many non-freemen chose what they considered to be the side of the godly.

* * *

It is important to not overstate the colonists' radicalism. Apart from exceptional figures such as John Eliot, they did not venture into anti-monarchical language. They could sound like republicans at times, drawing on the language of Hebraic or classical republicanism in their efforts to protect local institutions from arbitrary interference. They were animated, as many republicans were, by an opposition to "private interest politics" and by the belief that rulers should govern for the common good.[88] But most colonists did not follow the English Levellers or Milton into a critique of monarchy itself. It was their critics who accused petitioners of wanting an "independent" state.[89] If they were republicans, they were closer to those "monarchical republicans" who carved out self-governing towns in quiet corners of Elizabethan England, ready to hold the queen accountable if necessary to the idea that "monarchy is a ministry exercised under God and on his behalf."[90] Colonial men and women wanted civil liberties, but they were liberties compatible with some monarchical prerogative.[91]

Another important but unspoken context for the petition campaigns involves the structure of towns themselves. The level of organizing undergirding the petitions would have faced far more difficulty if colonists had lived in more dispersed fashion across the landscape, as they did in other, less dense colonies. In the Chesapeake, for example, urban projectors repeatedly tried to create towns that fostered robust civic life, some looking to New England for models. Entrenched class conflict, however, often stymied their efforts.[92]

Bay townspeople drew from a deep pool of biblical, civil war, and Reformed traditions as they advocated for their local institutions. Many understood the patent as a divine guarantee of their civil and religious liberties, both of which, in sinister and connected ways, seemed under attack. Compromising with the crown even in minor matters might mean letting go of a sacred bulwark against arbitrary government in either church or state. The energy and animation with which townspeople mobilized would baffle the royal commissioners and the Privy Council, who inhabited a royalist culture that tended "to restrict both public involvement in and discussion of politics."[93] In the Bay, the petition campaigns mark the formation of a markedly different constitutional culture, more committed to consensus building and open to widespread opinion. More voices—not all, but at least more—now had the right to be heard.

CHAPTER 7

Propositions

The Testing of New England

As Sir Robert Carr, George Cartwright, and Samuel Maverick traveled through southern New England in early 1665, their shared strategy of dividing New England and isolating Massachusetts became increasingly apparent. They gave only a cursory look at law and practice in the smaller colonies, hoping these examples of submission would pressure the Bay into compliance. Courted by disaffected colonists such as Samuel Gorton and the Quaker missionary Elizabeth Hooton, the royal commissioners listened closely to accounts of the Bay's overreach of their charter and the supposedly large numbers of disgruntled colonists eager to receive a royal governor. Overall, the royal commissioners' efforts to sow long-term division or raise a royalist party fell short of success, except in small, heterodox communities. Pressured to relax their constitutional convictions or turn on one another, most colonists declined to do either. Following along with the royal commissioners on this journey through Plymouth, Connecticut, Rhode Island, Narragansett, and, in Quaker company, back to Boston gives us new insights into the pivotal role played by these smaller colonies and less-studied groups in shaping constitutional sensibilities.

Launching their New England tour in February 1665, Carr, Cartwright, and Maverick decided to deal first with tiny Plymouth. Richard Nicolls did not join them: he had found it more urgent to govern New York, but he delegated authority to the other three, who would remain in close communication with him. Of Plymouth, Cartwright said, "we hope for a better complyance" than they had seen in Boston, where recent petition campaigns had given the commissioners "some ground to fear that the phancy of a commonwealth is yet in some of their braines."[1] Surely Plymouth, unlike those brain-addled Bay colonists, would cooperate with the king and his councillors' agenda.

Although likely aware of Plymouth's separatist past, which included a rejection of the king's church that hinted at sedition, the three men also might have known of Plymouth's quick proclamation of the king as lawful ruler.[2] Colony leaders had written to Charles II in June 1661 to declare the Plymouth colonists "truely Loyall subjects." With the help of some creative imagination, they had claimed that the original migrants had left their temporary refuge in the Netherlands out of "duty, love and loyaltie to our naturall Lord" James I, and out of a "desire to enlarge his dominions & injoy his protection." This letter also followed the Bay's lead in strongly requesting "confirmation of our Religiouse and Civill liberties & priveledges," supposedly "conferred by pattent" from "your Royall Grandfather," who "well knew the ends your servants Aymd at in our transplantation."[3] King James I probably did know their religious ends, and because of them had not actually supported the group, only agreeing to "connive at them," or look the other way. Plymouth's governor Thomas Prence would have been keenly aware that the 1620 Pierce Patent (and the subsequent 1630 Bradford Patent) did not bear royal seals from James I or his son Charles I and were not meant to authorize long-term colony government.[4]

The Plymouth letter had avoided any direct mention of separatists' complicated relationship with the monarchy or nonconformists' role in the English civil wars. It did, however, draw on the biblical story of Joseph and the many-colored coat, to say "it is enough Our Joseph (or rather) our Charles is yet alive." Charles Stuart, like Joseph, had been cruelly exiled before finding his way to power; perhaps Charles might now use that power to pronounce mercy on his nonconformist subjects, just as Joseph had shown mercy on his brothers. But, Prence had hinted, if the king were to withdraw his mercy, taking away Plymouth colonists' "Gospell liberties," a contented population would quickly transform into a "murmuring" one, as people who had lost their most essential, life-giving comforts.[5]

Charles II had eventually responded positively to Plymouth's letter, promising to defend the colony from all foreign foes. In this letter he also announced the royal commission, which would solve boundary disputes and communicate his "resolution . . . to preserve all your libertys & privileges both Ecclesiastical & Civill, without the least violation." The king hoped his generosity would lead Plymouth "to manifest by all wayes in your power . . . Loyalty & affection to us."[6] Colonists would indeed try to manifest or demonstrate their loyalty, but they would not prove as compliant as the king or Privy Council expected.

On hearing about the royal commission, Prence summoned "the body of the freemen" to the June 1664 General Court. On an issue of this magnitude, he preferred to involve the larger body politic. The population of Plymouth was probably around two thousand at the time, and the freemen not more than two hundred, with attendees at the court fewer.[7] After a long debate, those present finally "agreed and voated" to continue asking the king "for the further confeirmation of our pattent"—implying his endorsement of their current form of government—and to authorize the magistrates and deputies to raise funds for the effort, a difficult task in cash-strapped Plymouth.[8]

Aware of the small colony's shaky legal grounds and slim resources, Bay magistrate Thomas Danforth sent an encouraging letter, perhaps also fulfilling the United Colonies' previous agreement to share information regarding the royal commission.[9] A full generation younger than Plymouth's governor, Danforth first honored Prence, and then affirmed their shared faith that God would "have his Churches to acknowledge Him King: and might our Judah" or civil government "be his sanctuary, & compleat dominion." Mentioning the extraordinary spirit of unity throughout New England ushered in by the fast days, Danforth prayed that "our shakings and testing" would result in God's "Honor" and his people's "comfort." Danforth next let Prence know that the royal commissioners had not yet "acted anything" or revealed more of their instructions, although three had returned to Boston. For the political situation, Danforth said, colonists still hoped to keep "our present establishment in Church & Commonweale . . . the continuance whereof is our all, the more then all." Nothing mattered more. Encouraged by the king's recent letters, the Bay colonists' "great care," he argued, was that "no impresion may be made, to the infringement of our pattent."[10] Danforth hoped and expected Plymouth's care would be the same.

Arriving in Plymouth on horseback in late February 1665, the royal commissioners first communicated the king's assurances and demands in person to the General Court. "All houshoulders" should take the oath of allegiance, they declared, and all legal documents should be drawn in the king's name—a low-hanging fruit, for Plymouth inhabitants had already implemented this latter demand back in October 1660. Next, "all men of Competent estates and civill Conversation" should become freemen, or voters eligible for political and military leadership. People of "orthodox opinions competent knowledge and Civell lives (not scandalous)" should have access to the sacraments. Finally, the king wanted a revised law code that contained no "deregatory" holdovers from "these late troublesome times."[11] Seemingly reasonable, in practice these demands would overturn deep-rooted principles and open up colonial leadership to wealthy royalists. Historian John Gorham Palfrey (and others following him) said that in Plymouth the royal commissioners "conducted themselves with moderation, and experienced no difficulty," in contrast to the Bay, where colonial defiance set off royalist fury.[12] In fact, however, the Plymouth colonists responded with intense and protracted negotiations. "Moderation" is not the word that first comes to mind when we look carefully at their reactions.

Rather than giving Carr, Cartwright, and Maverick an immediate response, the Plymouth magistrates said that they needed time to deliberate. At the court meeting in early March, they considered the king's demands but still made no decision. Many colonists saw even the oath requirement as alarming. Oaths required by the restored Stuart regime were, in one scholar's words, "phrased with a fine mesh of words, to sieve and exclude the dangerous or unwanted."[13] While parliamentarians in the era of the English civil wars had argued that oaths were "mutual" and conditional, the Cavalier Parliament sought to reverse this view, initiating a revival of oaths as an instrument of the state, a strategy designed "to render any prospective constitutional resistance to the monarchy impossible."[14] The 1660 English Oath of Allegiance included unqualified acknowledgment of Charles as "lawful and rightful king of this realm," against whose person or government no one might "bear arms" or "raise Tumults." The oath had to be taken without any "secret reservation whatsoever . . . heartily, willingly . . . upon the true faith of a christian." The latter standard clause barring equivocation referred to the casuistic theory developed by Elizabethan Jesuits, who had revived still older methods that incorporated a "mental reservation"—an inaudible mental addendum—to an oath if a particularly tender conscience otherwise could not take it.[15] In the cultural mesh created by the oath, people emerged either royalists or Catholics. Many puritans understandably found Restoration oaths difficult. Back in Guernsey in 1660, Increase Mather had refused an oath required by General Monk "that now wee beleeved the Times were and would be happy," almost losing his salary over the refusal.[16] The poet and ejected minister Robert Wild's gently satirical poem, the "Nonconformist's Oath," circulating in the colonies in the 1660s, captured this dilemma: "I feare an oath, before I sweare, to take it, / And well I may, for 'tis the oath of God. . . . And yet I may and must sweare, for 'tis due. Both to my heavenly and my earthly king."[17] As Romans 13 instructed, "the powers that be are ordained of God." But monarchies and monarchs were no longer inviolable, if indeed they ever had been.

Plymouth leaders, including Prence, Josias Winslow, and Thomas Southworth, finally said "wee Consent" to the demand for an oath; however, it is not at all clear they consented to the official Restoration Oath of Allegiance. Rather, they agreed to keep doing what they had been doing since 1660, which was "to ensert in" their own "oath of fidelitie" a line about being "truely Loyall to our Sovereign Lord the King, his heires and successors." This line had been part of their 1636 freeman's oath, later replaced with "the State of Government of England as it now stands." Now they simply reverted to earlier practice, expressing loyalty on their own terms.[18]

Regarding the franchise, the Plymouth leaders also consented, though again by claiming their current policy basically aligned with the king's desires: "it haveing bine our Constant practise to admitt men of Competent estates and civell Conversation though of different Judgments . . . to be freemen" as well as "officers." But they added a stipulation: "yett beinge otherwise orthodox," a qualifier also in the king's 28 June 1662 letter to Massachusetts.[19] Freemanship in Plymouth was not linked to church membership as in the Bay. To become freemen, inhabitants only needed the approval of the freemen in their town and of the General Court. A 1658 law against Quakers, however, denied the franchise to "manifest opposers of the true worship of God or such as refuse to doe the Countrey service."[20] By leaving the definition of "orthodox" within their own purview, the Plymouth leaders' 1665 response essentially allowed them to continue their previous policies unchanged. Again, they consented; again, they did so on their own terms. They also took another line of argument, emphasizing to Carr, Cartwright, and Maverick that they sometimes had to "perswade" or even "compell" men "to be free men, so farre they are from hindring any." Finding men willing to serve on juries was not always easy, even among those who otherwise qualified for freeman status.[21] Notably, there was no influx of heterodox colonists to the ranks of Plymouth freemen following the royal commissioners' visit.

In lengthy negotiations over sacramental access, Plymouth did not consent but drove a hard bargain. There is evidence that Prence, Winslow, and Southworth negotiated with the royal commissioners to "underwrite" or insert lines below one of their propositions. Membership would be opened up, the insertion stipulated, "either by Admiting them into the Congregations alreddy gathered or permiting them to gather themselves into such Congregations where they may [enjoy the] benifitt of the Sacraments."[22] Rather than altering their own churches, in other words, the colony would allow an additional church to be established, under certain narrow conditions. Claiming liberty of conscience as a "high favour" from both God and king, the Plymouth leaders reminded the royal commissioners that purifying their worship was "the maine end of transplanting our selves into these Remote Corners of the earth" (an echo of Prence's 1661 letter). All "naighbours" were welcome to "adjoyne themselves to our societies according to the order of the gospell," but those who disagreed and were "truely Conscientious" could start a second gathering in a town, as long as the regular town minister did not suffer for support. If the king was serious about "his Royall purpose to continew our libberties," surely he did not mean that the Church of England could uproot "such Congregations as are alreddy in being"? Why, in any case, would prayer-book conformists want to settle in Plymouth? There were plenty of "other places to accommodate men of different perswasions in societies by themselves"; surely for the "preservation of peace and Charritie," high church ceremonialists could find another spot.[23] On the matter of church government, Plymouth held firm.

The colony's ability to negotiate may have been facilitated by the trader and magistrate Thomas Willett. A member of John Robinson's Leiden flock in his youth, Willett spoke fluent Dutch. Noting the magistrate's good relationships with Dutch leaders, Richard Nicolls had asked Willett "to assist in . . . reducing the affaires of these parts into good English," promising that such service would "render me ambitious" to demonstrate royal friendship to Plymouth. In spring 1665, Willett had, in his own words, taken every opportunity "to beget in them a good opinyon of our Colloney." His obligation to "the Churches of Crist," he said, "will stir me up" to use "all the intreste I have in aney of the Cumiscionars for thar good."[24] Sounding a little like a double agent, Willett was certainly using his influence on behalf of Plymouth while serving Nicolls and other royalists.

Regarding the royal commissioners' demand to revise their laws, the magistrates claimed knowledge of none "deragatory to his Majestie" but pledged to repeal or alter any they might discover going forward. On legal procedure, the royal commissioners later boasted that Plymouth had allowed them to hear appeals, but that claim was not really accurate. The only person who tried to appeal was William Nicarson [Nickerson], who had illegally purchased land from "an Indian" without going through local magistrates. Having been denied the purchase, he continued to develop the land; and the

General Court, not the royal commissioners, ended up deciding the case.[25] The magistrates were highly offended that Nicarson had tried to go over their heads to Carr, Cartwright, and Maverick. Aware of his offense, Nicarson submitted a formal apology to the court, saying he regretted his actions. The court did remit Nicarson's fine in order to "gratify" the royal commissioners, but they, not the commissioners, dealt with the appeal.[26] Nicarson would continue to write to Nicolls in 1666–1667. He was later taken to court for "abuse" of the Plymouth magistrates and "the body of the freemen" in these letters, as well as for "approbrious speeches against Mr Thomas Thornton," the Yarmouth minister.[27] Most likely, the population distrusted the idea of royal agents overriding local courts, especially in support of ethically questionable people like Nicarson. The royal commissioners did make a ruling that favored Plymouth on intercolonial boundaries—Rhode Island, especially, was trying to encroach on Plymouth's territory—but even this injunction was temporary, pending the king's review. When it came to tiny Plymouth, the commissioners wielded far less authority than they would have people believe.

At some point during these negotiations the royal commissioners tried a new tactic. They asked if Plymouth would trade the right to elect their governor directly for a royally confirmed charter. The commissioners were essentially offering to pay the fees necessary to get the Bradford Patent renewed in the form of a royal charter, sponsoring it personally. In exchange, the king would choose a governor from three of the colonists' nominees, for a three- to five-year term. The problem with this proposed arrangement, however, was that any governor so chosen would be obligated to the king in a new way. And longer terms meant less ability for local inhabitants to hold their leaders accountable. Further, entrusting royal commissioners with charter negotiations meant colonists would have very little say on its specific terms. The court again put the commissioners' proposal before all the freemen, who—not surprisingly—voiced strong opinions. Assembling in June 1665 to consider the commissioners' offer, they brought up "divers particulars" and "largely agitated" for them.[28]

The majority advocated writing directly to Charles II, pleading "for the renewall of our pattent," continuing their strategy from the 1664 assembly and also perhaps aware of the Bay's attempted "Petition from all the Freemen."[29] This petition, from the king's "Most Loyall Subjects" in the entire "Collony," is extant, and there is good evidence it was sent to Charles II.[30] The petition began in praise of loyalty—sort of. Although a "naturall duty," loyalty as they defined it remained contingent on the king's "fatherly Care," which was expressed through his continuance of their "Civell and religious liberties." Unlike Prence's earlier letter, this address dealt with the Interregnum directly, asking for amnesty if they "in any thing unwillingly bee found transgressers in those Evill times." Praising Carr, Cartwright, and Maverick for braving a winter visit, the authors claimed that Plymouth colonists had "aplyed our selves to give your Majesty full satissfaction" in the ensuing negotiations, as they knew the three men would relay, as well. The royal commissioners had "well observed the Constitution of our government, and disposition of our people." If all was accurately reported, Plymouth colonists knew that they would "finde place with the most Loyall in your princely breast." The colony as currently arranged, governed, and inclined, they argued, was fully compatible with the monarchy. But all was not as good as it could be. The authors described Plymouth colony as "but a little neck . . . very much trespased on," and nearing ruin at the hands of Rhode Islanders, despite a patent "more ancient by above thirty years." In a postscript, the writers mentioned fear of inroads from the Bay as well.[31] Rather than capitulation to the crown, then, the letter represented yet another attempt at constitutional negotiation.

A few colonists might have thought trading a freely elected governor for a royal charter a necessary sacrifice. Others wanted to send an agent to England as Connecticut and Rhode Island had successfully done.[32] However, supporting an agent would have incurred an extraordinary financial burden. While the Plymouth Court record says the matter was only referred to "future consideration," in fact colonists resolutely made their decision. As the royal commissioners' later accounts make clear, Plymouth inhabitants rejected their quid pro quo offer: "The General Assembly, with many thanks and great protestations of loyalty, chose to be as they are."[33] Plymouth freemen would continue to elect governors outright and even for the most part maintain their boundaries for the next two decades.

Continuing their negotiations, Carr, Cartwright, and Maverick asked Plymouth to break with the United Colonies if any other members—Massachusetts Bay, Connecticut, and, until it was annexed, New Haven—"refuse[d] his majesty's authority." They did not "have the least imagination" of Plymouth's disloyalty but simply wanted to shut down rumors, such as one currently circulating that the United Colonies "was a war combination" founded as part of "a design to throw off their dependence on England." A statement expressing Plymouth's willingness to break ranks with the United Colonies would encourage the king even further, the royal commissioners temptingly declared, "in his good opinion of your loyalty."[34] This strategy appeared to work: in the June 1665 assembly of Plymouth freemen, participants decided that while self-governance was worth protecting, their relationship to the United Colonies was not. They added a line to their official response to the four propositions: "The leage between the four Collonies was not with any Intent (that ever we heard of) to Cast of[f] our dependance upon England; a thing which wee utterly abhor; Intreating your honors to beleive us for wee speake as in the presence of God." They voted to send "a loveing, curteous letter" to Massachusetts saying that "wee see not light to persist" in "the confederation."[35] Later on, the United Colonies commissioners would make an effort to placate Plymouth's concerns, allowing the confederation to continue in somewhat altered form; but in this particular moment, the historically separatist colony decided it was safer to go it alone.

On the recommendation of the assembly, Plymouth leaders did ask Cartwright to act in London on their behalf regarding the boundary issue.[36] The royal commissioners expressed disappointment with Plymouth's rejection of their offer regarding the governorship. Carr, Cartwright, and Maverick thought if this plan "had succeeded well in this the first Colony they had visited, it might have been a good Example to the rest."[37] In other colonies, they would not make the same offer, attempting instead to influence elections covertly.

* * *

While Plymouth freemen were deliberating, Carr, Cartwright, and Maverick had moved on to Rhode Island, whose territorial claims conflicted with those of most of their neighbor colonies. Rhode Island, however, had an advantage: through agent John Clarke's work in London, in 1663 the colony had received a royal charter. But this important benefit did not resolve all conflicts: Connecticut, too, had a royal charter granting overlapping territory, thanks to Governor John Winthrop's work in London.[38] By the time royal officials realized the discrepancy between the two charters, Winthrop had already taken his sealed charter back to Connecticut.

Despite these and other boundary issues, Rhode Island's July 1663 charter was extraordinarily generous. An eloquent Roger Williams saw it as God's act "to turne the Kings heart towards us as Rivers of Water . . . [God's] Favour towards us fallen like Deaw upon Gideons fleece while all the World lies round about us drie and barren of such Liberties."[39] For their part, the members of the Privy Council probably considered Rhode Island a potential royalist base to counter the regional dominance of the Bay.[40] The Rhode Island charter specifically included the right to appeal to the king to settle intercolonial disagreements, itself a "direct challenge" to Massachusetts's autonomy.[41]

In addition to overlapping with Plymouth's and Connecticut's grants, the charter also included the Narragansett territory. When Rhode Island magistrates had informed the sachems Quissuckquansh (Pessicus) and Ninigret in late 1663 that through their new royal charter the king had taken "all the Narragansett Indians and lands into his gracious protection, as subjects unto himselfe" under Rhode Island's government, the Native leaders' initial response was positive. They assumed it meant they were free of the Atherton Company, a multicolony investment group headed by Winthrop that owned a mortgage on their territory.[42] Pessicus and Ninigret "returne[ed] his Majesty great thanks for his gracious reliefe in releasing their lands from those forced purchases and mortgages of theyr lands."[43] The issue, however, was far from resolved, especially because in June 1663, just before granting Rhode Island's charter, the king, under the influence of London lobbyists, had written in support of the "just propriety" of the Atherton Company's claim, rebuking the "unjust oppressions and molestations" of Rhode Islanders against them.[44]

When Carr, Cartwright, and Maverick arrived in Rhode Island in early March 1665, they thus faced a complex set of challenges and expectations. Grateful for their charter, Rhode Islanders assumed the high level of autonomy it granted would be respected. Further, Governor Benedict Arnold and Deputy Governor William Brenton thought the royal commissioners' assignment "in promoteing the Kings Royall intrest in these Parts" would mean defending Rhode Islanders from the injustices they had "suffered . . . under strange pretences from the Neighbour Colonyes."[45] Excluded from the United Colonies and hopeful to continue benefiting from the new regime, Rhode Island residents probably looked forward to the royal commissioners' visit. They must have been surprised, then, at the three men's scrutiny of their militias and their evident reluctance to confirm the boundaries Rhode Islanders believed to be their land.

Carr, Cartwright, and Maverick first presented a royal letter promising preservation of their liberties and protection from "any forraine Power" or "any disturbance from your Neighbours Countrymen."[46] On the franchise, the royal commissioners found that Rhode Islanders "remitt all to be freemen who desire it"; on legal documents in the king's name, the colony was already issuing them. The commissioners then moved to communicate demands similar to those shared with Plymouth, with two exceptions. To the franchise requirement they added a qualifier that freemen, in addition to being "of competante estates and of civill conversation," must "acknowledge" and be "obediante to the civill magistrate." Whether Rhode Island leaders negotiated the added phrase or the royal commissioners took the initiative, this line effectively acknowledged Rhode Island's long-term challenge: disruptive inhabitants who would rather live under no government at all. Second, the royal commissioners tacked on another demand regarding the militia: the colony must "be put in such a posture of defence" that its members could repel an invasion. Rhode Island would be the only colony the royal commissioners asked to invest in arms and militia training, preparing it to serve if needed as a royalist staging ground.[47]

How did Rhode Islanders respond to these demands? In their negotiations, colony leaders proclaimed "cheerful obedience," although insisting on a "loyall and resonable engagement" instead of an oath, a concession to tender consciences already in the charter.[48] On freedom of worship, Rhode Island leaders said, "it hath ben a principall held forth and maintained in this Collony from the very begining thereof." They did not immediately undertake a review of the law code, but promised to do so, and declared "voyd" any laws made "in the late troblesome time . . . in any sort derogatory to his Majestye," referencing the pardon issued at Breda. Regarding the militia, the Rhode Island Assembly acknowledged their "great defect in training" and "store of arms," ordering it addressed through a series of reforms, backed by fines.[49]

On appeals to the royal commissioners, Rhode Island magistrates actually described this request as "most reasonable," choosing to use the appeals issue as a deliberate statement of loyalty. As they began looking at appeal cases, Carr, Cartwright, and Maverick sometimes sent them back "in Civility" to the magistrates, perhaps because they were too time-consuming. In a few instances, the magistrates sent these cases right back to them, "againe remit[ing] to the Commissioners to be determined."[50] When it came to the Plymouth-Rhode Island boundary, however, the royal commissioners declined to outsource the decision, communicating that they had decided temporarily in favor of Plymouth, pending the king's review. Rhode Islanders did not wind up with the territory they had hoped for, as they complained repeatedly in subsequent letters.[51] Outside the colony, their eagerness to let the king decide boundaries, along with their "having yeilded so much to the

Commissioners" in appeals, was widely "derided."[52] Happy with their charter, Rhode Islanders ceded the most authority of any colony to the royal commissioners, but it did not necessarily redound to their benefit.

* * *

The royal commissioners next traveled to Narragansett territory and the town of Warwick, Rhode Island, fulfilling their instructions to investigate the Narragansetts' 1644 submission to Charles I and to enforce Native treaties, supporting the king's purpose of converting the "infidells." These instructions may have been influenced by Robert Boyle, a member of the Council for Foreign Plantations who served as governor of the New England Company, which funded John Eliot's mission. A strong advocate for that mission, Boyle believed that a focus on Native evangelism might heal misunderstandings between king and colonists. Benevolence toward Natives, however, also secured moral authority, an aspect of sovereignty. Sending the king freshly printed Algonquian Bibles a few years earlier, colonists had claimed the Eliot mission's success as a sign of the colony's flourishing under the patent, suggesting that the king's "securing . . . of our Civil Priviledges, and Religious Liberties hitherto Enjoyed" would confirm "this Good Work of Propagating Religion." In the royal commissioners' view, however, the converse might also be true. The Bay colony's injustice toward Natives might invalidate New Englanders' authority in the region.[53]

They could not have found a more eager proponent of the latter view than Samuel Gorton, who impatiently awaited their arrival in Narragansett. Gorton, who had drafted the 1644 declaration of Narragansett submission, would triumphantly present the signed document to Carr, Cartwright, and Maverick. Although Gorton liked to position himself as a champion of Native peoples, he and the Gortonists—his followers—navigated a contentious, sporadically violent relationship with neighboring Shawomets and Pawtuxets, sometime-tributaries to the Narragansett. The Gortonists had their eye especially on a beautiful, fertile piece of Shawomet land today called Warwick Neck, which offered prime access to Narragansett Bay fishing and clam-harvesting. Understanding Gorton's backstory and the royal commissioners' decision to partner with him helps us comprehend the other colonists' rising distrust of the royal commissioners' agenda. It also casts new light on Narragansett, Shawomet, and Pawtuxet contributions to the Restoration-era constitutional contest.

A clothier and lay preacher, Gorton held to an eclectic combination of spiritist mysticism and royalist legalism. Although never attending university, he had some classical and legal training—and he possessed irrepressible confidence. Along with his wife and at least two children, he had migrated first to Boston and then to Plymouth, where he received a quick order of banishment in 1638. The family then moved to Pocasset (Aquidneck or Portsmouth), where Gorton joined Anne Hutchinson in an attempt to overthrow William Coddington, who had Gorton whipped and again banished by 1640. Next they traveled to Providence, where they nearly incited an armed battle with local men before Roger Williams ejected Gorton and his followers. Gorton thus boasted an unenviable status as the only man to be ejected from three colonies. His utter disdain for the authority of local government drove these incidents. Colonists would later say Gorton had a knack for "inflaming of the malignant passions of many other malcontented persons" and a "dangerous tendency to the utter consumption of both our civill & ecclesiasticall constitutions." He preached messages seen as wildly heretical in both religion and politics, rejected literal concepts of heaven and hell, and dismissed any authority not directly backed by the crown.[54] He did, however, respect the king.

Ongoing tensions between the Narragansetts and the Mohegans in the mid-seventeenth century meant that smaller communities such as the Shawomets and the Pawtuxets needed protection. Although Shawomet and Pawtuxet sachems Pomham and Sococonoco had pledged tribute to the powerful Narragansett sachem Miantonomo, they took offense when in 1642 Miantonomo gave some of their lands to Gorton and his followers.[55] Seeking to exit their tributary relationship with Miantonomo, Pomham and Sococonoco had approached Massachusetts, accusing Gorton of unlawfully taking their land. They had signed the deal under duress, they said, and had received no payment. The two sachems then chose to submit to the Bay in order to protect their land from neighboring English or Narragansetts or both.[56] In doing so, they became the first of a series of Native leaders to make this difficult choice—if it could even be called a choice. The colonists leaped at the chance. John Winthrop (the father) had long seen advantages in having better access to "a verye faire Baye" with a "deepe channell" and proximity to Cape Cod, as well as a potential base for "sending out against any Indians of Naragansett" if relations soured.[57]

In September 1643, Massachusetts, with the support of the United Colonies, had called the Gortonists into court. When they repeatedly refused, the

Bay sent a captain and forty soldiers to Warwick to "ask" them again, and a skirmish ensued. Bay soldiers, with the help of "many of their Indians," probably Shawomet and Pawtuxet warriors, besieged and finally captured ten Gortonists; several more escaped. After a trial and several months' imprisonment during which the prisoners had to labor hard to support themselves, the Bay changed its sentence to banishment. Massachusetts leaders seemed most worried about Gortonists spreading their heterodox opinions among the population. Banishment seemed the best solution, with the penalty of death if Gortonists returned to the colony or "any of the lands of Pumhom or Sochonocho."[58] The Bay also helped arm the Shawomets and Pawtuxets for self-defense, anticipating conflict.[59]

When war broke out between the Narragansetts and their old rivals the Mohegans and the Narragansett leader Miantonomo was captured, the United Colonies recommended the sachem be executed. In 1644, Gorton presented Miantonomo's successors Canonicus, Pessicus, and Mixano with a document he had drafted that submitted the Narragansetts directly to Charles I, an attempt (at least in part) to retaliate against the Bay. Similarly aggrieved at Bay leaders and eager to hold them accountable, Canonicus, Pessicus, and Mixano agreed to sign, rewarding Gorton with more land.[60] Eagerly he sailed to London with their petition, although it was never acknowledged: with civil war now raging, he was unable to present it to the king. But he "procured the printing of it, that publique notice might be taken thereof."[61] When he finally obtained a hearing from Charles I's Committee on Foreign Plantations, Gorton spoke against the Bay's departure from English law and its expansion beyond their patent, grounds for revoking the charter. And, backed by the Earl of Warwick, he managed to get the Council on Foreign Plantations in 1646 to confirm his Shawomet (Warwick) land claim.[62]

After Gorton's return, his followers continued to engage in ongoing violence against neighboring Native Americans. The Shawomet sachem Pomham petitioned the Bay in the late 1640s "for Redresse and Reliefe" from "the great damedges and trouble occasioned" by the Warwick settlers. The General Court provided one hundred bushels of corne in restitution for that "spoyled by those of Mr Gortons society," and, the following year, sent commissioners to investigate. In 1649, there erupted "a great Fray betweene Warrick men and those Indians and blood spilt and many Cuts and hurts on both sides." Roger Williams tried unsuccessfully to arbitrate the conflict.[63] In 1656, Williams counted yearly damage above £60. About Warwick inhabitants, he minced no words: "they are so dangerously and so vexatiously intermingled with the Barbarians, that I have long admired the wonderfull power of God in restraining . . . mutuall slaughters, breaking forth betweene them."[64] In March 1659, Pomham led an "insurrection" to release an imprisoned Shawomet man, and Warwick authorities, fearful for their lives, tried to arrest him.[65] Supported by the Bay, Shawomets and Pawtuxets remained on their land, in uneasy and sporadically bloody proximity to Gorton and other Warwick inhabitants.[66]

These tensions continued after the Restoration. Furious about the Atherton Company mortgage, as well as Pomham and Sococonoco's supposed intransigence, Gorton did everything in his power to shore up Warwick's land claim. As early as March 1661, he sent a threatening letter to Atherton Company men reminding them of the Narragansetts' 1644 submission to the king and appointing himself, along with John Wickes and Randall Houlden, as Narragansetts' "attourneyes or trusties." If Atherton men wanted to "avoid . . . high Contempt" against Charles II, Gorton declared, they should stop their proceedings.[67] Most Narragansett sachems had actually preferred to have Roger Williams speak for them; in 1654, Ninigret and others had asked Williams to take a petition "to the high Sachems of England," and he had presented it to Oliver Cromwell. Ninigret and Pessicus also trusted the Rhode Islander John Nixon (or Nickson) to present a petition for them.[68] But Gorton declared himself their representative in any case.

In August 1661, Gorton and six followers had tried their hand at leveraging the Restoration with Bay leaders, sending a petition and threatening to go to Charles II if denied. They blamed Massachusetts for "incouraging of the Indians to oppresse us intollerably to this day." And they eagerly rehearsed the Bay's sedition: "When we did hang out the Kings Coulers to signifie to whome we did adheer" during the 1643 skirmish, Bay soldiers had, they claimed, "shott them thorow and thorow imediatly."[69] Although Gorton had no idea if Charles II would back his claim, he gambled that an invocation of Stuart power would disconcert the Bay long enough to prompt them to reimburse his financial damages.

The Bay did not deign to respond. An exasperated Gorton, styling himself a "commissioner" of the "Chief Sachems in America," sent a lengthy petition directly to Clarendon in 1662, asking him as he thought fit to share it with the king. As he reminded Clarendon of the Narragansetts' 1644 submission, Gorton emphasized the value of this Native territory, especially its "Rich mineralls," of which the men of Boston were, he said, already availing themselves.[70] Both Governors John Endicott and John Winthrop had deliberately downplayed the potential for mining in New England, information of keen interest at Whitehall.[71] Gorton, by contrast, alerted the king to the Narragansetts' wealth of natural resources, as well as his own ability to broker them. He rehearsed his men's capture, imprisonment, and banishment, claiming that they suffered because "we would not Relinquish our religion." He declared Pomham and Sococonoco to be "pettie Sachims" Massachusetts had drawn away from the Narragansett "grand Sachims," in order to "exersis authority out of their Jurisdiction." Territorial overreach, Gorton knew, was potential grounds for revoking the charter and replacing the colony's leadership.[72]

When he learned that Carr, Cartwright, and Maverick planned to visit Rhode Island, Gorton pulled out this recent letter to Clarendon and revised it for a new audience in early 1665. He might have already met Cartwright at some earlier date in London, in which case he could have "supplied the material that fueled Cartwright's scorn for Massachusetts." Regardless, Gorton earned the royal commissioner's trust: by May 1665 Cartwright would, in an affectionate letter to Gorton, promise to "represent your sufferings and your loyalty" in England.[73] The royal commissioners' decision to ally themselves with Gorton and his agenda severely undermined their credibility with puritan colonists, not to mention Pomham and other neighboring sachems.

Predictably, Gorton and his followers positioned themselves during the royal commissioners' visit as righteous upholders of the king's interest against evil and persecuting usurpers in the Bay. Warwick inhabitants were appalled, they said, when the Bay had issued writs and oaths without acknowledging the king, when they refused appeals to England, and when they extended their power beyond their patent bounds, acting "as sole lords of the whole country." Gortonists had learned their religion, they said, "in our constant frequenting the publick assemblies in our native country" (not caring to mention that the kind of churches Gorton had frequented in London were those of Baptist radicals such as Thomas Lamb). The Warwick men claimed they had suffered because they "would not falsify our faith to God and the king." The eighty cattle that Bay leaders had seized back in 1643 for court costs and to pay the forty-plus soldiers sent to secure the Gortonists, taking into account "ordinary increase," would require compensation of "divers thousands of pounds." (Gorton omitted to say that at least four of the ten men had successfully stolen or sued to reclaim their cattle.) According to Gorton, the followers of Pomham and Sococonoco, "under the fallacy and irregularity of the subjection of these revolting people" (the Bay leaders), had for two decades been "planting our best ground, burning up our wood, killing our cattle, pilfering and purloining our goods, breaking open our houses, offering violence to the inhabitants, resisting the king's officers, violently and riotously."[74] By the "king's officers" he may have meant Rhode Island magistrates, who for years had been trying to negotiate these disputes, many involving roaming livestock eating valuable crops.[75] The royal commissioners would later bring the Gortonists' March 1665 petition to the General Court in Boston and "urge" upon it "a necessity" of responding to Gorton and his followers' complaints.

After examining the 1644 Narragansett deed of submission, Carr, Cartwright, and Maverick met with one of the original signers, the elderly Narragansett sachem Pessicus, on 20 March 1665. When asked if the document was authentic, Pessicus owned it "with some ceremony, giving up himselfe and country into the King's protection." The decline in furs, the reconfiguration of Mohawk alliances, and intense demographic pressure from an expanding English population made the 1660s an especially precarious time for Native communities in the region, so the royal commissioners' offers of protection held much appeal.[76] Pessicus would later send gifts to the royal family, including "a feather mantle and a porcupine bagg" for the queen, although these offerings did not make it to England. The royal commissioners accepted Pessicus's submission, presenting coats as gifts and assuring his people of their protection. They required an annual tribute of "two wolves skins" and a promise "that you neither make war nor sell land, nor doe any thing of great consequence without acquainting us, or such as his Majesty will appoynt for that purpose." They then renamed the entire Narragansett territory the "King's Province," voiding the claim by the Atherton Company—whose members, they scornfully said, "pretend a Mortgage"—in exchange for a Narragansett payment of 735 fathoms of peag or wampum to the proprietors.[77] Carr, Cartwright, and Maverick would soon order any settlers, including Atherton proprietors, to leave the territory within six months, contradicting their instructions to avoid "disturbance" of any settled inhabitants (Nicolls would soon overturn the order, to Pessicus's dismay). When one inhabitant objected, the three men told him he was "henceforward . . . the King's tenant," owing "seven pounds a year" in rent.[78]

The royal commissioners had used the Narragansetts' submission to create a sprawling royal province. Although Rhode Island justices, including some Gortonists, received temporary jurisdiction over Narragansett, the land and its resources were now effectively the king's. In this case, as in others, "the Crown's attribution of a subject status to Indians was largely self-serving."[79] Pessicus's main—and poignant—request went ignored: he had "desired the commissioners to pray King Charles that no strong Liquors might be brought into that Country, for he had had 32 men that dyed by drinking of it."[80] Recent royal investment in the slave and rum trade would have made any prohibition of liquor unlikely. There was too much money to be made.

The royal commissioners then turned to the dispute between the Gortonists and Pomham and Soconónoco. They ordered that, after receiving £20 from the Gortonists, Pomham "and all the Indians with him shall remove to some other place, out of the King's province," either one provided by Massachusetts Bay or one assigned by Pessicus.[81] This relocation must be accomplished by planting time the following year. The commissioners did not grasp the nuances of Native politics well enough to understand that the Shawomets and Pawtuxets would have no interest in resubmitting themselves to Narragansett authority. In fact, Pomham had already entered into a relationship with Wampanoag leader Philip Metacom, who had promised aid in the case of a Narragansett attack.[82] Pomham cooperated with the royal commissioners' court but had no intention of moving his people. We will learn more about Pomham's protracted conflict with the royal commissioners—and its significance for the constitutional culture under formation across the colonies—in Chapter 9.

Carr, Cartwright, and Maverick's alliance with Gorton would seriously undermine their credibility with most colonists. Why then were they so willing to embrace him? The three men had to have known something about his controversial reputation prior to their Rhode Island visit. When the Privy Council gathered information about the colonies in the days following the Restoration, they made note of the geography of Boston's "seven hills" by way of a reference to "Gorton's Simplicity's defence agst. the 7 headed policy of Boston in New England"[83]—a 1646 diatribe in which Gorton had characterized the Bay as "that Servant so Imperious in his Masters Absence Revived."[84] Cartwright would later report that he and his colleagues had twice heard Gorton preach and were impressed. They saw no "spirit of malignity in his sermons, nor no sparks of revenge in his discourse," but rather "a great deal of learning . . . of zeal in his prayers, & of loyalty in his actions."[85] Gorton appears to have been a master of disguise, hiding his heterodoxy well. His true beliefs would probably have alarmed the commissioners: as their later actions testify, the three royalists were not exactly tolerationists but rather supporters of the Church of England's current exclusionary stance.[86] But they chose to dismiss previous reports about Gorton as misguided, attracted to his staunch royalism, local knowledge, and usefulness in opposing the Bay. Later informing Gorton that he would be unable to help dislodge Pomham, Cartwright commented, “These Gentlemen of Boston would make us beleeve that they verily think that the King hath given them soe much power in their Charter to do unjustly, that hee hath reserved none to Himselfe to call them to an account for doing soe.”[87] At least in part, supporting Gorton was about empowering anyone who could counter the Bay’s regional power.

* * *

The royal commissioners’ next colony, Connecticut, invested the most in their visit, both locally in entertaining the royal commissioners and across the ocean in mobilizing London supporters. Of all the colonial governors, Winthrop seems to have had the strongest grasp of the inner workings of charter renegotiations, probably gathering information on commissioners for the Corporation Act during his extended London residence. While acting as the colony’s agent, Winthrop spent almost two years and hundreds of pounds on Connecticut’s charter renewal, finding it “so much care & trouble” that only “the comfortable settlement of a people so pretious, & dearly esteemed by me” could have motivated him to this exhausting effort.[88] The charter finally issued to Winthrop raised almost as many questions as it solved. Not only did it conflict with Rhode Island’s charter, but it also included all of New Haven Colony, and it overlapped with grants to the king’s brother the Duke of York. Even though Connecticut enjoyed the benefits and prestige of a charter, the colony would need to proceed carefully.

In the case of the commissioners’ visit, proceeding carefully meant rolling out the red carpet. In October 1664, Connecticut Court members had voted to give the royal commissioners a present of “five hundred bushels of Corn,” the kind of gesture English city corporation officers might have extended to Corporation Act commissioners. The court also encouraged Connecticut’s churches to consider further expanding the sacraments, a direction already approved by a 1657 Connecticut synod. Winthrop, who had helped mediate the Dutch surrender, later visited New York “to congratulate” the royal commissioners on their conquest, and if possible to settle the Duke’s eastern line.[89] Additionally, Connecticut’s court had worked to negotiate boundaries with the Bay and Rhode Island and to absorb New Haven into its jurisdiction as granted by charter.

Although some New Haven towns longed to join Connecticut, others strongly opposed this move and, with the support of the United Colonies, initially tried to push back. In response, Connecticut leaders quickly took up royalist tropes: "where the word of a king is there is power, & we haveing the word of a king with a religious loyalty we are to observe it," unless that word was sinful.[90] It is likely that news of the royal commission pressured New Haven into submission. Major conflicts—either political or territorial—among the colonies gave the royal commissioners "a great advantage," and New Haven residents knew it. They felt betrayed by Winthrop, but if forced to choose between him and the "rakish" Duke of York, whose patent also included New Haven's territory, they would choose Winthrop. Writing to Connecticut leaders in late 1664, New Haven magistrates said they would rather continue as part of "the ancient confoederation," but they were now "chuseing rather to suffer then to begin any motion hazardfull to N. England settlements."[91] They joined Connecticut rather than provoke further royal interference.

Carr, Cartwright, and Maverick had asked Winthrop to send representatives to meet them near the Rhode Island border so they could decide the two colony's bounds, but there is no evidence that he carried out this request. When the three men arrived in Connecticut in April 1665, the magistrates and deputies entertained them generously and thanked them profusely for their concern, although they actually made few concessions.[92] The royal commissioners' propositions for Connecticut dealing with oaths, writs, the franchise, and the law code were relatively standard. Their proposition on religion, however, evinced a broader scope than normal, stipulating that those of "civill lives may freely enjoy the . . . worship of God in that way which they thinke best, provided that this liberty tend not to this disturbance of the publique." The final clause resembles the outcome in Plymouth: any changes would not tend "to the hindrance of the mayntenance of ministers regularly chosen in each respective parish or township." Connecticut, like its smaller neighbor, had negotiated a way to preserve its church order. And in the broader negotiations, Richard Nicolls also became involved, sending in a request "for assistance, in case of forraigne invassions."[93]

On writs and oaths, Connecticut leaders responded that they had already complied with the crown's directives. Although including phrases from the standard oath of allegiance, Connecticut leaders also added a clause to their oath: "as duty binds according to the word of God," an allowance for conscience.[94] Back in 1662, New Haven leaders had also added qualifications to their own oaths, stipulating that "in case of the alteration of the government in the fundamentals thereof, then to be free from the said oath."[95] In May 1665, the government of the newly joined Connecticut and New Haven colonies would declare that the new oath should be a strict requirement of freemanship—strict, that is, with exceptions for all formerly admitted freemen and all current colony officers, an astoundingly large loophole.[96]

On the franchise, Connecticut leaders said their "order" was already "consonant"; regarding laws, they were not aware of any that might be "derogatory" to the king but would repeal them if found, a duty to which they had already agreed during charter negotiations. There is some evidence that Nicolls requested a copy of Connecticut's law code but that Winthrop delayed sending it; royal commissioners let the matter drop. On Nicolls's request for a pledge of military assistance, "a matter of waighty importance," the court punted, deferring "to the serious consideration of the General Assembly in May next." Court members likely hoped to involve more freemen, including New Haven leaders, in these deliberations.[97] And to the (possibly altered) proposition on freedom of worship, the Connecticut Court simply responded that they were unaware of anyone "troubled by us for attending his conscience, provided he hath not disturbed the publique."[98] They did not actually consent on this issue, although the royal commissioners gave them a pass. Secure in the advocacy of Robert Boyle and other Royal Society connections, Winthrop would continue over the next few years to engage in a strategy of "positive noncompliance," effusively loyal rhetoric punctuated with small concessions—a tactic that included quietly withholding maps, military assistance, and, importantly, any real legal or constitutional changes.[99]

The royal commissioners later reported that all three colonies—Plymouth, Rhode Island, and Connecticut—had graciously promised loyalty and submitted to the king's demands, in contrast with their rebellious larger neighbor. But even humble Plymouth had negotiated strategically and given up little ground.[100] The smaller colonies had proven to be deft strategists. It is clear from their letters that Carr, Cartwright, and Maverick's quick visits and generous interpretation of the negotiations in these areas were conducted in light of their overall strategy: isolate the Bay. Yet colonists as a whole were not so easily maneuvered. Much of New England was moving toward a shared constitutional culture, carefully evaluating any potential concession to the crown and defending however possible their legal and ecclesiastical arrangements.

* * *

As they lodged in Boston during the winter and traveled throughout the smaller colonies in the spring, Carr, Cartwright, and Maverick made other alliances. The king's private instructions had encouraged them to avoid the appearance of partiality and to be careful about entertaining those with financial schemes or religious grievances, but the three men for the most part ignored this advice.[101] They played favorites during that 1664–1665 trip, and the faction they favored most was the Quakers. Known for disrupting court and church meetings with hellfire curses, Quakers had increasingly tested the constitutional issue of whether chartered colonies had the right to say who could or could not join the civic community. The royal commissioners' decision to befriend these missionaries, like their alliance with the Gortonists, would appall most colonists. Far from being simply victims, Quakers such as Elizabeth Hooton and Wenlock Christiansen actively positioned themselves as champions of the king's interests.

The relationship between royal commissioners and Quaker missionaries at first seems strange. Quakers, or Friends, generally rejected hierarchies in both church and state as forms of idolatry. True authority came to rulers through spiritual conviction and righteousness, not divine right or even popular consent.[102] Quakers were notorious for their rejection of tithes, oaths, and hat honors, as well as their prophetic signs such as dressing in sackcloth and ashes or breaking bottles in court chambers. They were widely viewed as threats to civil order. In June 1660, Quaker leader George Fox went to prison as "an Enimie to our Soveraigne Lord the King" and a leader of "insurrections" intended "to embroile the whole kingdome in blood."[103] Overall, Quakers bore the brunt of anti-nonconformist repression in Restoration England, hundreds dying of disease and malnutrition while incarcerated.[104]

Although the two made strange bedfellows, Quaker leaders expressed strong loyalty to Charles II even from prison. They could not state this loyalty in the expected terms, however, such as proclaiming him king "by Inherent Birth right" or submitting to his "heirs and posterities for ever."[105] Fox and most Quakers saw the king's rule as a divine gift, not a divine right, and a gift contingent on righteous action. The noblewoman Margaret Fell, who would marry George Fox, eloquently expressed this conditional model of kingship: "we do Love, Own, and Honour the King and these present Governours, so far as they do rule for God and his Truth."[106] A savvy petitioner, Fell wrote to Charles II asking him to release Quaker prisoners, including Fox himself, which he did.[107] The Quaker rejection of carnal weapons, a stance later termed a "peace testimony," also helped to ease their access to the king.[108]

And they may well have preferred Charles II's government to Cromwell's, which they found few reasons to praise.

The young Quaker polemicist Edward Burrough proclaimed that even if they engaged in civil disobedience, castigating judges with prophetic curses, Quakers' upright lives honored the king more than all those who honored him by "Drinking Healths, and Bonfires." Burrough also developed another strategy that would become increasingly popular with Restoration-era Quakers: he set out to affirm Quaker loyalty by highlighting puritan rebellion overseas.[109] Anti-puritanism may have been intrinsic to Quakerism, which borrowed puritan critiques of the Church of England but found different solutions. Quakers may also have astutely perceived that Charles II was more inclined to toleration than parliament, and more able to implement it in his colonial dominions. In any case, attuned to royalist animus toward puritans, Friends discovered an attractive opportunity to express their loyalty by contrast to these suspicious colonists. Burrough dug up old anti-Stuart correspondence from Bay leaders as evidence of their sedition. In recent years Bay leaders, he insisted, were "derogating from the Honour and Authority of the King" whenever they prevented Quaker movement "in any part of the Kings Dominions." In effect, to spit on a Quaker was to spit on the king himself. Friends might even, Burrough hinted, help the king raise a colonial royalist party.[110]

It makes sense, then, that Quaker missionaries in 1664–1665 approached Carr and Cartwright, offering to help them gather information about New England. One such volunteer, Elizabeth Hooton, had especially good reason to do so: George Cartwright had been her neighbor back in Nottinghamshire and had warmly called her "my country woman." Not just any Quaker, Hooton was also George Fox's first convert, a distinguished preacher and missionary, and a member of the gentry. Astonishingly, she carried with her a royal license from Charles II to buy land anywhere in the colonies. After being whipped, imprisoned, and released in Massachusetts Bay in 1661, Hooton had returned to her estate in England to find that her three mares had been seized and her son imprisoned for attending a Quaker meeting. She had appealed personally to the king based on her rights as an English subject, on Quakers' economic contributions, and on the possibility of divine vengeance.[111] While dispelling "false accusations" and promising Quaker loyalty, Hooton told the king he was punishing the wrong people, the "upright & hones[t]" such as Quakers rather than "turn[ing] your sword against sinne and Iniquity" found in "play-houses" or theaters, in which "the kingdome of

Sattan . . . is sett up." She might not have known about Charles II's frequent theater attendance, but her prophetic language in some way guilted or provoked Charles II to give her a license "to purchase land in any of his plantations beyond the seas."[112] Quakers like Hooton were a force of nature.

Bay leaders denied her the land she desired for a Quaker base and cemetery in Boston, but eager to avoid confrontation, they did offer her land "in the Cuntry" or countryside, which she declined.[113] As she engaged in missionary work, debating and cursing local leaders and enduring painful whippings, Hooton gathered evidence of sedition among the Massachusetts colonists. She also freely rebuked magistrates for "breaking both of Gods Law and the Kings Law."[114] And during the royal commissioners' visit, Hooton appointed herself their unofficial spy.

What were her findings? First, Hooton discovered that "the Church members" had organized themselves to be ready within twenty-four hours "to have fought against thy comisioners."[115] This statement might refer to the decision made by the General Court to strengthen military readiness after they had learned about the coming warships. Or it might be related to the story that, on a training day, Major William Hathorne had supposedly said, "You that are for the king's commissioners stand, and you that are for the country, follow me."[116] There is no corroborating evidence suggesting a planned revolt against the royal commissioners, although the situation in Massachusetts was certainly heated; and as we have seen, multiple towns pledged their lives to the defense of the charter. Hooton said she tried to argue the colonists down: fighting against the royal commissioners, she told them, would be a sure way to destroy themselves and their colony, for "the king would gett the better."[117] Further, she asserted, "there were enough that would take the Kings Commissioners parts." The colonists, she believed, should "suffer rather then fight, or else conforme as some of your brethren in old England doe." A colonist supposedly responded to her that Cartwright was a papist or Jesuit, "& they had a purpose to seeke his life." This Jesuit rumor was not limited to the colonies; no less a man than Joseph Williamson, secretary to the Privy Council, had thought "Cartwright persuaded himself to be a Jesuit by old Bellingham, of the Society of Jesus." Hooton did not agree. She defended Cartwright's Church of England credentials and issued a warning: "take heed what you doe, for the lord will give you into their hands because you have . . . persecuted the Just."[118] And she quickly sent a message to the royal commissioners about the supposed plot, telling them "to take heed how they came." Later, she boasted to the king that she "was a meanes to stop" the colonists' violent "Designe."[119] If the royal commissioners were not already suspicious of Bay inhabitants' intentions, they were now.

At a later face-to-face meeting with Cartwright, Hooton passed along the rumor that he was a papist, as well as the gossip that he "kept a naughty woman," and she shared that colonists saw Maverick as "their profest enemy." The Bay ministers were in a "secret councel" (probably a meeting of local clergy to advise the General Court), she warned, and who knew what they were planning? Cartwright responded to her with steely calm: "Many factious speeches fly up & down. . . . If these men will rebell I can as easily tell the King so, as that they are his good subjects."[120] Hooton also loaned the royal commissioners her horse when no locals would do so. Cartwright later certified to the Lord Chamberlain that "Elizabeth Hooton was very serviceable to his Majestyes Commissioners in new England."[121]

Commissioner Sir Robert Carr also befriended a Quaker missionary, Wenlock Christiansen, even traveling with him back to Boston in May 1665. A veteran missionary like Hooton, Christiansen had stood among the first to publicly challenge Bay laws as repugnant to those of England. Already banished once, he fearlessly chose to return to the Bay in early 1661, in full knowledge that a death sentence awaited him.[122] That same year, he debated members of the General Court not only on theology but also on their relationship to the king, asking how could they be good subjects when their laws differed so greatly from England's?[123] Stunned by Christiansen's question, which implied repugnancy, grounds for vacating the charter, Secretary Edward Rawson had replied, "What good will that do you?" Christiansen had a retort ready: Quakers' loyalty was "as good as you, if not better," a comment that deftly targeted Massachusetts's own recent profession of allegiance. He capped this comment off by taunting, "if the King did but know your Hearts, as God knows them, he would see that your Hearts are as rotten towards him, as they are towards God."[124] He then demanded to be tried by English laws as a test of the magistrates' loyalty to the king, attempting to force magistrates either to compromise their authority or to admit sedition.[125] One did not go toe to toe with a man like Christiansen lightly.

In part due to these provocations, in mid-1661 the Massachusetts Court had revised their Cart's Tail ordinance, which had permitted tying offenders to a cart and whipping them from town to town. This code now applied only to vagabonds, rather than to those with a specifically Quaker identity; it made "seditious Quakerism, in effect, a misdemeanor to be enforced by the colony's smallest legal unit."[126] The court also told Christiansen he could have his liberty if he agreed—for real—not to return. William Leddra, who was executed a few months earlier, the last of four Boston Quaker martyrs, had been offered this bargain and refused. Christiansen accepted. Interestingly, however, Christiansen did not explicitly promise to stay away forever; instead, he wrote simply that "I know not that ever I shall com into it any more."[127] This slippage was either missed or ignored. Christiansen settled in Salem and continued his missionary work, and somehow managed to make the acquaintance of Sir Robert Carr.

Carr and the other royal commissioners' sympathy emboldened Quaker action. In early spring 1665, Christiansen, along with two other missionaries, Mary Tompkins and Alice Ambrose, preached openly in Boston and were predictably arrested. Christiansen used the opportunity to test the colonists' allegiance. During the trial, Deputy Governor Richard Bellingham said that the three Quakers should be whipped as vagabonds, and Christiansen pressed him on his loyalty to the king. What was a vagabond? Christiansen asked. If it was a person of "no certain dwelling-place," as the magistrates defined the term, "then go and whip out the King's Commissioners from among you, for they came out of England since I did." Christiansen's strategy succeeded in enraging the magistrates, who sent the three missionaries to prison. When the next day Christiansen asked for an appeal before the royal commissioners, the magistrates retorted that they themselves "were Commissioners, and more than Commissioners." But appeals were a weighty constitutional issue, and Christiansen pressed his point: "Do you own these Men whom the King hath sent among you?" With the royal commissioners' and the Quakers' agendas now rhetorically fused, this question was nearly impossible to answer. One magistrate tried to dodge the issue, saying, "We will let that alone now." But another magistrate snapped, "If thou hadst been Hang'd, it had been well."[128] Christiansen retorted with a curse, and all three Quakers were whipped out of town.

A couple of months later, in May 1665, the royal commissioners invited Hooton, Christiansen, and other people with grievances, including wealthy Ipswich non-freemen, to gather with them in Boston. Bay colonists would later say it seemed like they designed "to gether [gather] all the combustible matter of discontented spirits among us into one, to make a flame in the country."[129] As we will see, converging in Boston, leading Quaker missionaries and others would stage a powerful political spectacle in front of the royal commissioners, a dramatic effort to prove the sedition of Bay leaders.

As with Gorton, the royal commissioners' decision to ally themselves with Quakers drastically undermined their ability to gain other colonists' trust.

Even those desiring compromise with the king had a hard time envisioning a colony where Quakers could disturb court meetings, church services, and funerals. Massachusetts officials such as Edward Rawson saw the weakening of anti-Quaker laws as opening the door to "men of such turbulency; as renders them not only disturbers of the peace, but professed enemies to all established Governments; and the trueth."[130] Boston minister John Wilson, who signed the moderate petition in 1661, urged colonists to "honour the King" but not to let Quakers come in and "rob you of the Ordinance of God." It would be better to die and "kiss the stake," he asserted, than to endure the kind of soul-death brought by allowing Quakers to desecrate their worship.[131] In a similar vein, the moderate Salem minister John Higginson—whose own ordination service had been disrupted by a Quaker—pleaded with the court to dissolve the Quaker base in Salem, which was starting to become a "nest of Quakers, from hence to infect the rest of the Country." Even if corporal punishment was no longer viable, he said, there had to be another way to protect local communities.[132]

Beyond concerns about religion and civic peace, the Bay's relationship with Quakers was fraught with constitutional significance. As we saw earlier, although the colony had in practice stopped executing Quakers, these dissenters remained the primary test case of whether colonial governments had the right to prosecute capital crimes, a marker of sovereignty. Quakers also tested the appeals issue. If each Quaker could appeal his or her case above the local courts to England, that meant years of expensive legal battles as well as truncated local authority. On these issues, the Friends' priorities aligned with those of the royal commissioners. Highlighting the significant differences between colonial and English laws, or legal repugnancy, Quaker missionaries proved very useful to Carr, Cartwright, and Maverick in their efforts to bring the Bay into genuine submission to the crown. At the same time, the commissioners' alliances with these dissidents, as well as with the Gortonists, compromised their trustworthiness in the eyes of many colonists. Defiance of the royal commissioners now seemed almost inevitable.

CHAPTER 8

Boston

The 1665 Negotiations and the Declaration by Trumpet

At eight o'clock in the morning on 23 May 1665, three colonists on horseback—a trumpeter, a deputy, and a marshal—rode up to an intersection right next to royal commissioner George Cartwright's lodging. The trumpeter sounded off, probably awakening Cartwright with a start, and a crowd quickly gathered. This moment marks the pivotal next phase of the constitutional struggle between colonists and crown. Cartwright and his three fellow commissioners had scheduled a nine A.M. appeals court, during which they planned to try the entire leadership of Massachusetts Bay in a case involving violation of the Navigation Acts. After the trumpet's blast, the deputy read a bold declaration from the General Court. The planned appeals court, this statement proclaimed, would infringe the charter. The royal commissioners had overreached the king's instructions and encroached on the colonists' liberties. Bay leaders would maintain the charter's "rules and prescriptions," including the right to elect those who enacted justice over them. By doing so, they would uphold their own government "so long injoyed and orderly established." Defiance of the royal commissioners, the statement concluded, was "absolutely necessary for the peace and well being of His Majesties good subjects here."[1] With the proclamation read, the three horsemen wheeled around and headed back the way they had come, leaving Cartwright and the crowd to ponder what they had just heard. The colonists had trumpeted a constitutional limit to the reach of monarchy, one that would resound from New England to Whitehall, and whose full import would not be heard for a century.

In the days leading up to the declaration by trumpet, Bay colonists had rapidly assembled and organized, using any means at their disposal. A great deal had happened in a short time, with events accelerating in May 1665. The season began with a deep loss, the death of beloved governor John Endicott in March 1665. Grief fused with anger when Quaker missionary Elizabeth Hooton disrupted his burial. With the royal commissioners' return to Boston looming, acting governor Richard Bellingham called a meeting of the Council. No rookie civil servant, Bellingham had trained in law, served as MP for Boston, England, in 1628, and served as magistrate in Boston, New England, for many years, including two as governor. In this fraught moment, Bellingham invited twenty-two named ministers to attend the Council meeting in case their assistance was required.[2]

It was. The magistrates asked the ministers to help formulate a strategy for upcoming negotiations over the king's demands. The ministers started by saying that dialogue should be conducted "in an amicable and respectfull way," but on revision added "as farre as may be"—there was such thing as too much courtesy, they had realized. Still, court members should take care to avoid unnecessary offense or provocation. Importantly, the court should assign "meet persons" as direct negotiators, men able "to begett or maintain a good understanding." These negotiators should clearly communicate the loyalty of the court and the people as a whole, giving "due respect" to the royal commissioners personally. They should also find out exactly what the king had instructed the four men to accomplish, for the latter still had not communicated their full public instructions, much less their private ones. Indeed, it would take a talented person to elicit transparency on the full extent of their mission. The negotiators, the ministers said, could promise that the court would "returne a <satisfactory> answer to the utmost so farre forth as they may with the preservation of their Patent"—a confirmed royal grant, in case anyone needed reminding—and with "their Consciences voyd of offence towards God & towards men."[3] In other words, comply with the royal commissioners' demands as far as possible but without jeopardizing patent liberties or commitments to God and to each other.

The clergy assured the colony's leaders that this "way of proceeding is warranted by the Scriptures." They provided classic biblical texts for political deference, such as "if it be possible, as much as lyeth in you, live peacably with all men," and "honour all men, love the brotherhood, Fear God & honour the King." They also, however, referenced "the advise given by the aged Counsellors of Rehoboam," a passage that suggested a conditional model of kingship, especially in the Geneva translation. It is likely the ministers knew the Geneva Bible's marginal notes for this passage, which stated that the only way for the king "to win the people's hearts" was "to grant them their just petition."[4] In short, the ministers advocated for a negotiated, constitutional defiance.

As we will soon see, the Council took the ministers' advice seriously. They also ordered further precautions regarding the upcoming election, arranging for guards to be on hand in case "any person do presume to disturbe or impeade the Election in word or writeing or otherwise."[5] They most likely intended this order for Quakers, for non-freemen who tried to vote, or even for the royal commissioners themselves. What we know for certain is that they were not taking any chances.

* * *

Perhaps aware of rumors about the taxpayer burden from entertaining royal commissioners, Richard Nicolls decided to arrive in Boston in early May unannounced, "by which meanes some troubles of reception were avoided." Sir Robert Carr did the same, traveling from Rhode Island with Wenlock Christiansen and other Quakers. But the Bay colonists had carefully prepared for their arrival. They were frustrated this secrecy "prevented the civility and respect that was both intended and prepared for them in sundry places."[6] Things were not off to a good start.

Nicolls spent some time those first days gathering news about local happenings, probably from wealthy Bostonians such as Thomas Breedon. Much had occurred while he was away in New York. He was surprised to find that "many false and malitious reports had gaind so much creditt not onely with the people but with the cheife Magistrates," and he decided to approach Bay leaders and demand an immediate formal meeting to clear the air. The magistrates, however, again declined to operate on his timetable. Incensed, Nicolls, in his own words, "was faine to put the question to them in plaine words whether they would refuse to heare at that instant of time the Message which his Majesty had commanded us to deliver." Thomas Danforth and Edward Rawson then spent several hours debating with the royal commissioners, and other leaders spent another few hours debating among themselves. These debates were unofficial, because the formal session had not yet begun. Only those court members tasked with preparing for the election had arrived.[7] But from Nicolls's point of view, the problem remained: charter negotiations were not supposed to work this way. If he had been a Corporation Act commissioner arriving in an English town, he would have enjoyed quite a different reception, one can imagine him thinking. Of Bostonians, he observed grimly, "some Guilty consciences suspect their shadoewes, and generally men are more scard than hurt but I hope that ill men will have little power in the Generall Court."[8] In the end, Bay leaders agreed to the requested meeting, and the royal commissioners jump-started the negotiations with an incomplete court.[9]

Nicolls, Carr, Cartwright, and Maverick had deliberately arrived immediately before the May election. As their private instructions had indicated, they needed to influence both the mode of election and the persons elected, with the optimal outcome of Nicolls as a five-year term governor and Cartwright as major general, and among colonists "men of the best reputation" chosen for leadership.[10] Although these instructions were initially kept secret, after the October 1664 letter from the General Court asking that the royal commission be recalled, Charles II had communicated openly (through Secretary of State William Morrice) that Endicott, governor "during all the late revolutions," was not considered "well affected to His Majesty's person and Government" and that the king "will take it very well, if at the next election, any other person of good reputation be chosen." Endicott had died, of course, effectively rendering the king's concern a moot point, although had he not passed away, he almost certainly would have been reelected. The election interference endorsed in the king's instructions was not an isolated occurrence: Charles II also told Londoners to elect an appropriate, and preferably wealthy, candidate to their Corporation.[11]

The commissioners' election engineering faced an uphill battle. Maverick's attempts to "undeceive the deceived" and "prepare" Bay colonists "for the election" had not been as successful as he had hoped.[12] Cartwright had all but given up when he wrote to Nicolls in February 1665, "I cannot conceive how it is possible for us to get a good election made for the next Generall Assembly, seeing none can elect nor be elected but such as are Churchmembers, and of them there is never a barrel better herrin" (meaning, they are all just alike).[13] On their May arrival, the royal commissioners tried even more directly to influence the election, pointing out the king's desire that "there be only consideration had of the wisdome, virtue, & integritie" of the nominees, rather than "of any faction in refference to their opinnions or outward professions."[14] This command diametrically opposed the constitutional culture of the Bay, in which most colonists considered godly—and professing—leaders crucial to promoting ongoing reform and blocking outside incursion. When the royal commissioners expressed their wish (or warning) that the colony would "be prosperous in the choice of a Governor,

& that he also may be prosperous in the execution of his office," it was clear to many colonists that the royalist vision of prosperity differed markedly from their own.[15]

The royal commissioners also tried to orchestrate the 3 May election day rituals. They insisted that the entire population be called to Boston for the election, in order that the four men might personally assure colonists of the king's favor. The Council thought it unwise to leave frontier towns undefended. But Cartwright angrily insisted on his plan, going so far as to say "the motion was so reasonable, that he that would not attend it was a traitor."[16] When the Council again refused, the royal commissioners tried to get the word out themselves, especially among non-freemen and religious minorities. In John Hull's view, "the honored commissioners seem to be elaborate in turning every stone to find the faults of this Colony and government, and to manage them to our disadvantage."[17] For colonists already concerned about a smooth transfer of power, the royal commissioners' attempts to summon people to Boston must have heightened their apprehension.

Arriving in Boston at the royal commissioners' request, Wenlock Christiansen, Elizabeth Hooton, and other Quakers used the occasion to enact an extraordinary political spectacle. If the Friends could again provoke the magistrates to seditious speech, this time the royal commissioners might witness it. Bellingham quickly rounded up the Quakers and questioned them before the General Court about why they were all in town at once. Hooton and the others replied that the royal commissioners had invited them. One magistrate lost his temper and responded: "they would whip the Comission[e]rs upon the Quak[e]rs backs." His statement was exactly what Friends had hoped to hear: Bay leaders had given proof of their sedition. The Quakers were whipped yet again, raw wounds crisscrossing old scars. This time, however, Nicolls, Carr, Cartwright, and Maverick were forced to watch as the gruesome scene played out, resenting their lack of power to prevent it. In Hooton's words, the "Kings Comission[e]rs were grieved . . . because they knew" the magistrates' "enmity was to them as well as to us." She relished her role in "speking for the king," proclaiming that the magistrates would indeed have whipped the royal commissioners themselves, just like they did the Quakers, but "the Country" (people in the region) would have "risen ag[ain]st them."[18] The Friends probably could not have imagined a clearer message of puritan disloyalty and Quaker allegiance.

On the election day itself, the royal commissioners' attempts to wield influence extended so far as to include the Council guards—they handed out gold pieces to each one. They watched as "about seventy freemen" were "admitted" into the voting area, "sundry whereof were not members of any particular church."[19] The election returns, however, must have been a shock to men like Nicolls and Maverick: there was very little turnover. The freemen, "apprehending the danger of some change, resolvedly fixed their choice upon such persons as they judged most likely to maintain the government in that same state wherein it hath been heretofore, without the least alteration."[20] Despite the royal commissioners' many efforts, no royalist majority emerged. Most Bay voters continued to support the magistrates and deputies who upheld the current constitutional arrangement.

* * *

With elections past and the full General Court present, the royal commissioners now began negotiations in earnest. The stakes were high; in some sense their earlier actions, including their tour of other colonies, had all been a prelude to this moment. Early on it became apparent that both sides were making requests that seemed small to them but mountainous to the other side. Nicolls, Carr, Cartwright, and Maverick kept asking for maps. But for the Massachusetts leaders, as for those of Connecticut and Plymouth, a detailed map meant a clear view of natural resources available for exploitation or land available for gifting as royalist estates. It was a major point of frustration to the royal commissioners that colonists seemed to "wholly forget" this particular request (although they eventually conceded).[21] For their part, following the ministers' advice, Bay leaders asked for a full set of the king's instructions, so they could assess them all at once. The royal commissioners demurred, proceeding on a "need to know" basis by compelling the magistrates and deputies to respond to each set of propositions in turn before presenting any further information. Truth be told, however, the commissioners had already contravened the instructions at several points and were improvising on some propositions as they went.[22]

Before discussing the king's demands, the royal commissioners wanted first to deal with seditious speech, specifically William Hathorne's. Given the widespread rumor that Hathorne had claimed their commission was created under a "hedge," the four men felt the need to defend their legitimacy.[23] As "private men," they could forgive slanders, but as agents of "his sacred majesty," they said, "we must not suffer his honor to be eclipsed by a cloud of black reproaches, and some seditious speeches, without demanding justice." The General Court's own reputation was at stake: "you cannot use a better argument to convince the whole world, or the king," of your innocence of sedition "than by severely punishing" Hathorne and other offenders.[24] No doubt there was much discussion behind the scenes. The magistrates and deputies responded they would welcome the royal commissioners' advice on stopping "scandalous & false rumours," but tracing their origins was nigh unto impossible.[25] Not placated, the royal commissioners wanted a "remonstrance of detestation"—a full apology—and "due examinations and depositions."[26] Although the Massachusetts Court refused to bring Hathorne to trial, he would come forward voluntarily to make a circumscribed apology approximately two weeks later, confessing what he could: "that I spake many words rashly, foolishly, & unadvisedly, of which I am ashamed." He also expressed a "desire [for] all that took offence to forgive me, as his majesties commissioners have Freely donne," referring either to the royal commissioners' earlier statement that they forgave slanderers in their private capacity or to an unrecorded conversation.[27]

When they turned to the king's demands, the royal commissioners first—and unsurprisingly—raised the issue of the regicides, still at large, as well as the Navigation Acts, still not generating adequate revenue. Notably, they did *not* repeat the demand they had made in Rhode Island about increasing military readiness. In fact, since the Restoration, and especially since hearing that four warships were headed their way, Bay colonists had invested significantly in defense.[28] They did not need any more encouragement in that department.

When it came to the standard demands—writs or legal documents in the king's name, the oath of allegiance, expansion of sacraments and the franchise, and a revised law code—only the writs had been fully attended to. The franchise, although slightly expanded in August 1664, was still at issue.[29] The royal commissioners objected that under the altered law, new freemen remained subject to "the approbation of the Court," and members of the Church of England might still be excluded from voting, even though "the church of England understands and follows the rules in God's word as much as this corporation." In the royal commissioners' minds, the Massachusetts Court's concessions on the franchise were so inadequate they feared they might "highly offend" Charles II. "Abuse not the kings clemency too much," they warned.[30] Later, Cartwright would bluntly call the new law "a mere juggle to deceive his Majesty."[31] He also would reveal another major concern with the franchise: the problem of poor people and servants having the vote; in his view, it was ridiculous that a full church member "though he be a servant, & pay not 2d may be a freeman."[32] But in May 1665, the Massachusetts Court was unwilling to go further in making wealth the threshold for political access.

On the king's demand to admit "good & honest" people to the Lord's Supper "& their children to baptisme," the magistrates and deputies replied briefly, saying only that they were "voluntary exiles from our deare native country" in order to set up these churches, and that to change "devotions. . . . will disturbe our peace in our present enjoyments."[33] Internally, they struggled to come to a consensus on the best response. In a draft, the magistrates referred to the "late Synod," which "extendeth baptism as far (for substance) as the words of his Majesties [1662] letter do import." But the deputies took issue with this language and declined to sign off on it. The court simply told the royal commissioners that they "commended to the ministry & people here the word of the Lord for their rule therein," pointing to the Body of Liberties' section on churches.[34] This section said that any who were "orthodox" and "not scandalous" had "full Liberty" to form churches as long as they did so according to the "Rules of Christ revealed in his word." Religious liberty for Bay leaders meant all were free to form biblical churches as long as they did it publicly and openly, with the approval of elected leaders and other churches, so as not to undermine "common peace & love."[35] Within the court, there seems to have been a low-key suggestion to allow high church conformists to set up their own towns, apart from congregationalist settlements, where they might use the prayer book, perhaps modeled on Plymouth's negotiations. But this gesture toward compromise did not pass the deputies.[36] For Bay colonists, an imposed toleration "oddly became associated not with freedom but with tyranny," linked with the Stuarts' broader ambition to consolidate control through royalist rituals and a "neo-feudal" network of wealthy landed elites.[37]

Oaths formed another major unaddressed issue. As we have seen, Plymouth and Connecticut had not agreed to the full oath of allegiance, and Rhode Islanders got by with an "engagement." The royal commissioners did not, however, press the issue in these smaller colonies. They were interested in extracting full allegiance only from the Bay. They presented the Massachusetts magistrates and deputies with a copy of the standard oath of allegiance, presumably also what they had asked of other colonies. The oath primarily comprised forswearing the pope's authority to depose kings or to absolve subjects from their civil allegiance.[38] On the surface, it seemed reasonable enough. However, as we have seen, the oath (by design) squeezed out any room for conscience or constitutional resistance.

Bay leaders wasted no time drafting their objections. Asking the oath of "all the Inhabitants" seemed beyond English requirements, beyond those of other colonies, and beyond the terms of the patent. Some magistrates were willing, following Plymouth's model, to add to their regular oath the language: I "sweare to be good & true unto our Soveraigne Lord King Charles his heires & successors." But the deputies would not consent. In its formal response, the court referred to their August Resolution to "beare faith & true alleagiance to his majestie, & to adhere to their patent," saying this resolution "will be a witnes against us, should wee be found to act contrary thereunto."[39] Their allegiance would be conditional, on constitutional terms.

A historically minded member of the court remembered that Matthew Cradock, their first governor, had taken an oath administered by a Master of the Chancery before departing England. Colonists had followed suit by administering similar oaths to all freemen, officeholders, and other householders.[40] Colonial leaders considered showing this older oath to the royal commissioners but in the end decided not to refresh their memory on its exact wording.[41] After all, in 1643 they had changed that oath, striking the part about bearing allegiance "to our sovereign Lord King Charles" because he "had violated the privileges of parliament, and made war upon them."[42] For more than two decades now, Massachusetts freemen had sworn only to be "true and faithfull" to the "Commonwealth" of Massachusetts, to support it, submit to its laws, vote according to conscience, and "truly endeavour to maintain and preserve all the liberties and priviledges" of the colony.[43] This kind of statement would not impress the royal commissioners.

After further discussion, court members did finally agree to add the king back into their oath, but they referred to a generic king, not to Charles II by name. And they carefully limited their obligation to the terms of the charter. The new clause read, "Considering how I stand obliged to the kings majestie his heires and successors, by our Charter & the Government established therby; do Sweare accordingly by the great and dreadfull name of the everliveing God that I will bear faith & true alleageance to our Soveraigne lord the king his heires & successors."[44] Displeased, the royal commissioners chastised Bay leaders for what they viewed as an anemic effort, saying "your charter commands" the oath of allegiance, "yet you make provisoes not there exprest; and, in short, would curtail the oath as you doe allegeance, refusing to obey the king."[45] Their accusations left Bay leaders worried but unmoved.

Nicolls personally stood up before the court on 18 May 1665 and took it to task for an inadequate response. The charter itself included a provision for an oath of allegiance, he reiterated, and "no faithful subject will make it less than according to the law of England." Eyeing Bellingham, Nicolls urged, "I hope the governour will show that fair example to begin it first. I am sure his majesty expects it from him." The king's "love and favour," Nicolls continued, were conditional on "duty and obedience." He expected his demands not only to be met but to "be done cheerfully." Secretary of State Morrice's letter, which had rebuked the colony for its resistance to the royal commission, "ought to be read over more than once." Nicolls warned, "the king will not suffer himself to be deluded. . . . I hope you will find better counsels about you, and tell us plainly and truly whether you will submit to that commission, without any shuffling."[46]

Yet shuffling ensued. On 24 May, magistrate Daniel Gookin finally took the oath of allegiance but modified it, saying he "would be so understoode as not to infringe the libertys & privlidges granted in his Majesties royall Charter" to Massachusetts Bay, "whereof hee is a member & unto which hee is sworen formerly."[47] Two days later, Thomas Danforth similarly qualified his oath, recording it proudly in a notebook: "When the oath was given me, I thus openly declared, and a copy hereof is left on file under my hand." On the same day, Governor Bellingham, along with the deputy governor and other assistants, took the oath as well, also declaring "that the same is to be understood not infringing the liberties of the patent."[48] The royal commissioners were irate. Cartwright later pointed out that the additional clause effectively rendered the oath worthless, saying "it will easily appear how farr that oath binds them."[49] But the court members held their ground, keeping to their August Resolution: as far as they could, they would "beare faith & true alleagiance to his majestie, & to adhere to their patent." In the Bay's constitutional culture, allegiance stopped where charter liberties were violated.

The most volatile issue of the May 1665 negotiations centered on the royal commissioners' insistence on their right to set up a court of appeals, especially a royal prerogative court that operated without a jury. More than simply refining legal procedure, appeals established who held real authority in a given region. From the time of Henry VIII, appeals had been heatedly contested in English jurisprudence, with some complaining that they involved great expense and delays, especially for those far from London. Those who supported appeals linked them to equity, or fair, merciful, individualized justice. Puritans had long criticized prerogative courts such as the Star Chamber for rehearing cases without juries and with seemingly unrestrained power, although they did not usually criticize appeals themselves, generally supporting ideals of equity. Appeals from lower or county courts to a higher court (the Court of Assistants) within the colony had been formalized in the 1641 Massachusetts Body of Liberties, possibly drawing on precedents such as Virginia's 1620 Orders and Constitutions. After 1648, Massachusetts law required appeals to a higher court to include juries if regarding matters of fact rather than law or interpretation. At issue with the royal commissioners now was not appeals in themselves, as Bellingham clarified, but authority. When a corporation charter gave its governors power without appeal, it assured them "complete legal authority."[50] Bay leaders supported appeals to their own higher court, but appeals to the king or royal courts were a different matter. The patent included no appeal beyond the colony. As the 1661 patent-study committee had stated, the General Court had "full power & authoritie . . . for the government of all the people here . . . without appeale" except where the law was "repugnant" to that of England.[51] Allowing royal judges to hear appeals—especially without a jury, and according to English rather than colonial law—would have been a major concession of authority. Court members argued based on the patent, and they also took up older arguments against appeals, such as their potential to entangle colonists in expensive and complicated legal battles, at great distance, any time convicted persons disagreed with their sentences.

The appeals issue formed a sore spot for Samuel Maverick. He had been involved, along with Robert Child and others, in a confrontation with the General Court back in 1646 over the political rights of non–full church members; losing in Massachusetts, they had tried to appeal their case in England. Samuel Gorton, too, had been trying for an appeal in England, arguing that if colonists did not allow it, they were denying the king's sovereignty. Traveling to England in the colonies' defense, Edward Winslow was finally able to secure a favorable agreement from parliament, declaring "we intended not . . . to encourage any appeals from your justice, nor to restrain the bounds of your jurisdiction." This statement did not technically say anything about appeals to the king, but the year was 1647 and so it would not really be an issue until the Restoration. John Winthrop (the father) was adamant that appeals to England were both impractical and destructive of local authority. As early as December 1660, Massachusetts leaders instructed their London agents to prioritize their judicial independence because appeals to England "would be such an intolerable & unsupportable burthen as this poor place (at this distance) are not able to undergoe, but would render authority & government vain & uneffectual." But Maverick was working against this opinion, advising members of the Privy Council to revoke the charter unless the colony allowed appeals.[52] He would not let the issue slide.

Appeals drew a constitutional line in the sand that Bay leaders were vigorously prepared to defend. Their October 1664 letter to the king asking for the royal commission to be withdrawn had pleaded that "we are like to be subjected to the arbitrary power of strangers, proceeding not by any established lawe, but by their oune discretions!"[53] Endicott had followed with another letter to Clarendon protesting that the four men's "commission to exercise government here it seemes altogether inconsistant with our charter & priviledges."[54] Clarendon curtly responded that he saw no conflict between the charter and the royal commissioners' hearing appeals. This was especially the case because in their instructions, which Clarendon had either drafted or approved, and which colonial leaders had not fully seen, "they are expresly inhibited from intermedling with, or instructing the administration of justice, according to the formes observed there," except in an "extraordinary case" involving "irregular" proceedings or a case "particularly recommended to them by his Majesty."[55] But Clarendon's careful legal distinctions were not at the forefront of the royal commissioners' minds in May 1665 when they claimed a much broader power to hear appeals.

Massachusetts leaders would have liked to dodge the conflict altogether. In the September Declaration of 1664, the Council had tried to prevent an appeals case from arising by ordering people not to "openly or willingly defame any Court of Justice, or the sentences & pleadings of the same."[56] The royal commissioners saw this order as itself a violation of sovereignty, calling it "a paper to deter and affrighten all from making any complaints to the Commissioners."[57] They did not press the issue of appeals in Plymouth or Connecticut, and in Rhode Island they did not need to raise it, as magistrates there encouraged appeals. But in the Bay they made a point of inviting disaffected people to present cases before them, and had two appeals ready as test cases in May 1665, one involving a previously convicted felon, John Porter, and another involving a violation of the Navigation Acts that, in effect, would put the entire General Court on trial. The royal commissioners were prepped and ready. Indeed, they initially hoped to hear many more cases, including possible treason cases that might target the regicides' colonial hosts, the royal commissioners functioning as "Judges . . . of the Kings Bench, of his Chancery, and Admiralty too." They soon realized, however, that they would need to scale back their ambition, focusing instead only on the two appeals cases.[58]

* * *

A brief look at the Porter case helps explain some of the charged emotions around the issue of appeals. That the royal commissioners would rehear this kind of case made them appear either oblivious or sinister. The young Salem man John Porter seemed to be tearing both his family and community apart. When his father trusted him with a Barbados trading venture, son John "riotuously expend[ed]" the investment, ending up in debtors' prison. Bailed out and forgiven, he soon engaged in abusive, violent behavior against both family and servants. He "frequently . . . threatned to burne his fathers house, to cutt doune his house & barne, to kill his catle & hoses." He took an axe and cut down his father's fences on multiple occasions, also setting fire to a woodpile "neere the dwelling house, greatly endangering it." He also "reviled, & abused, & beate his fathers servants, to the endangering of the life of one [of] them," and tried to "stab" one of his brothers. His actions were more than his parents knew how to handle. They asked for help from the Salem court, which imprisoned John briefly. The family then took him back in, but his dangerous behavior continued. The parents finally went to the Boston court for assistance. At his trial, witnesses included family, neighbors, and servants, all of whom feared for their safety. The court enacted a "symbolic execution" (an hour on the gallows with a loose rope), a whipping, and imprisonment. In late March 1665, however, Porter escaped, fleeing to the royal commissioners to ask for their help.[59]

In his petition, Porter claimed that his family only pretended he was rebellious in order to get "land which is his own." He charged Bay magistrate William Hathorne with serving as accuser, attorney, and judge while having an interest in the case because of his daughter's relationship with Porter's younger brother, who stood to benefit if Porter was disinherited.[60] Cartwright later admitted the decision to protect Porter was influenced by "so many informations" of Hathorne's "seditious speech at the head of his company" (the "hedge" speech mentioned earlier).[61] Porter thus appealed to the royal commissioners' worst assumptions about New England leaders: that they were greedy for land and that men like Hathorne could act with impunity. The subtext in Porter's petition was that "Massachusetts, not himself, was the true undutiful child."[62] Porter also claimed that on his deathbed, Endicott himself had "befriended" him, advising the young man "to be sure to escape to the Commissioners as soon as he was dead." That the royal commissioners were willing to believe Porter on this point shows their complete unfamiliarity with Endicott, not to mention the likelihood that a felon would be allowed near the late governor's bed. But they did believe him. The royal commissioners—Maverick, Carr, and Cartwright, but not Nicolls—gave Porter protection, ordering "all officers both military & civill" to refrain from "molestaccion or restraint."[63]

Learning that the royal commissioners were protecting the escaped Porter, many Massachusetts colonists felt blindsided. For anyone to take the side of someone like this young man without even looking into the judicial proceedings against him was simply mind-boggling. Further, the royal commissioners had arrogantly assumed the authority to tell the colony's officers how to treat a convicted felon, now at large. The court issued orders for the Marshal General to apprehend Porter, advising him to take whatever aids he needed. They immediately informed the royal commissioners, "wee apprehend our patent, & his majesties authority therein committed unto us, to be greatly infringed."[64] For their part, the royal commissioners continued to insist on sheltering Porter.

But their protections would not last. Over time, they began to back away from their close association with Porter; as the May negotiations ground on they gradually realized the inflammatory nature of the young man's case and appeal. The royal commissioners suggested a "conference"—thus far, they had mainly been trading position papers.[65] Carr, Cartwright, Maverick, and Nicolls met with eight representatives from the General Court to discuss whether hearing an appeal constituted an infringement of the charter.[66] According to Cartwright, "coppies of the Kings letters, & their charter were produced & very many arguments were used."[67] The royal commissioners' points did not convince Bay leaders, who were sure that "his majesties charter doeth give to the Governor & Company heere full & absolute power & authority for the government of his subjects of this colony." These powers included making laws not repugnant to England's and executing those laws, and for these powers "the said charter is their royall warrant & discharge."[68] They were happy to give an account of their actions in any proceeding, and to retry a case if need be, but they would not compromise the privilege of self-government.

In addition to standing by the charter, court members argued based on "the unreasonableness, and unsufferableness of such a burden," an argument that had been employed by Winslow and Winthrop in the 1640s.[69] If appeals were allowed, criminals from decades of trials would come flooding into the courts. But the constitutional issue held sway. Allowing people to appeal decisions of "the highest authority heere established by our constitution, according to his majesties royal charter," would in effect put the General Court, or even "the whole colony, to stand aequall with them [the convicted criminals] at the barr of another tribunall, divers from that established heere." It would mean a "breach . . . in the wall of our government" that "would be an inlett of much trouble to us" as people came forward "to trample upon the authority that sentenced them." The colony's leaders would rather move back to England, they vehemently declared, "then to be under the arbitrary determination of the commissioners, whose rule is their discretion."[70] It would have been a major concession to let royally appointed judges overrule local elected officials. They would be opening the door to arbitrary rule, without accountability or limits.

When the royal commissioners finally demanded a response, colonists "alleged our charter for exemption from appeals in all cases proper to our cognizance." In other words, laws "repugnant to the law of England" could be reviewed under the charter, but not regular cases. The General Court's representatives offered that "if we could be charged with bribes or malice in dispensing justice, we would not justify the same, but if otherwise, we were excused." The royal commissioners insisted, however, that they had the right to review individual decisions, not just breaches of justice such as bribery.[71] Toward the end of the debate, one magistrate (perhaps Bradstreet) made a last-ditch effort at compromise, asking whether the royal commissioners would allow a jury on their appeals court. The answer was an emphatic no. Calling their commission one of "oyer & terminer," the four men said that "they would have no jury." In other words, they were royally appointed judges, like those in England sent to a given region by the king to hear certain high-level criminal cases. No jury would be allowed.

Would they judge by English or colonial law? When asked this question by the magistrates, the royal commissioners said, "by the law of England." Finally, would they admit new evidence or witnesses? To this the royal commissioners said yes.[72] At this point the colonial representatives sought refuge in the tradition of English common law extending back to the Magna Carta. By the charter, they said, they possessed "all the privileges of any the naturall subjects within any of his dominions," including and especially "that no judgment shall passe on any mans person or estate but by the lawfull trial of his peeres, & that the rule of triall shall be the lawes of the land."[73] The royal commissioners dismissed this argument, insisting that theirs was a royal court and so exempt from these requirements.

The jury, however, was no small issue. In William Hubbard's summary: "there was a pretty large debate betwixt them, and the General Court were very slow to grant what was proposed in the subjecting of the power of the country to a Court of Appeals, wherein things were to be issued by the power of the Commissioners without any jury."[74] Cartwright later clarified that if the commissioners "were to hear a cause, where matter of fact was to be proved, they would use a jury" but that "where the fact was already proved, & confessed, they would use none." At another point, Cartwright further argued, "If all causes heard in the King's court of Chancery require not a jury, these gentlemen needed not to have troubled themselves" about the jury issue. In Cartwright's view, the colonists simply did not understand how royal courts worked. He reflected, "but that was a mistake, and had been easily pardonable, if they had asked their question for speeding of the businesse, & not for quarrelling." In his view, the colonists were determined not to submit, and thus "it did not concern them how we would proceed in a tryall, when they were resolved before hand, that they would not be tryed by us."[75] In his mind, the constitutional question over juries was not that important. Colonists, however, saw it as crucial.

When the debate seemed to be going nowhere, one colonist, perhaps Edward Johnson, launched into an emotional appeal. These privileges, he stated, were the bases on which they had "left theire deare relations, & parted with their inheritances in their native country," risking "the lives of themselves & families." At no expense to the king, out of their own labor they had "raised up a colony of people to his majesty." The royal commissioners' proposed appeals court "would be a great addition to their former sorrows." They wanted neither to deny the king's authority nor to "yeild to the prostrating of his majesties authority, orderly established heere according to the grant of his royall charter . . . & submit themselves, their lives, & estates, & thier liberties, farr dearer then them both, to another authority, whose rule is their oune discreation."[76] Colonists had risked so much to build a society based on mutual accountability. This impassioned constitutional plea against arbitrary rule left Carr, Cartwright, Maverick, and Nicolls unaffected.

* * *

The second case the royal commissioners chose to investigate involved the Navigation Acts and was at least as inflammatory as Porter's. A few years earlier, the Boston merchant Thomas Deane had supposedly complained to the king that Massachusetts had hindered him from enforcing the ban on trading with the French (he later denied voicing this complaint).[77] Deane had intervened in 1661 when he saw a local merchant couple, Joshua and Lydia Scottow, dealing in smuggled French wares, brought in from Maine.[78] When Deane and the royalist Thomas Kirke—the same Kirke who hunted the regicides—approached Governor Endicott with these allegations, Lydia Scottow challenged them. Although he expressed sympathy for her, Endicott still secured the goods and called for a trial. It never happened: Kirke and Deane requested a delay and then dropped the case.[79]

The king's initial instructions had told the royal commissioners to see that "the Act of Navigation be punctually observed." The four men's much-expanded proposition to the Massachusetts Court on the topic said they knew that "some men [were] pretending as if some acts made . . . during the last Rebellion, were still in force," or that older, less restrictive trade laws were still operative. Mentioning Deane's complaint specifically, the commissioners said he was "in plain terms denyed justice, even with reproaches for requireing it."[80] (Deane later clarified "it was the not doing of justice, & not injustice, was the complaint.") Court members responded vaguely that the acts for trade "hath for some yeares beene observed heere" but denied that they had committed any injustice, "or that any in authority heere discountenance[d] or reproached" Deane for his actions.[81]

Scribbled lines sent back and forth between magistrates and deputies indicate that at one point in this debate, the magistrates expressed willingness to "acknowledge <ourselves> responsable to any complaint legally exhibbited against us . . . not fearing to have our errour appeare in the Light," and to look over Deane's complaints. A court of appeals, however, was a different matter. "Wee must professe," they said, "our inabilitie to sattisfy ourselves" on allowing appeals, "much less his majesties subjects in this Colony, which are so nearely concerned in our concessions therein."[82] The magistrates, it seems, were acutely aware that the people were watching. With the urgings of the resistance petitions perhaps in mind, the deputies decided they were not satisfied with even this soft language, pushing for the harder statement that eventually made it to the commissioners: "Our charter under the great seale of England, giveth full power unto the authority here established according thereto, to governe, all the people of this place, whither Inhabitants or straingers," a power that "seems Inconsistent" with the royal commissioners' plan to hear appeals.[83]

The royal commissioners understood that at stake was who had authority to interpret the charter. In icy language they responded, "wee are heartily sorry to finde, that, by some evill perswasions, yow have put a greater value upon your oune conceptions then upon the wisdome of his majesty & council, which argues either an unreasonable jealousy & distrust of his majesty so often repeated graces & favours intended towards his subjects heere, or that his majesty is not a competent interpreter of your charter."[84] The royal commissioners then tried, as one historian has phrased things, to "elicit a treasonable utterance." They asked point blank if the court did "acknowledge his majesties commission . . . to be of full force to all the intents & purposes therein conteyned?" In other words, did they submit to the royal commissioners' authority or not? Bay leaders had no interest in falling into this trap. They evaded the question: "why you should put us on the resolve of such a question wee see not the grounds therof."[85] Next they reminded the royal commissioners that the king's instructions—of which they finally had a copy—forbade any disturbance of their charter liberties.

When Carr, Cartwright, Maverick, and Nicolls continued to press their authority, reminding the court of Morrice's rebuke, the court again declined to answer, simply asserting, "It is enough for us to acquaint you what wee conceive is granted to us by his majesties royall charter." If the royal commissioners were unsatisfied, the court continued, "it is our trouble, but wee hope it is not our fault." They concluded with an expression of faith: "It is knoune to Him that knows all things, that it . . . hath been our endeavor, according to our best understanding, to give his majesty & yourselves all due sattisfaction, saving only our duty to God, & the priviledges of our charter, so dearely purchased, so long enjoyed, & so graciously confirmed by his majestie." At this point, civility went out the window. The royal commissioners insulted the colonists' "dilatory answers" and mocked their religious language: "you might well have spared that salvo of your duty to God, & the priviledges of your charter." The court of appeals was no violation of their "liberties, civill & ecclesiasticall," the commissioners argued. It was simply the reality of living in the Stuart empire.[86]

The royal commissioners decided to continue with their planned court of appeals. Beyond the Scottows, the case fundamentally took on the colony's entire leadership for the way it had dealt with Deane's attempt to enforce the Navigation Acts. As Bellingham later observed, the royal commissioners were, in effect, "summoning this Courte, to apeare as delinquents at their Barr."[87] That was when the court sent three men on horseback to issue their declaration by trumpet, as we saw in the chapter's opening. The colony would not submit to arbitrary rule. Even so, the declaration by trumpet still ended with "God Save the King." While continuing, at least in theory, to honor the monarchy, this declaration meant that inhabitants must now choose between their local leaders and the royal commissioners; participants in an appeals court would be considered "abbettors."[88] Some colonists who supported "the royal interest" in the Bay took great "offence" at this order to boycott the royal commissioners' court "by sound of a trumpet."[89] Most colonists approved, however, siding with their elected leaders. One account said if the magistrates and deputies had "adhered to the [royal] Commissioners mandates," most of the inhabitants "were so resolved, that they would . . . have utterly protested."[90] Another colonist wrote in his diary, "Much revived & exhilirated with action of Court yesterday in declaring for liberties."[91] The court of appeals was defeated.

* * *

Astounded by how negotiations had ended, the royal commissioners accused the Bay Colony of using "that authority which [the king] hath given you to oppose that soveraignty which he hath over you."[92] In defending their right to hear appeals, they took up a line that would ring false almost anywhere but London: that the crown gave the charter so it could interpret or even modify its terms. For most English subjects, a charter's constitutional legitimacy derived not only from the crown but also from inherited rights and the sedimentation of custom over time.[93] Insisting on having a say in the charter's interpretation would emerge as one of colonists' most significant and enduring constitutional claims.

The General Court tried to soften the blow of its defiance, finally sending that long-requested map and inviting the royal commissioners to attend their own hearing of the Deane case. The commissioners declined. Cartwright put a more sinister spin on the invitation: "This order was made in their hott bloud," intending that "the Commissioners should sitt by, & hear them examine the businesse, & affirm in it, that this was the entent of his Majesties Commission, & instructions to them."[94] Carr, Cartwright, Maverick, and Nicolls instead spent their time reviewing the colony's law code, which we will explore more momentarily. They were out to identify colonial laws repugnant to the laws of England, the first step in a *quo warranto* proceeding.[95] Thomas Danforth had managed to get his hands on the colony's earlier *quo warranto* notice "sent over to the country sundry years since," carefully transcribing the 1636 document into his notebook. It had named many Bay freemen, including John Endicott and Richard Bellingham, demanding them personally to answer "by what warrant they claim to have divers liberties, privileges and franchises." Danforth was also reviewing the colony's trade advantages from the 1642 Long Parliament.[96] He knew the magistrates and deputies would have to defend their recent actions.

Even moderates like John Hull were irate at the latest developments. Hull scribbled in shorthand in his diary: "why are we imposed upon? why do any, in his majesty's name, protest against us, discourage magistrates, and sit . . . without our consent in our jurisdiction?" The colonists' constitutional arrangement had not been built on a whim. "God, in the king, has committed the care of rule to the government here." The royal commissioners had no biblical justification for their authority, and the colonists "may not suffer any rule to be publicly practised which is not of divine ordination." The royal commission was operating out of bounds, beyond both religion and law: "Strangers, though Englishmen, have no R[ight?] to think they may come hither, and seek the subversion of our civil and ecclesiastical politics," Hull protested.[97]

Cartwright later admitted that the General Court's account of both Porter's and Deane's cases "may be tru." The royal commissioners, he said, had protected Porter without knowing his actions: "their shoe wrung not here," meaning they were unaware of the pain Porter had caused others. Much later, Cartwright also said that the royal commissioners would actually have tried Porter under colonial rather than English laws. But all of this, in his view, was beside the point. In their August Resolution, the magistrates and deputies had decided to hold fast to their charter privileges, regardless. Details mattered little, Cartwright said, "as they had resolved . . . to adhear to their patent, the duties & priviledges thereof, & to be their own expositors . . . they were resolute not to forgoe that priviledge of being their own judge."[98] At issue was their attachment to, and interpretation of, the charter itself.

Royalist-leaning colonists chose to emphasize the inflammatory nature of the Porter and Deane cases. "Some that were the more cordial asserters of the royal interest in the Massachusetts, wished that some other cases had fallen under their cognizances, than those that were pitched upon."[99] For most, however, this claim missed the forest for the trees. At issue was not any one particular case but the threat of arbitrary rule.

* * *

The appeals court had been defeated, but Carr, Cartwright, Maverick, and Nicolls were not finished yet. Even though the Massachusetts charter, unlike Rhode Island's, did not grant the king review of laws, the royal commissioners now set about revising the law code. In other colonies, they had accepted assurances that the laws would be reviewed. Not so in the Bay. Determined to review these laws personally, the commissioners asked the General Court to lend them "a booke of your lawes."[100] It is interesting—and perhaps telling—that they did not already have a copy. Thomas Breedon had brought the 1660 *Book of the General Lawes and Libertyes* to the Council for Foreign Plantations in London in March 1661. Presenting the lawbook then, Breedon had reported colonists as saying "they will die before they will lose their liberties and privileges." Everyone should know by now, Breedon had declared, that puritans could not be true monarchists; just look at their laws and see how far their interests diverged from the king's.[101] Most likely the Council for Foreign Plantations had kept Breedon's lawbook, and with Bostonians probably unwilling to share theirs, the royal commissioners had to issue a formal request.

In reviewing the laws in late May 1665, Carr, Cartwright, Maverick, and Nicolls's immediate concern seems to have been any that contravened the Navigation Acts. They also looked, as instructed, for language derogatory to the king.[102] In the end, however, their revisions extended well beyond those initial guidelines. While official correspondence indulgently reassured the colonists of their charter's security, the law code revisions tell a different story, reflecting the ambitions of the regime more accurately and openly. These final acts of the royal commission in the Bay confirmed colonists' fears that constitutional lines they perceived clearly were blurry on the other side.

The royal commissioners began by demanding the laws' title page declare "his majesty . . . to be the fountaine" from which they "derived their lawes & liberties, by a charter."[103] It was true that Charles I had signed their charter, and describing the king as a fount of justice was a commonplace in early modern England. But puritans would have had trouble saying an earthly king was the sole fountain of their laws and liberties. The four men might not have had any idea just how much effort the colonists had put into legal reform, an attempt to implement biblical, humanist, and common-law ideals.[104]

Finding no less than twenty-six offensive aspects of the law code, the royal commissioners demanded changes. They first attended to the extension of a culture of royalism, requiring "commonwealth" language to be expunged from the code and the king made aurally and visually present in the colony.

His name, coat of arms, and colors must be prominently displayed, from courtrooms to merchant ships to militia companies. Even during the Interregnum, the king had never been absent from the colony, especially as men and women reflected on coreligionists' role in the regicide. But now the Stuart regime was asking for loud, bright, frequent markers of the royal presence. Appearances mattered.

Second, they turned to royal prerogative in the diplomatic realm. The Bay should start acting like a colony rather than a state, commissioners instructed, avoiding negotiations with "forraine parts" and shunning warfare except for immediate self-defense.[105] And the confederation known as the United Colonies, which itself usurped royal authority (and violated the charter), had to go. Third, the royal commissioners aimed to extend royal control over land and money. They wanted escheats—the lands of those who died without heirs—to revert to the crown rather than the colony. The king could then institute a form of patronage by giving those lands "to whom he pleaseath." The current law, which held that no one could "take wood or timber" without permission from local authorities, should be repealed—a move that would grant the royal navy unfettered access to the region's forests, a stark contrast to the king's reforestation projects at home and his garden cultivation in Jamaica. As for the colony's mint, it seemed to be a clear violation of "royal prerogative." Here the commissioners jettisoned even the facade of neutrality, adding that for the mint's "usurping" of the king's authority, "the act of indemnity is only a salvo." A one-time pardon, parliament's Act of Indemnity and Oblivion did not cover ongoing blatant acts of sedition, such as coining one's own money. And the commissioners wanted the colony to turn away French and Dutch merchant ships, enforcing the Navigation Acts.[106]

Fourth, the royal commissioners objected to colonists' language regarding Indian land. Colonial law assured Indians' right to lands they had "Possessed and improoved by subduing the same" including "fishing places" and citing Genesis 1:28, 9:1, and Psalm 115:16. The four men questioned the colonists' exegesis of these biblical passages, which, they said, made it seem like Indians "were dispossessed of their land by Scripture," an implication violating "the honor of God & the justice of the king." The language "replenish the earth," taken in context, referred, the royal commissioners claimed, to "generation, not husbandry." Therefore, Indians rightly possessed all the lands on which they dwelt, not just those they had "improved." The commissioners further accused colonists of excluding Indians from the Psalmist's phrase "children of men," although there is no indication that the colonists' law code sought to do so.[107] The commissioners ignored the Bay law code's guarantees of land allotments the same size as English plots to any Indians who settled within English towns; of land grants to Native families who came together to form towns, just as to English families; and of access to justice in court for Indians, no different from English. The royalists' assumption that colonists saw Native peoples as less than human, denying them legal rights, marked an attempt to discredit the colonists' moral authority, and therefore their authority to rule. It fits within larger contestations over moral high ground with regard to Native peoples during the Restoration period. Rhetoric aside, the royal commissioners would not enact these generous principles in their own land dealings with Native Americans in Rhode Island and Maine. Nicolls in particular seems to have had a low threshold for violence against Natives, writing in February 1665, "I am firmly of the judgment that it is more than equivalent to the loss of some trade that a little war be fomented between themselves [Native groups] to divert their restless, barbarous thoughts from a war with Christians."[108] Nonetheless, in late May 1665, the commissioners' insistence that Natives had a right to lands both improved and unimproved, coupled with their declaration elsewhere that the Bay did not wield authority to grant land outside of original patent boundaries, must have deeply unsettled the court.

Last but definitely not least, religious laws also required attention. In a later report to London, the commissioners highlighted the most egregious colonial offense as a £5 fine on people celebrating Christmas, a Church of England feast day.[109] Back in December, Maverick had engaged in a heated debate with Increase Mather over the holiday, which most puritans viewed as idolatrous because scripture made no mention of it as an annual celebration.[110] Reviewing the law code, the royal commissioners focused much of their energy on promoting prayer-book worship.[111] But they also tended to broader ecclesial matters. In their minds, not only should the Church of England set up local churches, but its adherents should have the franchise and full access to political power. In their ideal scenario, new churches would no longer have to be approved by magistrates and neighboring church leaders; and local preachers would no longer be forced to satisfy "Gospel-qualifications" as determined by the magistrates. Those who persistently rejected local church authority or absented themselves from worship would not undergo fines. The commissioners also urged expanding the franchise beyond only members of approved churches.[112] It is clear from a close reading of these proposed revisions that the commissioners were primarily concerned about the Church of England, not other religious groups. If Quakers such as Wenlock Christiansen and Elizabeth Hooton had read the document, they would have appreciated seeing that Quakers would be free to "quietly passe about their lawfull occasion." They would have been quite surprised, however, to read on and find that those Quakers who were less than quiet could "be punisht."[113]

In a related vein, Carr, Cartwright, Maverick, and Nicolls wanted to add two royalist holidays to the local church calendar: an annual thanksgiving day to celebrate the country's "miraculous preservation" from the gunpowder treason along with Charles II's "birth, miraculous & happy restauration to his crownes"; and an annual fast day for "that most barbarous & execrable murder of . . . Charles the First." The current colonial law code gave every church "freedom to celebrate" fast and thanksgiving days "according to the word of God" and gave the General Court liberty to appoint public fast and thanksgiving days for the entire colony.[114] Colonists highly prized this liberty to declare their own spontaneous fast and thanksgiving days, which, as we have seen, were central to a puritan ethos. As early as 1661, they had worried about Charles II's proclamation of fast days throughout England and punishment for those who neglected them.[115] The liturgy for the king's restoration included "suffrages" or oaths acknowledging divine right monarchy and promising unqualified obedience to both God and the king: "promising in thee, and for thee all loyal and dutiful allegiance to thine Anointed servant, and to his heirs after him."[116] This final revision to the law code may have been the hardest for Bay colonists to swallow.

Regarding the offending laws, Cartwright would later say that he, Carr, Maverick, and Nicolls only "coppyed them out" rather than demanding actual changes.[117] But a letter from the royal commissioners dated just after the thwarted appeals court states that they perused the law book and "finde just reason to propose, in his majesties name, that these ensuing alterations & necessary additions be made." And in the four men's final report, they recounted having "made a breviat" of the laws "and desired that they might be altered," faulting the colonists for having "yet done nothing in it."[118] From the colonists' perspective, the royal commissioners' law code revisions constituted a very real—and very concerning—part of the king's demands.

Bay leaders' responses to the royal commission might have seemed flatfooted in comparison with Winthrop's graceful evasions back in Connecticut. Perhaps aware of their inelegant efforts, they transitioned to a more familiar idiom, the language of fast days. Magistrates and deputies knew they acted in the presence of a God who "loves trueth in the inward parts, & will have no fellowship with iniquity, though in the greatest step of outward dignity." Trusting in the divine presence for protection and vindication, they "cast ourselves at the feete of his majestie" and asked for Charles II's continued favor. This was their "time of trial," they declared, and for obtaining the king's favor "wee are lying lowe in ourselves before the King of kings, in solemne humiliation with the order for which wee here conclude."[119] The court's secretary, Edward Rawson, copied in the fast day proclamation directly after the court's final statement, even though he had already transcribed it in an earlier May 1665 section. For many colonists, the fast day itself would constitute the final episode in the negotiations with the royal commissioners.

The fast proclamation nimbly placed the court's constitutional resistance to an expanding royal prerogative within both transatlantic and providential contexts. The stakes could not be much higher. Yes, the Bay had entered into a dark "howure of temptation" but so also had "the Protestant Christian interest in the world." For colonists, the Lord had sent providential warning signals. Environmental blights, low migration, comets, wars, and impending deaths among the founding generation all called out for repentance. Bay colonists now should repent especially of "the great indisposition . . . of our spirits to . . . submit unto the yoke of Christ" and "wantones under the peace & liberties wee partake of." They had not fully appreciated the divine gift of their civil and ecclesiastical liberties. The court saw "great reason to stir up all the inhabitants of this colony" to fast and pray not just on the June fast day but also to "be instant in season & out of season with the Lord, by prayer for his mercy towards his poore servants." The magistrates and deputies knew they could be held accountable for their response to the king's demands, possibly suffering for treason as Hugh Peter had done.[120] Indeed, the entire colony's participation in prayer would be needed to overturn the royal commissioners' vilifying report and win back the favor of the king. Therefore, the court asked that

> all may unfeignedly humble themselves in the sight of God, lifting up holy hands without wrath & doubting, & may turne from the evill of theire doings in the way of a reall & thorough reformation, that so the Lords anger maybe turned away from us, & wee may obteine reconcilliation with him, & the continuance of his gracious presence with us & ours, that this worke may appeare to his servants & his glory unto

> theire children, together with the favour of the kings majesty towards us, whence wee may be encouraged in this wildernes still to offer up the sacrifices of sweete savors unto the God of heaven & pray for the life of the king, that under him wee may live a quiet & peaceable life, in all godlines & honesty.

Like the Bartholomew's Day sermons of ejected ministers in England, this language was deferential toward the king. At the end of the day, most colonists did not want independence from the monarchy. Rather, they longed for a constitutional settlement in which they could both honor the king and continue their project of reform. Accounts from local churches on the fast day reflect the intensity of this intellectual, political, and deeply personal moment for Bay colonists. Noting the court's "many difficulties in the transaction of affayres with his Majesties commissioners," Salem called on "all the churches as people of God" to repent, "apply themselves to Humiliation and Reformation and to cry mightily unto God that he would be reconciled to us and that in particular he would graciously encline his Majesties heart to favour us."[121] At some level, colonists still yearned for the king's approval.

Yet the royal response had damaged or undercut this conciliatory impulse. The attempt of the royal commissioners to set up a court of appeals and revise the law code left even moderate colonists feeling like their backs were against the wall, gradually moving them into a stance of constitutional resistance. Above all, these seventeenth-century men and women resented "arbitrarines," that is, submitting to capricious ecclesiastical or political impositions from nonelected officials, a surrender that, in their increasingly defiant view, amounted to "prostituting our lives, liberties, peace, & comfort." Bay colonists' declaration by trumpet and the actions surrounding that eight A.M. sounding marked the formation of a shared constitutional culture, a widespread and "passionate solicitude for our liberties."[122]

CHAPTER 9

Borderlands

The Contest over Piscataqua, Maine, and Narragansett

As they rode and hiked their way through the thickly wooded forests of Piscataqua (later New Hampshire) and Maine in the summer and fall of 1665, the royal commissioners made their designs on New England clearer than ever. These months also ushered in another stage in the constitutional struggle, on the part of both Massachusetts Bay leaders and rural inhabitants. On paper and on the ground, the situation in the Northeast was messy. It is here that Massachusetts's jurisdictional claims were weakest. Colonists in these small remote towns had many different loyalties, fears, and concerns. Some cooperated with Sir Robert Carr, George Cartwright, and Samuel Maverick in their attempt to take over the Northeast for the crown, attending meetings and accepting offices in a new provincial royal government. Those who most reliably aligned themselves in this way tended toward high church, ceremonial worship or were otherwise disaffected with puritan culture. Some men and women vacillated, simply wanting to live under whichever authority promised long-term stability. Others chose constitutional resistance to the royal commissioners' plans. More so than elsewhere, the northeastern settlers who defied the Stuart regime put themselves at risk. They chose defiance because they liked outright ownership of land rather than proprietary systems, because they were drawn to the puritan vision of a godly society, and because they feared that under direct royal governance they might lose their civil and religious liberties. The latter fear was partially confirmed when Carr, Cartwright, and Maverick began to impose a high Church of England establishment on Maine. Shortly thereafter, in late 1665 the royal commissioners, especially Carr, turned their attention again to Narragansett. As they zeroed in on this Native territory, they demonstrated all too clearly just how far they would go to claim land for the king—and for themselves.

The northeastern settlements had come under the Massachusetts government relatively recently. On paper, this region consisted of "an overlapping patchwork of patents and land grants" held by English elites such as Ferdinando Gorges and Robert Mason.[1] The Bay colony's charter stipulated that their northern boundary extended three miles beyond the Merrimack River, commonly measured from the mouth of the river at Newbury (today Newburyport). Aware of multiple attempts to secure or reconfirm patents for the northeastern territories in the early 1650s, Bay leaders had explored the region and happily discovered that the Merrimack's source was actually about one hundred miles further north. "In an exercise of creative geography," they decided their territory extended three miles past that point.[2] Throughout the 1650s, towns in this region gradually voted to submit to the Bay, drawn to the security of freehold land titles, reliable courts, and protection from powerful Abenaki peoples.[3]

Their submission would not last uncontested. After the Restoration, men representing competing claims in the Northeast formed one of the loudest groups accusing Massachusetts of sedition. Former Maine governor Edward Godfrey characterized Bay colonists as "Gente inemica," or people unfriendly "to loyalty." Prior to Massachusetts's usurpation of their territory, he reported, the northern colonists had "ever lived according to his Majesties lawes." But now the region was full of rebels, people resembling Hugh Peter, or worse, Thomas Venner, who had led a 1661 revolt against the king.[4] The information these claimants provided to the Council on Foreign Plantations and the Privy Council must have influenced those groups' original plan for the royal commission. Clarendon was especially concerned about improving the region's trade, with the goal of "supplying the King and the Nation with Timper, Masts, Cordage, Tarr etc." Royal officials and colonists alike coveted the rich resources of Abenaki territory. Clarendon further eyed the Northeast with a view to securing the king's interest, so as to "give his majestie a good footing and foundacion for a farther advance of his Authority" through a royalist base.[5] In the borderland territories, legal and constitutional struggles were most conspicuously enmeshed with contests over land and natural resources.

* * *

After the disastrous negotiations in Boston, Richard Nicolls dutifully went back to govern New York, while Carr and Maverick waited for Cartwright's health to improve. Cartwright, it seems, had other reasons to drag his heels on departing Boston. Even while ill, he met with Simon Bradstreet and Daniel Denison regarding "Mr Deans businesse," still trying to make headway on that appeal and on the Navigation Acts. The two men listened carefully to Cartwright's insistence that the king had directly commanded the royal commissioners to hear this case.[6] When General Court members, energetically led by Bellingham, had decided to block the royal commissioners' appeals court and hear the Deane case themselves, Bradstreet had intervened, saying "the Governor did not speake the sence of the hous": in his view, most magistrates wanted to ask Deane if he was willing for his case to be handled locally. Brought in for questioning, Deane had confessed that he was simply carrying out instructions: he had been "commanded by a great minister of state in England to put his cause to the Commissioners." It was their case now, he had maintained, and he "could not alter it." The identity of the "great minister of state" who had issued this command remains unknown, but it is interesting to consider if Clarendon or someone like him had arranged Deane's case as a test of constitutional boundaries from the beginning. This news of a metropolitan design had probably only fortified court members in their resistance. Bradstreet and Denison had left the Town House in frustration; and, unwilling to proceed amid so much dissension, the court had "dissolved."[7] In the later meeting with Bradstreet and Denison, Cartwright was attempting to reopen the constitutional contest. He was disappointed.

Boston negotiations thus finished, if unsatisfactorily, the royal commissioners turned to pulling northeastern territories out from under Massachusetts's rule. On 8 June 1665, the three set off on horseback to visit the "Eastward parts" in person. They brought convicted felon John Porter with them, probably both for his continued protection and as a temporary manservant.[8] Their distrust of and revulsion toward the Bay, as well as their personal desire for land and influence, drove the royal commissioners' actions in the East. The region's vast old-growth forests and unspoiled fishing waters were tempting, to be sure. If they could not return to London having successfully fulfilled their instructions, the royal commissioners could at least acquire some richly resourced territory, for themselves and for the crown.

The English hunger for land shows up in their interactions with Native American leaders on their journey. One "Sagamore of Wesapaguaqueg" supposedly "came & surrendered his Country . . . to his Majestie humbly craveing his protection of them," a submission perhaps modeled on that of the Narragansett. According to William Hubbard, the royal commissioners also tried to set up a procedure for arbitration in case these Native groups and the English should injure each other. Maverick eyed the territory with approval, probably the area near Lake Winnipesaukee. He wrote, "It is a far better country then Narraganset, Colonel Cartwright hath the deede in his keeping." After mentioning the "Indian Sachem" and his request for protection, Cartwright commented, "the more northerly the country, the better the timber is accounted."[9] The natural resources of the Northeast were highly motivating to royalist visitors.

On the route northward the royal commissioners stayed with wealthy merchant families, the Curwens and Brownes in Salem, and the Denisons and Appletons in Ipswich.[10] Inhabitants from these towns, along with some Bostonians, would organize petitions in 1666 to encourage the Massachusetts General Court to compromise with the king on his next demands. Carr, Maverick, and Cartwright also made a stop in Hampton, where they found several men willing to show them the location of the "bound howse." Erected in the 1630s, the bound house supposedly marked Massachusetts's original boundary three miles north of the Merrimack's mouth.[11] By 1665 the house was gone, but a local man told them that "when the howse fell, he placed a barrell of a gun in the place where it stood," so the colony boundary was still marked. The commissioners rode out to inspect the site and later used this information as evidence for the colony's original northern line.[12]

On arrival in Piscataqua, Carr, Cartwright, and Maverick did what they had been prevented from doing in the Bay: they called the entire population of Portsmouth (including Strawberry Bank), Dover, and Exeter, around 1,500 non-Native people total, to a meeting "to heare his Majesties letters read." At the time, Anglo-American Piscataqua was a diverse mix of former Massachusetts residents and fishermen and traders from scattered northern settlements. According to Maverick's account, the people generally came and "shewed us very great respect." He sent off a report to Richard Nicolls in New York, with felonious Porter as messenger, also asking that Nicolls shelter Porter and find him work (evidently Maverick was finished with Porter's company). The three royal commissioners did not, however, at this point make any decisions about Piscataqua. Perhaps they were reluctant to act without Nicolls's consent. Not only was Nicolls supposed to weigh in on major decisions, but he had also recently agreed to serve as attorney for Robert Mason, who claimed proprietary rights to the region through his grandfather. Complicating matters further, the grounds for Mason's claims were not the strongest, as Cartwright himself later admitted. Maverick thought that violence might be brewing among supporters of the Bay, and a rash move by royal commissioners in Piscataqua "might animate them to resist to [the point of] blood shedding." And there seems to have been some disagreement among the three men about their own authority in the region; Cartwright had refused to sign their most recent order.[13]

Of more immediate concern, Bay magistrates Thomas Danforth and Samuel Symonds arrived in Piscataqua "to oppose us in our proceedings," as Maverick and Carr later wrote.[14] In one of their last acts, the May 1665 General Court had taken steps to reinforce their jurisdiction over the northeastern settlements: commissioning Danforth and Symonds, issuing firm instructions to local leaders to maintain their posts, and encouraging church and militia leaders across the region to resist any attempted royalist takeover. Everywhere they went, the royal commissioners later complained, colonists had been warned against cooperating. Maverick saw "spies every where upon all our actions and particularly upon our letters." The General Court had ordered a watch on the three men, but it seems likely that ordinary inhabitants would have kept track of them regardless. Carr, Cartwright, and Maverick decided to move on to Maine.[15]

The Piscataqua story might have stopped there, but the arrival on 9 July 1665 of a long-delayed royal letter made the royal commissioners rethink their decision to leave the territory alone. The letter warned of the escalating war with the Dutch and commanded the commissioners to "looke after the fortification of these parts." Carr, Cartwright, and Maverick decided to return to Piscataqua and call the inhabitants together again, determined to assert royal authority more directly and emphatically within the region.[16] The Portsmouth town selectmen must have been surprised to receive the royal commissioners' warrant demanding a one o'clock multitown meeting on 13 July. They wrote urgently to the Massachusetts Court, asking for "your Advice and Counsell with all Expedition upon what Point of the Compasse it wilbe our safety to steere, so as not to hazzard either our Alleigance to his Majesty or our Oathes to the [Massachusetts] Government."[17] Was there a way to maintain allegiance to both the king and the Bay? Portsmouth had its doubts.

There was no time to spare. A messenger raced the letter and a copy of the warrant to Boston, waking up Governor Bellingham in the middle of the night.[18] Lighting a candle to read the documents, Bellingham declared them to be a matter of "great consequence." By one A.M. he had called a meeting of the Council for six A.M., sending Major General John Leverett to personally deliver the message to Council members, waking them up one by one in their homes.[19]

On hearing that the royal commissioners were again asserting authority over Piscataqua, Bay Council members were incensed. In their subsequent communication to Portsmouth leaders, Bellingham and the Council expressed sympathy for the bind that Piscataqua inhabitants found themselves in. They understood the colonists' desire to "avoyd all unecessary disputes." Avoidance of conflict had been their own strategy at times. But they did not trust Carr, Cartwright, and Maverick for a moment. "Its matter of no small wonder," they wrote, that the three had come back "to breed you such trouble; as to presume to sumon & Require your Inhabitants to meete together at their pleasure, under pretence of communicating a letter lately received from his Majestie." The king's letter "cannot but be accounted a figg leafe." If Charles II had something to communicate regarding fortifications, he would write to colony leaders. The royal commissioners' real goal, they argued, was to turn Piscataqua into a royal province. The Council instructed the Portsmouth constable to "warne all persons" en route to the commissioners' multitown meeting "to depart home to their respective places." If any refused, their names should be sent in a list to Boston. To be safe, they included a warrant for the constable's own arrest in case he behaved "contrary to his oath."[20] In making this statement, Council members had effectively demanded a decision from their colonial neighbors: Piscataqua inhabitants would have to choose between the royal commissioners and Massachusetts Bay.

* * *

The choice was not easy. Some reports, especially Maverick's and accounts by Mason family members, assumed that the great majority in Piscataqua wanted to be freed from the domination of the Bay.[21] But even Nicholas Shapleigh, a royalist and Quaker, later admitted that "many" were drawn to "stick to the Government of the Massachusetts," owing, he said, largely to the influence of a few prominent pro-Massachusetts freemen.[22] Those loyal to the Bay might have seen the "liberty" the royal commissioners offered as "liberty for those that were bold in sinn & wickednes, to rant it amongst them at a high rate," preferring instead to stand up for godly social norms.[23]

Puritan-leaning inhabitants also feared royalist control might leave them "destitute of an able ministry," a thought that "filled their eyes with teares, & hearts with sorrow."[24] The role of young Portsmouth minister Joshua Moodey in promoting constitutional defiance remains intriguing. Learned and diligent regarding church discipline, he seems to have enjoyed a relatively successful ministry.[25] We know that local royalists targeted him with insults as they tried to rally people to their cause. Given his later career defending ecclesiastical liberty while imprisoned under royal governor Edward Cranfield, it seems likely that Moodey also helped shepherd this earlier movement.[26] Exeter minister Samuel Dudley would play a role the following year, acting as spokesman for his town and assuring Bay leaders that Exeter inhabitants did not side with the royal commissioners. Dover's minister John Reyner also later signed local inhabitants' petition expressing loyalty to the Bay.[27] Like Bay inhabitants, these ministers and some Piscataqua colonists likely resisted the royal commissioners out of fear of being forced to use the Book of Common Prayer, viewing its ceremonies as tinged with idolatry. Knowing the royal commissioners were still open to Mason's proprietary claims, others probably resisted in order to protect their freeholds.

On the other side, some colonists who welcomed the royal commission probably hoped for a reestablishment of the high Church of England. The outspoken royalist Henry Sherborne, for example, had served as warden of the Church of England parish that operated in Portsmouth from around 1638 to 1642. The church had closed when its priest, Richard Gibson, had, according to Winthrop, "provoke[d] the people, by way of arguments, to revolt from us."[28] Sherborne or someone like him had saved the thirty-year-old document that established a parish house and glebe lands for Gibson. A copy of this document appears in the Portsmouth town records for early 1665, perhaps indicating hopes for a revival of the parish.[29] Certainly their exclusion from the Lord's Supper by Moodey, and their children's lack of access to baptism, weighed heavily on colonists like Sherborne. The choice was vexed—for townspeople on either side of the equation.

The constitutional contest in the Northeast increasingly involved sharp words and threats. Arriving in Portsmouth on 10 July, Carr, Cartwright, and Maverick tried to convince local inhabitants of the "advantage" of being "taken into his Majesty's government" and called for a regional meeting.[30] When Portsmouth inhabitants tried to speak out in opposition to the meeting, the royal commissioners angrily retorted that their words were "no lesse then treason in a high degree." Even a youngster sparked their wrath. Told by his grandfather not to "open the doore" to the royal commissioners, a Portsmouth youth, a servant in a neighbor's household, held firm and would not offer them hospitality. Carr fumed that any such "disrespect" to the royal commissioners was tantamount to disrespecting "his majestie." When he found out the boy was acting on orders from his grandfather, Carr, "in a high

& resolute manner," supposedly said before a gathering crowd that "if the rest of the commissioners would have joyned with him, he would have hanged" the grandfather "at the next tree."[31] Not all the royal commissioners were as volatile as Carr. Cartwright, who would increasingly distance himself from his two companions, spent more time scanning documents than arguing with colonists. He continued to peruse papers related to the Masons' proprietary claim, eventually concluding it faced serious legal difficulties.[32]

Both the royal commissioners and those intending to defy them waited and watched on the appointed Thursday morning, 13 July 1665. Would Piscataqua colonists reject the Bay, obeying the royal commissioners' summons to appear? Neither party was probably satisfied with the turnout. Many residents did come—probably about one hundred inhabitants—but "Many did not." Some had planned to join but were later thankful that, "prevented by the providence of God . . . they could not attend the meetings."[33] July was a busy month for New England farmers and their families, and a summer thunderstorm or broken fence could have major consequences for their livelihoods. The residents of Dover, Exeter, and Hampton would have had to walk or ride at least ten miles to get to the meeting. The Portsmouth constable, out of either loyalty to or fear of the Massachusetts Court, stood on the roadside holding the Bay's warrant that forbade the meeting, and "Divers" of those who came turned right back around at the sight of him and "departed."[34]

When inhabitants had assembled, Carr, Cartwright, and Maverick began by reading the king's letter regarding the Dutch war and the required military preparations. They then asked the colonists present to vote for two representatives who could make decisions regarding fortifications. Clearly unfamiliar with local practice, the royal commissioners then had to ask who was eligible to vote. Sherborne "cryed out . . . One & all."[35] This was not quite true. Neither the Bay nor the royal commissioners were advocating universal manhood suffrage at this point. The royal commissioners had only invited "householders" to the meeting. Sherborne's phrase, however, implied criticism of the Bay and its restrictions on the franchise. Probably the royal commissioners let those who were present vote, and two men were chosen, although they would end up playing little role. The royal commissioners then briskly "declared unto them that they were out of the Bayes Jurisdiccion." Citing the supposed location of the no-longer-standing bound house, Carr, Cartwright, and Maverick promptly took over Piscataqua for the king. They renamed the region the "province of New Hampshire" and promised "speedily to settle the Government thereof." They also promised protection against the Bay, although how they planned to carry out this promise is unclear. Always careful to gather a paper trail, they grabbed the Massachusetts warrant from the Portsmouth constable. They also threatened the former constable with prison if he did not hand over papers sent from the Bay the prior year.[36]

The royal commissioners' abrupt takeover, with scant local input on its terms, probably led some wavering inhabitants to embrace Massachusetts's constitutional culture more firmly. Yet defying royal power was a fearful thing. Reporting to Boston on these events, the Portsmouth selectmen observed grimly, "Thus their Designe is now obvious, our people the five to one are in their hearts for the Bay, yet are readily & dreadfully affrighted with the names of K[ings] Commissioners," accounting "every thing sayd by them for Law." "Wee feare," they continued, "they will gradually take advantage upon us by secret seducing the Ignorant & Ill affected, & then will openly prevaile with the rest." The selectmen needed help and, they said, were looking first to God and then to Bay leaders "for farther direccion what to doe, & power" to do it. Although not opposed to monarchy, these Piscataqua inhabitants did not see the royal commissioners' actions as legitimate. Their hope, they concluded, was twofold: first, "that we may be neither by force nor fraud deprived of that fellisite [felicity] wee Long have had & hope for the future to enjoy under yor happy Government," and second, that we may not "be or accounted to be delinquents either to his Majestie or yorselves." They then included the names of royalist party leaders in the region, including Henry Sherborne and Abraham Corbett.[37]

The meeting regarding fortifications occurred at the mouth of the Portsmouth harbor the following Saturday. The royal commissioners had long eyed this "excellent harbour, larg & safe," with "great store of masts" nearby.[38] What a perfect place for a fort from which to attack Dutch ships or, if need be, Massachusetts ones. It was a grand vision, but no one in their company had the resources to carry it out. The Portsmouth representatives pleaded poverty, and the royal commissioners did not press the matter.[39] Local royalists, however, wanted further assurances of the crown's support. As they stood outside discussing fortifications, Corbett took the opportunity to present a petition from "the Inhabitants of New-Hampshire . . . to Be taken from under the massachusetts Goverment under his [the king's] own." Some Portsmouth colonists put their signatures or marks on it right then. Carr, Cartwright, and Maverick agreed to present the petition to the king. It was, however, sparse on signatures. Presumably with the royal commissioners' encouragement,

Corbett continued to solicit signatures for the next week or so by gathering people in his home or in the woods.[40]

Corbett's petition campaign seems to have had an anti-clerical bent. As he went about gathering signatures, he reportedly said "that Mr Moodey's prayers were but babblings."[41] For someone who liked formal prayer-book worship, the puritans' spontaneous prayers could easily be seen as long-winded or incoherent, although Moodey, a former Harvard fellow, was probably a capable speaker. More important than differences in homiletic style, however, the petitioners missed high Church of England liturgy and sacraments. The petition included in its list of grievances against the Bay the fact that the selectmen had "denyed us in our publique meeting the Common prayer Sacraments and decent buriall of the dead." It also called the Bay "an usurped power whose laws are derogatory to the laws of England," claiming that a small group of puritan inhabitants oppressively controlled the local government and kept the petitioners "under hard servitude."[42] Corbett managed to secure thirty-two signatures from Portsmouth and Strawberry Bank men.[43] Around the same time, he might have urged Dover inhabitants to start a petition campaign of their own, although there is no evidence this petition materialized.

Corbett also helped organize another petition later in July, this time including inhabitants of Exeter and Hampton. According to this second petition, inhabitants "were much transported with joy and hope of settlement" when they heard Charles II had sent royal commissioners "for the appointing of bounds and government amongst us here." It was their "great griefe," however, that the Bay was "denying that authority which your Majestie gave your Commissioners" and so had "hindered" the royal work. They asked for "Royall protection and government" so that they might have English law and both sacraments, "which they have bin too too long deprived of." They also offered to "dayly pray for the increase of all the earthly honors Untill yow arive at the heavenly kingdom."[44] This petition boasts sixty-one signatures, twenty-nine originals and thirty-two in the same hand, with the "vera copia" attested by Corbett. A few months later, leaders in Exeter and Hampton vowed "that the people of the said tounes had not acted in, or consented unto, the said remonstrance." In other words, Corbett had forged their signatures.[45] There is no way for us to determine now who actually signed the document.

Carr may have helped with this second petition. Recently learning he would not be given a Delaware governorship, he was working hard to find alternate sources of revenue. A similar petition to the king from several justices at Wells, Maine, around the same time (18 July) asks for the king to appoint "Sir Robert Carr Knight to bee & continew as under your Command our Governor." According to Maverick, Carr was the moving force behind this Wells petition.[46] Further evidence that Carr was pursuing the governorship of New Hampshire appears in his letter informing Secretary of State William Morrice that "the people in the Eastern parts were very desirous that I should be their Governour, and would have altered their peticion to the King, but Col Cartwright could not stay." The same packet included a letter from Carr asking Charles II for the governorship of either New Hampshire or Maine, as well as a large tract of land in Narragansett.[47]

While some in Piscataqua signed Corbett's royalist petitions, others considered the form their defiance would take. Richard Cutt, a leading Portsmouth merchant loyal to the Bay, said of Carr, Cartwright, and Maverick that he would have "a daggar putt into theire . . . gutts." When Maverick retorted that he would add Cutt's name to a list of "those which I conceived to rebellious"—a list soon to be presented to the Lord Chancellor—Cutt grudgingly backed off. Likely aware that a scuffle would do more harm than good, the royal commissioners agreed to a settlement by which they would not report on Cutt so long as he agreed to "never molest" the two men who had informed against him, one of whom was the high-ranking recent migrant Henry Greenland, a physician already disfavored due to a conviction for sexual assault.[48] Still others during this same period considered relocating, "seeking how they may remoove themselves & estates from thence as fast as they cann."[49] As we saw in the case of New Haven, for some colonists, the idea of direct Stuart rule was threatening enough to prompt resettlement elsewhere.

The three royal commissioners might have intended to start governing the region by setting up their own court. Dover selectmen worried about this possibility.[50] A Boston marshal arrived with a scathing letter from the Massachusetts Council, however, and possibly a few guards, effectively putting a halt to any possible plans. Bay leaders decried the royal commissioners' "irregular proceedings," seeing themselves as "bound to provide for the peace of His Majesties subjects, against such unreasonable mandates." Back in late May, the royal commissioners had said they would "cease further actings," but now, the Council said, they were clearly doing the opposite. Had they seen the latest royal message (possibly passed along in one of Clarendon's or Nicolls's rebukes of Carr) directing them "in a more orderly method then this that you observe"?[51]

After they read this letter, Carr, Cartwright, and Maverick abandoned all pretense of restraint. They pulled rank, scoffing that the Council's letter was "so full of untruth, & in some places wanting Grammer construction," that they could hardly believe it was authored by Council members. They had left Boston because "it was great reason and high time" to cease "treating in private" with Bay leaders, "who by sound of trumpet denied that authority which the King had over them." The now-notorious trumpet blast could not, however, "enervate the King's commission." The eastern territories did not belong to Massachusetts, despite "all the false and fraudelent expositions of their Charter."[52] They had seen the bound house marker and knew better.

The commissioners next accused the Bay of being "mislead by the spirit of independency." "The King did not," they wrote, "grant away his Soveraigntie over you when he made you a Corporation," or make you the "supream authority" over his colonial subjects. Bay magistrates' eyes had been "darkened" by "ambition and covetousness or something as ill." And, they warned, the king's promises might easily be retracted: "Tis possible that the Charter which you so much idolize may be forfeited," or likely was already "many ways forfeited." What Bay magistrates needed was a royal pardon, a prospect so far-reached as to be almost laughable: it was neither obtainable nor "effectuall to those who deny the King's supremacy." The bottom line was clear. Those who could not accept Charles II as supreme governor of both church and state could not be loyal subjects. Cartwright, Carr, and Maverick understood true religiosity. "Gentlemen," they wrote, "Remember . . . you profess yourselves to be Christians and pretend to be of the best sort. Pray make it appeare that you are so, by your obedience to the Kings authority."[53] Being a Christian meant obeying the king—end of story.

At this point, the royal commissioners finally admitted the elephant in the room, namely the regicide. The well-deserved execution of men who had "made use of the King's authority to oppose His Majesties power, and raised armes and fought against his Majestie and yet pretended the defence & safety of the King," they said, "we think might deterr all from broaching or acting according to such illusive and destructive sophisms." Massachusetts leaders in the 1660s were exactly the type to start another civil war. Trying to prevent the royal commissioners' success in Portsmouth was the kind of action that "give[s] us just grounds to fear that, if you had power, you would try your success the same way" as the parliamentary armies had in the 1640s. These searing words, and the anger behind them, were spoken in the spirit of having nothing left to lose: the royal commissioners had been defeated. They would have to leave Piscataqua as they found it.[54] Yet in Maine they would not be thwarted.

* * *

A contingent of Maine inhabitants were suspicious of the constitutional culture expressed in the Boston trumpet blast, deeming it rebellious or even treasonous. Carr, Cartwright, and Maverick discovered Maine to be a volatile region, flush with a nascent royalist movement propelled in part by local high church conformists. A brief recap of recent Maine events may prove useful. Privy Councillors had backed the proprietary claims of Ferdinando Gorges, who in May 1661 appointed his own local justices to the colony. One of these justices, Robert Jordan, was a Church of England priest, intertwining spiritual and civil authority in ways many puritans found dangerous. When Jordan and other justices tried to collect rents due to Gorges as proprietor (owner of the colony and its land), many inhabitants refused to cooperate, backed by reinforcements from the Bay, which resumed control of the court. (Gorges's justices would, however, still try to issue orders, even imprisoning the Kittery constable.) After a fresh election in 1662, ten of eleven deputies voted to stay under Massachusetts's government rather than Gorges's, at least until the king's will could be made known.[55] Petitions from four Maine towns then asked the Bay for defense against the Gorges justices' "pretended power" and "insulting threats," expressing their desire for "wholesome government, as the greate preservative of civill & religious order."[56] In 1663, Bay leaders also tried unsuccessfully to purchase Gorges's Maine patent.[57]

Amid these uncertainties, compounded by unstable relationships with Abenakis, rumors flew around the colony. Had the Bay's London agents traded "the whole conty of Yorksheire" for Bostonian liberties?[58] A leading royalist who had earlier faced prosecution in the Bay, Jordan supposedly called Governor John Endicott "a Rog[u]e," the rest of Massachusetts "Trators & Rebells aganst the King," and the late John Cotton, who had defended the regicide, a cursed liar. Jordan warned that New England would have to submit to a royalist agenda and high Church of England worship. Far from a tolerationist, he threatened to "hang" rebels "or burne thier houses." Maine inhabitants' complaints led to his arrest and imprisonment, although after promising "to live peaceably" if his conscience allowed, Jordan was quickly released and went right back to work organizing a royalist party.[59]

Maine congregationalist minister Seth Fletcher had also previously faced discipline in the Bay for "unfitnesse," a charge brought by his own congregants. He, too, however, was reinstated and seems to have joined the deputies in opposing the Gorges justices' authority. From the pulpit, he urged prayer for "the Lord to direct them In respect they were under 2 Claymes of Goverment." This acknowledgment of competing claims infuriated Gorges supporter Francis Hooke, Samuel Maverick's son-in-law, who rebuked Fletcher.[60]

Laypeople too expressed strong opinions across Maine—and all over the map politically. George Cleeve supposedly called Charles II "an Athi[e]st, a papest & a damned wretch in hell." Although resenting the Gorges justices, Cleeve was unsure of the Bay's protection—from either Gorges or the Abenaki.[61] A royalist layman, Jeremiah Sheeres, expressed anger at another colonist for "goeing to the Eastward to delude the people & to speake treason against the King." A colonist named Thomas Booth claimed his neighbors, presumably Bay supporters, were "a Company of hypocritical Roges" who "feared neither god nor the king." A "Mis[s] [Sarah?] Mi[t]chell" allowed Bay supporters to use her home as an information hub. "Goody [Susanna?] Greene," angry at a Gorges justice who had harassed and imprisoned a local constable, asked him if he would "carry in a dish of meat to the bay magistrates"? In other words, would he poison them? The justice answered affirmatively: "by god if it were poyzen hee would Carry itt to them."[62] Conflict in Maine escalated as laypeople, mincing no words, traded accusations and insults, all but abandoning the search for consensus.

The arrival of an official letter from Charles II to Maine inhabitants backing Gorges's claim did not resolve these tensions. Some Maine inhabitants, Cartwright complained, especially "church members, & military officers," still "stand out, & will not submit . . . but will adhear to the government" of Massachusetts.[63] Scrambling to compile their legal case, Bellingham and others admitted that previous governors had not seen the northern bound so clearly but nonetheless resolved to fulfill their "Obligation . . . to see the People within Our Patent govern'd according to God."[64] To everyone's surprise, on their arrival in Maine, Carr, Cartwright, and Maverick did not follow through on the king's recent decision backing Gorges but instead overrode both Gorges and the Bay and took the province directly for the crown.[65]

Gathering Kittery inhabitants at the spacious home of Quaker Nicholas Shapleigh, the royal commissioners read their commission aloud. Their listeners, they later claimed, then "generally petitioned us to take them into His Majesties more immediate government."[66] Other records paint a more complex picture, describing the three men trying to persuade their audience of the benefits of submission and claiming that loyalty to the Bay meant "innevitable ruine," because Massachusetts "rebells & traytors" would soon meet royal punishment. The royal commissioners claimed other Maine towns, too, had petitioned for a royal governor, although no such petitions survive. It seems unlikely that Kennebec, Sheepscot, and Pemaquid inhabitants cooperated, given the royal commissioners' later assessment of them as "the worst of men," escaped debtors turned fishermen who "share in their wives as they do in their boats."[67] No doubt some inhabitants disliked both Gorges and the Bay, but it is improbable that a majority preferred a royal governor.

Declaring Maine a royal province was, at least in part, a retaliatory move against Bay leaders who styled themselves, according to the royal commissioners, "the supreame power in these parts . . . derogatory to his Majesties Soveraignty." "It would be of ill consequence" if Maine colonists were "seduced by those . . . who have already by sound of Trumpet denied to submitt themselves unto his Majesties authority," the commissioners argued.[68] Maine was also an ideal royalist base, comparable to Rhode Island. With the Duke of York's claims to New York, as well as to Nantucket and Martha's Vineyard, the royalist territories would encircle the puritan-led colonies. In Maine, the royal commissioners assumed control of the local militia and would soon start training exercises.

Taking over Maine was also a religious cause. Their power, the royal commissioners said, was that of "his sacred Majesty," and "the Worship of god" was "the Cheife end of us, our lives & all our actions." Once God's glory and the king's honor had been "secured," newly appointed royal justices, including Rev. Robert Jordan, should "strenuously" work toward "the peace safety and wellfayr" of Maine inhabitants. While allowing justices to "Continew that worship Which you find," somewhat contradictorily the royal commissioners also commanded, "We must desire that all people may bee Convinced of the necessity of the 2 sacraments & that the sacraments may bee administred to such as are qualifyd for them according to the Church of England."[69] The royal commissioners here moved toward enforcing high Church of England practice in Maine. Maverick might finally have his chance to "see how they like the act of Uniformitie" in New England.[70]

On hearing word of the royal commissioners' actions, Bay magistrates hastily traveled north to counter them. Arriving in early July, they declared the commissioners' orders invalid because they contradicted "his majesties authoritie" as already expressed and upheld in "the constitution, & laws of this

Jurisdiction" of Massachusetts. Their efforts to set up a court on 4 July 1665, however, were thwarted by Carr, Maverick, and a "foot company in armes." We "doe find we are obstructed," the Bay magistrates hotly declared, "& the trained band summond to attend [Carr's] motions." For the time being, Maine continued a royal province, awaiting Charles II's final determination.[71]

Divisions among the royal commissioners deepened as Carr sought power for himself during this same period. In Maverick's account, when Carr found out he was "not to have the government of Delawarr," he began working hard "to be very popular" in Maine, even accepting "Courtesies from such as are not of the roghtest" and encouraging "Inhabitants . . . to petition that he may be Governor over them."[72] Two royalist petitions to the king resulted from these machinations: one from seven of eleven royal justices, and one from an unknown number of Maine inhabitants. The royal justices' petition, dated 18 July 1665, noted the "usurpations of the Masatusetts pouer over us" as well as "the Invalidd defence of our persons & propretys by . . . Gorges & his succeders." The justices then pleaded for Carr "to bee & continew as under your Command our Governor." Apparently, he was already acting as such. This petition was signed in an odd way, from "your distracted & disordered, yett Most Faithfull & loyall subjects."[73]

The second petition to the king from the "Inhabitants of the Province of Mayn In New England" accepted crown control but on terms resonant with the constitutional culture seen elsewhere. It exists as a modified copy with no signatures. The petitioners stated their main concern up front: "wee are much afrayed least wee bee further Intangled by Mr Gorges In our Lands . . . If not deeply oppressed by two high cheefe rents" (quitrents, annual fees to the landlord or proprietor). Like the royal justices, these inhabitants worried mostly about keeping their freehold lands. Although pleading with Charles II to continue Maine as a royal colony, their vision of its government differed from the royal commissioners'. They asked the king to "preserve us our estats, civill lybertys, by settleing sober & pyous persons In Goverment, & the true protestant Religion without <obligation to> ceremonys, as granted to other Collonys which wee doubt not through gods blessing."[74] Their puritan-leaning religious sensibilities and request for a "sober & pyous" governor are significant. Carr later said they would have added his name if Cartwright had delayed a bit.[75] More likely, these colonists lacked confidence in Carr and in his grandiose vision for Maine. They desired a governor solicitous for their interests rather than his own, and someone who would not enforce high church ceremonies.

These royalist-leaning petitions were countered by a declaration signed by twenty-two inhabitants of Falmouth (Casco Bay/Cape Elizabeth) asking to continue under Massachusetts's government. Thanking his "sacred Majestie" for his "fatherlie care," these petitioners said they would "chearfullie submitt" to Gorges's proprietorship if the king willed it but that they far preferred the Bay. Massachusetts leaders, they wrote, "have exceeded others in pietie and sobrietie," and "so God hath blessed them above others." Under the Bay's jurisdiction, religion and justice had flourished in Maine, so much so "that wee have found Gods blessing in our lawfull callings," with more prosperity in one year than in several years under the Gorges government. Their neighbors had tried to push them into signing the earlier royalist petition by "threatning" them—a rare example of coercion at work in a petition campaign—but they hoped the king would not interpret their refusal to sign as "any disloyaltie in us." Finally, they promised to pray that God would pour "upon your Majestie all the blessings heaven and earth can afford, both spirituall, temporall and eternall."[76] These petitions reveal many Maine inhabitants' primary concerns: rent-free lands, accountable leadership, and ceremony-free worship. Despite Carr's lobbying efforts, only the royal justices actually requested him as governor. Everyone else hoped for another option.

Quickly dispatching more officials to the Northeast, the Massachusetts Court asked Carr, Cartwright, and Maverick for a conference regarding their actions concerning "the disturbance of the peace of his majesties good subjects" in the region. Unsurprisingly, they declined.[77] Maverick did, however, come back to Boston in September to "watch their motions."[78] The General Court also decided to enforce Sabbath laws, including in the Northeast, a move that incensed the royal commissioners, who reported this news back to London.[79]

In response to royal justices' concerns about their "Imperious neighbours of the Massachusets," Carr returned to Maine, continuing to organize local militias. In early October 1665, a Kittery-based militia prepared to fire on Massachusetts men "if they came over the River." The Massachusetts contingent, led by Major General John Leverett, decided not to risk an armed confrontation. Retreating to Portsmouth, they probably thought to wait and see if Carr and Maverick would brave a Maine winter (they did not). While standing by in Piscataqua, the Massachusetts group worked to reestablish a functioning, consensual government, gathering inhabitants of each town and asking any who had grievances or concerns to speak freely.[80]

Inhabitants from Portsmouth and Dover then organized petitions to the General Court declaring their loyalty to the Bay and hoping to clear their names from collusion with Carr, Cartwright, and Maverick. Dover's petitioners expressed themselves "well contented with the privileges" of the Massachusetts charter and prayed for the Lord's "presence in the midst of yow." Dover's minister John Reyner signed, and the Exeter minister Samuel Dudley also sent a letter on 10 October trying to clear Exeter of having a "hand . . . directly or indirectly" in Abraham Corbett's earlier royalist petitions.[81] Despite Carr's warning to "forbeare troubling or molesting" local royalists, Massachusetts did prosecute Corbett, not for petitioning but for disturbing the peace and "keeping a house of comon entertainment . . . a seminary of much vice and wickedness."[82] Wisely, Corbett skipped town, although later he was "convicted of a seditious practize."[83] The magistrates and deputies made a strategic decision not to engage Carr or Maverick directly (Cartwright had already departed) regarding the Northeast. Better to wait for a more opportune time, they decided.

* * *

Despite hearing that the king was "unsatisfied" with his "actinge, in these partes," Carr was determined to acquire a colonial estate, if not in Delaware, Piscataqua, or Maine, then in Narragansett.[84] As we saw earlier, it was accepted practice for royal agents to receive gifts and benefits through their service, but Carr took things to an extreme. Nicolls, however, had complicated the landscape in Narragansett, nullifying Carr, Cartwright, and Maverick's order the previous March that had expelled colonial landowners from Narragansett, including Atherton Company proprietors. In this reversal, Nicolls was heeding the royal commission's original instructions, which clearly stated that they should not remove colonists from Narragansett lands. Narragansett sachems Pessicus and Ninigret must have been shocked that their lands so quickly reverted back to the Atherton proprietors and that the royal commissioners' promises had proven so temporary.[85] Carr pressed on, undeterred. In December 1665, he petitioned Secretary of State Morrice "to assist my sonne" in acquiring a patent grant for a large tract in Narragansett that ran from Cowesett to Point Judith.[86]

Securing this land would require several steps. First, he needed to finish his earlier campaign to remove the Shawomets from their nearby lands. Learning that the Shawomet sachem had ignored his earlier order, Carr went personally to Pomham "& caused him to take the moneys ordered, which he seemed unwilling to receive, & depart." Carr still seemed to think that Pomham would have no problem moving within Pessicus's territory, even though Pomham had left that tributary relationship. Carr arranged a meeting between Pomham and Pessicus to resolve the matter, which Pomham declined to attend. Pomham's son Cheesechamut was willing to come, but, Carr said, "I could make no conclusion with him according to that our order, for he was unwilling to submit to Pessicus." Carr thought throwing money at the problem might solve it. Cheesechamut eventually did accept a double payment and promised to leave, but this transaction had no effect on the Shawomets' willingness to give up their lands.[87] The actions of Carr and Pessicus, however, worried Pomham enough that he approached the minister John Eliot, whom he had known since the late 1640s, for help.

Eliot may not have been an avid monarchist but he knew how to appeal to royalist sensibilities. When Pomham informed him of the situation, Eliot wrote directly to Carr, framing a defense of Pomham with reference to the king's best interests. "It is his Majesties pleasure to command us to deale well with the poore Indians," he wrote, "which I hope your owne generous mind, and disposition will incline you to exemplarily to perform." He then took up the Shawomets' case. A people who had "suffered much hard and ill dealing by some English," including "both force and fraud," the Shawomets "are in no wise willing to part with that little which they still hold." Eliot urged Carr to treat the Shawomets in such an honorable way "that your actings may leave upon their hearts an impression of the Royall and beneficent affection of his Majestie towards them" and ended the letter with a prayer.[88] Eliot probably consulted with Governor Richard Bellingham, who was with him when he gave the letter to Pomham and his men.

After spending the coldest months in Providence, Carr returned to Warwick again in late February after hearing that Pomham was still disregarding his order. Some Shawomets gave the royal commissioner Eliot's letter, telling Carr of Bellingham's presence. Carr later mused that this letter, along with "some other actions of theirs, puts it out of question that the Massachusits are as unwilling to let the people in those Southern parts, rest under his Ma[jes]ties Government, as them of the Eastern, in the Province of Maine."[89] Convinced of the Bay's opposition to both the king and himself, Carr dispatched another order to Pomham for the Shawomets' removal. He testily replied to Eliot that the command for "Pumhams removall" was "made upon good grounds" given by "gentlemen and inhabitants of Warwick," including "divers injuries from the said Pumham and his adherents" and their inability to "peaceably injoy and possess that their lawfull possession . . . honestly purchased." As for Warwick settlers' mistreatment of Pomham, the royal commissioners had seen or heard no evidence; in fact, Carr did not even know which men Eliot could be talking about. Those involved were "well satisfied" with the king's "beneficent affections towards the Indians" and would continue to communicate those affections, arranging the new royal province's government without Eliot's direction. Concerned that his recent actions might cause the king or his commission to be "rendered obnoxious to the reproach and contempt of infidels and others," Carr also "require[d]" Eliot to circulate the letter. Although signing it "your loving friend," Carr's words were far from loving. He aimed to put Eliot and his fellow Bay colonists in their place. At the same time, he decided as an afterthought to send Eliot copies of his orders to Pomham, "for your satisfaction," he added, noting that even though the Shawomet sachem still had not relinquished any lands, Carr had "not acted ill towards him."[90]

Soon afterward, the Rhode Island magistrate and long-time mediator Roger Williams joined Pomham's cause. Whether Pomham appealed to him personally is unknown, but Williams had "heard of a late confederacy amongst great numbers of these barbarians to assist Pumham, &c." Rumors of Native American confederacies or pending attacks were common in those days and sometimes served as a diplomatic strategy among sachems. We do know, however, that some kind of protective agreement existed between the Wampanoag sachem Philip Metacom and Pomham. Expressing concern for Carr's own safety, Williams told him that "this is an old ulcerous busines, wherein I have been many yeares engaged." He had tried to negotiate the Shawomets' departure before, "but Pumham would not part with that Neck, on any termes." He confirmed, however, that Pomham was "the ancient possessor of this Lordship" or domain. And he questioned "whether it be just to dispossess him (not only without consent, which fear may extort, but without some satisfying consideration)."[91] Carr had no right to order his removal.

Williams then advised Carr that he would never conclude the matter before Carr "reduced the Massachusets to the obedience of his Majestie, and then these appendants (towed at their stern) will easily (and not before) wind about also." It was Gortonists who wanted the Neck, Williams explained, and they were unpopular with Native Americans as well as with other Warwick inhabitants. Pomham's people understood themselves to be "oppressed, and wronged" both by English and by Narragansetts, and were aware that almost everyone would be "please[d]" if "Mr. Gorton and his friends had been long ere this destroyed." Even if Carr were to "knock out their braines," the Shawomets would not give up their land.[92]

On reading Williams's letter, Carr called for him to come to Warwick. In his later report, Carr dismissed Williams as "an ancient man" who meant no harm but was simply "misinformed as others are by ill affected persons." A not-so-ancient Williams arrived within a few days and, according to Carr, "received satisfaction" and "was very much instrumentall in forwarding Pomham's removall, who with his company are removed." Carr, however, was likely mistaken about Williams's "satisfaction," and definitely mistaken about Pomham's removal. The Shawomets continued on their land, protected, it seems, by both the Bay and Plymouth.[93]

If we fast-forward almost a year, we find Warwick inhabitants still trying to continue Carr's mission to evict Shawomets (and possibly allied Cowesets) from their lands. In early February 1667, the Warwick constable brandished a warrant, signed by Carr, which told the Native families "to depart, And Come noe moor one the town lands, to plant or inhabit." Pomham was present, and he or another Native leader threw the warrant to the ground, declaring "that they would take no notice" of it. Pomham and others then encircled the constable and other Warwick inhabitants. "Threatning" that they might make the colonists carry the warrant right back, some "did behave themselves very ryotusly." The outraged constable then evoked Charles II's authority, charging them "to keep the kings peace, And not to Adhear to Any that did deny to yeeld obedyence thereunto." At this order, the group of Native men "in A Scornfull manner did deryd the kings Athoryty represented in the Constable."[94] For reasons of their own, these Cowesets and Shawomets had joined the movement to defy royal power.

As Pomham discovered, the royal commissioners' interest in Native American land was personal as well as political. Massachusetts men were involved in the Atherton Company, so the sachem was well aware that the Bay colony already supported expansion into nearby territory. His main concern, however, involved protecting the Shawomets' own small, much-reduced piece of ancestral territory. To stay on this land, Pomham made the strategic choice to ally with the Bay, whose leaders had at least supplied him with ammunition. Perhaps he reasoned that Bay magistrates, while far from perfect, were a local, relatively stable force in the region, able to quickly send reinforcements if needed. Pomham's ability to go to John Eliot for help with resisting Carr demonstrates he understood how to mobilize English advocates on his behalf. Weighing long-term as well as short-term realities, Shawomets and allies made a strategic decision to "deryd the kings Athoryty" and declare lines that even royal commissioners could not cross.[95]

Enraged by Bay leaders' interference with their designs, the royal commissioners doubled down on defending their actions, even trying once more to isolate Plymouth from the rest of the puritan-led colonies. Bay leaders supplied Carr, Cartwright, and Maverick with copious information about Gorton's abuses of multiple colonies and Native communities, along with news of his associated curses and heterodox preaching, but the three men continued to defend Gorton and his followers.[96] In March 1666 Cartwright tried for a second quid pro quo with Plymouth, asking Governor Prence to send someone to locate the "branch of Charles his river, from whence the Massachusets measures their 3 mile, southward" (also the northern boundary of the "King's Province" in Narragansett), helping him make the case for the Bay's territorial overreach. If Prence would assist, Cartwright would make it worth his while: "For now the interest of the kings province will make me, & all the other of his Majesties Commissioners, strive to doe you that service, which your own act debard you from asking," to obtain a royal patent. There is no record that Prence took Cartwright up on this second quid pro quo offer.[97] Although the relationship was far from perfect, Plymouth inhabitants shared constitutional and religious sensibilities that bound them closely to the Bay.

After the royal commissioners' visit, the borderlands of Narragansett and Maine saw continued instability. Rhode Islanders would continue to struggle for control of Narragansett against the Bay and against Atherton claimants, who preferred Connecticut's government. The Rhode Island Assembly went so far as to offer one thousand acres of Narragansett territory to Clarendon in September 1666 as it pleaded for this valuable land to remain part of Rhode Island. The region descended into near-lawlessness, with no effective governance over the Anglo-American inhabitants, who would increasingly commit acts of violence against Narragansett and other Native peoples.[98] In Maine, political uncertainty would also make life difficult and heighten tensions with Abenaki leaders. Maine's royal justices complained to Nicolls that their "different considerations are apt to divide our Judgments, if not disunite our affections," leading to "weakned" authority and disrupted peace. In the end, Maine inhabitants would become so impatient in their desire for a more settled government that they would petition the Bay again, and in 1668, Massachusetts leaders would formally reassert jurisdiction.[99]

* * *

There were more royalists in the borderlands, and more difficulty forging consensus. But even among these outlying regions, we can glimpse the pull of a constitutional culture that would resist the crown's tendencies toward arbitrary rule. The question remains whether the royal commissioners' actions in Piscataqua, Maine, and Narragansett were in keeping with the agenda of Charles II and his government or if they emerged out of an idiosyncratic personal agenda of the three men themselves. Hearing of his fellow royal commissioners' actions in these regions, Nicolls wrote with disapproval, "I will not excuse Sir R. Carr's hastiness unseasonably putting Plaistead [Maine] into possession, yet I heare that he received some extraordinary provocations upon the place." To the king, Bay leaders said that Carr, Cartwright, and Maverick had acted wildly outside the bounds of the royal instructions. Clarendon, at least, was not buying this claim. The Earl was furious about the trumpeted shutdown of the court of appeals, and not long after, Charles II formally rewarded and thanked Maverick and Cartwright for their service. Carr would die on arrival in England, so he never found out what the king might have thought of his various escapades.[100] Even so, the Stuart government delayed making a final decision about Maine. The royal commissioners' rashness, especially Carr's, probably did meet with some backroom frowns in London. But their actions did not diverge wildly from the government's overall policies, especially the king's private instructions, which had expressed hope for an eventual high Church of England establishment and for royal control of colonial governorships and militias. Similarly, Clarendon's early plan for the royal commission had designated the Northeast as a royalist base from which to expand the king's authority—a design the commissioners had done their best to uphold.[101]

Despite their protests about the royal commissioners' departure from the king's agenda, Bay leaders overall saw Carr, Cartwright, and Maverick's actions in light of the Cavalier Parliament's suppression of fellow nonconformists in England. The royal commissioners' willingness to use intimidation and force, together with their expressed desire for the establishment of prayerbook ritual, reaffirmed many colonists' fears about arbitrary rule and the loss of civil and religious liberties. Bay leaders' quick organizing and support for resistance in Piscataqua, Maine, and Narragansett also sent a pointed message. As Maverick had warned, the only way to reduce the Bay to obedience would be to use force: economically through seizing estates in England, militarily through frigates stationed in Boston harbor, or personally through ordering—with "force to backe it"—"refractory persons" such as Richard Bellingham, Daniel Gookin, and William Hathorne to face serious consequences in London.[102] Charles II had not yet seized colonial estates or sent more frigates, which in any case were needed to protect the West Indies from the Dutch. He did, however, heed Maverick's advice about calling individual magistrates to account, an order that opened the door to the momentous constitutional struggle of 1666.

CHAPTER 10

Crown

Paths to Divided Sovereignty and Charles II's Response

Sitting in the quiet Town House chamber in the aftermath of the declaration by trumpet, Governor Richard Bellingham and his colleagues steeled themselves for what lay ahead. They knew they had to explain their actions, quickly and effectively. In letters to Lord Chancellor Clarendon, Secretary of State Morrice, and Robert Boyle in late May 1665, they pleaded their case, tackling the appeals issue, boundaries, and self-preservation in the face of what they saw as an overwhelming threat of arbitrary rule. Using deferential, monarchical language, they acknowledged that the king's grace and favor remained contingent on the colonists' dutiful actions, and they expressed an "ardent desire" to demonstrate their "innocency, Loyalty & good affection" to Charles II.[1] But they did not guarantee their allegiance. It, too, remained contingent, resting on the king's willingness to allow them to govern rightly.

Bellingham and his colleagues' courtroom predicament reflected broader conversations taking place across Massachusetts Bay. While the royal commissioners traversed the borderlands, Bay colonists entered into a period of sustained constitutional reflection. Did Charles II, "having a more absolute Soveraignty over his Plantations in Generall then these his Kingdomes at home," also wield "more absolute power" over the colonies, as one seventeenth-century commentator assumed?[2] Colonists' rationales for limits on royal power involved tentative attempts to theorize divided sovereignty. Their discussions culminated in an extraordinary October 1666 in-person debate over the king's power to command Governor Bellingham, magistrate William Hathorne, and others to appear in London to face the consequences of the colony's defiance. In this tense moment, many colonists turned to eclectic sources—ancient, medieval, and contemporary—to defend local authority.

Increasing pressure from the Stuart regime pushed these colonists both to defy the regime and to explain their defiance, thus articulating—and helping solidify—their distinct constitutional culture.

Knowing that Clarendon believed an appeal in "any extraordinary case" advised by the king was entirely consistent with the charter, Bellingham and the others did not try to oppose appeals in general.[3] The king's colonial subjects were not "without hope of redress": decisions of "inferiour Judicatures" (the county courts) could be appealed to "superior" (the General Court). Further, colonial leaders were prepared to give "a faithfull & humble account" for any decision if the king requested it.[4] They were happy to revisit the case of John Porter, that "notorious malefactor" whom the royal commissioners had chosen to protect. In the case of Thomas Deane and the Navigation Acts, however, when Richard Nicolls, George Cartwright, Sir Robert Carr, and Samuel Maverick had asked magistrates and deputies themselves "to appear as Delinquents at the barre," the royal commissioners had not only undermined the colonists' authority but also deprived them of the "native priviledges of Englishmen," such as "sworne judges, knowne lawes & peeres."[5] To submit would, in reality, have meant colony leaders "forfeiting our Allegeance" to the king by "betraying the trust" of good governorship, their obligation under the royal charter.[6] In this framework, true loyalty to the king meant defending their privileges.

The colonists' defense did not stop there. Regarding the royal commissioners' accusations that they had oppressed neighboring colonies by inflating their bounds, Bellingham and his colleagues reminded their opponents that the court had already sent a map and justification. Even Native Americans knew, they argued, that if they desired protection for their boundaries they should go to the Bay, where they might have "recourse from time to time" to the General Court, "for releife from the injurious practices of others." The royal commissioners, however, had "sequestered the lands" and "secured [the] estates" of families "without ever hearing them speake for themselves," violating basic due process.[7]

And such insults had continued. Maverick, the colonists noted, had "liberally vented" invectives and threats, repeatedly declaring Bay colonists "Traytors," their government's authority short-lived, their boundaries in need of a "clip," their patent a "mad peece of work," and the United Colonies a "usurped authority." Perhaps worst of all he had threatened "the dividing of our publike meeting houses for worship" between congregationalists and high church conformists. Facing such threats, Bellingham and his associates argued, colonists had acted for their own protection. Bay leaders could apologize for their "rudeness" or "unskilfulness" of language, and they might have even been "overforward." If they had overreacted, however, "we intreate it maybe imputed to" passion for "liberties which being to us of so high concernment, & purchased by us at so deare a rate, cannot but be deare unto us." Better to "prevent trouble," they thought, than "remoove it" afterward.[8]

They concluded by appealing to the widespread nature of the opinions and convictions they had just stated. The General Court's actions were not "the contrivance of some few," as Morrice's last letter had intimated. Rather, Bellingham maintained, they emerged from long constitutional deliberations among many. With "the cry of the poore," he and his colleagues pleaded, "God knows it is the affliction of our soules to be thus constreined to dissent" from the royal commissioners. They wanted to obey the king's agents. Their inability to do so was not, finally, their own failing. It all came down to self-preservation. Because "self preservation doeth enforce us," they hoped to be "both pittied & pardoned for the same."[9] Like parliamentarians in the 1640s who had argued from natural law that it was "rebellious to nature" for any nation to allow someone to "destroy it without injury," Bay leaders protested the notion that anyone—even a king's representative—could set about destroying their colony without incurring resistance.[10]

* * *

In the days following the May 1665 negotiations, a committee that included leaders from Edward Rawson to Daniel Gookin worked diligently to "Collect & transcribe a true narrative" of those negotiations and to improve or interpret them to the colony's "advantage." They added reports of Carr, Cartwright, and Maverick's actions in the Northeast as they went.[11] Although in some ways isolated from current English debates, colonists had access to a wide spectrum of political theory, including civil war–era treatises on the nature of law and the royal prerogative.[12] These men no doubt read widely and debated vigorously as they prepared their narrative.

On the areas in which the court did not fully obey the king's demands, they argued that their constitutional differences from England lay within the realm of permissible divergence (rather than repugnance). The royal commissioners clearly had violated powers granted in the charter, such as the power to "correct, punish or pardon all offences," to oversee civil and military officers, and to make and execute "wholesome & reasonable" laws not repugnant to England's. Even though the colonists' franchise law seemed to favor poor church members above wealthier inhabitants, still those who designed "the constitution of civil & ecclesiasticall order" were motivated not by "private interest" nor the desire to oppress but rather the "promoting of piety, religion, & honesty, the professed true interest & knoune ends of this plantation."[13] Part of a distinct constitution, the franchise privileged piety over wealth not out of selfishness or some sort of revolutionary scheming but from the colonists' bedrock commitments to equity, godly reform, and the public good.

Here and elsewhere, these colonists began to imagine their "true interest" as distinct from that of England or other English colonies—another tentative yet crucial step toward theorizing divided sovereignty.[14] New Englanders might have "interest in other respects"—legal, economic, and so forth—but their "predominant interest & cause" was reformation, "the great end" of their migration. Compelling and beautiful, this reformation "would dazzle the Eyes of Angels, daunt the Hearts of Devils, ravish and chain fast the Affections of all the Saints."[15] Overwhelmingly valuable, this interest demanded fierce protection, even if doing so conflicted with the interests of other regions or the crown.

If earlier letters alluded to the Magna Carta, this committee took the research a step further, pulling out a copy of that revered document and citing specific statutes. Carr, Cartwright, and Maverick's summary ejection of those with deeds to lands in Narragansett "to the ruine of themselves & families; & that without any complaint legally exhibbited" had violated "the "Magna Charta of England." Colonists, like all the king's "natural subjects," possessed "immunities & priviledges," such as "that no man shall be deseised of his freehold" or be tried without "the lawfull judgment of his peeres, & by the lawe of the land." The royal commissioners had also violated the Magna Carta by insisting on judging in these cases "according to their own discretions." Their denial of a "jury of trialls" was a direct infringement, colonists said, of their ancient liberties.[16]

This committee also continued to defend the United Colonies as both necessary and reasonable. "Scattered at great distance" with "no walled tounes or garrisons of souldiers for their defence," colonists had scrambled to protect themselves by creating "a league of amity & union . . . in case of any unjust & fresh assault." Calling the United Colonies a "usurped authoritie"—as the royal commissioners had done—stood "contrary to the light of reason," which allows those on the same path "to combine for their mutuall help in all things common & just." The four men seemed to have a "speciall designe to disunite the colonies, & so to bring us unto ruine."[17] Although tradition held that only sovereign powers such as kings could form confederations, in this case it was just and reasonable that the colonies could form them as well. Self-preservation required it.

In defending their constitutional arrangement, the committee further elaborated on earlier natural law arguments about self-destruction. They had taken the only safe course between "dashing on the rocke of his majesties just displeasure by neglecting his authority in his commissioners" and "prostituting our lives, liberties, peace, & comfort" unto an entirely unacceptable "arbitrariness," or power unconstrained by law and due process. They had relied on "principles of reason & religion," as well as on "royal warrant" in the charter and the king's own promises to uphold it. In defying the royal commission, they acted "by common consent . . . upon deepe consideration" to avoid having "utterly undonne ourselves & this his majesties colony," whose "watchfull care" had been entrusted to them by both "God and our soveraigne."[18] Staving off an imposed arbitrary power was not rebellion; it was itself loyal governance.

The committee also argued for divided sovereignty based on geography, their "remoteness of place . . . from his royall throane." A long-distance relationship with the king was harder to keep up than one conducted from home. They did not have the ability, they said, "to prostrate ourselves afresh" before the king each time a difficulty arose, or in times of "urgent necessity" to go to the king in person. Unlike subjects in Ireland, Scotland, or England, sending for and receiving an answer could take as much as a year. If they had "yielded to an arbitrary Court of appeales" and wanted to contest its findings, the distance to London would "have prooved a perpetuall & intollerable burden." And any sense of weakness in local authority led to "distracting feares & cares" among English colonists, not to mention "eminent danger from the salvage natives."[19] The demands of geography and safety, they pleaded, required strong local authority.

The supposedly "savage" Native Americans, however, were cited as testimony in the committee's next subject, a defense of the colony's "patent right" to Maine over and against Carr, Cartwright, and Maverick's mid-summer takeover. They listed testimony from Natives about the Merrimack River's course alongside depositions from colonial surveyors appointed in the 1650s. Contrary to "all lawe & custome" that allowed people "quiet possession" of land unless legally dispossessed of it, the royal commissioners had "sought to wrest Yorkshire out of the quiet possessors government" without "sufficient legal warrant" from the king, Gorges, or the Bay. Their actions in Maine to overturn local justices and "to raise the militia of the shire toune against his majesties authority here setled" violated their own royal instructions to settle boundaries by "mutuall agreement," or in the last resort by "pleas of both parties to his royall self." And although Carr, Cartwright, and Maverick had acted "covertly," Maine inhabitants saw quite clearly that they "doe aime more to have other mens just rights for themselves then to be instrumentall to the peace" of "the right ouners thereof."[20] The royal commissioners' actions in Maine against the welfare of the local population and the Bay colony had crossed a line from unconstitutional to potentially criminal.

The committee also included a previously prepared refutation of Samuel Gorton's accusations, highlighting his heterodox beliefs about religion and government and reminding readers of the Gortonists' injuries against both English and Native Americans. They defended the Shawomets' actions, although saying they were no longer involved in maintaining peace in the region, presumably leaving it to Plymouth or Rhode Island. When the sachems Pomham and Sococonoco had in earlier years "importunately solicite[d] our help," Bay leaders had used force against the Gortonists according to charter mandate to repel those who sought harm. Even if the king "observe[d] any circumstantiall error" in the case, they hoped he would "out of his princely grace . . . indulge it" and support the colonists in their "suppression of such insolent & turbulent spirits" as these Gortonists, actions contributing to their larger quest to "peaceably . . . feare God & honor the king."[21]

In all these things the royal commissioners had used the "pretence" of "his majestys authority" to try to overthrow local rule by "threatning the destruction of our constitution." Bay leaders, in contrast, had acted according to "the conscience of our oune integritie . . . being carefull to render unto God the things that are Gods, & to Caesar the things that are Caesars; yea, to all men that which in justice belongs to them." They had "yeilded" as far as their consciences allowed, "without prejudice to religion & his majesties government in these parts."[22] Theirs was a monarchical, conscience-based argument for local constitutional resistance.

* * *

The committee's next letters, written to English sympathizers, shifted to a more biblical idiom that showcased their vulnerability. Bay leaders knew that their London enemies, "with al[l] imaginable mischief & spite," stood ready to echo the royal commissioners' characterization of them as "Rebells & traitors." They felt overwhelmed, they now wrote, "not much unlike Israel at the red sea." And while trusting "their cause to God" above all, they would not neglect any means available to inform friends about "the state of our Affaires (or rather the affaires & case of christ with us)." Carr, Cartwright, Maverick, and Nicolls had done all in their power to "frighten our Confederation from their [duty] to the people from their duty to God his Majestie & this Government established under him." But their fear tactics had fallen short: "blessed be God they doe not attyne much that way." Committee members knew that interceding on the colony's behalf would be a risky venture, "a worke of selfe denyall," and did not want their friends to "expose themselves to hazard in our cause," such as losing their jobs or facing fines and imprisonments. Only "if in a secret & safe way God gives any opportunity," perhaps then someone could intercede, "either by inclining the heart of his Majestie" or prevailing upon anyone close to him "to speake a word in our cause"?[23] Colonists, too, welcomed advice on how to control the flow of information. Should they print a report of the May negotiations, as the royal commissioners had requested, or might it "be Ill construed" or even "accounted a kind of remonstrance"?[24]

These more transparent letters reveal the colonists' keen awareness that the constitutional arguments so convincing at home might seem highly offensive in London. Bay leaders especially hoped for help from Robert Boyle, who sat on the Council for Foreign Plantations. He had previously helped push through a charter for Connecticut and for the New England Company as its governor and a prime defender of the philanthropy's landholdings against royalist claims. Boyle, however, believed an inclusive global Protestant revival would be derailed by any whiff of factionalism, sectarianism, or disloyalty. Bay magistrates probably did not know that Boyle had already concluded "the Massachusites . . . have disrespectfully used the Commissioners" and had decided to limit his advocacy to Connecticut and John Eliot's mission.[25]

Colonists also hoped for help from puritan merchant and New England Company treasurer Henry Ashurst. Like many English nonconformists, however, Ashurst was walking a tightrope. He had a long and close relationship with New England as trading partner since the 1640s and as agent in 1661. As a nonconformist, however, he had been ejected from his councillorship in the City of London under the 1661 Corporation Act. In order to maintain a position from which he could do some good, especially in his quest to fundraise for ejected ministers' families, Ashurst needed to guard his reputation with extreme care.[26] Receiving "a great Bundle of papers" from Massachusetts in late 1666 (probably the final version of the "improved" narrative summarized above), he decided he could not offer direct assistance, telling Boyle, "I shall neither excuse them, nor plead for them." Having established this distance, however, Ashurst did inform Boyle about the packet he had received, asking him if he felt comfortable giving it to Clarendon or Morrice. He also prayed for God to "pouer a forth a spirit of . . . self deniell, & uprightnes" on all, one that would create "amiable subjects. . . . to god & the King." Perhaps out of the political catastrophe for nonconformists in England, a revival of both righteousness and peace might spring forth, although believers such as Ashurst now walked a precarious line, unable to offer New Englanders much if any public support.[27]

Seeking advice closer to home, magistrate John Leverett sent a narrative of the May 1665 events to John Davenport, the revered and well-connected pastor of New Haven. Davenport's response affirmed the Bay leaders' defiance of the royal commission, conflating their resistance with work for Christ's kingdom. A "power of darknes" prevailing in parts of Europe was, Davenport said, working "also, to subvert the kingdom of Christ in these ends of the earth." But hope was not lost. Even though New Englanders' "unthankfulness" and "unfruitfulness" deserved otherwise, "God hath not yet said that this is theire hour in reference to N[ew] E[ngland]."[28] The colonists had done well to defy the royal commissioners, Davenport affirmed, just as they had in the earlier movement to resist Charles I:

> I would hope that the same onely wise God who disappointed the councel of that archprelate in the raigne of the last king (whereby your pattent was once and againe demanded by the said king, and as often refused by your generall court, to be returned to England) would also still appeare, in this juncture, by frustrating the present designe and making it . . . a mere tryall of the country, whether they will stand to their church rights and priviledges or permit them to be invaded and violated. . . . For the Lord is and will be with his people while they are with him.[29]

Davenport compared the Bay colony's situation to that time in the mid-1630s when Charles I and Archbishop William Laud, then head of the Commission for Foreign Plantations, had tried to revoke the charter, and John Winthrop and others had refused to send the document back to London.[30]

Davenport believed the royal commission's failure to influence or disrupt the colony's May 1665 election was a direct act of God in answer to prayer. And he concurred that allowing an "arbitrary" court of appeals would have laid the "ground worke to undermine your whole government" or "plucked downe with your own hands that house which wisdom had built for you and your posterity." Such self-destruction would have violated natural law. Even verbally "publishing" the trumpeted declaration against the court of appeals was "prudent," he approvingly declared, because the colonists had done it "in the kings name," and it was crucial to declare "the courage and resolution of the whole countrey to defend theire charter liberties and priviledges" in that moment. Holding onto a royal charter could not "rationally be accounted an opposing the soveraignty" of the current king because "*id possunt reges quod jure possunt*"—rulers may only do those things they have legal rights to do. Davenport stood with Bay leaders in their decision "not to yeeld up theire right voluntarily, so long as they can hold it, in dependance upon God in Christ, whose interest is in it."[31] Faithfulness to these liberties was faithfulness to God.

The elderly Davenport did not speak of these matters lightly. He had just lost the fight to keep New Haven Colony independent from Connecticut. He had conceded in part to avert further royal interference in New England as a whole. With New Haven now lost, the Bay's perseverance appeared even more important. Davenport recommended that Leverett and others quickly gather up and send their "grievances" to England, including the complaint that the royal commissioners had disrupted Eliot's mission, along with an account of the non-freemen's petitions. On receiving these materials, he hoped, Charles II and Clarendon would "plainly understand that the whole country (for the generality of them) are much aggrieved" and desired to "be freed from those new encroachments."[32] Davenport gave Leverett permission to share his advice with Governor Bellingham, who generally adopted it.

The August 1665 General Court's official letter to the king borrowed from the earlier committee's work, leaning heavily on language of the ancient constitution. Emphasizing their long-standing liberties as Englishmen rather than biblical or apocalyptic tropes was not a sign of secularization, as some have argued, but of knowing their audience.[33] The court asked Charles II to believe that they did indeed have "a just . . . allegiance unto your majestie, according to the charter," but saw no reason to submit "unto that arbitrary, absolute, & unlimited power" the royal commissioners tried to impose, contrary to "the liberties of Englishmen." Although willing to "cleare our innocency" from complaints by English or Indians, look, they said, at the kind of people complaining: in addition to Native Americans, "Quakers, libertines, & malefactors." Bay leaders exonerated Nicolls, a deft political move. Carr, Cartwright, and Maverick, not Nicolls, had "steered a course . . . different from, if not contrary to," the king's instructions. These three had destabilized the colonists' relationship with Native Americans both directly and through undermining the "unity of the English colonyes" and had taken control of Maine towns, "declining to heare our just pleas therein." In conclusion, the court "committ[ed] our cause unto the Lord God, & under him to your royall self"—sort of. For this court also did not neglect securing "meanes" of their own by further investing in military defenses.[34]

In the meantime, colonists in churches, in private homes, and in the body of the General Court continued to fast and pray.[35] To many, subsequent events seemed a providential answer. November 1665 Roxbury church records note that "Colonel Cartwright one of the king's Commissioners, was taken by the Dutch" at sea, "and all his writings against the Countrie, made void." Cartwright captured, along with all his papers detailing the colonists' misdeeds? A supernatural intervention was obvious to John Hull, who excitedly added a postscript to a diary entry on the Boston fasts: two ships, he said, were in harbor. One, Mr. Harrison's, carrying the royal commissioners' letters, had just set sail when "the Country's letters to the king's majesty and to other of our friends, whereby our innocency was to be cleared," arrived. A man took a shallop "with six oars to put those letters aboard, but could not. . . . Harison's ship, we hear since, is taken by the Dutch," along with Cartwright's own.[36] The "Country's letters," however, went safely by the second ship.

Even those who, like Hull, leaned toward compromise rallied behind the General Court's declaration by trumpet and rejoiced at Cartwright's capture. William Hubbard noted the "miscarrying of sundry papers and writings . . . full of complaints against the country of New England, many of which were . . . lost in the vessel by which they were sent." He added to the story a Jonah-like episode where guilty carriers "flung overboard" the anti-New England papers in hopes of calming the waves. Hubbard further noted that Cartwright's Dutch captors put "a gag into his mouth," just as Cartwright had "threatened" to gag "some in New England that pleased him not," a classic providential reversal.[37] Even Bellingham concluded about the "many great providences of these tyme[s]": "the Lord knoweth how to deliver his."[38]

Hearing these comments, Maverick reported to Clarendon that Bellingham had ordered a public thanksgiving day on the news of Cartwright's capture. "Some frivioulous reasons they give for it," Maverick sniffed, "but the maine is, that God hath yet been pleased to lengthen out the injoyment of their liberties."[39] In reality, the thanksgiving day for "the continuance of our peace & liberties hitherto,—in which favour many mercies are conteined" had been planned back in October, before news of Cartwright's misfortune. Maverick may have had information that local churches, in observing the thanksgiving day, had mentioned Cartwright's capture in their prayers.[40] At this point, however, Maverick could only fume.

A bedraggled Cartwright finally stumbled into London around December 1665, and although relieved of his papers, he retained his memory—and garnered an eager audience. His lengthy report demonstrates the extent to which he had internalized the Quakers' and Gortonists' views of the political landscape. Cruelty toward Elizabeth Hooton and Samuel Gorton, kindness to Edward Whalley and William Goffe, and the refusal to allow appeals together proved the colonists' disloyalty to the king. The report glossed over events in Plymouth, Rhode Island, and Connecticut, contrasting their loyalty to the utter sedition of the Bay. It also gave plentiful information about ports, natural resources, and potential fortifications, especially in Rhode Island, Piscataqua, and Maine.[41]

Finally hearing things firsthand, Clarendon bristled. "His Majesty," he said, "will not sett downe by the affronts which he hath received."[42] Clarendon had personally advocated sending the royal commission as a milder policy than the Council of Foreign Plantations' idea to immediately demand agents to renegotiate the charter.[43] He was aware of the royal commissioners' personal failings, especially Carr's land grabs and Maverick's old animosities. Even so, Massachusetts's rejection of appeals went too far.

With Clarendon's guidance, Charles II signed a strong rebuke in April 1666: "Notwithstanding many expressions of great affecion and duty," he wrote, the governors of Massachusetts "in truth . . . believe that His Majestie hath no Jurisdiction over them," as was evidenced by the Bay's denial of the royal commissioners' right to hear appeals.[44] He also made it clear that Abraham Corbett, the organizer of the Piscataqua petition campaign, should be released from prison.[45] The king also ordered that Governor Bellingham and Assistant William Hathorne be sent over as agents, with two or three others (Maverick's suggestion). Hathorne was probably chosen because of the rumor that he had called the royal commissioners' instructions a forgery.[46] The Stuart government wanted to settle the constitutional matter in London, on its own terms, and, Clarendon warned, "if they do not give obedience to it, wee shall give them cause to repent it."[47]

Yet by mid-1666 England itself was in trouble. Colonists took up collections at fast days for London after the previous year's plague. A citywide fire would soon devastate the metropolis. Clarendon's own position was increasingly precarious; he would be impeached the following year.[48] War against the Dutch required an enormous outlay of funds, funds increasingly scare due to an agricultural downturn. In summer 1666, Bay colonists housed several hundred refugees from St. Christopher's Island after it was seized by the Dutch-allied French.[49] Colonial aid, along with Nova Scotia's, was requested to "reduce Canada."[50] At the very same moment the Stuart regime most strongly asserted the royal prerogative, it also stood most in need of its colonies' financial and military assistance.

* * *

While the king's official letter demanding agents somehow did not arrive in the colonies promptly, another document surreptitiously did, an earlier petition from Maverick to the king "stolen out of the Lord Arlington's Office in Whitehall."[51] If New Englanders had any question about Maverick's contempt for them and their project of self-government, they now had undeniable proof. The petition was possibly one from 1663, complaining that royalist New Englanders had for three decades "been debared all Liberty Civill & Ecclesiasticall" and urging Charles II to send someone "to regulate all things there" to prevent violence.[52]

Probably oblivious to the theft of his own writing, Maverick received an unofficial copy of the king's delayed rebuke-filled letter and impatiently decided to present it to the recently reelected Governor Bellingham. Arriving on Bellingham's doorstep early in the morning on 11 August 1666, Maverick was probably relishing the moment of his vindication. The requested agents, including Bellingham, would be expected to renegotiate the charter and faced possible imprisonment if they balked—or perhaps even the terrible fate of Hugh Peter and Henry Vane if they were found treasonous. According to Maverick, the letter that he showed Bellingham "I feare tooke of[f] his stomacke for breakfast."[53]

The governor, however, was not queasy enough to call the Council as Maverick had demanded. With plague, war, and political intrigue causing profound disruptions back in England, time might favor the colony. Bellingham delayed for several weeks before finally allowing Maverick to submit the letter to the Council. But when Maverick presented only a copy without "seale or Direction" (marks of authenticity), some of the magistrates and deputies displayed "agitation," suspecting a scheme. In Bellingham's words, the message was "of very high Concernment to us in <touchinge> our all, wee have in this world."[54] Should they trust a piece of paper backed only by Maverick's word? Rumors began flying: the suspicion that Maverick had forged the letter was "commonly reported about the Countrey" a year later, along with the story that the king, after reading the letter, explained "hee never ordered any such thing to bee sent."[55] The debate over the letter's authenticity and the king's demand for agents would severely challenge the colony's ability to achieve a working internal consensus.

Most Bay colonists had supported the declaration by trumpet that shut down the royal commissioners' court of appeals. The king's 1666 order for agents represented a different constitutional question. It was one thing for a colony to voluntarily send agents but quite another for the king to demand specific people to be sent back to England. At issue was the "distinction between the king's sovereignty and his power to command," a topic also central to constitutional debates in England during the 1640s.[56] Those arguments were available to colonists through pamphlets in libraries such as the Mathers' and through people like John Leverett, who had fought in the civil wars.[57] William Goffe, too, could have told colonists about New Model Army debates over whether "we are bound so absolutely to personal obedience" to a ruler "that if they work to our destruction we may not oppose them."[58]

The demand for agents met a more divided colonial response, including on one side arguments for a more unitary version of sovereignty. What were the limits on a king's power to command? Nearly identical petitions in 1666 from inhabitants of Salem, Newbury, and Ipswich agreed on the answer: very few.[59] This was not the first time North Shore inhabitants had asserted their political will. As we saw earlier, back in 1661, inhabitants from Newbury and Ipswich (along with Sudbury and Boston) had petitioned the General Court to compromise with the king. North Shore colonists had long been a major force in the colony's political debates.[60]

In 1666, the North Shore petitioners found themselves joined by a group of Bostonians, mostly "recently arrived merchants without church affiliation or the franchise." Among these were Thomas Kellond, the regicide-hunter; Richard Wharton, a "confirmed Anglican and royalist"; Thomas Breedon, host to the royal commissioners; and Thomas Deane, who had tried to enforce the Navigation Acts.[61] Moderates like Simon Bradstreet were not involved; he later said "I neither knew nor saw any thing about the petitions."[62] Bradstreet's adult son Samuel was a signer, however, perhaps without telling his father. Council member and Ipswich resident Daniel Denison, who would later use arguments similar to those in the petition, did not sign.

Both freemen and non-freemen, the 1666 petitioners accused the General Court of interpreting the patent "to the divesting of a sovereign prince of his royal power of his natural subjects and liege people." They were grateful for the Bay leaders' "abundant care and pains" in governing and "endeavouring to uphold the liberties" of colonists and would "run any hazard" with them in the colony's defense. But they needed to speak up in this matter so greatly concerning "the honour of God, and the credit of religion," as well as "their own persons and estates." They paraphrased Ecclesiastes 8, an exhortation to obey the king and not "be hasty to go out of his sight." The king was already displeased with them, the petitioners noted, and refusing to send agents might "plunge ourselves into great disfavour and danger."[63]

North Shore clergy similarly emphasized pious obedience to kings in other declarations and writings. In fast day sermons, William Hubbard of Ipswich had called believers to demonstrate faith through patient suffering, finding "victory" only "by the Blood of the lamb." Remember David, who "would not put forth his hand against the Lords anointed," King Saul? Saints would soon win the battle. Therefore, Hubbard urged, "Let us not by unlawful means cast of[f] the yoake" or embrace disobedience.[64] Hubbard did not sign the 1666 royalist petition, perhaps out of respect for his Ipswich colleague Thomas Cobbet, chosen to preach the May election sermon that same year and a likely opponent of sending agents. But Thomas Parker of Newbury and his nephew John Woodbridge did sign.

Ejected from his English parish under the 1662 Act of Uniformity, perhaps Woodbridge thought sending agents might forestall similar legislation from reaching New England's shores.[65] Parker, Presbyterian in his sympathies and an outspoken royalist, had been allowed to preside over an outpost in congregationalist-led New England out of respect for his Cambridge teacher William Ames, and Parker's brilliance at Hebrew, generously doled out to aspiring Harvard students. Parker had penned a dedicatory preface to Charles II for a treatise that defended "the sacrednesse of the persons and authority of Kings against Sacriligious usurpation and King-killing." He had attributed the monarchy's restoration to "the finger of the Almighty," anticipating that God would work through Charles II's reign to enact "not onely the restauration of the Church defaced, but also the rising of Christs Kingdom to a greater height . . . then in former times." He wrote those lines during the first months of the Restoration, when Presbyterians still hoped for inclusion in the Church of England.[66] Even if that hope had now faded somewhat, Parker's version of Christian duty still supported, and in no way undermined, obedience to the king. Other scholars have assumed that merchants Thomas Breedon and Thomas Deane, spurred by Maverick, "instigated" the 1666 petitions, but it is likely that Hubbard, Parker, and Woodbridge were providing theological arguments for an expansive royal prerogative.[67]

Although much of the petitioners' language fell within acceptable frameworks for expressing dissent, they took things a step too far, some colonial leaders would say, when they threatened to write directly to the king "to clear themselves from the least imputation of so scandalous an evil, as the appearance of disaffection or disloyalty."[68] In October 1666, Breedon sent a copy of the Boston petition to Clarendon and declared in his accompanying note that some Bay leaders "have with Oliver joyned." If Cromwell had been buried in New England, Breedon scoffed, these colonists would "rake up his ashes" or even "have raised him from the dead."[69] The court would consider the North Shore petitions, but some members would resent their colonial colleagues for crossing over into threats.

* * *

Opposition also makes its way into a remarkable 1666 royalist manuscript treatise. This document records the constitutional arguments circulating in Massachusetts that year, although its authors clearly took the side of the 1666 loyalist petitions, going even further in their support for crown authority. They understood charter-based claims for the General Court's power to govern and make its own laws. But they embraced the French lawyer Jean Bodin's understanding of a "soveraigne Athority" that could not be shared. A ruler could delegate power to governors or courts and hold them accountable; but the ruler's own sovereign power was absolute, accountable only to God.[70] Neither time nor distance mattered. The English king had never given away his "right of jurisdiction" or "Empire" claimed for him by explorer John Cabot in 1497. Either Massachusetts leaders submitted to Charles II as sovereign, therefore acknowledging his right to hold them accountable, or they did not. And if they did not, they were seditious; and not just the General Court but all the people could be punished.[71]

In this crown-affirming scenario, the colonists could neither modify their government nor interpret the patent, nor could they draw lines the king must not cross. In simple terms, "against a King there is no rising up." Across the continent, reformers such as Bohemians and Huguenots had tried to overstep in times past. But seeking "externall power and dominion" in an attempt to protect the church was "fatall to tymes of reformation, scandalous to Reformers, and a wofull snare," often leading to bloodshed, the authors argued. A powerful God could carry out "his own Cause and glorie in the world without the additional help of man's polecie." Like some early apostles who expected Jesus to rule a secular kingdom, many New Englanders "inordinate[ly] desire after Civile power," these royalist writers went on. But even if the king opposed "true religion," no casuistry could justify "evill that good may come thereoff." Selectively quoting John Calvin and John Owen in addition to scripture, the royalists' arguments were more than Bodinian, they were deeply religious.[72]

Having declared their own preferred position, the treatise authors next turned to articulate the ideas of their opponents, which I am filling out with other sources. In response to royalists' assertion of the king's sole "right of Empire" through Cabot's discovery, some Bay leaders asserted a rather remarkable argument: the colonists' right of dominion came primarily not from king or charter but from Native rulers. When they made their purchase from Native "princes," the colony's founders acquired "not only the soil, but the dominion, the lordship, and sovereignty" of the region. Native leaders' "right to lordship and sovereignty" had, they claimed, already been acknowledged by English kings. Without purchase, before God and men, colonists "had no right or title to what they possessed." Early settlers also obtained a charter and bought out royally issued titles, to be sure; but doing so was simply to "prevent molestation" from competing claimants.[73] Native leaders such as Miantonomo, of course, would have had much to say about the extent, nature, and legitimacy of these "purchases." For these colonists in the mid-1660s, acknowledging Native sovereignty became a way of shoring up the colonists' freeholds and blocking the king from acting as the region's landlord, effectively preventing him from granting large swaths of land to royal favorites. As a colonist exclaimed elsewhere, if the king could just start redispensing colonial territory "it annyhilates pattents."[74] The authors of the 1666 royalist treatise countered that "the Barbarous People that inhabited those deserts" had no "fixed habitations," nor had they "Improved any part thereoff," and so had never wielded sovereignty or true possession over the region.[75] These assumptions differed markedly from the high rhetoric concerning Native Americans in the king's instructions to the royal commissioners.

Wrestling further with the constitutional implications of geography, some Bay leaders delved into "the nature of civil subjection" itself, arguing that subjects in faraway places had a different relationship to the English government than did people in England. Subjection, Bay leaders said, could take two forms: "necessary and voluntary." Necessary civil subjection derived from "actual residence within any government" rather than from birth and incurred "an obligation to submit to the laws and authority" of that place. Subjects could remove to another place so long as they did not weaken the state; on removal necessary subjection "ceased." They then might enter into a "new kind of subjection" that was voluntary. The Bay colonists' charter was a "mutual compact" that established the terms of their voluntary subjection, "to which they were held, and from which they would never depart."[76] In their geographical remove, colonists therefore were exempt even from the king's demand for their presence: "there can be noe lawfull summons to call them to Answer in England." Distance necessitated a different kind of subjecthood. Royalist-leaning colonists did not buy this argument: the duties of subjects were the same "be they naturall subjects by descent or necisary subjects by force of Armes . . . or voluntary subjects by consent . . . iff any please themselves with such a distribution it comes all to one pass." "Privileges" granted by patent might "dignifye" an individual, they argued, "yet they make not a new kind of subject." The idea that faraway colonists could refuse appeals or demands for agents was simply ludicrous: "It would puzle all the logicians lawyers and divines in Europe to find under what tropick to place such kind of subjects as will allow none to have jurisdiction over them."[77] Neither the charter nor geography divested Charles II of absolute sovereignty.

At issue, as well, was the reach of parliament. Did colonists have to submit to its laws "at soe great a distance?" Drawing on the work of the jurist Sir Edward Coke from the late 1620s, Bay leaders insisted "the common law is included within the four seas" and did not reach American shores.[78] The General Court in the 1640s had argued similarly: "our Allegeance bindes us not to the Lawes of England, any longer then while we live in England."[79] In 1666, colonists claimed charter-based "liberty to make lawes of their own"; because they were "not sending Burgesses to the Parliament of England," they were exempt from parliament's laws. In response, the colonial royalists said that point might hold if Massachusetts was a "distinct kingdome or Government," but it was not. The royalists wavered, however, on the reach of parliament—this issue was not so clear. But whether under parliament's laws or their local court's laws, colonists should still submit to the king's "Jurisdiction," which was absolute; of that they remained certain. Any dispute would thus be settled according to "sence and reason," meaning the law of England and judges authorized by "the fountain of Justice," namely the king. Charles II could either send delegates (like the royal commissioners) or call for the "personall appearance of some in behalfe of the supposed offendors" (like Bellingham and Hathorne).[80] These arguments, provoked in part by the king's demand for agents, engaged some of the most fundamental constitutional questions of the seventeenth century.

* * *

The Massachusetts Council now faced a weighty decision, both theologically and politically, as its members put forth arguments for and against sending the requested agents to England. As Clarendon had said earlier, he could not imagine a colony having "the Courage to refuse" the king's demand for "any Person . . . Though it were the Governor himselfe."[81] Could refusing a king's direct command ever be right? The Council spent time in prayer before deliberating.

Six prominent ministers, including Boston's John Wilson and Cambridge's Jonathan Mitchell, helped the Council "call God to guide them what to do."[82] One of the six exhorted the group to put all their trust in the Lord rather than putting "any confidence in man." Although they were now "poor and afflicted," the Lord "hath many wayes to save his people." How many? "He hath 1000 wayes," the sermon's refrain. If God "could turne the heart of Saul to David can he turn the heart of the K[ing] to u[s]? The answer: h[e] hath many wayes let there be decree[s] [sent] forth. God can alter such a decre[e]." Fearing God rather than men, they should cleave not to earthly powers but rather to godly worship. Echoing the language of recent election day sermons, the preacher linked New England's glory or cause with godly institutions, and divine presence with political safety. The ministers held their regular lecture in Boston the following day, then returned to the

Town House to participate in the General Court's intense debate "concerning the duty we owe to his majesty."[83]

Prior to the debate the loyalist petitions were formally "exhibited," although it seems the magistrates were already aware of them. Thomas Danforth recorded the towns and number of signatures with no comment in his notebook. He did, however, jot down some of the debate in detail. This significant act of preservation marks the first time since 1637, with the possible exception of the 1666 royalist treatise, that a magistrate had recorded divisions within the colony's leadership. Ipswich minister Thomas Cobbet also wrote an account of the meeting, no longer extant.[84] Later nineteenth-century historians would pore over the debate at length, finding it a dramatic contest between European and American politics, one that America would ultimately win at the Revolution.[85] It does not diminish the debate's significance, however, to see it first within its seventeenth-century context rather than pushing forward to the 1770s. The debate brought colonists squarely into the most pressing constitutional issue of their time: the limits of royal prerogative and the reach of law.

As strong voices emerged on both sides, the contest quickly heated up. Up to this point the court had maintained a working, if fragile, consensus. But now deep division threatened. Bellingham started by asking whether "the king's offence taken against us . . . may come to a legal issue," meaning, could Charles II legally demand agents and hold them accountable? Simon Bradstreet answered first, speaking from his recent experience as the colony's agent in London. He acknowledged that the colony had its own laws; they were not under the jurisdiction of English courts. Even so, the king's "prerogative gives him power to command our appearance, which before God and men we are to obey." The king could demand that any subject board a ship for England. Stopping short of the 1666 royalist treatise, Bradstreet acknowledged "legal process in a course of law reach us not in an ordinary course." But a king's direct command was different from run-of-the-mill governance issues. The Christian and legal duty was obvious: send the agents. Ipswich's Daniel Denison concurred, arguing that "ordinary process" of law did not reach them, but the "king's commands" did. Holding a Cambridge degree and formidable legal talents, Denison had led the colony's 1658 effort to revise and consolidate its law code. On agents, Denison now added two arguments also present in the 1666 royalist treatise: first, that the king's sovereignty reached to "Calais, Dunkirk" (English-controlled territories on the coast of France), so geography must not be regarded as any limit; second, colonists possessed legal rights in English courts, and these privileges of subjecthood, in turn, implied duties of obedience.[86]

Francis Willoughby offered the first counterargument. His political experience was notable: after helping build the colony's government in the 1640s, he had spent the 1650s as a commissioner of Cromwell's navy, serving briefly in parliament before remigrating post-Restoration.[87] Willoughby now took up Denison's examples of Calais and Dunkirk, pointing out that they had never "been governed by [royal] commission." The king's sovereignty might reach far, but not so far as to contravene local government. If it did, "how easily may the king in one year undo all that he [God] hath done"? "We must," Willoughby continued, "consider God's displeasure as [well as] the king's, the interest of ourselves and God's things, as [well as] his majesty's prerogative." Like some in the New Model Army two decades earlier, Willoughby wanted to allow the "hand of God" to directly oppose a king's will. Preserving God-given liberties, civil and ecclesiastical, eclipsed the king's demands. And "if the king may send for me now, and another to-morrow," Willoughby reflected, "we are a miserable people."[88]

In his response, Denison quickly rehearsed the traditional monarchical formulation that "Prerogative is as necessary as law, and is for the good of the whole." It was a truism of English political thought that violating royal prerogative could plunge the realm into chaos. Denison did not approve of Charles II's actions; like William Hubbard in his fast day sermon and the authors of the 1666 royalist treatise, he knew weak or impious kings were "apt to miscarry." Even abuses of power, however, did not entitle colonists to deny the king's right.[89] That remained sacrosanct.

Next William Hathorne, whose presence (along with Bellingham's) the king had specifically demanded, took on Denison by noting that more than one theory of kingship existed. "This age hath brought forth many treatises about prerogative." There would be no going back to the simpler days before the civil wars. Some royalists, including Laudian theologians, had argued in the 1640s that kings were above ordinary law or at least had veto power. Many puritans, on the other hand, and parliamentarians more broadly, maintained that kings must rule according to law and could be held accountable. Hathorne sided with the latter: "prerogative is not above law, but limited by it." The elderly Ipswich merchant Samuel Symonds here chimed in, voicing his disagreement by comparing the colony's situation to that of English corporations, protected by law but with certain privileges granted (or withheld) by the king. Symonds's opinion was not a popular one.[90]

The Council returned to its pressing issue: should agents be sent to England? Bellingham and Hathorne had not been legally summoned, nor had

Charles II issued a specific accusation against them. But the two men had been ordered to come by a legitimate monarch. Further, the king had significant leverage in his ability to confiscate the English estates of colonial families. Council members, even those on opposite sides of the spectrum, sought some sort of balanced response to the royal challenge. Those members who leaned farthest toward compromise still held back from supporting the 1666 royalist treatise that defended the royal commissioners' court of appeals, which would function "to stop justice." But they did believe the king could hear complaints and require answers to those complaints. The General Court's "absolute power to determine" justice within the colony "must not abate the king's prerogative." In a related manner, even those Council members most willing to defy the king knew they had to submit in some way, by either sending agents or some other symbolic demonstration of loyalty. No one desired a free state or republic but rather a favorable constitutional balance between colony and crown.[91]

Ministers weighed in on both sides. Some, probably including John Wilson, thought Bellingham and Hathorne should go and "obey for conscience sake," drawing on Romans 13:5. Others such as Jonathan Mitchell, who had preached against compromise since the early 1660s, opposed this view, arguing "that if two might be sent for, ten might." Advancing a very limited view of the royal prerogative, Mitchell said, "the civil magistrate was the minister of God for the good of the people, and so far as his commands tended to their good, they ought to obey." For him the issue was simple: "none would say it was for the good of the colony to send away their rulers."[92] These and other arguments against sending agents finally prevailed. In September 1666, the Massachusetts Council voted to defy the king's command.

* * *

No agents sailed to London. The magistrates would tell the king that their written report contained all the information they had to offer. "The ablest persons among us," they said, could not "declare our cause more fully."[93] The breakdown of consensus, however, had consequences. Bradstreet asked his dissent to be recorded, stating, "I fear we take not a right course for our safety." After thinking on the matter for a few days, Denison also registered his dissent and went a step further, asking for notice of his opinion to "be sent to Secretary Morrice" in London.[94] Bradstreet's and Denison's statements marked the inability of the court and ministry to achieve a working consensus. Very few of these puritan leaders were fond of the Stuart regime, but some understood safety to rest in obeying the king even if he abused his authority, and others thought the safest option was to hold their ground.

They did generally agree, however, that they needed to offer some conciliatory gesture. Their refusal to send agents must be accompanied by some compensatory sign of loyalty. One option was to contribute troops for the second Anglo-Dutch war. After a dinner consultation with Thomas Temple, however, John Winthrop and Bay leaders agreed jointly that it was "not feasible" for Massachusetts and Connecticut soldiers to help fight the Dutch-allied French on New York's border.[95] Massachusetts did, however, make a substantial commitment of supplies for the war effort, first sending masts from timber felled in New England's forests. The masts constituted "tribute payment," a ceremonial gesture of "honor and respect" that simultaneously communicated an expectation: leave us alone.[96] With a keen sense of ceremony, the magistrates asked royal navy commissioner John Taylor, along with the English timber magnate William Warren, to give the masts to the king "as a testimony of loyalty & affection from the country."[97] The Royal Navy was desperate for these long, straight trunks from old-growth forests no longer readily found in England. That the masts were a substitute for agents was obvious. But the ship's captain, John Pierce, made it literal, naming "the one Governor Bellingham, the other major Hawthorne."[98]

Agreeing to send masts was easier than financing their voyage; at more than one hundred feet long and three feet in diameter, the masts required a very large ship. The September 1666 General Court debated whether to levy an immediate rate (a tax on inhabitants) or borrow from local merchants, knowing that lenders felt skittish regarding a possible *quo warranto*, under which the colony might default on loans. Would a direct rate "provoke and raise a tumult" among colonial inhabitants? Queried informally about loans, some compromise-leaning merchants said they would finance the masts only if agents accompanied them. Danforth observed, "no orderly debate can be had to know the mind of the Court. . . . some fearing these actings will precipitate our ruin, and others apprehending that to act further, will necessitate our ruin."[99] Pressures from both merchants and populace made consensus elusive.

Thus stymied, the General Court formed a mast-finance committee, including Danforth, to resolve the problem. "Here is man's weakness and extremity," Danforth subsequently reflected. "What a favour will it be, if it may be God's opportunity." God had reversed dark circumstances before, and he might do so again. His prayer was "That it may be so, for mercy to us and ours, the Lord grant."[100] Another member of the mast-finance committee, the wealthy recent migrant Humphrey Davie, might have guaranteed the loan himself. Although the "particular persons" financing the effort remained private, the credit appeared. The October court ordered an additional shipload of masts and empowered an enlarged finance committee to raise even more capital "for the good of the country . . . in order to the continuance of our precious liberties without interruption, through the blessing of the Lord smiling upon our endeavours." They also authorized London friends to borrow and spend an additional thousand pounds.[101] As Winthrop in Connecticut had learned much earlier, advancing the colonial constitutional effort required a great outlay of capital.

Still convinced of the court's error, Boston selectmen John Hull, Hezekiah Usher, and Joshua Scottow made a last-ditch effort to send agents. Prominent merchants and church members, they were the kind of people who normally stepped in to help the colony in a financial pinch. A few years before, all three had helped finance the colony's last agents, Norton and Bradstreet.[102] Now they petitioned privately, in a language of intense shared piety, for submission to the king's command. They sent up "moanes to God," longing to satisfy their duty to the Lord, their "Allegiance & Honour to our Sovereigne the King," and their "Fidelity & love to this our Commonalty" or commonwealth.[103] Hull was personally furious about the royal commissioners' actions: how could "strangers," without the colonists' consent or divine mandate, think they could "seek the subversion of our civil and ecclesiastical politics," he asked, intervening in ways that "will ruin the constitution of the country"?[104] Along with Usher and Scottow, he wanted the General Court to continue its "zeale unto & Interest in all the aforesaid liberties & priviledges granted by his Majesties Charter." But—and this was quite a conditional clause—the colony needed all their "solemne protestacions of the sincerity of our loyalty" to "manifestly appeare to be reall." If agents were withheld this time, the three men feared, the king might not provide colonists with another opportunity to plead their case.[105] The court considered this petition but was unmoved.

It is important to observe the extent to which the court accepted or disapproved of dissent within its own orbit. Having risked the king's ire to protect their liberty of self-government, how much liberty of expression could the court now allow on its own shores? Bradstreet's and Denison's statements of dissent were respected, and no objection was made to Hull, Scottow, and Usher's petition. But the deputies thought the 1666 royalist petitions from

Boston, Ipswich, Newbury, and Salem had gone too far. In examining these petitions, they took on a role traditionally held by the House of Commons, drawing a line between acceptable and unacceptable expression of grievances.[106]

How exactly they drew that line tells us something about the constitutional culture under formation within these debates. The deputies' first concern was that the petitions "have a tendancy to divide the Court & the Country." It is easy to pass over this language as reactionary, but colonial leadership had recently found consensus difficult, and, as historians have demonstrated for Providence Island and Lygonia, factionalism was no small contributor to a colony's success or failure.[107] The 1666 loyalist petitions also used the language of "dangerous mistakes" committed by "persons inclinyng to disloyall principles," implying the General Court itself was untrustworthy. The main problem, however, was the petitioners' "Threatening the Court . . . to make their addresse to the kinge, & declare to the world against the Court." No other post-Restoration petitioners except Samuel Gorton and some Quakers had threatened to go over the court's head to London. In the deputies' estimation, the petitioners "herein . . . professe themselves to be enemyes, and underminers of the Government here established by his majestyes royall charter." The deputies asked the magistrates to consider whether the petitioners had not violated the charter, the Bible, and the laws of the colony by using such language, although if any were to "acknowledge their error," they should be treated with "moderation."[108]

The magistrates agreed to bring in the leaders of the petition campaign for questioning. Almost all cooperated and "freely . . . professed" that their intention was "not in the le[a]st to reflect against the Court," claiming a "reall and unfained desire that the Charter libertyes should Continue." The deputies were satisfied, not only discharging these men but excluding the entire matter from the formal court record and communicating goodwill toward the remaining petition signers.[109] John Appleton, however, refused to answer the deputies' questions, only submitting a combative letter. He had forged close ties with the royal commissioners, even hosting them on their expedition to Piscataqua and Maine.[110] His response, which he (mistakenly) expected other petitioners to sign, claimed that he was actually calling the October 1664 resistance petitions' authors "dangerouse" and "disloyall," not the court. And, because his own co-petitioners acted according to the "publique good & Intrest" in the hopes of "preventing" danger, it was impossible for their words or potential London complaints to be construed as harmful.[111] The court was not impressed. Threats were unacceptable, as was refusing to answer the deputies' questions. It seems that Appleton alone was verbally censured before the court. No further action followed. Overall, the court members upheld the right to petition, if done respectfully and within a local arena.[112]

Perhaps the most succinct and vivid expression of New England's constitutional culture—monarchical, pious, and defiant—came just after the vote against sending agents. William Hathorne and Thomas Danforth, under the joint anagram "Nadhorth," wrote a letter directly to Secretary of State Morrice.[113] While they claimed their letter was produced without "authority or advise" from others, they must have had Bellingham's approval. Far from disliking "monarchicall power," they wrote, colonists "highly honour and esteem" it. After migrating, they had sadly lost "the benefit of those priviledges in the Parliament of England," but the sacrifice was worth it because they had gained "the free passage of the gospell, far dearer to them then all their other comforts whither naturall or civill." They launched the colonies with the encouragement of a charter that allowed "absolute power of ruling & governing." With enormous pain and cost, they had successfully created "some small beginnings of a common weale." They now wanted nothing more than to "stand among the rest of His Majesties dominions . . . as the shrub among the Cedars, growing upon their own root." To accept arbitrary, non-elected leaders would destroy what they had built. For "if the wall of civill government be pulled down, the wild boar will soon destroy the Lords vineyard . . . it is impossible . . . to keep the waters of the Sanctuary when that Venice-glass which holds them is broken in pieces." The king should know, Hathorne and Danforth continued, that "the body of the people have a higher esteem of their liberties, sacred and civill, then of their lives," and that these same people, undaunted, "are resolved to bury their estates & liberties in the same grave." Not enacted by a mere few, the "obstruction" of the royal commissioners marked the will of the people. But if the king confirmed their liberties, he would have "no subjects more faithful."[114]

* * *

Nicolls, the other royal commissioners, and their sympathizers had decided that the Bay colony's position was incompatible with the king's interest. They condemned the General Court's decision about agents in biblical language, hoping to provoke shame. The king did not want "sacrifice," he wanted "obedience," they said.[115] Wondering how the colonists could "fly higher in contempt of His Majestis Authority," and expressing disdain for their "false Sophistry," Nicolls pondered the severity of potential consequences. The use of force was tempting but might further radicalize the populace. A "Temporary Embargo" on Boston might be more effective; it would divide the colonists, and soon those "well affected" to the Stuart regime would "give up the Ringleaders" of the resistance.[116] It would not hurt the economy of New York, where he still served as acting governor, either. Maverick and Carr urged Clarendon to "procure some speedy order . . . for the quelling of the rebellious," which might include "seisinge on their estate where ever found," "prohibitinge them all trade," and "the keeping of a small frigott or two" in Boston harbor.[117]

After sending the masts, colonists waited prayerfully for the king's response, celebrating both a day of thanksgiving and a fast day. They gave thanks that the Dutch had not yet invaded, that some harvest had come in despite mildew and drought, and that their "civil & spirittual liberties" still continued. Then they fasted—for the war, the London plague, the "low estate" of professing Christians everywhere, and "in particular, that the Lord would yet continue our precious liberties & injoyments, civil & spirituall . . . [and] blesse all good meanes to those ends," including "the fleet of ships lately gonne" carrying masts and letters to the Stuart government and English friends.[118]

When the masts finally arrived, carefully lashed to a massive vessel, the Privy Council received them with surprising warmth. The situation for England was grim, with Scottish Covenanters rebelling on top of the Anglo-Dutch war. The nobility was not cooperating with the king in raising troops because he had not fully recompensed them for previous efforts. Samuel Pepys wrote of the "very good newes" of the masts' arrival, calling them "a blessing mighty unexpected, and without which, if for nothing else, we must have failed the next year."[119] In the meantime, colonists had also sent provisions for the relief of the Royal Navy in the West Indies, also gratefully received.[120] The king acknowledged both presents—the masts and the provisions—as "expressions of your Loyall Sincere affection unto us. . . . exceeding acceptable." Their contributions to the Royal Navy, he wrote, "doth continue good inclination & purposes in us towards you which we have allwayes had as towards all other our Loyall subjects."[121] The colonists' constitutional arguments might have been more convincing in Boston than in London, but their tribute spoke loudly enough. Their political gamble was, for the moment, a success. In Bodin's theoretical formulation, sovereignty might be indivisible. But in Restoration Massachusetts, the king's ability to command had run up against a sturdy constitutional culture.

CHAPTER 11

Impressions

Constitutional Legacies

Hearing from Richard Nicolls about events in the Bay, Governor William Berkeley of Virginia, who associated New England with "that Accursed Cromwell," wrote mockingly, "For our Bretheren I shal confidently say that as long as his Majestie suffers the government to be in their hands there wil never be wanting seditious men to nourish discontents and upbrayde the least defects and escapes in Government."[1] Berkeley's association of puritanism with vigilance about government overreach may not have been too far off. Not interested in being upbraided, the high church governor instituted measures paralleling English legislation, excluding nonconformists from Virginia offices and banishing ministers lacking episcopal ordination who persisted in preaching.[2] A brief look at Virginia and other Atlantic colonies will help us understand the larger story of the crown's Restoration-era policies and New Englanders' dramatic resistance to royal governor Edmund Andros in the 1680s.

Despite Berkeley's dislike for frequent elections, long sermons, "free schooles," and a free press—the latter two, in his view, nurtured "disobedience . . . and libells against the best Government"—as a constitutional royalist he too would grow alarmed by the Stuart monarchy's vision of empire.[3] After Berkeley's 1660 reinstatement to the governorship, he worked to maintain his colony's status as a semi-autonomous commonwealth, rather than merely an extension of the English state. Drawing on older traditions of Christian humanism, Berkeley urged Charles II to perform his true monarchical duties, prioritizing Virginia's godly flourishing, rather than seeing it only as a source of commercial income. Alarmed by Charles II's drift toward absolutism and his Hobbesian advisors' denial of reciprocal obligations between kings and colonies, Virginians too reminded Charles II of their unshakeable loyalty, and of the risks they and their forebears had undertaken, urging him to keep his promises.[4]

Further, after Charles II started granting large chunks of Virginia's land and revenues to royal favorites or creditors, in 1675 Virginia leaders would attempt to negotiate a charter codifying their liberties and privileges.[5] They argued for taxation only by consent, citing the example of other colonies such as "New England." When London officials noted those northerners' lack of obedience, Virginia's agents protested that, unlike New Englanders, who had "imagine[d] great felicity in their form of government, civil and ecclesiastical, under which they are trained up to disobedience to the crown and church of England," Virginians liked having a crown-appointed governor and close royal ties. Even so, they hoped their loyalty might be rewarded with expanded "liberties and privileges."[6] In part because of Bacon's Rebellion, an armed uprising of colonists against Berkeley's government in 1676, the desired charter never materialized. Instead, Virginia received royal commissioners, whom Berkeley found insulting and irritating when they "undermined his authority and issued orders."[7]

New York, too, would try for a charter. After the Duke of York finally instructed its royal governor to allow a general assembly in 1683, the assembly at its first meeting passed a "Charter of Libertyes and priviledges." The Duke initially signed this charter but then, once he became king, declined to confirm it.[8] Expansion of local liberties was not so easy to come by.

Over time, colonial leaders realized that Charles II cared less about the older colonies than he did about his investments in the Royal African Company (created 1660, rechartered 1663) and the slave trade. Having acquired Tangier and Bombay through marriage to the Portuguese Catherine de Braganza, his interest also turned to controlling the seas from the Caribbean to Ceylon. Not content with pressuring Dutch rivals through the Navigation Acts, he attacked Dutch forts in West Africa in an attempt to draw more of the slave trade under English control, provoking a war in the process. And rather than giving up Jamaica, recently conquered under Cromwell's Western Design, he kept that territory, instructing Jamaica's governor "to roote the dutch out of all places in the West Indies."[9] One of Charles II's few exemptions from the Navigation Acts allowed Jamaica and Barbados slave traders access to Spanish buyers. His royal governor in Jamaica, Thomas Modyford, implemented economic policies that promoted the importation of enslaved Africans and gave planters an additional thirty acres per person.

Social divisions among different populations within the Caribbean made it difficult for locals to push back against increasingly autocratic royal governors, who generally preferred their own interests and the crown's.[10]

When England stabilized following the Anglo-Dutch wars, Charles II's government renewed its program of imperial consolidation. In both England and the colonies, he siphoned power from localities, detaching subjects from "local customs, privileges, and liberties."[11] In New England, local institutions came under more severe threat during Charles II's later reign; it became more apparent than ever that the constitutional culture formed through the crisis of the early Restoration was not the province of an elite strata of puritan intellectuals but rather popular and widespread. By the 1680s, the colonies needed the constitutional culture they had forged in the 1660s for their very survival.

Prodded by Robert Mason and Ferdinando Gorges—who still claimed New Hampshire and Maine for their own—the newly reconstituted Committee for Trade and Plantations (or Lords of Trade) now turned again to New England. In 1676, Edward Randolph, a cousin to Mason and an ambitious royal official, arrived in Boston to demand agents and to investigate the colonists' loyalty. The past appeared to be repeating itself.

Randolph did not step onto colonial shores at the optimal moment. Colonists and Native Americans were embroiled in the devastating conflict known as King Philip's or Metacom's war. Randolph seemed clueless that the earlier royal commission might have itself destabilized Anglo-Native relations, either by attempts at diplomacy with various sachems that undermined their relationships to the United Colonies or by their takeover of New Netherland, which undercut the wampum economy and deprived Native groups of more stable Dutch alliances. Randolph must have been aware that Bay leaders had declined to request military aid from London, a decision rooted at least in part in the royal commissioners' erosion of trust a decade earlier.[12] When the governor John Leverett had informed Whitehall of the war, the king's immediate concern was that the "hostilityes" might be a "generall Conspiracy" that would infect his other dominions. By contrast, during Bacon's Rebellion, the crown sent 1,200 soldiers to Virginia.[13]

Randolph's complaints, however, focused on New Englanders' disloyalty. He observed that they only enforced local laws, which still included some "most derogatory and contradictory" to England's, the people counting it "a betraying of the liberties of their commonwealth" if pressured to observe English law or royal commands. He noted the mint and ongoing violations of the Navigation Acts, and he accused colonists of sheltering any who "fly to them for succour from tyranny or oppression." Here he gave the example of "Whalley and Goffe and other traytors." Citing Leverett's role "in the late rebellion, under the usurper Oliver Cromwell," Randolph argued, as had the royal commissioners in 1665, that truly loyal colonists "groan[ed] under the yoake" of Leverett's government and yearned "in dayle hopes" for a royal governor. The association between puritans and regicide had not faded; instead, royalists such as Randolph increasingly deemed nonconformists incapable of true loyalty.[14] Randolph's report would lay the groundwork for another attempt to vacate the charter.

To the king's 1676 demand for agents, the General Court this time found a compromise. On the advice of local ministers and friends in England, they sent William Stoughton and Peter Bulkeley "in way of information," giving them very little authority but sending them along with a special "tribute" of codfish, cranberries, and cornmeal. They also passed a law enforcing the Navigation Acts. At first the Lords of Trade were conciliatory, but over time they became frustrated with the agents' lack of powers, the colony's ongoing violations of sovereignty, and the surprising news that Massachusetts had finally bought out Gorges in Maine. They recommended a *quo warranto* against the charter, a prelude to installing a royal governor, and they sent the agents home. In England and Scotland, the fictitious conspiracy that became known as the Popish Plot would soon divert everyone's attention. But the king did appoint Randolph to be New England's customs collector, with the job of prosecuting illegal trade. Charles II also took advantage of New England's weakness to turn New Hampshire into a royal colony.[15]

Colonists, still reeling in the aftermath of war, wondered what God was doing. Eighteen ministers proposed a Reforming Synod in 1679, asking what evils had led to such divine judgments, and how might their sins be reformed? The early 1680 return of Randolph, an unelected royal official once again sent to hold court in their midst, exacerbated their concerns. When Randolph struggled to find housing in Boston, like the earlier royal commissioners he made alliances with Quakers, who provided hospitality. His attempts to seize and prosecute violators of the Navigation Acts were most often acquitted by local juries, a perceived injustice that he diligently reported, along with many others, to London. Finally, in late 1680, the king demanded new agents—and real ones this time, that is, representatives empowered to negotiate the charter.[16]

The new constitutional contest had now begun in earnest. The General Court assembled quickly. Although in the previous session they had declined to ask the ministers for advice, this time they did. Too much was at stake. The ministers counseled sending agents, but without any powers allowing for "yeilding <up> or weakning this Government as by Patent Established." Echoing a logic forged in the 1660s, the ministers argued, "It is our Undoubted duty to abide by what Rights & Priviledges the Lord our God . . . hath bestowed upon us, & what Ever the Event may be, the Lord forbid that wee Should be any way active in parting with them."[17] Their civil liberties were a gift, and forfeiting them would be a betrayal of that gift.

Even this advice felt too much like compromise for some. Thomas Danforth, now deputy governor, opposed sending agents at all, saying the ministers' position "tended to cutt off some of the Countryes liberties."[18] He and Daniel Gookin now led the push against any move that might jeopardize civil and religious liberties. Gookin prepared an extensive but little-studied argument against sending agents that illustrates how strongly the constitutional culture of the 1660s informed that of the 1680s.

If he had to choose between sending men to England every time someone who "delights in giveing us trouble" brought up a case and receiving another set of royal commissioners, Gookin said he would choose the latter (although he preferred neither). In his memory, the royal commissioners had attempted "to try all cases civil criminal & military according to discretion . . . Anno 1664: 1665 But then God was pleased to influence his people with such a degre[e] of virtue & courage" to hold fast to their charter liberties, despite these royal pressures. And "God of his grace & goodnes . . . incline[d] his ma[jes]ties Royall hart . . . not to give us further trouble" for the next fifteen years.[19] The strategies of the 1660s had worked once; they could work again, he argued.

Gookin next picked up the civil gloss on Christian liberty that appeared in the 1664–1665 petition campaign, combining it with an appeal to the law of nature for self-preservation, English common law, and local consensus. He had learned most of these constitutional arguments from Cambridge-area sermons in the 1660s and from the process of defying the royal commissioners. In the 1660s, he remembered, God led the colonists "firmely to Adhere unto our charter & the Lawes and liberties therby established." Their actions were a form of "selfe preservation," which "is a moral duty & not only Reason & Religion but nature, doth teach us this." Their efforts to protect local institutions were also pious: “if this Gove[r]nment of ours bee of Ch[ris]ts establishing & gift & a fruit of his purchase <as I judge it is:> wil it not bee a morall evel for us to bee Active in parting with it”? Gookin thought the constitutional mobilizing of the 1660s was effective, and “surely our God is the same; yesterday & today & for ever; and our king is [the] same, inclin[i]ng to favor the Right[e]ous caus of his poore inocent & loyal Subjects.” He urged the colony’s leaders in 1681 to both honor the king and adhere to the charter, in “faith & prair,” expecting that “God will appere for us, in mercy, & make a good Isue.” These steps were consistent with “our liberties as Englishmen” in the Magna Carta and with a long-standing local government with which most colonists were still “wel contented.”[20]

Gookin knew that some might object to withholding agents as blatant disobedience of the king, and therefore as a violation of the biblical fifth commandment to honor fathers and mothers. In his reasoning, however, when superiors required “unlawful things,” Christians should respond by saying, the “Holy Ghost tels us our duty,” echoing Acts 4, when the apostles said to their respective rulers, “Whether it be right in the sight of God, to obey you rather than God, judge ye.” For Gookin, certain forms of obedience, when “Considered in their tendencies; & circumstances; & Comixture with religion,” were neither moral nor lawful: it was better to “Runne the Hazard of Suffering” than to “destroy our selves in our greatest Concernes.” Here, too, his language echoed that of the 1660s. New Englanders were not disloyal, he insisted; they wanted to and were willing to obey the king. But at stake was the “weale or woe of thousands of the Lords poore people . . . that for the testimony of Jesus transplanted themselves . . . here purchasing that right of the nat[i]ves” and “with great laubor & suffe[r]ings . . . have possessed & left to their posterity those inheritances.” For Gookin, as for other leaders of the earlier resistance movement, sovereignty was based in actual territorial purchases from sovereign Native leaders and in the long ensuing labor of clearing fields and building towns, as well as in the royal charter. Both bases had merit, in his view. Further, their charter government was a gift from God, purchased by Christ. In the 1680s, as in the 1660s, Gookin said, colonists should not willingly part with their local constitutional arrangement.[21] His arguments must have had a receptive audience: General Court members, although initially selecting agents, seem to have changed their minds, reporting to a member of the Privy Council that they could not find anyone willing to go.

As they contemplated sending agents and fended off Randolph’s incursions, colonists grimly sought news of the king’s decision to dissolve parliament in 1681, as well as the *quo warranto* against Bermuda, which would fail on procedural errors in 1682. With even more concern, they followed crown pressure on the corporations of Worcester and London, as local Tory factions solicited *quo warrantos* to purge nonconformists from town leadership. One charge against London was its petition opposing the 1681 dissolution of parliament. Colonists knew that the very "nature of corporations" was at stake in this latest debate: whether they could be controlled or even destroyed by the king, whether their leaders could be punished, and whether sovereignty lay "as a single power located in the monarchy or a power divided between national and local jurisdictions." One colonist, reflecting on news of Londoners being "forc'd to part with their Libertyes," wondered "what shall wee poor shrubs expect, when the stately cedars crack!" London and Worcester's corporate charters would end up surviving but would have to stipulate the king's "complete power to remove any corporation member at any time." If the colony sent agents and the charter was similarly altered, would the king try to purge their General Court?[22]

The Bay finally sent two agents, Joseph Dudley and John Richards, in 1682, funded as usual on credit from merchants such as John Hull. The General Court, however, followed the ministers' advice in not giving them real power to negotiate. The Lords of Trade then pressured the colony on this point, threatening a *quo warranto* if they did not give the agents authority to revise the charter. The court held another rousing debate, backing down on letting Randolph enforce the Navigation Acts but forbidding the agents from negotiating alterations to their civil or religious constitution as granted in the charter.[23]

As the *quo warranto* hung over them in 1683, New England magistrates and deputies again wrestled with the issue of "yielding or denying appeals." Like Gookin, they went back to the events of the 1660s. The 1661 study of the patent was readily available, so colonists could say firmly, "By our Pattent we have full and absolute power to rule and governe, pardon and punish, etc." Their previous arguments against appeals provided a resource for asserting confidently that "allways hitherto we have judged ourselves free from appeales." Either their General Court had real authority "or else appeals ly in all cases, which will make the Government here to be a meer cypher." As was "the case in 1664," the magistrates decided that allowing appeals would mean "every pragmatick person will refuse to submit to the judgment of our courts, hoping for relief in England, or by some commissioners here, to which our Government must be subordinate."[24] Appeals meant a loss of meaningful self-government; as such, they could not be permitted.

Colonists also organized a petition campaign in 1683, drawing on their experience from 1664–1665. Hearing that "Evill persons" had drafted a letter to falsely accuse Massachusetts leaders and had "labour[ed] to gaine Subscriptions from Sundry malcontents," the deputies designed a counterpetition. On 15 March, people gathered "in their several towns" to hear the deputies' statement. The organizers had instructed that only after those sixteen and older "fully understand the contents" should they decide to "put their hands" to it. Sent from freemen and non-freemen, this new multitown resistance petition countered the misinformation campaign by those of "ill will . . . not freinds to our constitution and order." The colony's enemies might say inhabitants were groaning under the present government, but in reality it "hath been abundantly satisfactory to us." The king's continuation of their "liberties and privileges which they hold in such high esteeme" under charter government would "knit and binde the hearts" of his subjects to him more than any other measure. New Hampshire's new royal governor Edward Cranfield, spying on these goings-on in Boston, disdainfully reported that the wealthiest colonists refused to sign, so that desperate town leaders had to appeal to "servant Boyes." More likely, as in the petition campaigns of the 1660s, people across the social spectrum participated from the beginning.[25]

Far from winning over the Stuart government, this petition became part of its ammunition as it moved to *quo warranto* in June 1683. The case against the colony, summarized by Randolph, included causing "inhabitants to signe a Mutinous addresse to his majestie altho' the best persons of estates in the Colony have refused."[26] Also problematic were the colonists' laws, taxation, oaths, courts, trade, and mint. Still hoping the colony might voluntarily submit, Charles II sent a declaration alongside the *quo warranto* stating that if they yielded up the charter, he would make sure they benefited. Trying to divide the colonists, he warned that colony leaders who did not submit would personally have to pay for their legal defense, whereas any colonists who submitted would be freed from any attempted "rates, Levyes and contributions" toward the *quo warranto* case.[27]

A position paper circulating in the General Court as they discussed this declaration further shows the extent to which the constitutional culture forged by New Englanders in the 1660s now empowered their opposition in the 1680s. To consent to "alterations . . . which will be destructive to the interest of . . . Christ's kingdom in that colony, cannot be done without . . . great offense to the majesty of heaven," this paper declared. Briefly evoking the *quo warranto* crisis of 1634–1638, the authors focused on the events of "the year 1664" when the crown tried "to impose commissioners upon the government of the Massachusetts, they did not submit to them." Clearly, the Lord was with "these worthy predecessors, in their being firm and faithful in asserting and standing by their civil and religious liberties." Colonists today should stand fast as well, not giving in to "fear and diffidence." The General Court should also keep in mind the will of the people: to give up the charter "without the consent of the body of the people, ought not to be," and "the generality of the freemen and church members throughout New England will never consent hereunto." Both the "laws of righteousness and equity" and natural law were on their side. And again, self-preservation held sway: "Men may not destroy their political any more than their natural lives."[28] The General Court did not submit the charter.

Their decision seemed confirmed by what court members soon observed of direct royal governance in New Hampshire. Governor Edward Cranfield had at first seemed conciliatory to local inhabitants, but he quickly became convinced that the people of New Hampshire were part of a puritan antimonarchical conspiracy. He dissolved their assembly and tried to exact high taxes and quitrents on their land. When these colonists increasingly refused to cooperate, Cranfield tried to force them to observe a fast day for the regicide on 30 January 1684 and eventually revived the campaign to impose high Church of England ritual on the region by force, believing congregational worship was, at its core, seditious.[29] The Stuart government did not support Cranfield's attempt to impose high church practice and eject puritan ministers. But the frustrated governor took matters into his own hands, demanding that clergy open up sacraments to everyone, according to the Book of Common Prayer rite. Portsmouth's Joshua Moodey refused, saying "I durst not, could not, should not, do it."[30] Cranfield forbade him to preach and ordered his arrest. With Randolph's cooperation, Moodey was sentenced to prison.[31] Moodey defiantly told friends to "provide against the day when these things should be overhauled"—meaning, to anticipate God overturning power structures—and he prayed with a martyr's confidence "that the cause of Christ will gain by my sufferings."[32] New Hampshire inhabitants were primed for resistance. When Cranfield sent revenue collectors to the area, local women warned them off with threats of "hot spits and scalding water."[33] On his release from prison, Moodey was rewarded by Bostonians with the pulpit of their most prominent church, which he used to preach coded messages "to resist the imposition of royal authority."[34]

Back in London, the *quo warranto* against the Massachusetts charter was dismissed because it had been delivered too late and expired, but the king's lawyers found another mechanism, *scire fascias*, and vacated the charter anyway, not even giving colonists time for a defense. On 23 October 1684, the charter was effectively destroyed. Charles II's death the following year would delay some of the effects of this monumental change, but colonists still had to face the long-feared reality: they were no longer a self-governing colony. They were not alone in this dramatic reversal of fortunes. The crown was working to limit local autonomy across the colonies in an effort to "make the King great and extend his real Empire" in North America.[35] By 1686, other colonies—including Connecticut, Rhode Island, and East and West Jersey—had found their charters under similar pressure from the new king, James II, the Duke of York. These colonies, along with the never-chartered Plymouth and the royal colonies of New Hampshire and eventually New York, became the consolidated Dominion of New England.

Their experience of royal governance under the Dominion did not change most New Englanders' view of the Stuart regime. When Dudley and Randolph arrived to set up a new government by council, with no elected assembly, the Massachusetts General Court adjourned without giving assent.[36] The Dominion's royal governor, Edmund Andros, arriving from New York in late 1686, fulfilled many of the colonists' worst fears, working to systematically dismantle local institutions. In addition to extracting heavy taxes and appointing high church royalist outsiders to rule, he insisted that the General Court had no power to grant land to towns, effectively invalidating grants made from towns to families (how land had generally been distributed) and requiring fees for revalidation. Having petitioned the king to recall the *quo warranto*, Connecticut's General Court would not surrender its charter, delaying and evading until Andros came personally to Hartford to attempt its seizure. The colony's charter oak legend dates from this time: Joseph Wadsworth supposedly extinguished the lights during a meeting of the General Court with Andros, whisking the document away to the hollow of an oak tree. Andros responded by simply taking over, appointing a few Connecticut leaders to his council and swearing in new judges, one of whom was the royalist-leaning clergyman Gershom Bulkeley. Connecticut leaders' petition to the king brought them no reprieve, but still they did not surrender the charter.[37]

In the Bay, it is not surprising that the three men who led the resistance against Andros—Daniel Gookin, Thomas Danforth, and Increase Mather—

had all actively opposed the royal commission back in the 1660s. By now they were seasoned hands at this kind of situation. Others such as Simon Bradstreet who had advocated compromise in the 1660s came to join their ranks, seeing the logic of constitutional, even forceful, resistance in the present situation. Above all, both elites and ordinary people now had access to a cogent, fully articulated constitutional culture, including language for criticizing arbitrary rule and evaluating the consequences of each expansion of royal prerogative, thanks to the contributions made in the early Restoration period. The hard-fought lessons learned during those years now helped the colonies navigate this new constitutional crisis. New Englanders were not the only ones to resist James II's consolidating agenda—revolts occurred across the colonies. Yet, it is true that "most accounts of the Glorious Revolution in America neglect . . . the distinctively unified quality of Boston's rebellion within the larger British Atlantic world."[38] In a remarkable act of violent resistance in spring 1689, Bay colonists would imprison Andros, overthrowing his regime. The constitutional mobilizing of the 1660s paved the way for the 1689 revolt in New England, a sustained, organized, largely consensual rebellion.

Some such as Edward Rawson who had generally advocated compromise in the 1660s now turned to resistance in the 1680s. Their arguments for concessions had largely been in service of preventing a wholesale takeover; now that the worst was happening, however, they readily joined the opposition. Even John Appleton, who had spearheaded the 1666 royalist petition campaign, even refusing to answer deputies' questions in court, now, along with the minister John Wise, led Ipswich citizens in refusing to assist in taxation that "doth infringt their Liberty, as free born English Subjects," because these fees had not been voted on by a representative assembly. Wise summed up his fellow citizens' position: "we had a good God, and a good King, and should do well to stand for our Priviledges." When arrested and tried, they pleaded charter liberties, common law, and the Magna Carta, as others had done before.[39] Rawson would further argue, in line with the ideas about voluntary subjection expressed in 1665–1666, that in the "Original Contract" between the king and the "first Planters," the king had promised that "if they at their own cost and charge would subdue a Wilderness, and enlarge his Dominions, they and their Posterity after them should enjoy such Priviledges as are in their Charters expressed," including taxation only by consent. "What Englishmen in their right Wits," he asked, would have risked their lives "if all the reward they shall have for their cost and adventures" was deprivation of

"English Liberties"?[40] Rawson would help lead the 1689 revolt against Andros. Those few colonists who sided with the Dominion's royal governor had either financial or direct personal ties to the Dominion's continuance.

The ranks of those choosing self-preservation over submission continued to swell. Salem minister John Higginson, who had generally advocated limited compromise in the 1660s (although reminding colonists of appropriate grounds for resistance), now personally debated Governor Andros in March 1689 on the question, "Whether all the Lands in New-England were not the Kings?" In line with Calvin's two-kingdom theory (recently disregarded by Bulkeley), Higginson at first tried to avoid the debate as a "State matter" rather than a ministerial one. When Andros pressed, however, Higginson agreed to give scriptural and rational, if not legal, counsel. He built on arguments that had circulated in 1664–1666. The lands, he said, had for sixty-plus years belonged to "the Kings Subjects," if previously unoccupied by right of the Book of Genesis's command to fill and subdue the earth, and if occupied "by a right of purchase from the Indians, who . . . had possession of the Land before the English came hither." With some fluency in an Algonquian dialect, Higginson had participated in some of these purchases as an interpreter. Andros replied that the charter was conditional, its terms were "not performed," and that therefore the lands had reverted to the king. His attorney general concurred, "vilifying the Indian Title, saying, They were Brutes"; and another royalist present argued, "Where-ever an Englishman sets his foot, all that he hath is the Kings." Higginson refused to back down. "The King had no right to the Lands of America before the English came hither," he said, and "therefore he could give no right to them." Andros finally threw up his hands, exclaiming in frustration, "either you are Subjects or you are Rebels."[41]

For eighty-seven-year-old John Gibson and eighty-six-year-old George Willis, Andros's exasperated outburst must have evoked memories of the royal commissioners' similar words two decades before. Both Gibson and Willis had signed the 1664 Cambridge petition protesting royal infringement, Willis with only a mark.[42] In 1688, they signed another petition, this one to the king on behalf of Cambridge inhabitants protesting Andros's actions. In this later petition, they first rehearsed constitutional arguments, claiming their right had been purchased from Native peoples, confirmed by royal charter, and "quietly possessed for near sixty years." Then they "cast our selves, and distressed Condition of our Wives and Children; at Your Majesty's feet," concluding "with the Saying of Queen Esther, If we Perish; we Perish."[43] Their arguments, their experience of petitioning, their use of Esther, and their refusal to give up all hearken back to the constitutional culture forged in the 1660s.

Amid these heated debates, colonists resisted in other ways as well, through various forms of clandestine communication, hiding correspondence, and avoiding royal censors—all tactics that they had developed in the 1660s. In addition, they would not always read the king's letters publicly when instructed to do so, refusing to relinquish control over the flow of information.[44] And when Andros "took all imaginable care to keep us ignorant of the News," these colonists, drawing on recent experience, worked hard to stay informed, keeping abreast of developments in England, Scotland, Ireland, and other colonies however they could manage.[45]

The unrest of the late 1680s, however, also involved newer elements. A heightened fear of Native attack unnerved many colonists. It was amplified by anxiety about a Catholic scheme behind frontier violence and behind James II's policies. The final capture of Andros was not a slow, deliberate legal process but an armed revolt. Hearing rumors of English corporations' resistance and William and Mary's arrival in England to oust James II, around five thousand colonial men converged on Boston in impromptu militias.[46] Ministers and magistrates might not have initially wanted to become involved, but they led this revolt nonetheless. Later accounts said that "the ancient magistrates and elders" had discouraged the militias, wanting to await "orders from England," but when the people started to act, they felt "compelled to assist with their presence and councells for the prevention of bloodshed." New Englanders had again found consensus on constitutional resistance, the people "universally crying up their charter priviledges."[47] Inspired by reports of William and Mary's coup, colonists wasted no time imprisoning their absolutist-leaning royal governor Andros.

Magistrates such as Thomas Danforth vigorously justified the revolt in language forged in the early Restoration. He explained that the defense of the charter was for "the felicity of this part of God's church." And, like Gookin, he argued that "Nature hath taught us selfe preservation: God commands it, as being the rule of charity towards our neighbour." Their resistance was not, however, anti-monarchical. Danforth pleaded, "We have alwayes endeavoured to approve ourselves loyall to the crown."[48] Other leaders concurred, noting that although "all our Concerns both Civil and Sacred have suffered by the Arbitrary Oppressions of Unreasonable Men," what remained notable about New Englanders was their "Patience": "for though our foul-mouth'd enemies have treated us a rebellious, because we are a religious people," in reality "if we had not been Religious, we had long since been what they would, if they durst, have called Rebellious."[49] Piety had informed their patience. Rawson told New England's accusers to go read Justin Martyr and Tertullian, and "see if Pagans did not accuse Christian[s] of Old . . . with the same Crimes." But the new king and queen could, in reality, "have no subjects more cordially and zealously devoted" than the colonists, who knew, Rawson said, "that the Scripture speaks of a lawful and good Rebellion, as well as of that which is unlawful."[50] Declaring flatly that "we have not so much Resisted the Ordinance of God, as we have Resisted an intolerable Violation of His Ordinance," colonists in the 1689 revolt eloquently and forcefully drew on a well-developed constitutional culture.[51] They were well prepared for the crisis this time around.

* * *

But not everything went according to their hopes. Massachusetts did end up losing its 1629 charter. In 1691, with great reluctance, Bay colonists had to accept a new one, and with it a royally appointed governor. Under this new charter, Plymouth was absorbed into Massachusetts. Ironically, Connecticut and Rhode Island, which before 1660 were charterless, in the long run maintained the most autonomy. Most colonists saw the new, firmly Protestant monarchs, William and Mary, as divinely sent to rescue England from the tyrannical Stuarts. Yet the contest for liberties continued unabated. Even with godly rulers, there remained an intractable transatlantic conflict between those "Eleutherians" who embraced spiritual and temporal liberty and those ceremony-mongering "Idumaeans" who believed kings "are above the Law and have an Absolute Authority" and so are "Irresistible."[52] Repeated efforts by the Stuarts to regain the throne—at least eight attempts were made between 1708 and 1759—kept memories of earlier constitutional battles alive, as did colonial high Church of England parishioners' efforts to hold fast days on the anniversary of the regicide.[53] A repertoire of hard-earned constitutional tropes and experiences remained available to colonists whenever a royal governor tried to push for expanded prerogatives.

Whether it was Jeremiah Dummer's defense against a parliamentary effort to undermine charter governments in the 1720s or newspaper letters protesting the Stamp Act in 1765, colonists drew liberally from the arguments and events of the 1660s as a basis for their constitutional mobilizing.[54] Excerpts from Restoration-era sermons on New England's interest—including

Jonathan Mitchell's 1662 *The Great End and Interest of New-England* and John Higginson's 1663 *The Cause of God and His People in New-England*—were reprinted in 1722 and again in 1774 as resources for fending off arbitrary rule.[55] Thomas Hutchinson, later royal governor of Massachusetts, did the most to make the constitutional debates of the 1660s readily available through his 1764 *History of the Colony of Massachuset's-Bay.* This volume included full texts of crucial statements, such as the General Court's 1664 letter to Charles II protesting the royal commission, that rapidly found their way into sermons and newspapers.[56] During the 1772 Gaspee Affair, when Rhode Islanders torched a British ship and Admiralty commissioners arrived to investigate, colonists marshalled the 1665 rejection of the royal commissioners' court of appeal.[57] In 1773, as the Massachusetts legislature debated the reach of England's authority, they gathered evidence from colonists' defiance in 1665.[58] The deep-seated constitutional culture forged in the 1660s persisted to mobilize the defense of local liberties against any power that seemed arbitrary.[59]

In the decades leading up to the American Revolution, the practice of voting in church meetings, as well as town and provincial elections, nurtured bedrock convictions about consent as crucial to a given leader's legitimacy and about the essential role of accountability in healthy institutions.[60] While Tories tended to despise assembling, petitioning, and forming committees as deplorable forms of "disorder," most people in New England insisted they "had a clear Right to instruct their Representatives" on any matter they deemed important and "to propose, and unite in such constitutional Measures as they shall judge necessary or proper, to obtain Redress."[61] Preachers frequently regaled congregations with stories of earlier generations who had resisted arbitrary rule and sacrificed much to gain both liberty of the ordinances and civil liberty, stories that were also passed down from grandparents to grandchildren. Election sermons said governors were supposed to rule for the common good, that liberties were gifts worthy of personal sacrifice, that men and women should emulate the public-spiritedness of Esther rather than the cursed passivity of the people of Meroz.[62]

Tropes regarding liberty and resistance circulated widely in the provincial Northeast. But the region was not monolithic. Baptists such as Isaac Backus took the language of Christian liberty and turned it against Congregationalists, as did—in more complicated ways—Native Americans and Africans, free and enslaved. Church of England conformists gained a strong foothold in the region with the Dominion of New England and continued to honor Charles I as martyr-king. Over the long eighteenth century, Church of England theologians and others tried to reconcile versions of divine right monarchy with contractual theories of government. There were moments when Stuart reputations enjoyed a revival among elites, especially those whose land claims rested on Stuart grants.[63] Yet the ranks of New Englanders who advocated divine right monarchy remained a tiny minority. A strong regional constitutional culture was difficult to uproot. It was continuously nurtured in the rich soil of town meetings, petition campaigns, sermons, and fast days. There was good reason that Massachusetts emerged as "the epicenter of the resistance" to infringements on colonial rights in the era of the American Revolution. Although later giving way to more generic natural law arguments, positions more conducive to cross-colony unity, there should be no doubt that a local, puritan-rooted "critique of monarchy and misrule" helped launch the movement to resist parliamentary overreach in the 1760s.[64]

Petitions, fast days, committees, ministerial advice, biblical commentary, claims based on labor and purchase—all of these endured in the decades moving forward, even as they continuously evolved and adapted to rapid commercial and intellectual change. The royalist accusation that puritans could never be truly loyal subjects also endured, from Clarendon's strategy to divide the United Colonies to Thomas Gage's efforts to isolate Massachusetts. Puritanism was not the only cultural influence at play, but it was a particularly deep source for a popular regional constitutionalism drawing on biblical, parliamentary, legal, and theological ideals. The crisis of the 1660s forged a distinct, widespread, and long-influential constitutional culture.

CONCLUSION

As they awaited the king's reaction to receiving timber masts rather than human agents, Bay colonists gathering for the May 1667 election heard a message that resonated deeply with their recent actions. The General Court chose for its election day preacher Jonathan Mitchell, who had authored the 1664 letter asking for the withdrawal of the royal commission—and who had been preaching constitutional defiance all along. Mitchell pulled out all the stops in his sermon. "The Publick good," not obedience to a ruler, he said, was the magistrates' only "Compass" or "Touch-stone." The supremacy of the people's welfare constituted a rational and historical principle as well as a biblical one: "Salus Populi Suprema Lex . . . is engraven on the Forehead of the Law and Light of Nature."[1] For Mitchell, no "Law, or Custome, or Consideration whatsoever" could bind governors to make decisions against the people's good: "If it be indeed contrary or destructive to the welfare of the people . . . it is impossible they should be bound in Conscience to do it." And if colonists held to "Righteous" and "Rational" ways, God would not disappoint: "never was God known to fail a people, that in a way of well-doing did trust themselves with him."[2] Colonists should stay the course, stick to "safe and sober Principles and Practices," and "avoid Irregular Extremes," finding, like the biblical Nehemiah, "discreet" and "prudent" ways to adhere to their liberties and garner support.[3]

Mitchell also gathered threads from other recent election sermons to urge colonists to courage rather than fear. Quoting Richard Mather's 1660 line, "the Sun shines not upon an happier people then we are in regard of this mercy" of thirty (now thirty-seven) years of godly rulers, Mitchell prayed, "the Lord . . . give us to know and prize the things of our peace, and faithfully to adhere thereunto." And he drew on Thomas Cobbet's plea from his 1666 election sermon on 2 Chronicles 15:2 to "faithfully keep with God, and then he will be with you." In the vein of John Winthrop's early "Modell of Christian Charity," Mitchell reminded colonists that "the eyes of the whole

Christian World are upon you," not to admire and emulate but rather to "observe how you Manage and Discharge this Trust now at such a time."[4] Like God's people of old, "Adversaries, and Ill-willers . . . did labour to affright them with the Accusation of Rebellion," urging "Fear, fear, fear; a discouraging Heart and Hand-weakning carnal fear." But God said, "Be strong, and of a good courage, fear not when in Gods way and work."[5] Weaving a biblical, humanist, and rational tradition of constitutionalism, Mitchell affirmed many colonists' deepest convictions. The conscience of faithful men, guided by reason, natural law, and scripture, would lead them to the path of ongoing reform.

* * *

In the 1660s, New Englanders were, in an unprecedented way, pressed to define their rationale for governance, their relationship to the crown, and their rights and liberties. Inevitably, their response to this challenge drew on familiar religious, historical, and philosophical sources. Nonetheless, their arguments and actions were both more sustained and, as they responded to the onslaught of criticism, more logical, sophisticated, and firmly embraced than ever before. This constitutional culture, forged to protect local institutions from the threat of arbitrary rule, remained intact through succeeding decades. It was deployed to great effect when in the 1680s royal governor Edmund Andros tried to fulfill some of the earlier royal commissioners' highest aspirations. Endowed with great affective power, New Englanders' commitments to civil and ecclesiastical liberties continued to be passed on and warmly cherished, still revered as traditional wisdom in the imperial crisis of the 1760s.

We should not lose sight of the fact that the colonists who mobilized for constitutional resistance in the 1660s were monarchists. The idea that they would be associated with rebels, or worse, regicides, was abhorrent to these men and women, as it would have been to most English people across the Atlantic. They valued their economic and cultural connections to the empire. But the span of an ocean did make a difference. Faraway from the crown's observing eye, New Englanders had created their local institutions, continuing the reforms of the sixteenth and early seventeenth centuries with little interference from entrenched landed elites. In thousands of manuscript pages responding to the demands of Charles II and his royal commissioners, these colonists declared that they loathed disobeying the crown but that they longed to keep what they had built.[6] What they had created together mattered. While enemies accused them of aspiring to a "free state" or republic, colonists themselves argued on monarchical, constitutional grounds for self-governance under their royal charter.

In addition to civil war-era practices such as petitioning and biblical sources such as the stories of Esther and Meroz, Reformation- and Renaissance-era convictions also informed their ability to mobilize. Many colonists had grown up immersed in puritan and reformed notions of a Christian's dual calling to a particular vocation and to the Christian life, a calling that could, in turn, justify a "prophetic mode of discourse" and certain kinds of "self-reflective" political agency in the religious and civic arenas.[7] Further, they participated in an older and broader Christian humanist tradition, one that prized public-spiritedness—sacrifice of private interests for the common good—and scorned "selfish passions."[8] This is not to overlook colonial brutality toward Africans and Native Americans, the subject of much outstanding and important recent scholarship. Rather, it is to identify one available tradition of political activism and hopefully to lay groundwork for further studies that might trace how many kinds of New Englanders, from Samson Occom and Phyllis Wheatley to Lemuel Haynes and Samuel Hopkins, found elements of this tradition useful, criticized it, or modified it for their own purposes in the century to come. Neither liberal nor democratic, puritan colonists do not fit neatly into our modern categories. Yet with persistence, and skill, they figured out how to effectively mobilize against absolutist-leaning regimes.

Agreement was often difficult and rarely complete. Nevertheless, these colonists achieved a remarkable level of hard-won, carefully articulated consensus regarding resistance to monarchical infringement of their political and ecclesiastical liberties. Regional alliances coalesced, most notably among an outspoken group of North Shore and Boston-based merchants who advocated for further compromise with the king. In this era, however, their disagreements were for the most part over tactics and methods rather than deeper ideals. Considering consensus building the mark of healthy politics, and factionalism a dangerous sign of its breakdown, colonists spent untold hours working toward rough agreements.[9]

When they did reach consensus, they achieved it in part through the orchestrations of the elites in their midst: town leaders who circulated petitions, magistrates who invited opinions and disseminated information, ministers who preached fast day sermons. Yet even non-freemen, people often seen as excluded, contributed in meaningful ways to the dialogue over what a king and his subjects owed each other, and generally identified with shared ideals. A few Quakers and Gortonists would have begged to differ, but colonists from many economic and educational backgrounds participated in this relatively open interpretive culture. Colonists' "Errand into the Wilderness"—their aim as a people—was not to transform England or take over the North American continent but rather to "study and practise true Scripture Reformation." And the slow, determined, painstaking labor of building large-scale, functional consensus was the only way to achieve it.[10]

Why did the Stuart government let Massachusetts get away with its defiance? Some scholars have emphasized the regime's weakness and inconsistency. Yet this was not the case in New England, where royal commissioners came with substantial funds, clear instructions, and four armed frigates. Whether or not they would have turned the frigates' guns on Boston after seizing New Amsterdam, these commissioners spent time estimating the strength of puritan-led colonial militias, attempted to revise laws and judicial procedures, identified local elites through whom they might exert influence, took over territories for direct royal governance, and catalogued local resources for metropolitan exploitation. In early Restoration New England, the Stuart regime presented a substantial threat.[11] More likely, Massachusetts colonists did not face immediate retaliation for their refusal to obey royal demands because the timing of events in London and throughout the empire worked in their favor. The crown was too busy and stretched to keep Massachusetts in line constantly. After all, just a few months after Mitchell's sermon, Lord Chancellor Clarendon was impeached. The London plague and fire sent the metropole into crisis on top of crisis. The year 1666 saw riots in England against the hearth tax, a rebellion of Scottish Covenanters, and uprisings in Montserrat and St. Christopher.[12] Last but certainly not least, the war with the Dutch required an enormous outlay of resources. Bay colonists' contributions of masts and provisions for the Royal Navy were not a small consideration. England's Privy Councillors were baffled by these misfit colonists, and they did not have a strong sense of the place of New England in the empire. But the nonconformist outposts had never cost the crown a penny (as colonists liked to remind them), and now they were supplying the Stuart war effort. In short, the king could not afford to pick a fight with Massachusetts Bay. Provoking these colonists could have led to a full-blown rebellion. Colonial defiance did, however, prompt serious thinking on the part of the king and his government about the costs and benefits of faraway territories for religion, trade, and overall imperial stability.[13]

A hundred years before the American Revolution, many New Englanders understood themselves to be living under a different constitutional relationship to the king and parliament than the men and women in Newcastle or even quasi-republican London. The charter's significance for defining the terms of this new relationship grew over the course of the early Restoration crisis. Colonists increasingly came to see their subjecthood as mediated through a document. With rising confidence, they turned to the charter as a binding, near-inviolable guarantee of their liberties and privileges, a gift from God as well as the king. These liberties were not so much individual as communal, a freedom to fulfill their social obligations. The Lord has given us, they said, our "mould & form of government . . . our frame civill & Ecclesiasticall," and his very "glory" is at stake in its "success."[14] We have a right, they insisted, to keep reforming our own government and churches as long as we avoid repugnancy to English law or other violations of the charter's terms, terms we have a role in interpreting. While some royalists were saying that only God could hold the king accountable, many colonists had come to believe that written charters, and the people who adhered to them, could stand up to arbitrary power. A formative moment in Anglo-American political history, the constitutional defiance of the 1660s shows us a cohesive local population rallying around the principle that neither the king nor his royal commissioners are above the law.

In the minds of people like Samuel Maverick and Sir Robert Carr, the colonists' "impertinent speeches" were simply "inconveniences" in the way of a Stuart ascendency, a "cloud of black reproaches" eclipsing the "honor" of the new regime.[15] For colonists such as Roger Clap, who served at the Boston castle during the crisis, however, the 1660s were a time "when Men Abroad (and doubtless some at Home) endeavoured to overthrow our Government" and almost "attained their Ends." Happily, though, God had "stirred up a mighty Spirit of Prayer in the Hearts of his People," and "put Wisdom and Courage" into the colony's leaders, so that they "did assert our Privileges granted unto us by Patent, and did adhere thereto." When colonists claimed to adhere to the liberties of self-government enshrined in a document, one protected by the people's vigilance and ultimately by God, they participated in forming an enduring and popular constitutional culture.[16]

NOTES

Introduction

1. Special Collections Washburn, 1666–1667, MHS; Thomas Hutchinson, *History of the Colony and Province of Massachusetts-Bay*, ed. Lawrence Mayo (Cambridge, 1936), 1:218; Suffolk Quarterly Court Files, Case 791, Massachusetts Judicial Archives, Boston; James Phinney Baxter, *George Cleeve of Casco Bay, 1630–1667* (Portland, 1885), 204n264.

2. At Mason's better-known trial later in 1667, Mason questioned the other royal commissioner Samuel Maverick's capacity as a witness and interrogated Maverick's loyalty to the crown; Maverick modified his charge. John Noble, ed., *Records of the Court of Assistants* (Boston, 1904), 2:187–188; Suffolk Files, Case 791.2; Court records, 22 May–1 June 1667, *Miscellaneous Bound*, MHS.

3. Special Collections Washburn, 1666–1667, MHS.

4. Special Collections Washburn, 1666–1667, MHS.

5. Special Collections Washburn, 1666–1667, MHS; MassRecs 4.2.305; see also Maverick to Sec. of State, 16 October 1667, DCHNY 3:160.

6. Special Collections Washburn, 1666–1667, MHS.

7. Mary Sarah Bilder, *The Transatlantic Constitution: Colonial Legal Culture and the Empire* (Cambridge, MA, 2004), 1–3 ("transatlantic"); Daniel Hulsebosch, *Constituting Empire: New York and the Transformation of Constitutionalism, 1664–1830* (Chapel Hill, 2005), 8 ("practical"); Mary Beth Norton, *Separated by Their Sex: Women in Public and Private in the Colonial Atlantic World* (Ithaca, 2011), xii ("meddlers").

8. The largest colony, Massachusetts, had around 22,000 inhabitants, with Connecticut and New Haven together at 8,000 and Plymouth and Rhode Island less than 2,000 people each. The status of certain Long Island towns was not yet settled. These numbers do not include Native American inhabitants outside praying towns. MassRecs 4.1.416–417; PlymRecs 3:187; ConnRecs 1:347–353 and https://ctstatelibrary.org/cttowns/counties; NHRecs 2:359–377; RIRecs 1:427–428; Franklin Dexter, "Estimates of Population in the American Colonies," *Proceedings of the American Antiquarian Society* 5 (October 1887): 31; "Estimated Population of American Colonies: 1610 to 1780," Series Z 1–19, in Colonial and Pre-Federal Statistics, United States Census Bureau, https://www2.census.gov/library/publications/1975/compendia/hist_stats_colonial-1970/hist_stats_colonial-1970p2-chZ.pdf; Herbert Osgood, *American Colonies in the Seventeenth Century* (New York, 1904): 1:166–167; Neal Dugre, "Repairing the Breach: Puritan Expansion, Commonwealth Formation, and the Origins of the United Colonies of New England, 1630–1643," *NEQ* 91, No. 3 (September 2018): 382–417.

9. Cornelia Hughes Dayton, *Women Before the Bar: Gender, Law, and Society in Connecticut, 1639–1789* (Chapel Hill, 1995), 27–34; David D. Hall, *A Reforming People: Puritanism*

and the Transformation of Public Life in New England (Chapel Hill, 2011), chap. 4; Barry Levy, *Town Born: The Political Economy of New England from Its Founding to the Revolution* (Philadelphia, 2009), chap. 1; Michael Winship, *Godly Republicanism: Puritans, Pilgrims, and a City on a Hill* (Cambridge, 2012), chap. 8.

10. For work on these limitations, as well as wider injustices committed against Native Americans and Africans, see, to start, Jean O'Brien, *Dispossession by Degrees: Indian Land and Identity in Natick, Massachusetts, 1650–1790* (Cambridge, 1997); Christopher Tomlins, *Freedom Bound: Law, Labor, and Civic Identity in Colonizing English America, 1580–1865* (Cambridge, 2010); Allan Greer, *Property and Dispossession: Natives, Empires and Land in Early Modern North America* (New York, 2018); and Margaret Newell, *Brethren by Nature: New England Indians, Colonists, and the Origins of American Slavery* (Ithaca, 2015).

11. David D. Hall, *The Puritans: A Transatlantic History* (Princeton, 2019), 235.

12. Stephen Foster, *Their Solitary Way: The Puritan Social Ethic in the First Century of Settlement in New England* (New Haven, 1971), 39; Dayton, *Women Before the Bar*, 27–34; George Haskins, *Law and Authority in Early Massachusetts: A Study in Tradition and Design* (New York, 1960); Hall, *A Reforming People*, chap. 4; Levy, *Town Born*, chap. 1; Winship, *Godly Republicanism*, chap. 8; David Konig, *Law and Society in Puritan Massachusetts: Essex County, 1629–1692* (Chapel Hill, 1979), chap. 1; William Nelson, "The Utopian Legal Order of the Massachusetts Bay Colony, 1630–1686," *American Journal of Legal History* 47, No. 2 (April 2005): 183–199; Mark Valeri, *Heavenly Merchandize: How Religion Shaped Commerce in Puritan America* (Princeton, 2010). For the line between "inhabitant" and "foreigner" in its relation to other legal categories, see Nan Goodman, *Banished: Common Law and the Rhetoric of Social Exclusion in Early New England* (Philadelphia, 2012), 108–112.

13. Mark Goldie, "The Unacknowledged Republic: Officeholding in Early Modern England," in *The Politics of the Excluded, c. 1500–1850*, ed. Tim Harris (London, 2001), 153–194.

14. Mark Goldie, "Restoration Political Thought," in *The Reigns of Charles II and James VII & II*, ed. Lionel Glassey (London, 1997), 13, 15 ("dwelt"), 28; Tim Harris, "Constitutional Royalism Reconsidered: Myth or Reality?" in *Politics, Religion and Ideas in Seventeenth- and Eighteenth-Century Britain*, ed. Justin Champion et al. (Rochester, 2019): 19–37; Gary De Krey, *London and the Restoration, 1659–1683* (Cambridge, 2005), 84 ("electoral"), 69–86; Blair Worden, *God's Instruments: Political Conduct in the England of Oliver Cromwell* (Oxford, 2012), 329 ("sole"). See also Jacqueline Rose, *Godly Kingship in Restoration England: The Politics of Royal Supremacy, 1660–1688* (Cambridge, 2011), 136–146; Mark Goldie, "The Theory of Religious Intolerance in Restoration England," in *From Persecution to Toleration: The Glorious Revolution and Religion in England*, ed. Ole Peter Grell, Jonathan Israel, and Nicholas Tyacke (Oxford, 1991), 354–358; Paul Seaward, *The Cavalier Parliament and the Reconstruction of the Olde Regime, 1661–1667* (Cambridge, 1986), 33; and Ted Vallance, "Political Thought," in *Oxford Handbook of the English Revolution*, ed. Michael Braddick (Oxford, 2015), 431. Later Tory theorists saw a role for consent as a "mode of designation" but not as authorizing the king's power; they encouraged passive resistance if a king contravened moral or divine law (Goldie, "Restoration Political Thought," 25).

15. Massachusetts to Charles II, 19 December 1660, MassRecs 4.1.450. Significant work in English and transatlantic puritanism has laid the foundation for these longer trajectories, much following Patrick Collinson in recovering strong links between puritans and institutional reform in both church and state. While highlighting puritan moderation, Collinson acknowledged that "like so many threatening missiles hidden in their siloes" were puritan

convictions that "as a public officer the monarch is accountable" to the people. Historians are now returning to puritan ideals of equity and accountability and their conviction that "even traditional authority . . . must be judged and discarded if found wanting." Patrick Collinson, "The Monarchical Republic of Queen Elizabeth I," in *Elizabethan Essays* (London, 1994), 44 ("threatening missiles"); Foster, *Their Solitary Way*, 39 ("even traditional"); Peter Lake, "The Historiography of Puritanism," in *Cambridge Companion to Puritanism*, ed. John Coffey and Paul Lim (Cambridge, 2008), 347; Michael Winship, "Freeborn (Puritan) Englishmen and Slavish Subjection: Popish Tyranny and Puritan Constitutionalism, c. 1570–1606," *English Historical Review* 124, No. 510 (October 2009): 1050–1074; Nicholas Tyacke, "Revolutionary Puritanism in Anglo-American Perspective," *Huntington Library Quarterly* 78, No. 4 (Winter 2015): 761–762; John Coffey, *Politics, Religion and the British Revolutions: The Mind of Samuel Rutherford* (Cambridge, 1997), 176–183.

16. New Englanders of course were also involved in Native American and African slave economies. Scholars from Charles Andrews to Jack Sosin have emphasized the disorganized weakness of the Restoration state; Stephen Saunders Webb by contrast saw it as militantly interventionist. Recent scholarship, however, has identified targeted regional pressure, especially in New England, but also in royalist colonies like Jamaica and Virginia, sometimes solicited by local factions or continuing policies initiated during the Interregnum, and often with an eye to royal investments in the slave trade. Charles Andrews, *British Committees, Commissions, and Councils of Trade and Plantations, 1622–1675* (Baltimore, 1908), 61–95; Jack Sosin, *English America and the Restoration Monarchy of Charles II: Transatlantic Politics, Commerce, and Kinship* (Lincoln, 1980); Stephen Saunders Webb, *The Governors-General: The English Army and the Definition of the Empire, 1569–1681* (Chapel Hill, 1979). Works on the early Restoration emphasizing targeted pressure include Robert Bliss, *Revolution and Empire: English Politics and the American Colonies in the Seventeenth Century* (Manchester, 1990); Walter Woodward, *Prospero's America: John Winthrop, Jr., Alchemy, and the Creation of New England Culture, 1606–1676* (Chapel Hill, 2010), 283; Ken MacMillan, "'Bound by Our Regal Office': Empire, Sovereignty, and the American Colonies in the Seventeenth Century," in *British North America in the Seventeenth and Eighteenth Centuries*, ed. Stephen Foster (Oxford, 2013); Alexander Haskell, *For God, King, and People: Forging Commonwealth Bonds in Renaissance Virginia* (Chapel Hill, 2015), chap. 5; Abigail Swingen, *Competing Visions of Empire: Labor, Slavery, and the Origins of the British Atlantic Empire* (New Haven, 2015), chap. 3; and Jonathan Israel, "The Emerging Empire: The Continental Perspective, 1650–1713," in *Oxford History of the British Empire*, ed. Nicholas Canny (Oxford, 1998), 1:428–433. For interventions solicited by local factions, see L. H. Roper, *Advancing Empire: English Interests and Overseas Expansion, 1613–1688* (Cambridge, 2017), chaps. 7–8.

17. Hall, *A Reforming People*, 15, 125; Tim Harris, *Restoration: Charles II and His Kingdoms, 1660–1685* (New York, 2005), 57. Legal writers of many persuasions allowed for arbitrary or unbounded monarchical powers in emergencies.

18. Bilder, *Transatlantic Constitution*, 2.

19. Daniel Richter, *Before the Revolution: America's Ancient Pasts* (Cambridge, 2011), 261–262; see also David Armitage, *The Ideological Origins of the British Empire* (Cambridge, 2000), chaps. 1–2; Jack Greene, *Peripheries and Center: Constitutional Development in the Extended Politics of the British Empire and the United States, 1607–1788* (Athens, 1986), 11–13; Craig Yirush, *Settlers, Liberty, and Empire: The Roots of Early American Political Theory, 1675–1775* (Cambridge, 2011), 56–63; and Tomlins, *Freedom Bound*, 178–183. For Locke, see

Holly Brewer, "Subjects by Allegiance to the King?" in *State and Citizen: British America and the Early United States*, ed. Peter Onuf and Peter Thompson (Charlottesville, 2013), 41.

Chapter 1

1. Francis Bremer, "In Defense of Regicide: John Cotton on the Execution of Charles I," *WMQ* 37, No. 1 (January 1980): 120; Brendan McConville, *The King's Three Faces: The Rise & Fall of Royal America* (Chapel Hill, 2006), 209. I use "nonconformists," "Independents," "puritans," and "congregationalists" mostly interchangeably, with an awareness that "nonconformists" is a broader category, that "congregationalist" denominationally belongs to a later time, and that not all designated "Independents" or "nonconformists" subscribed to congregational polity. Following Anthony Milton, I avoid "Anglican" as an anachronistic term that can elide ongoing contestation over the nature of the Church of England, using instead "high church" or "prayer book conformists." Milton, *England's Second Reformation: The Battle for the Church of England 1625–1662* (Cambridge, 2021), 9–10.

2. Matthew Neufeld, *The Civil Wars After 1660: Public Remembering in Late Stuart England* (Rochester, 2013), 25, 29; for conspiracy language, see James Heath, *A Brief Chronicle of the Late Intestine War* (London, 1663), A5v–A7r.

3. Peter Heylyn, *Aerius Redivivus* (London, 1670), 482 (quote), A1v; Heylyn, *Ecclesia Restaurata* (London, 1660–61), A2v, C1v; Anthony Milton, *Laudian and Royalist Polemic in Seventeenth-Century England: The Career and Writings of Peter Heylyn* (Manchester, 2007), 198–210.

4. John Morrill and Philip Baker, "Oliver Cromwell, the Regicide, and the Sons of Zuriah," in *Cromwell and the Interregnum*, ed. David Smith (Oxford, 2003), 17, 34; Philip Baker, "The Regicide," in *Oxford Handbook of the English Revolution* (Oxford, 2015), 155–162. The king's trial is debated in Sean Kelsey, "The Death of Charles I," *Historical Journal* 45, No. 4 (2002): 727–754; and Clive Holmes, "The Trial and Execution of Charles I," *Historical Journal* 53, No. 2 (2010): 289–316.

5. C. H. Firth, ed., *Clarke Papers* (London, 1891), 1:253–254.

6. Firth, ed., *Clarke Papers*, 1:282, 253–256, see also 262; Christopher Durston, "Goffe, William," ODNB; John Morrill, "The Puritan Revolution," in *Cambridge Companion to Puritanism*, ed. John Coffey and Paul Lim (Cambridge, 2008), 74. For Whalley's and Goffe's longer careers, see Matthew Jenkinson, *Charles I's Killers in America* (Oxford, 2019), 10–21.

7. Firth, *Clarke Papers*, 2:165, 168; Elizabeth Poole, *A Vision* (London, 1648 [1649]), 6; Manfred Brod, "Poole, Elizabeth," ODNB; Baker, "Regicide," 155–162; Raymond Stearns, *The Strenuous Puritan: Hugh Peter, 1598–1660* (Urbana, 1954), 316–317.

8. Crawford Gribben, *John Owen and English Puritanism: Experiences of Defeat* (Oxford, 2016), 95.

9. Stearns, *Strenuous Puritan*, 315–317n4; Samuel Pecke, ed., *A Perfect Diurnall of Some Passages in Parliament* (1855), Iss. 230, 20th–27th December 1648; Ian Gentles, *The New Model Army in England, Ireland, and Scotland, 1645–1653* (Cambridge, 1992), 288; Morrill and Baker, "Oliver Cromwell, the Regicide," 29–35; Gribben, *John Owen and English Puritanism*, 95–96.

10. Stearns, *Strenuous Puritan*, 331–334; Gentles, *New Model Army*, 306; Holmes, "Trial and Execution," 308–309.

11. John Owen, *A sermon preached to the Honourable House of Commons* (London, 1649), 66–67; Martyn Cowen, *John Owen and the Civil War Apocalypse: Preaching, Prophecy and Politics* (New York, 2018), 100.

12. Roger Williams to John Winthrop, 26 May 1649, *Collections of the MHS*, Ser. 3, 9 (1846): 286; Stearns, *Strenuous Puritan*, 334; Carla Gardina Pestana, "Peter, Hugh," ODNB.

13. Cowan, *John Owen and the Civil War Apocalypse*, 108; "retained sovereignty": Owen, *A sermon preached to the Honourable House of Commons*, 17, 5; Tim Cooper, *John Owen, Richard Baxter and the Formation of Nonconformity* (Burlington, 2011), 105.

14. P. M. Zall, introduction to *The Simple Cobler of Aggawam in America*, ed. Zall (Lincoln, 1969), xii–xiii.

15. Some judges refused to sign the death warrant. Morrill, "Puritan Revolution," 84–85; Baker, "The Regicide," 162–165.

16. John Maidstone to John Winthrop, 24 March 1659, *Collections of the MHS*, Ser. 3, 1 (1825): 187.

17. *Modell of Church and Civill Power*, in Roger Williams, *The Bloudy Tenant* (London, 1644), 136, 150; Darrett Rutman, *American Puritanism: Faith and Practice* (Philadelphia, 1970), 95; T. Dwight Bozeman, *To Live Ancient Lives: The Primitivist Dimension in Puritanism* (Chapel Hill, 1988), 157–160. Ephraim Huit and Thomas Hooker rejected this view. Hooker, *A Survey of the Summe of Church-Discipline* (London, 1648), 2:80; Hall, *A Reforming People*, 98–99.

18. John Calvin, *Institutes of the Christian Religion*, ed. John McNeill (Louisville, 1960), 4.20.1519–1520; Thomas Cartwright, *The Second Replie* (London, 1575), 403–404; John McNeill, introduction to *On God and Political Duty* (New York, 1986), viii–ix; Robert Kingdon, "Calvinism and Resistance Theory," in *Cambridge History of Political Thought, 1450–1700*, ed. J. H. Burns (Cambridge, 1991), 210; Coffey, *Politics, Religion and the British Revolutions*, 176–183.

19. Nathaniel Ward dissented from the other ministers' advice. Richard Dunn, James Savage, and Laetitia Yeandle, eds, *The Journal of John Winthrop, 1630–1649* [unabridged] (Cambridge, 1996), 140; Winship, *Godly Republicanism*, 202; Tyacke, "Revolutionary Puritanism in Anglo-American Perspective," 759.

20. Massachusetts General Court to Commissioners for Foreign Plantations, 6 September 1638, in Hutchinson, *History*, 1:422; see also Winship, *Godly Republicanism*, 202 203; and Richard Dunn, *Puritans and Yankees: The Winthrop Dynasty of New England, 1630–1717* (Princeton, 1962), 28–35.

21. Thomas Shepard, *Parable of the Ten Virgins* (London, 1660), 166. The Massachusetts magistrate Daniel Gookin remembered being influenced by these passages from Shepard in the 1660s. Daniel Gookin, Petition, 14 February 1681, in Frederick Gookin, *Daniel Gookin, 1612–1687: Assistant and Major General of the Massachusetts Bay Colony* (Chicago, 1912), 176.

22. Scottish National Covenant, 27 February 1638, in Samuel Rawson Gardiner, ed., *Constitutional Documents of the Puritan Revolution, 1625–1660* (Oxford, 1889), 54; Hall, *The Puritans*, 247, 255; John Walter, *Covenanting Citizens: The Protestation Oath and Popular Political Culture in the English Revolution* (Oxford, 2017), 36–49; David Cressy, "The Protestation Protested, 1641 and 1642," *Historical Journal* 45, No. 2 (June 2002): 255.

23. For political conclusions of Cotton's sermons, see Hall, *A Reforming People*, 96–97, 106–116; and Winship, *Godly Republicanism*, 183–184. For Cotton's Revelation sermons circulating in the 1660s, see Increase Mather, Diary [M.G. Hall Transcripts], February 1664, May 1664, January 1665, AAS.

24. MassArch CVI.26; MassRecs 2:69. The Court did allow royalists merchants and inhabitants liberty if "carrying themselves here quietly" (69). Henry Dunster ms. notebook, fol. 135, MHS.

25. John Brock ms. notebook, Amherst College Archives, Amherst, Massachusetts; "John Brock," *Biographical Sketches of Graduates of Harvard University*, ed. John Langdon Sibley (Cambridge, 1873), 1:127–131. A portion of Brock's notebook is in "Autobiographical Memoranda of John Brock, 1636–1659," ed. Clifford Shipton, *Proceedings of the AAS* (1943). For civil wars–era reemigration, see Susan Hardman Moore, *Pilgrims: New World Settlers and the Call of Home* (New Haven, 2007), 64–66.

26. Brock ms. notebook.

27. John Hull, "Diaries," *Archaeologia Americana: Transactions and Collections of the American Antiquarian Society* (1857), 3:172–173; James O'Toole, "New England Reactions to the English Civil Wars," *NEHGR* 129 (January 1975): 7; Timothy Sehr, *Colony and Commonwealth: Massachusetts Bay, 1649–1660* (New York, 1989), 14.

28. Dunster ms. notebook, fols. 135–137, MHS. Dunster studied at Cambridge and was influenced by William Perkins and Thomas Goodwin. Francis Bremer, "Dunster, Henry," ODNB.

29. Dunster ms. notebook, fol. 135. Jeremiah Chaplin mistranscribed "deserved to Die" as "deserted to Scotland." Chaplin, *Life of Henry Dunster* (Boston, 1872), 284.

30. Prov. 28:17, GNV.

31. Cotton mentions tensions over whether to have a fast or thanksgiving day. Colonists continued to fast for England in the 1650s. Bremer, "In Defense of Regicide," 114, 105; "Scituate and Barnstable Church Records," *NEHGR* 10 (January 1856): 40; MassRecs 4.1.52, 109, 200.

32. On Cotton's earlier preaching on legitimate political resistance, defending the Scottish revolt, see Tyacke, "Revolutionary Puritanism," 759; and Winship, *Godly Republicanism*, 183–184.

33. "How far Moses Judicialls bind Mass[achusetts]," *Proceedings of the MHS*, Ser. 2, 16 (October 1902): 282.

34. Bremer, "In Defense of Regicide," 120.

35. Bremer, "In Defense of Regicide," 117–120; Anon., *The New Oath or Covenant* (London, 1643), 5; see also Kirsteen MacKenzie, *Solemn League and Covenant of the Three Kingdoms and the Cromwellian Union, 1643–1663* (New York, 2018); and Dunster ms. notebook, fol. 136.

36. Bremer, "In Defense of Regicide," 120; Nathaniel Ward, *A Sermon Preached before the Honourable House of Commons* (London, 1647), A3v.

37. Bremer, "In Defense of Regicide," 107–108, 120–123.

38. MaineRecs 2:142.

39. Worden, *God's Instruments*, 264–265; Glenn Burgess, *British Political Thought, 1500–1660: The Politics of the Post-Reformation* (New York, 2009), 187–188. But see also Mark Kishlansky's argument that "all divine right rested upon conditions"—that the ruler "govern for the benefit of his people." *A Monarchy Transformed: Britain, 1603–1714* (London, 1996), 38.

40. Worden, *God's Instruments*, 269, 282–283. Milton's republicanism changed over time and was not always transparent. *Milton: Political Writings*, ed. Martin Dzelzainis (Cambridge, 1991), 80; Nigel Smith, "The Anti-Episcopal Tracts: Republican Puritanism and the Truth in Poetry," and N. H. Keeble, "'Nothing other then a Free Commonwealth': Milton's Later Vernacular Republican Tracts," in *Oxford Handbook of Milton*, ed. Nicholas McDowell and Nigel Smith (Oxford, 2011), 166–169, 305–309; Martin Dzelzainis, "Milton's Politics," *Cambridge Companion to Milton* (Cambridge, 1999), 81–82.

41. John Eliot to Edward Winslow, 8 July 1649, *Eliot Tracts*, ed. Michael Clarke (Westport, 2003), 186; Sehr, *Colony and Commonwealth*, 22.

42. John Eliot, *The Christian Commonwealth* (London, 1659), Blv, A4r, B2v, C2r, 2; see also *Eliot Tracts*, ed. Clarke, 191–192.

43. Hall, *A Reforming People*, 98–99, 120.

44. Mark Peterson, *The City-State of Boston: The Rise and Fall of an Atlantic Power, 1630–1865* (Princeton, 2019), 85–89; Sehr, *Colony and Commonwealth*, 36–45; T. H. Breen, *Character of the Good Ruler: A Study of Puritan Political Ideas in New England, 1630–1730* (New Haven, 1970), 89; Hutchinson, *History*, 1:149.

45. Christopher Hill, *The Experience of Defeat: Milton and Some Contemporaries* (New York, 1984) chaps. 6–7; MassRecs 4.1.417–418.

46. Thomas Shepard, "An Enquiry into the Reasons why God contends with his people & this Country," September 1665, Cotton Mather Papers, MHS.

47. *Records of the First Church of Dorchester, in New England, 1636–1734* (Boston, 1891), 34; MassRecs 4.1.417–418. Connecticut also observed the fast. Thomas Minor, *Diary* (New London, 1899), 40.

48. In 1662 Charles II sent an agent to negotiate reconciliation with Rome; in 1670 he promised the French king he would convert. *King Charles II. his Declaration* (Edinburgh, 1660); Ronald Hutton, *The Restoration* (Oxford, 1985), 200; Harris, *Restoration*, 71–73; N. H. Keeble, *The Restoration: England in the 1660s* (Malden, 2002), 68; Seaward, *The Cavalier Parliament*, 26–34.

49. Thomas Parker, "To the High and Mighty Prince Charles the Second," in James Noyes, *Moses and Aaron, or, The Rights of Church and State* (London, 1661).

50. Hull, "Diaries," 3:200–201; Bliss, *Revolution and Empire*, 132, 271n1.

51. Maverick to Clarendon ca. 1661–1663, *The Clarendon Papers* (New York, 1870), 22–32; Breedon, "Narrative and Deposition," 17 October 1678 [11 March 1661], CO 1/42, No. 133, in DCHNY 3:39–40; John Reid, *Maine, Charles II, and Massachusetts: Governmental Relationships in Early Northern New England* (Portland, 1977), 40–50. On returning to Boston, Breedon was fined £200 for "insolencies & contempt . . . tending to mutiny, sedition, and subvertion"; the fine was later mitigated through Thomas Temple's intervention (MassRecs 4.2.69).

52. Robert Mason et al. to the King, 15 February 1662, CO 1/16, No. 18. For other petitioners at court, see Sosin, *English America*, 88–93; and Jenny Hale Pulsipher, *Subjects unto the Same King: Indians, English, and the Contest for Authority in Colonial New England* (Philadelphia, 2005), 45, 53–59. My thinking on this point is indebted to Alison Games's presentation titled "400 Years Since Plymouth" at the January 2020 American Historical Association Annual Meeting.

53. Edward Godfrey to Sec. Nicolas, 15 July 1660 and 7 April 1663, *Collections of the Maine Historical Society* 9 (1887): 356, 359; Egerton Ms. 2395, fols. 299–300, BL. See also Reid, *Maine, Charles II, and Massachusetts*, 40–44. "Baker" may be parliamentary preacher Matthew Barker.

54. Quoted in Hutchinson, *History*, 1:187n (Mitchell's manuscript is lost). When serving as Cromwell's major generals in the 1650s, Whalley and Goffe were unpopular among non-royalists and royalists. Philip Major, *Writings of Exile in the English Revolution and Restoration* (New York, 2016), chap. 4.

55. For these connections, see Douglas Wilson, "Web of Secrecy: Goffe, Whalley, and the Legend of Hadley," *NEQ* 60, No. 4 (December 1987): 523–525; William Hooke to John Davenport, 2 March 1663, in A. G. Matthews, "A Censored Letter," *Transactions of the*

Congregational Historical Society 9 (1924–1926): 263–265; and Francis Bremer, *Building a New Jerusalem: John Davenport, a Puritan in Three Worlds* (New Haven, 2012), 282–284.

56. Treason Act, 1351, *Statutes of the Realm* (London, 1810), 1:319–320.

57. Goffe's later role as the "Angel of Hadley" who supposedly led colonists into battle during King Philip's War was a well-known nineteenth-century story. After Yale president Ezra Stiles popularized their tale as a heroic saga, it became a favorite of Romantic novelists looking for genealogies of revolutionary courage, only to fade into obscurity after the American Civil War. Lemuel Welles, *History of the Regicides* (New York, 1927) is the standard account, though see also Jenkinson, *Charles I's Killers*. Bremer, *Building a New Jerusalem*, gives the New Haven side with full attention to its religious dimensions, as does Owen Stanwood, "Crisis and Opportunity: The Restoration Church Settlement and New England," in *"Settling the Peace of the Church": 1662 Revisited*, ed. N. H. Keeble (Oxford, 2014), 197–198. For early versions, see Mark Sargent, "Thomas Hutchinson, Ezra Stiles, and the Legend of the Regicides," *WMQ* 49, No. 3 (July 1992): 431–448; and for literary context Lawrence Buell, *New England Literary Culture: From Revolution Through Renaissance* (Cambridge, 1986), chap. 8; and Michael Colacurcio, *The Province of Piety: Moral History in Hawthorne's Early Tales* (Cambridge, 1984), 206–220.

58. William Goffe, Diary, *Proceedings of the MHS* 7 (December 1863): 281.

59. Goffe, Diary, 281–282; Hutchinson, *History*, 1:184. Hutchinson possessed Goffe's shorthand diary (no longer extant).

60. Deposition of John Crown [1661?], CO 1/15, No. 82.

61. Hutchinson, *History*, 1:139n.

62. Goffe, Diary, 282.

63. Goffe, Diary, 281.

64. Charles R., *By the King, A Proclamation* (London, 1660).

65. Edward Hutchinson to Winthrop, 21 February 1661; Amos Richardson to Winthrop, 21 February 1661; Elizabeth Richardson to Winthrop, 22 February 1661, all in MsWP; Hutchinson, *History*, 1:184–185.

66. *Records of the First Church of Dorchester*, 37; Hull, "Diaries," 3:199.

67. Breedon, "Narrative and Deposition."

68. Hutchinson, *History*, 1:185n.

69. Endicott, Instructions to Kirke and Kellond, 6[–7] May 1661, CO 1/15, Nos. 50–51, orders to Michelson enclosed.

70. Charles R., "To our . . . present Governour . . . of New England," *Collections of the MHS*, Ser. 3, 7 (1838): 123; Hull, "Diaries," 3:201.

71. Temple to Morrice, 19 August 1661, *Collections of the MHS*, Ser. 3, 8 (1843): 325–326; ms. is CO 1/15, No. 80; Hull, "Diaries," 3:202.

72. Deposition of John Crown [1661?], CO 1/15, No. 82.

73. Maverick to Clarendon, ca. 1661–1663, *Clarendon Papers*, 32.

74. Breedon, "Narrative and Deposition"; Temple to Massachusetts, 4 March 1663, *Collections of the MHS*, Ser. 3, 7 (1838): 127.

75. Hull, "Diaries," 3:200.

76. Eliot, *Christian Commonwealth*, A3r; MassRecs 4.2.5–6; Hutchinson, *History*, 1:181–182; Richard Cogley, *John Eliot's Mission to the Indians Before King Philip's War* (Cambridge, 2009), 114–116.

77. Eliot to Baxter, 6 July 1663, in Richard Baxter, *Reliquiae Baxterianae*, ed. N. H. Keeble, John Coffey, Tim Cooper, and Tom Charlton (Oxford, 2020), 3:528.

78. John Davenport, *Saints Anchor-hold* (London, 1661), 191–199.

79. Davenport, *Saints Anchor-hold*, 191–199. William Hooke cowrote the preface. See also Bremer, *Building a New Jerusalem*, 284–289, 301; William Scheick, "An Inward Power and Authority: John Davenport's Seditious Piety," *Religion & Literature* 33, No. 1 (Spring 2001): 5; and Major, *Writings of Exile*, 152.

80. Hooke to Davenport, 1661, in Edward E. Atwater, *History of the Colony of New Haven* (New Haven, 1881), 441.

81. Davenport to John Winthrop, 6 August 1659, *Collections of the MHS*, Ser. 4, 7 (1865): 503. For rumors surrounding Davenport, see Bremer, *Building a New Jerusalem*, 300–301.

82. Bremer, *Building a New Jerusalem*, 290; Isabel Calder, *New Haven Colony* (New Haven, 1934), 217–219.

83. Leete had been acting governor since Francis Newman's death in November 1660. Bruce Stark, "Leete, William," ANB; Welles, *History of the Regicides*, 34–45.

84. Thomas Kellond and Thomas Kirke, Report to Gov. Endicott, Thomas Hutchinson, *The Hutchinson Papers* (Albany, 1865), 2:55.

85. Kellond and Kirke, Report, *Hutchinson Papers*, 2:52–57. The General Court later gave Kellond and Kirke land grants.

86. "Crampton," whom Francis Bremer has identified as Dennis Scranton, purportedly told Kellond and Kirke that Whalley and Goffe led a militia training, saying "if they had but two hundred friends that would but stand by them, they would not care for Old or New-England," a doubtful report. Kellond and Kirke, Report, *Hutchinson Papers*, 2:53–54; Bremer, *Building a New Jerusalem*, 286–287.

87. Wilson, "Web of Secrecy," 530; Jenkinson, *Charles I's Killers*, 42–50.

88. Edward Rawson to William Leete, 4 July 1661, *Hutchinson Papers*, 2:57–59.

89. Baxter, *Reliquiae Baxterianae*, 3:522.

90. John Davenport to Sec. Morrice, 19 August 1661, *Collections of the MHS*, Ser. 3, 8 (1843): 328–329; ms. is CO 1/15, No. 81. Davenport also asked Morrice to intervene, pleading "myne Innocyency in Referance to the 2 Collonells." He claimed "that uppon a faire hearing I should be acquitted, & some in Boston who raile against mee, should have their Injurious mouthes Stopped." It is hard to believe that Davenport was fully innocent. Leete also went to the Lake family for help: Thomas Lake to Edward Lake, 12 December 1661, MsWP.

91. Robert Newman to Gilbert, 12 February 1661, Mather Papers, *Collections of the MHS*, Ser. 4, 8 (1868): 182.

92. United Colonies Commissioners, Declaration, *Hutchinson Papers*, 2:64.

93. Hutchinson, *History*, 1:185n; *History of Milford, Connecticut, 1639–1939* (Bridgeport, 1939), 27–31; see also Jenkinson, *Charles I's Killers*, 56–70.

94. This story involves complex negotiations in England, arbitrated in part by William Hooke, who almost succeeded in helping New Haven retain its independence. Woodward, *Prospero's America*, 260–276; Bremer, *Building a New Jerusalem*, 294–298; Dunn, *Puritans and Yankees*, 117–149.

95. Carl I. Hammer, *Pugnacious Puritans: Seventeenth-Century Hadley and New England* (Lanham, 2018), 20–21.

96. MsWP, 28 May 1661; Pynchon to Winthrop, 23 May 1661, in Carl Bridenbaugh, ed., *Pynchon Papers* (Boston, 1982), 1:40–41; Hutchinson, *History*, 1:186n; Dunn, *Puritans and Yankees*, 120.

97. MassArch CVI.76; "Cartwright's Report," DCHNY 3:112; Nicolls, Carr, and Maverick to Richards, 31 October 1666, CO 1/20, No. 159; Gookin, *Daniel Gookin*, 110; Increase Mather, Diary, 10 April–20 June 1665, AAS; Michael G. Hall, *The Last American Puritan: The Life of Increase Mather, 1639–1723* (Middletown, 1988), 54–55; Jane Hooke to Rebecca Russell, 24 July 1672, Mather Papers, 260–261; Frances Goffe to William Goffe, ca. 1671, *Collections of the MHS*, Ser. 3, 1 (1825): 61. Cynthia Van Zandt is doing important work to explore this female network.

98. Kellond and Kirke, Report, *Hutchinson Papers,* 2:52–57. When Whalley and Goffe returned to the rocky "cave" briefly in 1664, "some Indians, in their hunting, discovered the cave with the bed" and reported it—to whom is unknown, but not to claim a reward. Hutchinson, *History,* 1:186n. For the skills of Native messengers in this period, see Katherine Grandjean, *American Passage: The Communications Frontier in Early New England* (Cambridge, 2015), 47–48, 53–61, 119.

99. Hutchinson, *History,* 1:186–187n. Dixwell, alias James Davis, lived at New Haven until his death in 1689. Goffe removed to Hartford around 1676 (Hammer, *Pugnacious Puritans*, 6–13).

100. As blood money the reward might also have been hard to spend locally.

101. Endicott to Sec. Nicholas and Sec. Morrice, late 1661, CO 1/15, No. 83; see also a similar letter, referring to this one in MassArch CVI.39; and another from Endicott, perhaps to Clarendon, in *Collections of the MHS*, Ser. 3, 1 (1846): 51–53.

102. Maverick to Clarendon, ca. 1661–1663, *Clarendon Papers*, 29, 39.

103. For Hunton, violent resistance was a negation of the constitutional order rather than a part of it; authority rested on consent of the governed as well as divine right. J. T. Peacey, "Hunton, Philip," ODNB; Philip Hunton, *A Vindication of the Treatise of Monarchy* (1651), 7–13, 24–25, 51–55; 62–79; Francis Osborne, *A Perswasive to a Mutuall Compliance* (Oxford, 1652), 4, 30. Shepard's copies are held by the American Antiquarian Society. Shepard was also reading and annotating *A Collection of Several Speeches* (London, 1642), a document that contained petitions, and *Touching the Fundamentall Lawes, Or Politique Constitution of this Kingdome* (London 1643). See also Burgess, *British Political Thought*, 198–199.

104. Thomas Shepard notebook, Octavo 5, Shepard Family Papers, AAS.

105. Hall, *The Puritans*, 184. See also Jonathan Mitchell, *Nehemiah on the Wall* [1667] (Cambridge, 1671), 28.

Chapter 2

1. Jane Kamensky, *Governing the Tongue: The Politics of Speech in Early New England* (Oxford, 1997), 47 ("greedily"); Grandjean, *American Passage*, 61 ("as eager"), see also 105; Alejandra Dubcovsky, *Informed Power: Communication in the Early American South* (Cambridge, 2016), 2–3, 214–215.

2. Sandra Gustafson, *Eloquence Is Power: Oratory and Performance in Early America* (Chapel Hill, 2000), xviii.

3. Richard Brown has argued convincingly that knowing the kinds of information people accessed leads to understanding a society's power structures. Yet his description of a "hierarchic diffusion pattern" where elites dispensed knowledge sparingly on the assumption "that the population at large need not and could not be generally informed on public matters" fits uneasily with the evidence for Restoration New England. Brown, *Knowledge Is Power: The Diffusion of Information in Early America, 1700–1865* (Oxford, 1987), 4–5, 28–36. New England was not, of course, the only region with high civic engagement; see, for example,

Jessica Roney, *Governed by a Spirit of Opposition: The Origins of American Political Practice in Colonial Philadelphia* (Baltimore, 2014).

4. Mitchell, *Nehemiah on the Wall*, 17–18, 23–24, 26; Davenport, *Saints Anchor-hold*, 195.

5. *The Intelligencer*, No. 1 (31 August 1663): 2; Richard Brown, *The Strength of a People: The Idea of an Informed Citizenry in America, 1650–1870* (Chapel Hill, 1996), 12; Andrew Pettegree, *The Invention of News: How the World Came to Know About Itself* (New Haven, 2014), 236–239.

6. Samuel Winthrop to John Winthrop, 20 October 1660, *Collections of the MHS*, Ser. 5, 8 (1882): 248. For surveillance, see Examination of Samuel Willson, Taylor, 3 April 1663, SP 29/71, fol. 24; Hooke to Davenport, 2 March 1663, in Matthews, "A Censored Letter," 262–283. Tim Harris notes both the regime's attempts to "silence critical voices" and their shortcomings. Harris, *Restoration*, 69.

7. Francis Bremer, *Congregational Communion: Clerical Friendship in the Anglo-American Puritan Community, 1610–1692* (Boston, 1994), 219–220; David Cressy, *Coming Over: Migration and Communication Between England and New England in the Seventeenth Century* (Cambridge, 1987), 225–226, 256–258.

8. John Allin [Allen] to Philip Hrith, 4 July 1665, John Allin ms. letters, 1663–1674, MHS. A similar story circulated during the Robert Child affair of 1646. David D. Hall, *Worlds of Wonder, Days of Judgment: Popular Religious Belief in Early New England* (New York, 1989), 103–104.

9. Adam Fox, *Oral and Literate Culture in England, 1500–1700* (Oxford, 2000), 336; Tim Harris, "Understanding Popular Politics in Restoration Britain," in *A Nation Transformed: England After the Restoration*, ed. Alan Houston and Steven Pincus (Cambridge, 2001), 135–139; Dagmar Freist, *Governed by Opinion: Politics, Religion and the Dynamics of Communication in Stuart London, 1637–1645* (London, 1997), 178–180, 210; Jonathan Barry, "Communicating with Authority: The Uses of Script, Print and Speech in Bristol, 1640–1714," in *The Uses of Script and Print, 1300–1700*, ed. Julia Crick and Alexandra Walsham (Cambridge, 2004), 204–205.

10. Leverett to Massachusetts, 13 February 1661, in Hutchinson, *History*, 1:182n. Benjamin Worsley told John Winthrop (via Samuel Hartlib) that a royal governor for New England was being considered: Woodward, *Prospero's America*, 257.

11. MassArch CVI.112; Danforth Papers, *Collections of the MHS*, Ser. 2, 8 (1826): 60; MassRecs 4.2.187; Royal Commissioners to Massachusetts General Court, May 1665, Danforth Papers, 61.

12. Davenport to Winthrop, 29 March 1660, MsWP; Richard Blinman assumed Winthrop and Davenport shared letters: Blinman to Winthrop, 9 March 1660, MsWP.

13. Davenport to Winthrop, 20 April 1660, *Collections of the MHS*, Ser. 4, 7 (1865): 511.

14. Hull to Leverett, 10 December 1660, MassArch 241.231.

15. Leverett to Massachusetts, 13 February 1661, in Hutchinson, *History*, 1:182n; see also Leverett to Thomas Temple, 1663, *Hutchinson Papers*, 2:106–107.

16. Blinman to sons, 4 August 1663, Mather Papers, 211.

17. Eleazer Mather to John Davenport, July 1662, in Hutchinson, *History*, 1:193n; John Hall, 3 May 1664, John Hall Letters, 1663–1685, AAS; T. M. Lawrence, "Goodwin, Thomas," ODNB; John Coffey, *Persecution and Toleration in Protestant England, 1558–1689* (London, 2000), 177; Gribben, *John Owen and English Puritanism*, 223; Francis Bremer, *Puritan Crisis: New England and the English Civil Wars, 1630–1670* (New York, 1989), 328–331; Moore, *Pilgrims*, 143–145, 269n13.

18. Freist, *Governed by Opinion*, 299.

19. John Davenport to Elizabeth Winthrop, 14 April 1662, MsWP.

20. Margaret Jacob highlighted the post-Restoration prevalence of a Newtonian view that "stability was possible without constant divine intervention" in *The Newtonians and the English Revolution, 1689–1720* (Ithaca, 1976), 18. Jane Shaw has argued for the persistence of belief in miracles among both the high church party and nonconformists, alongside a strand of skepticism, in *Miracles in Enlightenment England* (New Haven, 2006). On the general history of providentialism among post-Reformation Anglo-Protestants, see Alexandra Walsham, *Providence in Early Modern England* (Oxford, 1999); and on the tradition of prophecy, Andrew Crome, "Constructing the Political Prophet in 1640s England," *Seventeenth Century* 26, no. 2 (2011), 279–298.

21. Warren Johnston, *Revelation Restored: The Apocalypse in Later Seventeenth-Century England* (Rochester, 2011), 71.

22. John Davenport to William Goodwin, 1665, Mather Papers, 126; for the long tradition of prophetic infants, see Walsham, *Providence in Early Modern England*, 207–212. For the dogs: William Goffe, Journal, 12 May 1660, *Proceedings of the MHS* 7 (1863–1864): 281. For further portents surrounding the coronation, such as a massive thunderstorm, and royalists' attempts to redirect their interpretations, see Matthew Jenkinson, *Culture and Politics at the Court of Charles II: 1660–1885* (Rochester, 2010), 73. Woodward describes the Royal Society's interest in certain prodigies (*Prospero's America*, 290).

23. Probably the town of Montgomery in Wales. Hooke to Davenport, March 1662, Mather Papers, 196–197.

24. "Copy of the articles of complaint against Rev. Thomas Gilbert," 28 March 1666, Phillips Library, Rowley, Massachusetts.

25. Edward Taylor, "Lay-mans Lamentation . . . on Bartholomew day 1662," in *Edward Taylor's Minor Poetry*, ed. Thomas Davis and Virginia Davis (Boston, 1981), 13–18.

26. Jeremiah Blinman to John Davenport, 2 September 1663, Mather Papers, 211; Eleazer Mather to John Davenport, 4 July 1662, Mather Papers, 193.

27. Hooke to Davenport, March 1662, Mather Papers, 196.

28. Hooke to Davenport, 2 March 1663, in Matthews, "A Censored Letter," 267; Davenport to Goffe, 8 July 1662, Mather Papers, 198; see also 193.

29. Anon., *Mirabilis Annus*, A2r–A3r, 2, 55–56; Peter Elmer, *Witchcraft, Witch-Hunting, and Politics in Early Modern England* (Oxford, 2016), 176–179. On skepticism as built into the genre of portents, see Hall, *Worlds of Wonder*, 95.

30. The Presbyterian Matthew Poole had invited colonists to participate in an early stage of the project, prior to the Restoration. Richard Greaves, *Deliver Us from Evil: The Radical Underground in Britain, 1660–1663* (Oxford, 1986), 213; David Appleby, *Black Bartholomew's Day: Preaching, Polemic and Restoration Nonconformity* (Manchester, 2008), 136–148; Keith Thomas, *Religion and the Decline of Magic: Studies in Popular Beliefs in Sixteenth and Seventeenth Century England* (Oxford, 1997), 94–95; Michael Winship, *Seers of God: Puritan Providentialism in the Restoration and Early Enlightenment* (Baltimore, 1996), 37. The work was based on the Baptist Henry Jessey's earlier tract, *The Lords Loud Call to England* (1660).

31. Increase Mather to Davenport, 21 October 1662, Mather Papers, 205; H[ooke] to Davenport, 12 October 1661, Mather Papers, 178.

32. Hooke to Davenport, 2 March 1663, in Matthews, "A Censored Letter," 266; Davenport to William Goodwin, 2 November 1665, Mather Papers, 126. Davenport was appointed by the New Haven Court in 1657 to collect providential stories, as part of a larger plan by the

United Colonies commissioners to compile a general providential history of New England. NHRecs 2:217; Ebenezer Hazard, ed., *Historical Collections* (Philadelphia, 1794), 2:367.

33. Testimony of John Plumbe, 16 October 1665, Davenport and Winthrop Mss. 1638–1693, New York Public Library (printed in *Collections of the MHS*, Ser. 3, 10 (1849): 57). Winthrop endorsed Plumbe's testimony.

34. Davenport to Winthrop, 25 January 1665, MsWP. Davenport may have been writing as a service to his father. Bremer, *Building a New Jerusalem*, 399n27.

35. Davenport to Winthrop, 18 December 1665, MsWP.

36. *Mirabilis Annus*, 2–4, 30–31.

37. John Allin [Allen] to Philip Hrith, 4 July 1665, John Allin ms. letters, 1663–1674, MHS.

38. Hull, "Diaries," 3:218, 208.

39. William Hubbard, *A General History* [ca. 1680] (Boston, 1848), 580. Isam's criticisms are also recounted in a shorthand letter by Thomas Shepard, Octavo 6, Shepard Family Papers, AAS.

40. Simon Bradstreet, Diary, *NEHGS* 8 (October 1854): 325.

41. Thomas Shepard, "An Enquiry into the Reasons why God contends with his people & this Country," 1665, Cotton Mather Papers, MHS.

42. *John Saffin, His Book*, ed. Caroline Hazard (New York, 1928), 133–136.

43. Hull, "Diaries," 3:208–209, 218; Michael Wigglesworth, "God's Controversy with New England," in *Poems of Michael Wigglesworth*, ed. Ronald Bosco (Lanham, 1989), 99.

44. Roxbury Church Records, *NEHGR* 34 (January–April 1880): 84–89, 162–166, 297–301. On comets, see also Hull, "Diaries," 3:213–215; Minor, *Diary*, 65; Thomas, *Religion and the Decline of Magic*, 96; Hall, *Worlds of Wonder*, 78; and Woodward, *Prospero's America*, 290.

45. Samuel Danforth, *An Astronomical Description of the Late Comet* ([London], 1666), 17–18, title pg. verso; "Samuel Danforth," in John Langdon Sibley, *Biographical Sketches of Graduates of Harvard University* (Cambridge, MA, 1873), 1:88–92; Hall, *Worlds of Wonder*, 86; Bernard Capp, *English Almanacs, 1500–1800: Astrology and the Popular Press* (Ithaca, 1979). See also Roger Williams to John Winthrop, 8 September 1660, *Collections of the MHS*, Ser. 3, 10 (1849): 39–41.

46. Davenport (the son) to Winthrop, 7 January 1665, MsWP; see also *John Saffin, His Book*, 133–136. Davenport also sent Winthrop comet-based reflections of his father's. Colonists further reflected on the "vicissitude of providences upon our nation" as they debated difficult decisions such as splitting congregations. See Phillips Diary Ms., fol. 73, Congregational Library and Archives, Boston.

47. John Leverett to Winthrop, 31 January 1665, MsWP. Leverett continued, "Coll. Cartwright and Mr. Mavericke have not moved in any busynes here since they came. . . ."

48. Winthrop to Nicolls, 18 January 1665, MsWP; Winthrop to Robert Boyle, 29 October 1666, *Proceedings of the MHS* 16 (1878): 229.

49. Thomas, *Religion and the Decline of Magic*, 95–96. For Baxter's critiques of congregationalist factionalism, see Michael Winship, "Defining Puritanism in Restoration England: Richard Baxter and Others Respond to *A Friendly Debate*," *Historical Journal* 54, No. 3 (2011): 689–715; and for his autobiography, Baxter, *Reliquiae Baxterianae*.

50. *The Newes*, 28 April 1664, quoted in J. B. Williams, *Notes and Queries*, Ser. 2, 8 (1913): 203.

51. See also *A Perfect narrative of the Phanatick Wonders* (London, 1660); and the ballad *The Phanatick's Plot Discovered* (London, 1660).

52. *Kingdomes Intelligencer* for 14–21 October 1661, quoted in Williams, *Notes and Queries*, 82.

53. Shaw, *Miracles in Enlightenment England*, chaps. 1–2; John Spurr, "'Virtue, Religion, and Government': The Anglican Uses of Providence," in *Politics of Religion in Restoration England*, ed. Tim Harris, Paul Seaward, and Mark Goldie (Oxford, 1990), 29–47; Haskell, *For God, King, and People*, 292.

54. "The Play of the Puritan, 1661," in *Ben Johnson: The Critical Heritage*, ed. D. H. Craig (London, 1990), 227; Lang to Davenport, 28 October 1661, Mather Papers, 174; Hooke to Davenport, 12 October 1661, Mather Papers, 177–178.

55. Taylor, "Lay-mans Lamentation," 14.

56. Parker, *Bishop Parker's History of His Own Time*, 1:23–25. For anti-puritan historians, see Neufeld, *The Civil Wars After 1660*; Paul Lim, *In Pursuit of Purity, Unity, and Liberty: Richard Baxter's Puritan Ecclesiology in Its Seventeenth Century Context* (Boston, 2004), 217–223; and Appleby, *Black Bartholomew's Day*, 179–194.

57. John Spencer, *A Discourse Concerning Prodigies* ([Cambridge?], 1663), A3r, B1v. William Burns, "'Our Lot Is Fallen into an Age of Wonders': John Spencer and the Controversy over Prodigies in the Early Restoration," *Albion* 27, No. 2 (Summer 1995): 241; Elmer, *Witchcraft, Witch-Hunting, and Politics*, 177, 230–251. For increased politicization of prodigies and debates over authenticity, overlapping with new views of science, see Capp, *English Almanacs*, 90; Freist, *Governed by Opinion*, 302–303; Shaw, *Miracles in Enlightenment England*, chap. 3; Hall, *Worlds of Wonder*, 106–110; and Winship, *Seers of God*, 38–39.

58. Stearns, *Strenuous Puritan*, chap. 6. Peter's daughter Elizabeth was raised by the Shepards. Joseph Felt, *Memoir or Defence of Hugh Peters* (Boston, 1851), 46.

59. When William Coddington of Newport saw Peter's influence as chaplain to the Council of State in the 1650s, he jokingly called him the new "Arch B[ishop] of Canterberye." Coddington to Winthrop, 1651, *Collections of the MHS*, Ser. 4, 7 (1865): 281. Peter had returned to England in 1641 as agent and fundraiser for a Massachusetts sinking into economic depression. Louise A. Breen, *Transgressing the Bounds: Subversive Enterprises Among the Puritan Elite in Massachusetts, 1630–1692* (Oxford, 2001), 107–109. Peter helped bring Archbishop William Laud to trial and was reported to have wanted to exile him to New England as a punishment after the civil wars (probably a joke). He promoted broad-minded congregationalism, along with reformed legal codes, within Cromwell's regime. He was progressive for his time on toleration, women's education (even promoting female theologians), and inheritance laws, and saw state-sponsored poverty relief as crucial to the work of godly magistrates. R. P. Stearns, ed., "Letters and Documents by or Relating to Hugh Peter," *Essex Institute Historical Collections* 72 (1936): 57–67, 210–211; Stearns, *Strenuous Puritan*, 183, 370–382; Felt, *Memoir or Defense*, 47–49; Philip Gura, *A Glimpse of Sion's Glory: Puritan Radicalism in New England, 1620–1660* (Middletown, 1984), 202; Pestana, "Peter, Hugh," ODNB.

60. Peter was ill during the king's execution and was not formally accused of regicide; however, Presbyterians hoping to curry favor with the new king may have resuscitated older rumors that he *was* the masked executioner. Pestana, "Peter, Hugh," ODNB; Richard Gildrie, "Peter, Hugh," ANB; Francis Bremer, *First Founders: American Puritans and Puritanism in an Atlantic World* (Durham, 2012), 96–105.

61. Randolph to Leoline Jenkins, 14 June 1682, CO 1/48, No. 104.

62. Thomas Atkins, *Hosanna* (London, 1649), 3.

63. Alexandra Walsham, "Phanaticus: Hugh Peter, Antipuritanism and the Afterlife of the English Revolution," *Parergon* 23 (2015): 65–97, identifies Peter as central to the discourse of anti-puritanism in England from the 1640s to the later seventeenth century, when it morphed into a diatribe against "fanaticism." On sexualized satires interfacing with violence against women, see Sharon Achinstein, "Women on Top in the Pamphlet Literature of the English Revolution," *Women's Studies* 24 (1994): 131–163.

64. Nathaniel Briscoe to Thomas Broughton, 1652, *Collections of the MHS*, Ser. 3, 1 (1825): 32–35.

65. Stearns, ed., "Letters and Documents," 309–310.

66. Richard Blinman to Winthrop, 22 August 1659, MsWP, transcribed by Hans Rollman; see also Davenport to Winthrop, 28 September 1659, *Collections of the MHS*, Ser. 3, 10 (1849): 26.

67. For royalists' speculation about Peter's "regret of Conscience," see Daniel Axtel, *The Speech of Maj. Gen. Harison* (London, 1660), 4.

68. Davenport to Winthrop, 11 August 1660, *Collections of the MHS*, Ser. 3, 10 (1849): 38.

69. Peter, along with Henry Vane and John Owen, was accused of being involved in the Sowerby Plot. Bremer, *Congregational Communion*, 206; Greaves, *Deliver Us from Evil*, 30–31.

70. Nye was granted indemnity after abjuring officeholding in church or state. Barbara Donagan, "Nye, Philip," ODNB.

71. Davenport to Winthrop, 17 October 1660, *Collections of the MHS*, Ser. 3, 10 (1849): 42.

72. Hugh Peter, *The Speech and Confession of Hugh Peters* (London, 1660).

73. Anon., *The Most Vile and Lamentable Confession of Hugh Peters* (London, 1660).

74. Anon., *Hugh Peters Last Will and Testament* (London, 1660).

75. Hutchinson to Winthrop, 21 February 1661; Amos Richardson to Winthrop, 21 February 1661; Elizabeth Richardson to Winthrop, 22 February 1661, all in MsWP.

76. Testimony of John Stebbin, 5 May 1662, MsWP.

77. Hutchinson to Winthrop, 21 February 1661, MsWP.

78. Winthrop to Thomas Lake, 15 April 1661; Lake to Winthrop, 11 March 1661, both in MsWP. For *Speeches and Prayers*, see Laura Knoppers, *Historicizing Milton: Spectacle, Power, and Poetry in Restoration England* (Athens, 1994), 47–51.

79. Heneage Finch, *An Exact and Most Impartial Accompt* (London 1660), 153.

80. Finch, *An Exact . . . Accompt*, 154–155.

81. Finch, *An Exact . . . Accompt*, 155; Anon., *The History of the Life and Death of Hugh Peters that Arch-traytor* (London, 1661), 5–6.

82. Maverick to Clarendon, ca. 1661–1663, *Clarendon Papers*, 39; Egerton Ms. 2395, fol. 415v, BL.

83. Finch, *An Exact . . . Accompt*, 172–173.

84. Finch, *An Exact . . . Accompt*, 181.

85. Anon., *A Brief Account of the Behaviour* (London, 1660), 23.

86. Edward Godfrey to Sec. Nicolas, 7 April 1663, *Collections of the Maine Historical Society* 9 (1887): 356, 359.

87. Deposition of John Crown [1661?], CO 1/15, No. 82; modernized transcription in George Chalmers, *Political Annals* (London, 1780), 263–264.

88. Hugh Peter, *A Dying Fathers Last Legacy* (London, 1660) went quickly through six editions, a Boston one in 1717. The volume ends with a poem delineating expectations for godly rule and connecting faithfulness to suffering (118–121).

89. *Tryal of Sir Henry Vane* ([London?], 1662), 81; George Sykes, *Life and Death of Sir Henry Vane* (London, 1662), 124 (MHS copy inscribed J. Mayhew).

90. *Mirabilis Annus*, 79. Hugh Peter's widow, Deliverance, lived on the charity of *Mirabilis Annus* contributor George Cokayne's London congregation. Pestana, "Peter, Hugh," ODNB.

91. Samuel Parker, *Bishop Parker's History of His Own Time*, trans. Thomas Newlin (London, 1727), 23–25.

92. *Mirabilis Annus*, 4–5 (referencing Joel 2:30). A royalist's mocking epitaph on this scene: *History . . . of Hugh Peters that Arch-traytor* (London, 1661), 12.

93. Spencer, *Discourse Concerning Prodigies*, B2r.

Chapter 3

1. Foster, *Their Solitary Way*, 71–72.

2. Martha McNamara, *From Tavern to Courthouse: Architecture and Ritual in American Law, 1658–1860* (Baltimore, 2004), 14–19. The street was later "King Street." Partly funded by the wealthy Boston merchant Robert Keayne, the Town House may also have had a library. The merchants used the space below to deal in bonds or bills of credit, posting notices on the pillars of what they called the "exchange" or "'change."

3. Hutchinson, *History*, 1:180; MassRecs 4.1.432–448.

4. Perhaps they also wanted to make sure deputies were available to come. Council Executive Records, 1650–1661, MassArch GC3-327.

5. MassRecs 4.1.449.

6. Endicott and Bellingham to Lord Saye and Sele, 7 December 1660, MassArch 106.27. For the authority of longevity, see Bilder, *Transatlantic Constitution*, 38–39.

7. Elders' Advice, *Hutchinson Papers*, 2:50.

8. John Norton, *Three Choice and Profitable Sermons* (Cambridge, 1664), 14–15.

9. Elders' Advice, *Hutchinson Papers*, 2:50–51. David Hall notes the ministers' "reluctance to become involved in further controversy." *The Faithful Shepherd: A History of the New England Ministry in the Seventeenth Century* (Chapel Hill, 1972), 232.

10. MassRecs 4.1.450–452.

11. Stephen Winthrop to John Winthrop, 16 July 1649, *Winthrop Papers* (Boston: MHS, 1947), 5:356; Hall, *The Puritans*, 328.

12. Endicott and Bellingham to Saye and Sele, 7 December 1660, MassArch 106.27; Robert Boyle to Commissioners of the United Colonies, 15 May 1662, *Correspondence of Robert Boyle*, ed. Michael Hunter, Antonio Clericuzio, and Lawrence Principe (London, 2001), 2:20. For rhetoric of Native missions in the context of imperial rivalries, see Carla Gardina Pestana, "Cruelty and Religious Justifications for Conquest in the Mid-Seventeenth-Century English Atlantic," in *Empires of God: Religious Encounters in the Early Modern Atlantic*, ed. Linda Gregerson and Susan Juster (Philadelphia, 2011), 37–47; Pulsipher, *Subjects unto the Same King*, 17–18.

13. MassRecs 4.1.450–452; Hull, "Diaries," 3:197.

14. MassArch CVI.29c. See also Bliss, *Revolution and Empire*, 133; and Alonzo Lewis and James Newhall, *History of Lynn* (Lynn, 1865), 1:208.

15. Deposition of Samuel Benett, MassArch CVI.33a; Deposition of Thomas Tower, MassArch CVI.29a; Deposition of Robert Pingon, MassArch CVI.29 For English examples, see Harris, *Restoration*, 48–49.

16. For language of anti-popery, see Owen Stanwood, "Catholics, Protestants, and the Clash of Civilizations in Early America," in *First Prejudice: Religious Tolerance and Intolerance in Early America*, ed. Chris Beneke and Christopher Grenda (Philadelphia, 2010), 218–240; and Tim Harris, *London Crowds in the Reign of Charles II: Propaganda and Politics from the Restoration Until the Exclusion Crisis* (Cambridge, 1987).

17. MassArch CVI.31, 34a, 29a; MassRecs 4.2.7.

18. Also refusing to take the new oaths, Cheney pleaded lunacy; his sentence was remitted. "Proceedings in York County Court," *WMQ* 11, No. 1 (July 1902): 28; Noeleen McIlvenna, *Early American Rebels: Pursuing Democracy from Maryland to Carolina, 1640–1700* (Chapel Hill, 2020), 55.

19. Charles II to Endicott, 15 February 1662, CO 5/903, fols. 18–19, printed in *Hutchinson Papers*, 2:51–52.

20. Hull, "Diaries," 3:202; MassRecs 4.2.24.

21. De Krey, *London and the Restoration*, 75. Ministers Richard Mather, John Norton, Thomas Cobbet, and Jonathan Mitchell were among the most educated in the colonies, with multiple Oxford, Cambridge, and Harvard degrees. They may have served reluctantly, first pleading a prior urgent commitment to arbitrate divisions in the Barnstable church, then relenting. MassArch CVI.35.

22. MassRecs 4.2.24; Hull, "Diaries,":203; MassArch CVI.35.

23. MassRecs 4.2.24.

24. Answer of the Patent-Study Committee, June 1661, Hutchinson, *History*, 1:439–440; MassRecs 4.2.25–26.

25. MassRecs 4.2.24–26.

26. MassRecs 4.2.26.

27. Carla Gardina Pestana, *The English Atlantic in an Age of Revolution, 1640–1661* (Cambridge, MA, 2004), 214–216. Plymouth was also early, in October 1660. New Haven would follow the Bay in August 1661.

28. Sudbury petition, 18 June 1661, https://www.digitalcommonwealth.org/search/commonwealth:sj13bp849. A tear on the ms. makes the quote on law less certain.

29. Bilder, *Transatlantic Constitution*, 47–56.

30. Sudbury petition, 18 June 1661; Matt. 10:16.

31. MassArch CVI.36.

32. Boston Petition, 19 June 1661, MassArch CVI.36.

33. William Ames, *Marrow of Sacred Theology* (London, 1642), 314; Bremer, *First Founders*, 39–49.

34. This is not to say that puritanism led to a modern version of citizenship, or that puritans were the only ones promoting the "life of active virtue in the public interest," a common humanist ideal. J. P. Sommerville, "English and Roman Liberty in the Monarchical Republic of Early Stuart England," in *The Monarchical Republic of Early Modern England: Essays in Response to Patrick Collinson*, ed. J. F. McDiarmid (Aldershot, 2007), 208. See also Margo Todd, *Christian Humanism and the Puritan Social Order* (Cambridge, 1987), 28–42; Phil Withington, *The Politics of Commonwealth: Citizens and Freemen in Early Modern England* (Cambridge, 2005), 243–248; Patrick Collinson, "*De Republica Anglorum*: Or, History with the Politics Put Back," in *Elizabethan Essays* (London, 1994), 18; and Breen, *Character of a Good Ruler*, 27–31. For historiographical debates about New England church and civil politics as

dominated by elites, see James Cooper, *Tenacious of Their Liberties* (Oxford, 1999), 4–8. For broad lay participation, see Francis Bremer, *Lay Empowerment and the Development of Puritanism* (New York, 2015).

35. MassArch CVI.35a; MassRecs 4.2.26.

36. MassRecs 4.2.27.

37. Venner had been a church member and constable in Salem. Henry Wheatley, ed., *Diary of Samuel Pepys* (New York, 1892), 1.2:300; MassRecs 4.2.33; Hull, "Diaries," 3:200; Bernard Capp, *Fifth Monarchy Men: A Study in Seventeenth-Century English Millenarianism* (London, 1972), chap. 9; Richard Greaves, "Venner, Thomas," *ODNB*; De Krey, *London and the Restoration*, 71–78.

38. Joseph Caryl et al., *A Renuntiation and Declaration* (London, 1661), 8–9, 3, 5 (Nathaniel Mather, Thomas Weld, and John Oxenbridge were also signers). The commitment to pray was from the Savoy Declaration, a revision of the Westminster Assembly's work that would be adopted in modified form by New England's Reforming Synod of 1679–1680 and by Connecticut's 1708 Saybrook Platform.

39. Egerton Ms. 2395, fols. 299–300, BL; "Orders in Council," *Collections of the MHS*, Ser. 4, 2 (1854): 280. Lord Saye and Sele disagreed on linking the franchise to church membership. Karen Kupperman, "Definitions of Liberty on the Eve of Civil War: Lord Saye and Sele, Lord Brooke, and the American Puritan Colonies," *Historical Journal* 32, No. 1 (March 1989): 25.

40. Hooke to Davenport, 5 March 1663, Mather Papers, 207–209.

41. De Krey, *London in the Restoration*, 73–74.

42. Charles II, 1661: An Act for . . . Corporations, *Statutes of the Realm* (London, 1819), 5:321–323.

43. Hull, "Diaries," 3:203; MassArch CVI.37–39.

44. MassRecs 4.2.30–31; Hull, "Diaries," 3:203–204.

45. The historian John Gorham Palfrey did not think such a letter could have been sent, but it was received in the State Paper Office. MassRecs 4.2.32–33; MassArch CVI.40; Endicott to Charles II, 7 August 1661, CO 1/15, No. 77. For Stuart elites' embracing of the Davidic motif, see Goldie, "Restoration Political Thought," 15.

46. Warren Billings, ed., *Papers of Sir William Berkeley* (Richmond, 2007), 150; MassArch 106.40; MassRecs 4.2.31–32.

47. Delivered by Quaker Samuel Shattuck, the letter is often called "Shattuck's missive." Charles II to New England, 9 September 1661, CO 1/15, No. 85; Charles II to Endicott, 15 February 1661, *Hutchinson Papers*, 2:52–53; MassArch X.273.

48. In Nan Goodman's view, the law had a primarily "rhetorical function," to prevent Quakers "engaging . . . in further legal debate." Goodman, *Banished*, 92.

49. A flurry of prosecutions of English Quakers, soon formalized in the Quaker Act, followed Venner's revolt. MassRecs 4.2.21–21, 23–24; Coffey, *Persecution and Toleration*, 169–173.

50. Endicott too had heard that Baxter with "loving and cordial readiness" had helped "to further our Concernments." Baxter, *Reliquiae Baxterianae*, 2:520.

51. MassArch X.275a.

52. Charles II to Massachusetts, 28 June 1662, MassRecs 4.2.165; MassArch X.275a.

53. MassArch CVI.42–44b; Hull, "Diaries," 3:204.

54. MassRecs 4.2.37; MassArch CVI.44a, 461, 47, 64a; X.54; *Hutchinson Papers*, 2:90–93; 60–70 (marked-up draft in MassArch 241.245a–246); Hull, "Diaries," 3:205.

55. MassArch 106.44a; *Hutchinson Papers*, 2:66–74.

56. MassArch 10.276a; *Hutchinson Papers,* 2:76–89; Hull, "Diaries," 3:207. Cotton Mather's *Magnalia* most likely mixes up the drafts.

57. Hull, "Diaries," 3:205; *Hutchinson Papers,* 2:88–93; MassArch CVI.45–61.

58. Jeannine Hensley, ed., *Works of Anne Bradstreet* (Cambridge, 1967), 265–66; see also 269.

59. Hutchinson, *History,* 1:188n.

60. Peterson, *City-State of Boston,* 147–148; Andrew Eliot to Thomas Hollis, 25 May 1768, *Memoirs of Thomas Hollis* (London, 1780), 397.

61. Maverick to Clarendon, ca. 1661–1663, *Clarendon Papers,* 37–38.

62. Clarendon to Nicolls, undated, MsCP, fol. 141. Similarly, Clarendon tried to amend the Act of Uniformity to enhance the king's flexibility in dealing with nonconformists. Andrews, *British Committees, Commissions, and Councils of Trade and Plantations,* 62–79; Greene, *Peripheries and Center,* xi; Paul Seaward, "Circumstantial Temporary Concessions: Clarendon, Comprehension, and Uniformity," in *Settling the Peace of the Church: 1662 Revisited* (Oxford, 2014), 57–84; David Appleby, "From Ejectment to Toleration in England, 1662–89," in *The Great Ejectment of 1662,* ed. Alan Sell (Eugene, 2012), 67–124.

63. Charles II also mentioned the regicides, and in a second letter, the ironworks. John Hull traveled with the agents and may have assisted them. Charles II to Endicott, 28 June 1662, Danforth Papers, 53; MassRecs 4.2.58; MassArch CVI.53; Hull, "Diaries," 3:206.

64. Baxter, *Reliquiae Baxterianae,* 2:110–111.

65. Mark Goldie, *Roger Morrice and the Puritan Whigs* (Woodbridge, 2016), xv. Moderates in the Church of England such as Gilbert Burnet would support an inclusive church; for the most part they lost, however, to a more exclusive majority. Tony Claydon, "Latitudinarianism and Apocalyptic History in the Worldview of Gilbert Burnet, 1643–1715," *Historical Journal* 51, No. 3 (September 2008): 579–591.

66. Baxter, *Reliquiae Baxterianae,* 2:238.

67. N. H. Keeble, "Baxter, Richard," *ODNB*; Seaward, "Circumstantial Temporary Concessions," 76–80. Baxter had assisted the New England Company's charter renewal.

68. Baxter, *Reliquiae Baxterianae,* 2:111; Charles II, 1662: An Act for the Uniformity of Publique Prayers, *Statutes of the Realm,* 5:364–370; Keeble, *Restoration,* 141; Harris, *Restoration,* 52–53; Richard Greaves, *Enemies Under His Feet: Radicals and Nonconformists in Britain, 1664–1677* (Stanford, 1990), 137–142; Appleby, *Black Bartholomew's Day,* 174.

69. Danforth Papers, 53–54.

70. Breedon went so far as to say "he knew no Authority wee had to Comitt him nor would he obey any marshall." MassArch CVI.52b–53a; MassRecs 4.2.69, 75; see also Pulsipher, *Subjects unto the Same King,* 46–48.

71. Davie to Davenport, Mather Papers, 204.

72. Davie to Davenport, Mather Papers, 204.

73. MassRecs 4.2.58; MassArch CVI.52–52a.

74. MassArch CVI.52a.

75. Danforth Papers, 55; MassRecs 4.2.62, 73, 141. Censors were appointed in October 1662; the press was ordered "at liberty as formerly" in May 1663; censors were reinstituted during the royal commissioners' visit in May 1665.

76. Edward Rawson to [Thomas Thacher], 2 February 1663, Miscellaneous Bound Collection, MHS. Other towns read the letter as a routine matter: e.g., Charlestown on 6 October 1662: "The kings Letter directed to the generall Court was openly and deliberately reade

by Jacob Greene," a constable. Herbert Edes, ed., *Charlestown Town Records*, microfilm, New England Historic Genealogical Society, Boston.

77. MassArch CVI.61a–62; see also Richard Frothingham, *History of Charlestown* (Boston, 1845), 155; John Gorham Palfrey, *History of New England* (Boston, 1892), 2:531.

78. MassArch CVI.62c. Some townsmen may have requested the letter be resent. Letter of Thomas Dutton, 8 December 1662, in Edward Rawson Papers, MHS. For a discussion highlighting divisions among deputies and magistrates, see Paul Lucas, "Colony or Commonwealth: Massachusetts Bay, 1661–1666," *WMQ* 24 (1967): 96–97.

79. Massachusetts Council to Sec. Morrice, 25 November 1662, MassArch CVI.54; also in Danforth Papers (misdated), 47–49; Sudbury petition, 18 June 1661.

80. "Result of the Synod of 1662," in Williston Walker, ed., *Creeds and Platforms of Congregationalism* (New York, 1893), 301–339. Richard Mather had proposed expanding baptism at the Cambridge Synod of 1646–1648, where it was approved by the majority but tabled; more recently the Synod of 1657 involving Connecticut voted to expand baptism. Hall, *The Puritans*, 332–334.

81. Sudbury petition, 18 June 1661. Pestana has identified the Boston church's January 1661 covenant renewal, an implementation of baptismal reform, as "a gesture designed to rally the community to New England's distinctive way" in the face of threats from England (*English Atlantic*, 218). "Halfway covenant" is an eighteenth-century term; colonists used "large Congregationalism." Michael Winship, *Hot Protestants: A History of Puritanism in England and America* (New Haven, 2018), 192.

82. Preface to "Letter . . . to Mr John Dury," appended to Norton, *Three Choice and Profitable Sermons*. Signed eventually by forty-four pastors, teachers, and Harvard fellows, the letter circulated in Latin before being translated and printed in 1664. The original letter, with thirty-nine signatures, is in Mather Family Papers, AAS. Baxter too linked the baptismal synod to political circumstances (*Reliquiae Baxterianae*, 2:111).

83. MassArch CVI.54; Danforth Papers, 47–49.

84. Rawson mentioned petitions from Hampton, Newbury, Ipswich, Salem, and Sudbury, adding that "Boston, Rowley & some others" were also "Ready"; he may have been conflating earlier or later documents. Rawson to [Thacher], 2 February 1663.

85. Cotton Mather, *Magnalia Christi Americana* (London, 1702) 3:38. According to lore, Norton died of a broken heart. Humphrey Davie feared "a breach" in the Boston church because "Norton hath lost himselfe much in the Esteeme of the generallity, & will doe more," some calling for a new minister. Davie to Davenport, n.d., Mather Papers, 204; Hall, *Faithful Shepherd*, 232–233.

86. Rawson to [Thacher], 2 February 1663.

87. Hull, "Diaries," 3:207; Nicolls to Clarendon, 27 July 1664, MsCP, fols. 94–95. Connecticut leaders also worried about non-freemen trying to vote. ConnRecs 1:417–418.

88. MassArch CVI.65. Magistrates would have invited ministers for morning prayer but deputies declined, perhaps recalling Norton's October plea for compliance, or worried about crops back home. They did, however, turn to merchants for advice on the Navigation Acts.

89. John Higginson, *The Cause of God and His People in New-England* (Cambridge, 1663), 4, 12, 17. Calvin, drawing on Cicero, wrote, "those laws are preposterous which neglect God's right and provide only for men." *Institutes*, ed. McNeill, Book IV.XX.9.1495.

90. Higginson, *Cause of God and His People*, 13–14, 20–21; *Elijah's Mantle* (Boston, 1722), 1–5, MHS copy with Thomas Prince's annotations. Following Calvin, Higginson argued that civil government was "an Ordinance of God" with specific forms left up to men, as

long as its "ultimate end" was "Religion." See also Eric Slauter, *The State as a Work of Art: The Cultural Origins of the Constitution* (Chicago, 2009), 51.

91. Higginson, *Cause of God and His People*, 23; Perry Miller said election day preachers, though "not wishing unnecessarily to antagonize royal sensibilities . . . never left the people in doubt about their right to resist rulers who transgress the agreement." *The New England Mind: The Seventeenth Century* (Boston, 1961), 1:410. See also Meredith Neuman's distinction between perfunctory and true obedience in "Failures of Consensus: Contesting Election Sermons in Puritan New England," in *Stories of Nation: Fictions, Politics, and the American Experience*, ed. Martin Griffin and Christopher Hebert (Knoxville, 2017), 187.

92. Higginson to Massachusetts General Court, 6 June 1663, Higginson Family Papers, MHS.

93. Martha Howes and Sidney Perley, eds., *Salem Town Records* (Salem, 1913), 37.

94. Higginson to Massachusetts General Court, 6 June 1663.

95. For "reason of state" ideas circulating in Virginia and England, see Dean Mathiowetz, *Appeals to Interest in Seventeenth-Century England* (University Park, 2011), 61–68; and Haskell, *For God, King, and People*, 20–21.

96. Higginson to Massachusetts General Court, 6 June 1663; Bremer, *Building a New Jerusalem*, 172–176. For dating and authorship, see Bruce Steiner, "Dissension at Quinnipiac: The Authorship and Setting of a Discourse About Government in a New Plantation Whose Design Is Religion," *NEQ* 54 (1981): 14–32. Higginson cited Cambridge Platform, chap. 2.4. See Walker, ed., *Creeds and Platforms*, 204–205.

97. Higginson to Massachusetts General Court, 6 June 1663. For "tribute," Higginson drew on the continental Calvinist and Geneva Bible contributor Franciscus Junius. Higginson also pleaded for action to keep Salem from becoming a Quaker missionary base. Court members had Higginson's election sermon printed and appointed him to a franchise committee; his arguments may have informed their 1664 decision to minimally expand the franchise and gift masts and provisions to the royal navy.

98. MassArch CVI.66–66a.

99. MassRecs 4.2.74; Suffolk Files, Case 537. The committee at first was only magistrates and deputies; the deputies later proposed adding four elders or ministers, two named by each house. The magistrates chose Higginson and Mitchell, the deputies Dedham's John Allen, a Harvard graduate who served an English parish and was ejected post Restoration, and Dover's John Reyner, a Cambridge graduate who would later help resist the royal commissioners in Piscataqua.

100. MassRecs 4.2.73–74. A traditional phrase, also used in the *Modell of Church and Civil Power*, 125.

101. Nicolls to Clarendon, 27 July 1664, MsCP, fol. 95.

102. MassRecs 4.2.86, 134.

103. For the case of Simon Tuttle, who supposedly threatened "if we cannot have the libertye the King gave us we would winn it by edge of the sword" and who received, after repenting, a moderated sentence of twenty stripes or a £10 fine, see Edward Rawson Papers, MHS; MassRecs 4.2.110; and Pulsipher, *Subjects unto the Same King*, 37–38. Samuel Hunt was also prosecuted for seditious speech, and for refusing to dig up tree stumps on a militia exercise field, threatening that if punished "there would be great disturbance in the country, for there were hundreds in the country of his mind." For repeated offenses, in addition to a £10 fine he was ejected from the militia and disfranchised. George Francis Dow, ed., *Records and Files of the Quarterly Courts of Essex County* (Salem, 1913), 3:139.

104. Only the magistrates are listed as present. "Letters to the severall Governors," 24 June 1663, CO 5/903, fols. 11–15; MassRecs 4.2.86–87.

105. Haskell, *For God, King, and People*, 285–331; Paul Musselwhite, *Urban Dreams, Rural Commonwealth: The Rise of Plantation Society in the Chesapeake* (Chicago, 2018), 216–218; April Hatfield, *Atlantic Virginia: Intercolonial Relations in the Seventeenth Century* (Philadelphia, 2004), 50–55; Christian Koot, *Empire at the Periphery: British Colonists, Anglo-Dutch Trade, and the Development of the British Atlantic, 1621–1713* (New York, 2011), 87–106; Antoinette Sutto, *Loyal Protestants and Dangerous Papists: Maryland and the Politics of Religion in the English Atlantic, 1630–1690* (Charlottesville, 2015), 81–91; Osgood, *American Colonies*, 1:311.

106. MassRecs 4.2.86–87 (drafts in MassArch LX.2, 5–5a).

107. MassRecs 4.2.97–98; Massachusetts Court to Owen, 20 October 1663, Curwen Papers, AAS; Hull, "Diaries," 3:209.

108. Gribben, *John Owen and English Puritanism*, chap. 9. A December 1663 Council also dealt with Rhode Islanders' complaints to the king regarding land and disturbances to Atherton Company proprietors, and appointed a committee to engage London supporters (later backed with £400). MassArch CVI.67, 71a, 287.1; MassRecs 4.2.102.

109. MassRecs 4.2.98.

110. Coffey, *Persecution and Toleration*, 170; Greaves, *Enemies Under His Feet*, 137. For the range of opinions about toleration of dissent among proponents of high church ceremonies, see Harris, *Restoration*, 54–55.

111. *Journal of the House of Lords* (London, 1767-[?]), 11:575–580. Although vacillating and still wary of nonconformists, Charles II also "saw his role as healing and settling past animosities" and hoped to keep "laws elastic and subject to exception" in order to shore up royal authority. John Spurr, *The Restoration Church of England, 1646–1689* (New Haven, 1991), 30; Annabel Patterson, *The Long Parliament of Charles II* (New Haven, 2008), 146–147.

112. Higginson, *Cause of God and His People*, 21–22, 10; Hull, "Diaries," 3:213–214.

113. Sudbury petition, 18 June 1661 ("an universall"); Hull, "Diaries," 3:202 ("unanimous").

114. Mitchell, *Nehemiah on the Wall*, 30.

Chapter 4

1. Thomas Becon, *A Fruitful Treatise of Fasting* (London, 1551), Biiiir, Ciiiir, Iiiir; Walsham, *Providence in Early Modern England*, 142–153.

2. Becon, *A Fruitful Treatise*, Giiiir, Hiiiiv; Lewis Bayly, *Practice of Pietie* (London, 1660), 325–328; John Jewel, *The Second Tome of Homilees* (London, 1571), 173, 182.

3. John Wilson, *Pulpit in Parliament: Puritanism During the English Civil Wars, 1640–1648* (Princeton, 1969), 60, 62; H. R. Trevor-Roper, "The Fast Sermons of the Long Parliament," in *Essays in British History, Presented to Sir Keith Feiling* (London, 1964), 85–87, 117–120; Mary Morrissey, *Politics and the Paul's Cross Sermons* (Oxford, 2011), 68–69, 78–83; Natalie Mears et al., eds, *National Prayers: Special Worship Since the Reformation* (Rochester, 2013), 1:lxxi–cvi; Christopher Durston, "'For the Better Humiliation of the People': Public Days of Fasting and Thanksgiving During the English Revolution," *Seventeenth Century* 7, No. 2 (1992): 129–49. Auditors and note-takers might also filter out political messages. Ann Hughes, "Preachers and Hearers in Revolutionary London: Contextualising Parliamentary Fast Sermons," *Transactions of the Royal Historical Society*, 6th ser., 24 (2014): 57–77.

4. Anthony Fletcher, *Outbreak of the English Civil War* (New York, 1981), 92–94.

5. Matthew Brown, *The Pilgrim and the Bee: Reading Rituals and Book Culture in Early New England* (Philadelphia, 2007), 111; Richard Gildrie, "The Ceremonial Puritan: Days of Humiliation and Thanksgiving," *NEHGR* 136 (January 1982): 3–4.

6. Thomas Cobbet, *A Practical Discourse of Prayer* (London, 1657), 75–77, 448; Cobbet, "A Narrative of New England's Deliverances," 1677, *NEHGS* 7 (July 1853): 214. See also Foster, *The Long Argument*, 6, 97–99, 225–227; and Horton Davies, *Worship of the American Puritans* (New York, 1990), 60–68.

7. *Book of the General Lawes and Libertyes* (Boston, 1660), 27.

8. Stephen Foster, "Rereading Liberalism: Omission, Ambiguity, and Anomaly in New England Sermonic Literature, 1699–c. 1750," *NEQ* 92, No. 3 (September 2019): 484. The extent to which enslaved laborers or servants participated in fast days is a live question.

9. Brown, *Pilgrim and the Bee*, 111–113, 119, 121–124. Brown notes rightly that an emphasis on participation does not imply puritans were aiming for originality or a "Romantic autonomy" (133). Gildrie argues that "both the form and content" of fast days "asserted the official value system," although he allows that they fostered "a psychological climate more conducive to reconciliation" of political or ecclesiological differences ("The Ceremonial Puritan," 7–8). Francis Bremer includes fast days as forums for lay influence (*Lay Empowerment*, 26, 34). There is a rich scholarly literature on sermons and lay experience; see, for example, Arnold Hunt, *The Art of Hearing: English Preachers and Their Audiences, 1590–1640* (Cambridge, 2010); and Meredith Neuman, *Jeremiah's Scribes: Creating Sermon Literature in Puritan New England* (Philadelphia, 2013).

10. Thomas Danforth to Gov. Prence, 12 January 1665, Winslow Family Papers II, MHS.

11. Thomas Shepard notebook, 2 January 1662 fast day sermon, Octavo 5, Shepard Family Papers, AAS.

12. David Colclough, *Freedom of Speech in Early Stuart England* (Cambridge, 2005), 165.

13. Shepard notebook, 2 January 1662 fast day sermon.

14. Hull, "Diaries," 3:194; *Records of the First Church of Dorchester*, 34.

15. MassRecs 4.1.417–418; Suffolk Files, Case 397; Minor, *Diary*, 40.

16. *Records of the First Church of Dorchester*, 37.

17. *Records of the First Church of Dorchester*, 36–37. Hull records an additional private fast day: 21 November [1660]: "*for the state of our native country, it being like to come . . . under the bishops; the church countenancing the old liturgy, and formalities again to be practiced*" (Hull, "Diaries," 3:151–152).

18. *Records of the First Church of Dorchester*, 36–37; quote from Geneva Bible (1599). Eliot's Roxbury church fasted on 1 January 1661, probably along the same lines as Dorchester. Richard Mather most likely participated, reciprocating for Eliot's earlier Dorchester sermon.

19. Worden, *God's Instruments*, 329, 337, 344; Hall, *A Reforming People*, 15; Higginson, *Cause of God and His People*, 8.

20. Worden, *God's Instruments*, 342–348.

21. *Records of the First Church of Dorchester*, 37. For the "Epidem[ical] Cold," see William Hubbard's 27 February 1661 fast day sermon in Nathaniel Rogers, Sermon notebook, Ipswich Papers, 1653–1835, AAS. Hubbard focused more on the raging sickness than political events. He reassured his congregation that breaking one commandment did not mean a broken covenant, although warning against "Neglecting or changing the worship of God."

22. Hull, "Diaries," 3:199. In Ipswich Thomas Cobbet also brought up baptism, urging the community to "search and try our wayes," with "a neglect of baptizing children" first on the list. Cobbet, 27 February 1661 fast day sermon, in Nathaniel Rogers, Sermon notebook.

23. Hull, "Diaries," 3:200. Tompson preached at least one other sermon but soon relapsed. Salem held its own fast the following week for sickness, the Quaker threat, and "To seek the Lord for the peace and welfare of ourselves, and of our native land." Their minister John Higginson spoke from Rev. 3:10 and Psalm 50:5 regarding temptation and "our duty of Commandment keeping." Richard D. Pierce, ed., *The Records of the First Church in Salem, Massachusetts, 1629–1736* (Salem, 1974), 88–89.

24. Notes on sermons delivered in Boston, 1661, MHS. The sermon does not give the exact date.

25. ConnRecs 1:369, 390; Minor, *Diary*, 52–53.

26. While limited for Connecticut and New Haven and rare for Plymouth, extant fast day documents indicate similar sustained attention to political events and communal discernment. NHRecs, 465; Woodward, *Prospero's America*, 260–276; Bremer, *Building a New Jerusalem*, 294–298.

27. *Records of the First Church of Dorchester*, 39. The fast for most occurred on 4 December, but Salem inhabitants observed theirs later in December, focusing in a slightly more positive way on "preventing our fears, and continuing the blessings of Church and Commonwealth." Pierce, ed., *Records of the First Church in Salem*, 91.

28. Charles II, 1661 [effective 20 December 1661]: An Act for . . . Corporations, *Statutes of the Realm* (London, 1819), 5:321–323; Brewer, "Subjects by Allegiance to the King?" 27–28.

29. Hull, "Diaries," 3:204; Pierce, ed., *Records of the First Church in Salem*, 91–92.

30. MassRecs 4.2.34–35.

31. Shepard notebook, 2 January 1662 fast day sermon.

32. Shepard notebook, 2 January 1662 fast day sermon. Richard Mather drew parallels to Jerusalem's miseries when enemies "did mock at her sabbaths." *Records of the First Church of Dorchester*, 39; Lam. 1:7, KJV.

33. MassArch X.13a.

34. MassArch X.13a. The General Court's 21 May 1662 proclamation called for a 5 June fast day.

35. *Records of the First Church of Dorchester*, 40. Dorchester fasted for "thos that went to England for to negociate . . . that god would bless them in that worke."

36. Shepard notebook, 5 June 1662 public fast day sermon.

37. MassRecs 4.2.58; *Records of the First Church of Dorchester*, 40; Pierce, ed., *Records of the First Church in Salem*, 95.

38. Charles II to Massachusetts, 28 June 1662, Danforth Papers, 52–55.

39. Charles II to Massachusetts, 28 June 1662, Danforth Papers, 54.

40. Edward Rawson to [Thomas Thacher], 2 February 1663, Miscellaneous Bound Collection, MHS.

41. Isa. 30:20–21; Ps. 147:10–11.

42. Shepard notebook, 5 November 1662 public thanksgiving sermon.

43. MassRecs 4.2.60; MassArch X.14; Hull, "Diaries," 3:207.

44. *Elijah's Mantle*, 1–5 (MHS). Mitchell's December 1662 sermon does not indicate a fast day, but, sharply attuned to political events, it reads like an occasional sermon. The manu-

script version, used by Thomas Prince to correct by hand the printed version, more sharply advocates defiance of the Stuart regime.

45. *Elijah's Mantle*, 1–5 (MHS). For Christ's kingship over civil affairs, see Hall, *A Reforming People*, 96–99; and for Scottish Covenanters, Hall, *The Puritans*, 97–102. The Scottish Second Book of Discipline also advocated for the autonomy of the church. Scottish influences arrived personally through ministers such as Thomas Gilbert of Topsfield, who was furious at Charles II for betraying the Scottish Covenant (that of 1643, which the king took, insincerely, in 1650). *Historical Collections of the Topsfield Historical Society* 23 (1919): 67–70. Colonists also read reports of western Scots holding outdoor services, the Scottish bishops saying Charles II must either "give them Liberty and indulge them, or else make a Law to burne them." Hooke to Davenport, 5 March 1663, Mather Papers, 207–209.

46. Daniel Gookin, Petition, 14 February 1681, Thomas Prince Papers, 1661-1743, MHS. Gookin referred to a February 1661 lecture sermon on the same topic.

47. Thomas Cobbet, 3 December 1662 fast day sermon, fols. 87–91; William Hubbard, 3 December 1662 fast day sermon, fols. 92–95, notes in Nathaniel Rogers, Sermon notebook.

48. Anon., *Divine Consolations for Mourners in Sion* (Cambridge, MA, 1664), A3v–A4r; for a contextual reading of this text, attributing it to Joshua Scottow, see Anne Myles, "Restoration Declensions, Divine Consolations: The Work of John Foxe in 1664 Massachusetts," *NEQ* 80, No. 1 (March 2007): 35–68. For New Englanders' martyrdom rhetoric generally, see Adrian Chastain Weimer, *Martyrs' Mirror: Persecution and Holiness in Early New England* (Oxford, 2011).

49. Shepard notebook, 3 December 1662 public fast sermon.

50. John Milton, *Samson Agonistes* (London, 1671), 39; John Milton, *Complete Prose Works*, ed. Don Wolfe (New Haven, 1953), 5:3–4. Milton scholars generally do not read Samson's violence as a straightforward model for Restoration Dissent, especially given that Samson's destructive actions led to Israel's monarchy and fall into idolatry; there is little evidence, however, that Milton turned to quietism. Derek Wood, *"Exiled from Light": Divine Law, Morality, and Violence in Milton's Samson Agonistes* (Toronto, 2001), introduction, 172–191; Knoppers, *Historicizing Milton*, 55–56, 61–63; Sharon Achinstein, *Literature and Dissent in Milton's England* (Cambridge, 2003), 19. For nonconformists in exile, see Gaby Mahlberg, *The English Republican Exiles in Europe During the Restoration* (Cambridge, 2020), 26–28, 137–149.

51. Shepard notebook, 3 October 1662 private fast sermon. Shorthand transcription by Sarah Heavren.

52. Hull, "Diaries," 3:209; Gribben, *John Owen and English Puritanism*, chap. 9.

53. Hull, "Diaries," 3:153–154.

54. Although evidence is more scant, private fasts occurred throughout New England. Increase Mather, Diary, private fasts: 24 October 1664; 8 November 1664; 24 April 1665; 25 April 1666; January 1667; April 1667; 16 December 1668 (sermon notes in Mather Family Papers, AAS).

55. Appleby, *Black Bartholomew's Day*, 221–222. Increase Mather's inscribed copy of *A Compleat Collection of Farewel Sermons* (London, 1663) is in Mather Library 0714, AAS.

56. *Records of the First Church of Dorchester*, 41–42; Hull, "Diaries," 3:209; 1663 fasts: Dorchester, 18 August; Charlestown, 28 August; Cambridge, 2 September; Roxbury, 8 September; Boston, 18 September; Watertown, 23 September; Dedham, 7 October; Braintree, 14 October.

57. *Records of the First Church of Dorchester*, 42–43; Pierce, ed., *Records of the First Church in Salem*, 98; Hull, "Diaries," 3:210.

58. Shepard, *Parable of the Ten Virgins*, 10; Mather, *Magnalia*, 3:177; Hall, *The Puritans*, 232–234; Katharine Gerbner, "Beyond the 'Halfway Covenant': Church Membership, Extended Baptism, and Outreach in Cambridge, Massachusetts, 1656–1667," *NEQ* 85, No. 2 (June 2012): 281–301.

59. Jonathan Mitchell, *Propositions Concerning the Subject of Baptism* (Cambridge, MA, 1662), "Preface." The General Court ordered the synod on 31 December 1661 (MassRecs 4.2.38). Pulsipher argues that the Restoration dashed "hopes for a divinely mandated form of government in old England," leaving Massachusetts with "sole responsibility for creating such a community," leading to expanding baptism (*Subjects unto the Same King*, 89). Bremer concludes Davenport, absent from the synod due to the New Haven crisis, saw "efforts to 'obtain great alterations, both in civil government and church discipline,'" as connected, opposing both (*Building a New Jerusalem*, 313). See also William DeLoss Love, *Fast and Thanksgiving Days of New England* (Boston, 1895), 160–161, 186.

60. Increase Mather, Diary, 26 February 1664; Thomas Shepard, *Church-Membership of Children* (Cambridge, MA, 1663). In the preface Shepard (the son) argues for expanding baptism (B3r).

61. Shepard's sermon on this occasion is not extant. The Charlestown church, "after some discourse," had voted to approve the decision of the synod "for the substance thereof" earlier that year (4 February 1663) and implement baptismal reforms (27 November 1664). James Hunnewell, ed., *Records of the First Church in Charlestown* (Boston, 1880), ii–iii; Robert Pope, *The Half-way Covenant: Church Membership in Puritan New England* (Princeton, 1969), 55.

62. Shepard, "An Enquiry." Shepard also mentions sins of covetousness, sensuality, heresy or entertaining of heretics, and neglect of church discipline and Sabbath observance.

63. Increase Mather, Diary, 26 February 1664.

64. Historians have argued that supporters of the expansion of baptism generally wanted compromise with the king. It is true that the leading Boston ministers for baptismal reform—John Wilson and John Norton—promoted political compromise; and those against baptismal reform—John Davenport, Increase Mather, Eleazer Mather, Charles Chauncy, and John Mayo—were also generally for defying Charles II. But some advocates of baptismal reforms such as Richard Mather, Jonathan Mitchell, and John Eliot were also leaders of the movement to resist crown demands. Some ministers who supported the resistance petitions of 1664–1665 had a more difficult time denying the king's 1666 demand for agents. But the ministers who signed compromise petitions in 1666 were not congregationalists at all but Presbyterians Thomas Parker and John Woodbridge. Stephen Foster, *The Long Argument: English Puritanism and the Shaping of New England Culture* (Chapel Hill, 1991), 196–202; Lucas, "Colony or Commonwealth," 90–92. Robert Pope saw the visit of royal commissioners as a break in the baptism controversy that "temporarily silenced debate over the half-way covenant" (*Half-way Covenant*, 152). For congregationalist ministers' general aversion to publicizing their differences, see David D. Hall, *Ways of Writing: The Practice and Politics of Text-Making in Seventeenth-Century New England* (Philadelphia, 2008), 176.

65. Nicholas Street, Errata Synodalia, c. 1665–1666, Mather Family Papers, AAS. Another opponent of baptismal reform, John Russell argued that widening baptism changed the parameters of visible sanctity, which made it too easy for unregenerate men to gain political power. Hammer, *Pugnacious Puritans*, 38.

66. Davenport to Leverett, 24 June 1665, *Hutchinson Papers*, 2:118.

67. *Records of the First Church of Dorchester*, 43; Increase Mather, Diary, 25 February–10 March 1664. Increase was reading the German reformer David Pareus's commentary on Revelation, the sixteenth-century Italian Protestant Girolamo Zanchi's *De Ira Dei*, and a book about the early Bohemian Brethren reform movement. See also Julius Tuttle, *Libraries of the Mathers* (Worcester, 1910), 19, 17, 23.

68. Increase Mather to John Davenport, 2 June 1662, Mather Papers, 188; Hall, *Last American Puritan*, 54–55.

69. Massachusetts Council to Sec. Morrice, 25 November 1662, MassArch CVI.54 (printed in Danforth Papers, 48).

70. ConnRecs 1:424; Minor, *Diary*, 62; NHRecs, 542; Woodward, *Prospero's America*, chap. 8.

71. Increase Mather, Diary, 6 September 1666.

72. Nicolls to Clarendon, 27 July 1664, MsCP, fol. 94.

73. "Cartwright's Report," DCHNY 3:111–113.

74. MassRecs 4.2.144–145, 235–236 (May proclamation for 22 June 1665 fast).

Chapter 5

1. Maverick to Clarendon, ca. 1661–1663, *Clarendon Papers*, 21; see also Clarendon Ms. 74, fols. 232–235v, Bodleian Library. I owe the point about Maverick to Daniel Richter. Lou Roper has deftly uncovered the inner workings of these London committees. He claims that Winthrop, along with Maverick, instigated the conquest; my reading of these sources indicates Winthrop did supply information and desired Long Island to be part of Connecticut, but there is little evidence for his advocacy of the plan for conquest apart from presumed close association with Maverick. L. H. Roper, "The Fall of New Netherland and Seventeenth-Century Anglo-American Imperial Formation, 1654–1676," *NEQ* 87, No. 4 (December 2014): 683–685; Robert Ritchie, *The Duke's Province: A Study of New York's Politics and Society* (Chapel Hill, 1977), 20 ("overawe" [as "be overawed"]); Wim Klooster, *The Dutch Moment: War, Trade, and Settlement in the Seventeenth-Century Atlantic World* (Ithaca, 2016), 98; Daniel Richter, "Dutch Dominos: The Fall of New Netherland and the Reshaping of Eastern North America," in *Trade, Land, Power: The Struggle for Eastern North America* (Philadelphia, 2013), 100.

2. Hen. Parker to John Thomson [Edward Riggs to Sec. Bennet], 11 January 1664, SP 29/90 fol. 2; Jonathan Scott, "Sidney, Algernon," ODNB; Mahlberg, *English Republican Exiles*, 26–28, 137–149. The plot fizzled when Sidney failed when attempting to free Major General John Lambert from prison. The more committed anti-monarchist of the two, Ludlow refused to participate in the plot.

3. Maverick to Clarendon, ca. 1661–1663, *Clarendon Papers*, 32. Somewhat contradictorily, Maverick also implied royalist colonists might "remove to the Dutch" to escape the Bay's disorder (Petition, 30 August 1663, SP 44/13, fol. 356).

4. Stuyvesant, "Report on the Surrender of New Netherland," DCHNY 2:367, quoting a 23 April 1664 letter from Amsterdam's "Honorable Directors."

5. "Proposalls about Religious Matters," ca. 1662–1663, misfiled in October 1664 folder of MsWP.

6. Ritchie, *Duke's Province*, 18; Klooster, *Dutch Moment*, 98; Richter, "Dutch Dominos," 100. See also "Plan for Long Island," 29 January 1664, CO 1/18, No. 15. For larger imperial rivalries,

the perceived economic threat of the Dutch, and the struggle to enforce the Navigation Acts, see Koot, *Empire at the Periphery*, 97–109; and Israel, "The Emerging Empire," 425–433.

7. Clarendon to Nicolls, n.d., MsCP, fol. 141; Alison Olson, *Anglo-American Politics, 1660–1775* (New York, 1973), 46–47. Paul Seaward explores Clarendon's "rationalistic approach" in "Circumstantial Temporary Concessions: Clarendon, Comprehension, and Uniformity," in *"Settling the Peace of the Church": 1662 Revisited*, ed. N. H. Keeble (Oxford, 2014), 81. For other suggestions in Whitehall of setting up king-approved ministers in major towns and the Harvard presidency, see Egerton Ms. 2395, fol. 414v, BL.

8. Farmers of the Customs orders, DCHNY 3:48–50; see also Bliss, *Revolution and Empire*, 116, 122.

9. Ritchie, *Duke's Province*, 20; Pestana, *English Atlantic*, 221; Bernard Bailyn, *New England Merchants in the Seventeenth Century* (Cambridge, 1979), 112–114. Barbados was still much more lucrative.

10. Public Instructions for Massachusetts, DCHNY 3:51; see also CO 5/903, fols. 9–10. I owe the point about the lack of a real civil service pre-1690s to Stephen Foster.

11. Robert Ritchie, "Nicolls, Richard," ODNB; Geoffrey Gneuhs, "Nicolls, Richard," ANB; Hutchinson, *History*, 1:198–199; P. R. Newman, ed., *Royalist Officers in England and Wales, 1642–1660: A Biographical Dictionary* (New York, 1981), 62; Palfrey, *History of New England*, 2:580–581. Carr's son would marry Sec. Henry Bennet's sister Elizabeth.

12. On Maverick's several occupations, see Roper, "Fall of New Netherland," 681–698; on his project to "breed" enslaved persons by force, see Wendy Warren, "'The Cause of Her Grief': The Rape of a Slave in Early New England," *Journal of American History* 93 (2007): 1031–1049.

13. Clarendon to Maverick, 5 March 1665, DCHNY 3:92; His Majesties Commission, 25 April 1664, printed in MassRecs 4.2.161–162; see also Cartwright to Sec. Bennet, 16 January 1665, CO 1/19, No. 8; and Bailyn, *New England Merchants*, 114–115. By October 1664 Nicolls would empower the other three to act without his presence, though not without his consent. CO 1/18, Nos. 107, 156; MsCP, fol. 131; CO 1/19, No. 37.

14. Public Instructions for Massachusetts, DCHNY 3:51–53.

15. Public Instructions for Massachusetts, DCHNY 3:51–53; Public Instructions for Connecticut, DCHNY 3:53–56. Winthrop had left London with a sealed royal charter that was then realized to conflict with Rhode Island's. See Woodward, *Prospero's America*, chap. 8.

16. Public Instructions for Massachusetts, DCHNY 3:53–54; Public Instructions for Connecticut, DCHNY 3:56.

17. Public Instructions for Massachusetts, DCHNY 3:52–54.

18. Private Instructions, DCHNY 3:57–60. See also Cartwright's frustration, "I cannot conceive how it is possible for us to get a good election made for the next Generall Assembly" (DCHNY 3:87). Sosin emphasizes the instructions' "self-deception," symptomatic of the "weakness of the royal government." *English America*, 109–110. For more successful efforts to pressure the Corporation of London in elections, see De Krey, *London and the Restoration*, 26.

19. Private Instructions, DCHNY 3:58–61.

20. Charles II, 1661 [effective 20 December 1661]: An Act for . . . Corporations, *Statutes of the Realm* (London, 1819), 5:321–323. Thanks to Robert Bliss for this suggestion.

21. Paul Halliday, *Dismembering the Body Politic: Partisan Politics in England's Towns, 1650–1730* (Cambridge, 1998), 96–97 (quotes); Harris, *Restoration*, 67. London received thorough attention, especially because of the work of Bishop Gilbert Sheldon. De Krey, *London in*

the Restoration, 81; Elliot Vernon, *London Presbyterians and the British Revolutions, 1638–64* (Manchester, 2021), chap. 12.

22. Halliday, *Dismembering the Body Politic*, 153–161, 167–171. After 1668 elected mayors would require the lord lieutenant's approval and corporation members would have to take Church of England sacraments biannually.

23. "Estimate of the charge of sending the King's Commissioners to New England," [early 1664?] CO 1/66, No. 61.

24. Nicolls to Clarendon, 27 July 1664, MsCP, fol. 91.

25. Nathaniel White to Michael Wigglesworth, 12 September 1664, Miscellaneous Bound, MHS. White summarizes Wigglesworth's July letter, composed when "Frigots are dayly expected."

26. The boundary decided 29 May 1664 is in Massachusetts Collection, AAS.

27. Rhode Island's 1663 charter allowed for appeals of such intercolonial disputes to the king, a clause on which John Clarke insisted. Sydney James, *John Clarke and His Legacies: Religion and Law in Colonial Rhode Island, 1638–1750* (University Park, 1999), 81.

28. "Orders as to a Day of Humiliation and as to Pattent being kept safe," Suffolk Files, Case 633; Lucas, "Colony or Commonwealth," 98.

29. *Winthrop Papers* (Boston, 1943), 3:465; Dunn, *Puritans and Yankees*, 26–29.

30. Suffolk Files, Case 633; see also MassRecs 4.2.101–102.

31. Suffolk Files, Case 634; George Howell, ed., *Colonial Records: General Entries* (Albany, 1899), 1:72–73.

32. Richard Mather, fast day sermon, 15 June 1664 and William Stoughton, fast day sermon, 15 June 1664, both in John Minot notebook, Mather Family Papers, Special Collections, University of Virginia Library; see also Increase Mather, Diary, 8 June 1664. For the language and culture of "fellow feeling," see Abram Van Engen, *Sympathetic Puritans: Calvinist Fellow Feeling in Early New England* (Oxford, 2015).

33. Nicolls to Clarendon, 27 July 1664, MsCP, fols. 91–92. One of the ships may have stayed anchored off Nantucket. Nicolls and Cartwright to Sec. Bennet, July 1664, in Howell, ed., *Colonial Records*, 1:74.

34. Nicolls and Cartwright also attended an afternoon service at Boston's second church. Nicolls to Clarendon, 27 July 1664, MsCP, fols. 92–93.

35. Thanks to Evan Haefeli for the meaning of "Push a Pike." Nicolls to Clarendon, 27 July 1664, MsCP, fol. 94; John Pynchon and Thomas Clarke to Edward Rawson, 15 August 1664, Carl Bridenbaugh, ed., *Pynchon Papers* (Boston, 1982), 1:52.

36. Charles II to Massachusetts, 23 April 1664, CO 1/18, No. 53, printed along with the royal commission, the proposals regarding the campaign against the Dutch, and the General Court's official account of the meeting in MassRecs 4.2.157–164.

37. His Majesties Commission, 25 April 1664, printed in MassRecs 4.2.162; Pulsipher, *Subjects unto the Same King*, 285n62.

38. Bilder, *Transatlantic Constitution*, 47–56. Pulsipher suggests that the royal commissioners may have intended "to deliver jurisdiction back to the colony after first obtaining acknowledgement of their superior authority," but the magistrates' opposition derailed that possibility (*Subjects unto the Same King*, 49).

39. MassRecs 4.2.164. They also protested it was the harvest season. Howell, ed., *Colonial Records*, 1:75–78.

40. Nicolls to Clarendon, 27 July 1664, MsCP, fol. 95. Whether these men were involved in the petitions described by Rawson above is unknown.

41. Lucas, "Colony or Commonwealth," 99.

42. Thomas Danforth, notebook, MHS; mostly transcribed in Danforth Papers, 95. For Maverick's letters from Piscataqua, see CO 1/18, No. 86.

43. MassArch X.201; MassRecs 4.2.119. Increase Mather, Diary, 5 August 1664. For Mitchell's role in these meetings, see Cotton Mather, *Ecclesiastes* (Boston, 1697), 95.

44. MassArch X.201.

45. MassArch LXVII.148. For Protestant theories of just war, going back to Augustine, in relation to holy war, see Susan Juster, *Sacred Violence in Early America* (Philadelphia, 2016), 79–100.

46. MassArch LXVII.148.

47. MassRecs 4.2.117–125; Hull, "Diaries," 3:213; Pynchon and Clarke to Rawson, 15 August 1664, *Pynchon Papers*, 1:52.

48. MassRecs 4.2.118–119; MassArch CVI.87a, LXVII.148. Rawson's summary of the General Court's proceedings (transcribed by Shurtleff) makes it appear the resolution preceded the elders or ministers' advice, but Rawson often overrides chronological order; it is more likely the ministers, meeting 4 August, were involved earlier.

49. MassRecs 4.2.118–122, 125. As we saw earlier some court members would argue the 1662 synod's reforms partially addressed the king's concern regarding baptism.

50. MassRecs 4.2.73–74; MassArch CVI.66a.

51. MassRecs 4.2.117–118. A similar policy had been suggested in the 1661 Sudbury petition. The candidates' status as "freeholders" with estate "rateable to the country in a single country rate . . . or the full value of tenne shillings" would be certified by local selectmen. For the scholarly debate over whether the entire estate or the rate amounted to ten shillings (resolved on the latter), see B. Katherine Brown, "The Controversy over the Franchise in Puritan Massachusetts, 1954 to 1974," *WMQ* 33, No. 2 (April 1976): 212–241.

52. MassRecs 4.2.120.

53. MassRecs 4.2.117–119; see also MassArch X.14a (magistrates initiate, deputies consent); *Records of the First Church of Dorchester*, 44; Pierce, ed., *Records of the First Church in Salem*, 102; Hull, "Diaries," 3:213.

54. Howell, ed., *Colonial Records*, 1:93, 100–101.

55. Stuyvesant to Directors in Holland, 24 September 1661, DCHNY 14:506; Stuyvesant, "Report on the Surrender of New Netherland," DCHNY 2:367 (quoting 23 April 1664 letter from "the Honorable Directors" in Amsterdam); Ritchie, *Duke's Province*, 22; Roper, "Fall of New Netherland," 686. Papers of surrender: Howell, ed., *Colonial Records*, 1:95–98, 102–104. John Scott played a role in these uprisings, claiming to be representing royal interests. Connecticut prosecuted him but he escaped from jail. He also served (briefly and poorly) as agent for New Haven. NHRecs 1:420–423; John Davenport to John Winthrop, 22 June 1663, in *Letters of John Davenport, Puritan Divine*, ed. Isabel Calder (New Haven, 1937), 217, 240–241n2; Alan Marshall, "Scott, John," ODNB.

56. Remonstrance of the People of New Netherland, DCHNY 2:248. See also Stuyvesant, "Report on the Surrender," DCHNY 2:365–370. The Dutch would briefly retake New York in 1673.

57. I am indebted to Daniel Richter's analysis of these broader conflicts. "Articles agreed upon in Fort Albany," 24 September 1664, CO 1/18, No. 105, printed in DCHNY 3:67–68; Howell, ed., *Colonial Records* has Cartwright's commission (1:105), the Albany agreement (1:112–114), the Iroquois treaty (1:110–112), Carr's commission (1:104) and instructions

(1:125–126), Delaware agreement (1:127–128); Ritchie, *Duke's Province*, 23–25. For these Native alliances and the long-term ramifications of the Dutch arms trade, here resumed by the English, see Andrew Lipman, *Saltwater Frontier: Indians and the Contest for the American Coast* (New Haven, 2015), 190–202.

58. Stuyvesant, "Report on the Surrender," DCHNY 2:369; Ritchie, *Duke's Province*, 24–25; Mark Thompson, *Contest for the Delaware: Allegiance, Identity, and Empire in the Seventeenth Century* (Baton Rouge, 2013), 182–184; Klooster, *Dutch Moment*, 99; Carr to Nicolls, 13 October 1664, DCHNY 3:73–74. Any lands west of the Delaware were not actually included in York's patent.

59. Nicolls to Clarendon, 21 November 1664, MsCP, fol. 127; see also Nicolls to Arlington, October 1664, DCHNY 3:68–70; D'Hinoyossa to Nicolls [late 1664?], DCHNY 3:82–83; "Gerrit Van Sweeringen's Account" repeats the claim about Dutch soldiers "transported to be sold" and includes a list of the plunder, including "betweene sixty and seventy negroes . . . foure thousand pounds sterling . . . [and] foure and twenty great gunns." DCHNY 3:345–346.

60. Common punishment for soldiers, the "horse" was a triangular wooden structure on which offenders were made to sit, sometimes weighted down; strappado meant being tied to a rope and dropped. Nicolls to Clarendon, 21 November 1664, MsCP, fol. 130.

61. Order for ship *Guyny*, Howell, ed., *Colonial Records*, 1:133.

62. Hulsebosch, *Constituting Empire*, 46.

63. Duke of York to Gov. Andros, January 1676, DCHNY 3:235; Anon., *Conditions for New-Planters* ([Cambridge, MA], 1665); Nicolls to Clarendon, 30 July 1665, *Clarendon Papers*, 75.

64. *Colonial Laws of New York* (Albany, 1894), 1:24–26; Nicolls to Howell and Young, 1 December 1664, in Howell, ed., *Colonial Records*, 1:132–133; see also Ritchie, *Duke's Province*, 32–35; and Jaap Jacobs, *New Netherland: A Dutch Colony in Seventeenth-Century America* (Boston, 2005), 181–182. For the religious settlement, see Evan Haefeli, *New Netherland and the Dutch Origins of American Religious Liberty* (Philadelphia, 2012), 256–259 (who cites evidence that Nicolls may have been Catholic leaning). The cities of Albany and New York would eventually gain corporate charters and more autonomy.

65. Quakers probably reported the Hathorne rumor to the royal commissioners. Transactions of Royal Commissioners with Massachusetts, 26 May 1665, CO 1/19, No. 56, mostly printed in Danforth Papers, 56; George Bishop, *New-England Judged* (Philadelphia, 1885), 1:218n. See also "Cartwright's Report," DCHNY 3:110; and "Cartwright's Answer," *Clarendon Papers*, 94.

66. "Cartwright's Report," DCHNY 3:110.

67. Cartwright to Nicolls, 25 January 1665, DCHNY 3:85; Cartwright to Nicolls, 4 February 1665, CO 1/19, No. 20; see also Cartwright to Sec. Bennet, 7 February 1664, DCHNY 3:89.

68. MassArch CVI.81.

69. MassArch CVI.81. Even colonies whose charters included a provision for review of the law code, such as Jamaica, jealously guarded their authority to write their own laws. Bilder, *Transatlantic Constitution*, 55.

70. MassArch CVI.81; Lucas, "Colony or Commonwealth," 101.

71. PlymRecs 10:318.

Chapter 6

1. MassRecs 4.2.136–137. Gregory Stone was probably Hartford minister Samuel Stone's brother. Edward Oakes was father to later Harvard president Urian Oakes. Of the 106 male

signers in the first list 75 were full church members and 52 were freemen; of the 35 young men in the second list 17 would go on to become freemen. B. Katherine Brown, "Puritan Democracy: A Case Study," *Mississippi Valley Historical Review* 50, No. 3 (December 1963): 386–387. For breadth of participation in Cambridge town government, see *Records of the Town of Cambridge . . .* (Cambridge, 1901); Lucius Paige, *History of Cambridge* (Boston, 1877); Roger Thompson, *Cambridge Cameos: Stories of Life in Seventeenth-Century New England* (Boston, 2005); and Hall, *A Reforming People*, chap. 5. For the roots of this participatory culture in English parishes, especially traditions of local officeholding, see Goldie, "The Unacknowledged Republic."

2. Rebeccah [or Reana] Daniell is probably the "Widow Daniell" who was "granted liberty to fell timber on the Common" on 14 February 1659. *Records of the Town of Cambridge*, 126.

3. For the shift in English constitutionalist thought in the 1640s to an emphasis on "enforceable limitation," and its later contexts, see Glenn Burgess, *British Political Thought, 1500–1660: The Politics of the Post-Reformation* (New York, 2009), 197; H. A. Lloyd, "Constitutionalism," in *Cambridge History of Political Thought, 1450–1700* , ed. J. A. Burns (Cambridge, 1991), 255–258; John Reid, *Constitutional History of the American Revolution* (Madison, 1995), 3; Peter Onuf, *The Origins of the Federal Republic: Jurisdictional Controversies in the United States, 1775–1787* (Philadelphia, 1983), xiii–xiv, 13–17, 129–131; and Jack Greene, *Constitutional Origins of the American Revolution* (Cambridge, 2011), 2–14.

4. Increase Mather, Diary, 4 March 1664; W-W- to William Goffe, 18 December 1661, Mather Papers, 168; Harris, *Restoration*, 59.

5. Coffey, *Persecution and Toleration*, 169–173.

6. *Journal of John Winthrop*, 140; John Davenport to John Leverett, 24 June 1665, in *Letters of John Davenport*, ed. Calder, 248–253.

7. Nadhorth to Sec. Morrice, 26 October 1666, DCHNY 3:142. The idea of consolidating the New England colonies under a single governor had also circulated prior to 1660.

8. Thomas Danforth, notebook, MHS; mostly transcribed in Danforth Papers, 95.

9. For the Rhode Island case, involving Tobias Saunders and Robert Burdet, see MassArch CVI.67–70. For Maverick's rhetoric, see Maverick, *A Briefe Description* (Boston, 1885), 17–18.

10. Magistrates had also encouraged local responses to counter Robert Child's petition in 1646. Hall, *Ways of Writing*, 165–166; Robert Wall, *Massachusetts Bay: The Crucial Decade, 1640–1650* (New Haven, 1972), 171–175.

11. MassRecs 4.2.274.

12. Howes and Perley, eds., *Salem Town Records*, 37. The Woburn records are less specific but note heated debates in this year. Record for 7 March 1664, *Records of Middlesex County, Mass. Towns Through 1830: Woburn*, vol. 1 (Boston, 1975), Microfilm, MHS. See also Kenneth Lockridge, *A New England Town: The First Hundred Years* (New York, 1970), chap. 3; and Sumner Chilton Powell, *Puritan Village: The Formation of a New England Town* (Middletown, 1963), 107–108.

13. Paul Lucas argued that Edward Johnson wrote the petition as a more moderate alternative to the General Court committee's—moderate because it "contained no reference to Massachusetts's independence." But almost no one referred directly to the colony as a "free-state" or "independent" political entity; this was the language of their detractors, almost never of colonists describing themselves. In general Lucas's reading of the colony's politics in these years posits a Manichaean battle between "moderate" and "commonwealth" factions,

whereas my reading sees a more fluid political landscape. But even Lucas acknowledges that the town petitions were "signed by members of both groups" and exhibit a "blurring of factional lines" ("Colony or Commonwealth," 102, 101).

14. MassArch CVI.52–52a, 61a–62c; MassRecs 4.2.58; Letter of Thomas Dutton, 8 December 1662, Edward Rawson Papers, MHS.

15. MassArch CVI.80.

16. Patents or charters gave colonial leaders the power to make laws within their boundaries according to local needs, not requiring them to fully replicate English law, although legal repugnancy and divergence were continually negotiated. Bilder, *Transatlantic Constitution*, 40–46.

17. MassArch CVI.80.

18. Hobbesian theories held influence in both Cromwellian and later Stuart regimes. Within a royalist framework, William Berkeley would also advocate for Virginia as a distinct commonwealth. Haskell, *For God, King, and People*, chap. 5. For colonists' emphasis on a unique polity in the 1670s and 1680s, see Richard Ross, "The Career of Puritan Jurisprudence," *Law and History Review* 26, No. 2 (Summer 2008): 232–234.

19. MassArch CVI.80; Withington, *Politics of Commonwealth*, 241–249. The language of "honest men" was not unique to puritans or the civil war era.

20. The possible alliance between Presbyterians and Charles I in 1648, which could have excluded Independents, marked an important moment for merging fears about civil and religious liberty. In the 1640s some English puritans, along with Levellers, said that if they were deprived of the liberty of worshipping according to conscience, civil liberties had no meaning, they could not be enjoyed. Worden, *God's Instruments*, 316–317, 331–335, 346–348; John Owen, *ΟΥΡΑΝΩΝ ΟΥΡΑΝΙΑ: The Shaking and Translating of HEAVEN and EARTH* (London, 1649), 17, 35–36. For similar linking of civil and religious liberties among Elizabethan and Jacobean puritans, see Winship, "Freeborn (Puritan) Englishmen and Slavish Subjection," 1050–1052, 1056–1058, 1065–1073.

21. MassArch CVI.80. William Poole transcribes "regitate" here as "vegetate" but reagitate, or "stir up," better fits the word and context. "Reagitate," Oxford English Dictionary Online. Edward Johnson, *Wonder-Working Providence of Sions Saviour in New England*, ed. William Poole (Andover, 1867), cxxiii.

22. Woodward, *Prospero's America*, 257.

23. MassArch CVI.80. The English population of all New England was probably not over thirty-five thousand.

24. Esther 6–7, Geneva Bible (1599).

25. Geneva Bible (1599), 178v.

26. MassArch CVI.81.

27. Fletcher, *Outbreak of the English Civil War*, 191–193; Valerie Pearl, *London and the Outbreak of the Puritan Revolution* (Oxford, 1961), 229–235; John Morrill, *Nature of the English Revolution* (London, 1993), 75–78; Murray Tolmie, *Triumph of the Saints: The Separate Churches of London, 1616–1649* (Cambridge, 1977), 90–95.

28. Pearl, *London and the Outbreak*, 229; David Zaret, *The Origins of Democratic Culture: Printing, Petitions, and the Public Sphere in Early-Modern England* (Princeton, 2000), 224–225, 254–255; John Walter, "Confessional Politics in Pre-Civil War Essex: Prayer Books, Profanations, and Petitions," *Historical Journal* 44, No. 3 (2001): 677–701. For early 1640s contests over certain petitions' fraudulency, see Peter Lake, "Puritans, Popularity and Petitions:

Local Politics in National Context, Cheshire, 1641," in *Politics, Religion, and Popularity in Early Stuart Britain* (Cambridge, 2002), 259–289. For the increasing role of popular opinion in English politics, see Freist, *Governed by Opinion*, part 4; and Buchanan Sharp, "Popular Political Opinion in England 1660–1685," *History of European Ideas* 10 (1989): 13–17.

29. Nehemiah Wallington, *Historical Notices of Events Concurring in the Reign of Charles I*, ed. R. Bentley (London, 1869), 2:14.

30. Fletcher, *Outbreak of the English Civil War*, 195. The Essex petition of 1642 boasted at least ten thousand signers. There were other large English petitions campaigns, especially that of 1659.

31. Withington, *Politics of Commonwealth*, 243–248. There were exceptions, especially in the 1650s, for example when Oliver Cromwell retaliated against petitioners in 1653. C. H. Firth, ed., *Clarke Papers* (London, 1899), 3:vii–viii, 6–8.

32. Robert Child et al., Remonstrance and Petition, *Hutchinson Papers*, 1:214–223; MassRecs 3:90–94; *Journal of John Winthrop*, 624–625, 647, 655–671. See also Wall, *Massachusetts Bay*, chap. 6; Stephen Clucas, "Robert Child," ODNB; and Hall, *Ways of Writing*, 165–166. Maverick's initial fine was much smaller because he supposedly did not threaten to appeal the case to England. Five members of the General Court registered dissent from the decision to fine the petitioners, and the court allowed for the fine to be waived if an apology was given. The court later intercepted documents intended for London aimed at the revocation of the charter, leading to further prosecution.

33. "Body of Liberties. 1641," in William Whitmore, ed., *Colonial Laws of Massachusetts* (Boston, 1890), 35; Hall, *A Reforming People*, 92; see also 88–91.

34. Ministers who signed included Richard Mather, Eleazer Mather, John Eliot, John Russell, John Mayo, Jonathan Mitchell, Charles Chauncy, John Wilson (the son), and James Allen (an ejected minister who would be ordained teacher in 1668). Of twelve extant 1664–1665 petitions from inhabitants generally (excluding the two solely from non-freemen), nine were signed by ministers, teachers, or ruling elders.

35. Fletcher, *Outbreak of the English Civil War*, 96; Zaret, *Origins of Democratic Culture*, 226, 233–234. Fletcher argues that in England "responsibility for parochial subscriptions rested in the last resort either on constables or ministers" (195; see also 91–97). Pearl finds that in London during the Long Parliament the MPs' "chief agents for spreading information and later for raising subscriptions were . . . the Puritan ministers and lecturers of the City," although puritan aldermen and other city officials also played a role (*London and the Outbreak*, 230–235).

36. Pulsipher offers the most extensive treatment of the 1660s petitions, giving special attention to Native-Anglo relations. Pulsipher, *Subjects unto the Same King*, 86–87. For the Hadley petition, see Hall, *A Reforming People*, 191. The "one fourth" estimate is Pulsipher's (86–87). For the franchise debates, see Brown, "Controversy over the Franchise."

37. Conal Condren, *The Language of Politics in Seventeenth-Century England* (London, 1994), 33–46.

38. MassRecs 4.2.136.

39. Daniel Gookin, Petition, 14 February 1681, Thomas Prince Papers, 1661-1743, MHS. Gookin also mentioned the previous pastor of Cambridge Thomas Shepard's book the *Ten Virgins*, which "in the 1st part page 166: speakes to the same purpose." He concluded of Mitchell and Shepard, "these persons were burning & shineing lights in their Generation . . . much of Gods mynd did they know and speake."

40. Cambridge Petition in Paige, *History of Cambridge*, 74–76. For "wilderness" language among second-generation colonists, see Karen Kupperman, "Climate and Mastery of the Wilderness in Seventeenth-Century New England," in *Seventeenth-Century New England*, ed. David Allen and David D. Hall (Boston, 1984), 24–25; and for longer uses of the "wilderness" trope, see Zachary Hutchins, *Inventing Eden: Primitivism, Millennialism, and the Making of New England* (Oxford, 2014), 53–67.

41. MassRecs 4.2.119; Hull, "Diaries," 3:213.

42. The Concord petition is in the William Monroe Special Collections of the Concord Free Public Library. Thanks to Conni Manoli for sending an image and transcription. For a list of signatures, see Ruth Wheeler, *Climate for Freedom* (Concord, 1967), 199–200.

43. Anon., *The Foure Petitions of Huntington Shire, Norfolk, Suffolk, and Essex* (London, 1642), A2v; Anon., *The Humble Petition and Resolution of the County of Essex* (London, 1642).

44. Anon., *Foure Petitions*, A3r (Norfolk); Anon., *The Resolution of the Gentry and Commonalty of the County of Kent* (London, 1642), 5.

45. Henry Hazen, *History of Billerica* (Boston, 1883), 185.

46. The Medfield petition is printed as "Medfield Memorial, 1664," *NEHGR* 13 (1859): 346.

47. There was a private fast, for example, at "Brother Ways" the day before the Boston 25 October petition was drafted. Increase Mather, Diary, 24 October 1664.

48. B. R. Burg, *Richard Mather of Dorchester* (Lexington, 1976), 163.

49. MassRecs 4.2.24. Mitchell, Norton, and Cobbet were also on this committee, along with four magistrates and four deputies.

50. *Life and Death of Richard Mather* (Boston, 1850), 55, 56–67 (includes extracts from Mather's journal).

51. The Dorchester petitioners also included a longer section on financial concerns. They may have heard rumors that the royal commissioners were going to demand £3,000 as well as 12d per acre of improved land. Cartwright to Sec. Bennet, 7 February 1665, CO 1/19, No. 22. Other financial pressures included the enforcement of the Navigation Acts, the outlay of at least £500 to equip soldiers for the New Netherland campaign, and the royal commissioners' entertainment. MassRecs 4.2.122–123, 134; Breen, *Character of a Good Ruler*, 89–90.

52. Dorchester petition, September 1664 folder, Photostat Collection, MHS.

53. Dorchester petition, September 1664 folder, Photostat Collection, MHS.

54. MassRecs 4.2.5–6.

55. Roxbury petition, October 1664 folder, Photostat Collection, MHS; MassArch CVI.97.

56. *Report of the Record Commissioners of the City of Boston* (Boston, 1881), 7:26. This committee convened just after the town meeting when the deputy was chosen.

57. "Petition of the Citizens of Boston," Danforth Papers, 103–7; MassRecs 4.2.317–318.

58. Hull, "Diaries," 3:213–214.

59. These other petitions are lost, although the Woburn one could have been based on the "Petition from all the Freemen" discussed above, and Dedham non-freemen would later send in their own petition. MassRecs 4.2.136–137. See, for example, accounts of presentation at the end of Anon., *The Citizens of London's Humble Petition* (London, 1641); and Anon., *The Humble Petition of Divers Inhabitants of the County of Hertford* (London, 1659). Wallington, *Historical Notices*, 2:2–6, 11–13; Fletcher, *Outbreak of the English Civil War*, 196–197; Zaret, *Origins of Democratic Culture*, 228.

60. Cartwright to Nicolls, 25 January 1665, DCHNY 3:84; see also Cartwright to Nicolls, 4 February 1665, DCHNY 3:87.

61. MassRecs 4.2.86, 134.

62. MassRecs 4.2.129–132.

63. MassRecs 4.2.131–132; Woodward, *Prospero's America*, 288–301. Endicott wrote similarly to Boyle that giving power to men who would only "serve themselves" would drive colonists to leave. Endicott to Boyle, 19 October 1664, printed in Archibald Kennedy, *An Essay on the Government of the Colonies* (New York, 1752), 9.

64. MassRecs 4.2.132–133. The letter's final blessing was from Job 29:12–13.

65. "Morrice's answer to the New England petition," 25 February 1665, CO 1/19, No. 30.

66. MassRecs 4.2.175–177; Kamensky, *Governing the Tongue*, 105–115. The court's recent proclamation for a November 1664 fast, while similar to the previous one, also struck an especially somber tone, mentioning "threats of greater evils yet impending in severall passages of his providence towards us." Pierce, ed., *Records of the First Church in Salem*, 102; Hull, "Diaries," 3:214; Roxbury Church Records, *NEHGR* 34 (January–April 1880): 162; *Records of the First Church of Dorchester*, 44. MassRecs 4.2.135; see also MassArch X.15.

67. MassArch CVI.104. The pastor Eleazer Mather signed the petition but Trumbull identifies the handwriting as that of James Cornish. Trumbull estimates that "nearly every male person in the place, above 21 years of age" signed. James Trumbull, *History of Northampton* (Northampton, 1898), 1:156–157.

68. Corrine Weston, "England: Ancient Constitution and Common Law," in *Cambridge History of Political Thought, 1450–1700*, ed. J. H. Burns (Cambridge, 1991), 374–395; Burgess, *The Politics of the Ancient Constitution*, chap. 2. Modifying the work of J. G. A. Pocock, Burgess's "ancient constitution" is an evolving tradition, based in both reason and custom.

69. While Quentin Skinner saw "'a few wisps' of resistance theory lingering" in the Geneva notes, Patrick Collinson went further, insisting that Geneva readers learned "that God takes vengeance on tyrants, even in this life." Collinson, "The Monarchical Republic of Queen Elizabeth I," 45; see also Richard Greaves, "Traditionalism and the Seeds of Revolution in the Social Principles of the Geneva Bible," *Sixteenth Century Journal* 7, No. 2 (October 1976): 94–109; and Abram Van Engen, "Origins and Last Farewells: Bible Wars, Textual Form, and the Making of American History," *NEQ* 86, No. 4 (December 2013): 551–552.

70. Also Galatians 5:13: "For brethren, ye have been called unto liberty: only use not your liberty as an occasion unto the flesh, but by love serve one another." GNV; KJV omits word "your." For uses of this verse in the 1560s vestarian controversy, see Hall, *The Puritans*, 50.

71. Milton's *A Defence of the People of England* (Latin ed., 1651) said that rulers were always accountable to the people who had given them power in the first place; kings could not take away the people's liberty: "Our liberty is not Caesar's," he wrote, "but is a birthday gift to us from God himself." Colonists also shared Milton's appeal to natural law arguments but remained far shy of his radicalism, especially his argument that individuals could punish rulers who violated the laws of nature, or even depose them at will. *Milton: Political Writings*, ed. Dzelzainis, xv–xviii, 8–16, 182–184, 107; Tyacke, "Revolutionary Puritanism in Anglo-American Perspective," 767. There is a 1652 edition of *Pro populo Anglicano defensio* at the AAS, Mather Library 0532, inscribed: "Ex libris Johannis James / Samuelis Matheri liber." I am grateful to Meredith Neuman for conversations about books catalogued as the Mather Library, some of which are later additions.

72. MassArch CVI.107; Hall, *A Reforming People*, 191; Sibley, "John Russell," in *Biographical Sketches*, 1:110–113. Hadley's petition reads like a mini-sermon and was almost certainly

drafted with help from Russell, perhaps giving insight into the content of Russell's 1665 election sermon, never printed.

73. Hull, "Diaries," 3:207; Nicolls to Clarendon, 27 July 1664, MsCP, fols. 94–95.

74. Zaret, *Origins of Democratic Culture*, 259–260. Later in 1665 there is some evidence of Maine neighbors (and possibly the royal commissioners themselves) threatening others to sign a petition (MassRecs 4.2.249; *Hutchinson Papers*, 2:122–124).

75. The issue of the political resentments of enslaved Native Americans and Africans in New England households, as well as indentured servants, is a different and essential question. For an in-depth look at legal access across the social spectrum in Massachusetts see M. Michelle Jarrett Morris, *Under Household Government: Sex and Family in Puritan Massachusetts* (Cambridge, MA, 2013). For Narragansetts' interactions with the royal commissioners, see Pulsipher, *Subjects unto the Same King*, chaps. 2–3. For Native American petitions, a good starting point is MassArch 30, partially digitized by Harvard University's Massachusetts Native American Petitions project, https://iiif.lib.harvard.edu/manifests/view/drs:53822428$1i. For Anglo-American non-freemen and voting, see Brown, "Controversy over the Franchise," 228–229; and Lockridge, *New England Town*, 47–48, 53–54.

76. MassArch CVI.110. Lockridge has confirmed that none of the signers "was qualified to vote in colony elections and some could not participate in the town meeting" (*New England Town*, 54).

77. In a well-known 1642 parliamentary fast day sermon on this passage, Stephen Marshall had argued that "All people are cursed or blessed according as they doe or doe not joyne their strength . . . to the Lords people against their enemies" and if they do not their city would be destroyed or grow "unpeopled." Marshall, *Meroz Cursed* (London, 1641 [i.e., 1642]), 5, 8. AAS holds a copy of this sermon, rebound as Mather Library 0136I. See also Davenport, *Saints Anchor-hold*, 191–192. Samuel Maverick said this passage was also preached in the 1640s in Massachusetts to encourage colonists to fight for the parliamentary army. Maverick to Clarendon, ca. 1661–1663, *Clarendon Papers*, 39. Of the non-freemen's petitions, Davenport said they were part of a general aggrievement at the actions of Maverick and the other royal commissioners, as well as an "earnest desire" that the charter might be continued. Davenport to John Leverett, 24 June 1665, in *Letters of John Davenport*, ed. Calder, 251–252.

78. MassArch CVI.110; see also Gilbert Hawes, *Edward Haws, the Emigrant* (New York, 1895), 8–9.

79. MassArch CVI.111.

80. MassArch CVI.111.

81. On the frequent and voluntary nature of petitions in the eighteenth century, see James Hrdlicka, "Dr. William Douglass and the Constitution of Massachusetts Bay, ca. 1750" (forthcoming); and Abby Chandler, "'Unawed by the Laws of Their Country': Local and Imperial Legitimacy in North Carolina's Regulator Rebellion," *North Carolina Historical Review* 93, No. 2 (April 2016): 119–146. For their use in imperial diplomacy, see Hannah Muller, "From Requête to Petition: Petitioning the Monarch Between Empires," *Historical Journal* 60, No. 3 (2017): 659–686.

82. Maverick to Nicolls, 4 February 1665, DCHNY 3:88; see also Maverick to Nicolls, 5 March 1665, DCHNY 3:93.

83. MassArch CVI.139; although the formal deposition was taken later the story had probably already circulated.

84. MassArch CVI.125. The depositions regarding this incident took place at the height of the May 1665 negotiations between Bay leaders and royal commissioners.

85. Hubbard, *General History*, 579.

86. Joseph Williamson wrote, "Mavericke was of all men the worst to do it; debauched[?], idle, and under great prejudices." "Sir Joseph Williamson's Original Notes relating to New England," ca. 1663, *Proceedings of the MHS* (1868): 377; ms. is CO 1/17, No. 115. Cartwright also reported a colonial magistrate saying to him "that if we found not that respect which was due to us, as the Kings Commissioners, we might lay the fault on Mr Mavericke. For we found lesse, becaus he was with us." "Cartwright's Answer," *Clarendon Papers*, 104.

87. Maverick had supported Child's petition. For Quakers and the commissioners, see Jonathan Chu, *Neighbors, Friends, or Madmen: The Puritan Adjustment to Quakerism in Seventeenth-Century Massachusetts Bay* (Westport, 1985), chap. 5; and Adrian Chastain Weimer, "Elizabeth Hooton and the Lived Politics of Toleration in Massachusetts Bay," *WMQ* 74, No. 1 (January 2017): 43–76.

88. Jonathan Scott, "What Were Commonwealth Principles?" *Historical Journal* 47, No. 3 (September 2004): 595. For a view that emphasizes puritans' republican leanings, see Winship, *Godly Republicanism*. For the later importance of Hebraic republicanism in American political thought, see Nathan Perl-Rosenthal, "The 'Divine Right of Republics': Hebraic Republicanism and the Debate over Kingless Government in Revolutionary America," *WMQ* 66, No. 3 (July 2009): 535–564.

89. Hull, "Diaries," 3:213–214; MassRecs 4.2.185.

90. Collinson, "Monarchical Republic," 44. Collinson's analysis is now refined in Goldie, "Unacknowledged Republic"; the essays in McDiarmid, ed., *The Monarchical Republic of Early Modern England*; and Peter Lake, "The 'Political Thought' of the 'Monarchical Republic of Elizabeth I,' Discovered and Anatomized," *Journal of British Studies* 54, No. 2 (April 2015): 257–287.

91. Their concept of liberty was nowhere near capacious enough to include the Africans and Native Americans in bondage in their midst. For rationales for enslavement in seventeenth-century New England, see Newell, *Brethren by Nature*. For various definitions of liberty circulating at the time, and English puritan grandees' critique of Massachusetts colonists' ideas of liberty in the 1630s and 1640s, see Kupperman, "Definitions of Liberty on the Eve of Civil War," 17–33. For Tories' advocacy for liberty and property in the 1680s, see Tim Harris, "'Lives, Liberties, and Estates': Rhetorics of Liberty in the Reign of Charles II," in *Politics of Religion in Restoration England* (Oxford, 1990).

92. Musselwhite, *Urban Dreams, Rural Commonwealth*, 116–144.

93. Harris, *Restoration*, 59.

Chapter 7

1. George Cartwright to Sec. Bennet, 7 February 1665, DCHNY 3:89. For scattered evidence of Nicolls's empowering the other three, see CO 1/18, Nos. 107, 156; MsCP, fol. 131; CO 1/19, No. 37.

2. "Sir Joseph Williamson's Original Notes relating to New England," ca. 1663, *Proceedings of the MHS* (1868): 377; ms. is CO 1/17, No. 115. Williamson has Winthrop for Winslow. PlymRecs 11:129; see also Pestana, *English Atlantic*, 215–216.

3. Plymouth to Charles II, 5 June 1661, CO 1/15, No. 61. Issued to John Pierce by the Virginia Company, the Pierce Patent of 1620 was supplanted by the Bradford Patent in January 1630,

issued by the Council for New England, and surrendered to the freemen in March 1641. Charles Andrews, *Colonial Period in American History* (New Haven, 1934), 1:294–296. See also Winship, *Godly Republicanism*, 113–119; and Jeremy Bangs, *Strangers and Pilgrims, Travellers and Sojourners: Leiden and the Foundations of Plymouth Plantation* (Plymouth, 2009), 623–626.

4. William Bradford, *Of Plimoth Plantation*, ed. Kenneth Minkema, Francis Bremer, and Jeremy Bangs (Boston, 2020), 343–345; Edward Winslow, *Hypocrisie Unmasked* (London, 1647), 89–90; John Turner, *They Knew They Were Pilgrims: Plymouth Colony and the Contest for American Liberty* (New Haven, 2020), 85.

5. Gen. 45:28 (GNV); Plymouth to Charles II, 5 June 1661, CO 1/15, No. 61.

6. Charles II to Plymouth, 23 April 1664, CO 1/18, No. 56; see also Winship, *Godly Republicanism*, 111, 131.

7. Traditionally Plymouth freemen after casting their votes in person had attended the June court, but they had shifted over to voting by proxy. Freemanship already entailed a hefty civic burden; in October 1659 the freemen had voted 111 to 63 that they not be summoned to the June court. PlymRecs 3.115, 174. George Langdon, *Pilgrim Colony: A History of New Plymouth, 1620–1691* (New Haven, 1966), 81–82, 191.

8. At this 8 June 1664 meeting they also authorized funds for entertaining the royal commissioners "in a civill manor behoofull to theire condition." PlymRecs 4.62; Langdon, *Pilgrim Colony*, 191.

9. PlymRecs 10:318. For "the ethics of righteousness, peace, and amity" among the United Colonies as "not merely sentiments, but also policies" for members of the United Colonies, see Neal Dugre, "New Haven's Sacrifice: Regional Politics and the Anatomy of Restoration New England," *Connecticut History Review* 59, No. 2 (Fall 2020): 7–8.

10. Thomas Danforth to Gov. Prence, 12 January 1665, Winslow Family Papers II, 18–19, MHS.

11. Charles II to Plymouth, 23 April 1664, CO 1/18, No. 56; Propositions and Answers, 2 May 1665, Winslow Family Papers II, MHS; PlymRecs 4:85–86.

12. John Gorham Palfrey, *History of New England* (Boston, 1892), 2:600. See also Hutchinson, *History*, 1:214; and Bailyn, *New England Merchants*, 119.

13. Conal Condren, *Argument and Authority in Early Modern England: The Presupposition of Oaths and Offices* (Cambridge, 2006), 241. See also McConville, *King's Three Faces*, 15.

14. David Martin Jones, *Conscience and Allegiance in Seventeenth Century England: The Political Significance of Oaths and Engagements* (Rochester, 1999), 172–173.

15. Danforth Papers, 64–65; Condren, *Argument and Authority*, 249; John Spurr, "A Profane History of Early Modern Oaths," *Transactions of the Royal Historical Society* 11 (2001): 49–50.

16. Increase Mather, Autobiography, ed. M. G. Hall, *AAS Proceedings* 71 (1961): 284–285.

17. *Non-Conformist's Oath* (1666), in *Collections of the MHS*, Ser. 2, 4 (1816): 104–106; copy in MsWP.

18. PlymRecs 4:86, 11:129.

19. PlymRecs 4:86; Charles II to Massachusetts, 28 June 1662, MassRecs 4.2.164–166.

20. PlymRecs 11:101, 109; Langdon, *Pilgrim Colony*, 81–82.

21. "Cartwright's Report," 14 December 1665, CO 1/19, No. 143.

22. Evidently the royal commissioners had to make this amendment on their way back through the colony because they neglected to do it the first time. Carr, Cartwright, and Maverick to Gov. Prence, 1664 [1665?], *Collections of the MHS*, Ser. 1, 5 (1798): 192–193; Propositions and Answers, 2 May 1665, Winslow Family Papers II, MHS.

23. Plymouth to Royal Commissioners, 4 May 1665, Winslow Family Papers II, MHS. For the ways this policy benefited Rehoboth Baptists, who founded Swansea and its church in 1667, see New Plymouth to Nicolls, 4 July 1666, CO 1/20, No. 110; and Turner, *They Knew They Were Pilgrims*, 246–247.

24. Nicolls to Plymouth, 17 March 1665, Ms. L1.v1.11, Boston Athenaeum. I have altered some of Willett's mostly phonetic spelling to make it readable. Willett to Prence, 18 April 1665, Winslow Family Papers II, MHS; Articles between Cartwright and New York Indians, 24 September 1664, DCHNY 3:67–68; Cartwright to Nicolls, 4 February 1665, DCHNY 3:87; Robert Ritchie, "Willett, Thomas," ODNB; Elizur Yale Smith, "Captain Thomas Willett: First Mayor of New York," *New York History* 21, No. 4 (October 1940): 404–417.

25. "Cartwright's Report," 14 December 1665, CO 1/19, No. 143. The royal commissioners also received a petition for land from Peregrine White, a very early settler, which they referred to the Plymouth Court, and the court accommodated (PlymRecs 4:110).

26. PlymRecs 4:64, 87, 101–102.

27. PlymRecs 4:157–158, 168.

28. "Cartwright's Report," 14 December 1665, CO 1/19, No. 143; PlymRecs 4:92.

29. PlymRecs 4:92.

30. "The humble addrese of your Colloney of N[ew] P[lymouth]," 1665, Winslow Family Papers II, MHS; MassArch CVI.80. For this letter and surrounding evidence, see Adrian Chastain Weimer, "The 'Contynuance of Our Civell and Religious Liberties': Plymouth Colonists' 1665 'Humble Addrese' to the King," *Early American Literature* 56, No. 1 (2021): 219–232.

31. "Humble addrese."

32. PlymRecs 4:92. Massachusetts Bay had sent two agents but with little power to negotiate.

33. "Cartwright's Report," 14 December 1665, CO 1/19, No. 143. See also Langdon, *Pilgrim Colony*, 191.

34. Carr, Cartwright, and Maverick to Prence, 1664 [1665], *Collections of the MHS*, Ser. 1, 5 (1798): 192–193.

35. Prence to Massachusetts, 21 June 1665, PlymRecs 10:324–328. They were also frustrated that the United Colonies was letting Connecticut absorb New Haven and reluctant to keep paying United Colonies expenses. Propositions and Answers, 4 May 1665, Winslow Family Papers II, MHS; PlymRecs 4:92.

36. PlymRecs 4:92.

37. "Cartwright's Report," 14 December 1665, CO 1/19, No. 143. See also Carr, Cartwright, and Maverick to Sec. Bennet, 27 May 1665, DCHNY 3:96–97.

38. Rhode Island and Connecticut's differences had been mediated first by arbiters chosen by Clarendon (including Thomas Temple, Robert Boyle, and Samuel Maverick) and then by other arbiters, who helped them reach the tenuous agreement. Woodward, *Prospero's America*, 257–261; James, *John Clarke and his Legacies*, 59–83.

39. Roger Williams to the Town of Warwick, 1 January 1666, *Correspondence of Roger Williams*, ed. Glen LaFantasie (Hanover, 1988), 2:534–539.

40. Osgood, *American Colonies*, 3:170.

41. Pulsipher, *Subjects unto the Same King*, 29; RIRecs 2:20; for Clarke's strategies, see Jonathan Beecher Field, *Errands into the Metropolis: New England Dissidents in Revolutionary London* (Hanover, 2009), 6–12; and James, *John Clarke and his Legacies*, chap. 4.

42. Pulsipher, *Subjects unto the Same King*, 26–36, 55–56; Julie Fisher and David Silverman, *Ninigret, Sachem of the Niantics and Narragansetts: Diplomacy, War, and the Balance of Power in Seventeenth-Century New England and Indian Country* (Ithaca, 2014), 87–95; Hazard, ed., *Historical Collections*), 2:337–340, 432–434; "Mortgage Deed of Narraganset Sachems," *Collections of the MHS*, Ser. 3, 9 (1885): 25–26 (see also 27–45, 54–55, 70–71, 74–76, 82–83); John Frederick Martin, *Profits in the Wilderness: Entrepreneurship and the Founding of New England* (Chapel Hill, 1991), 62–73.

43. RIRecs 1:513.

44. Charles II to New England, 21 June 1663, *Collections of the MHS*, Ser. 5, 9 (1885), 54–55 (see also note on 41); "Boundaries of Rhode Island and Narragansett Purchasers," July–August 1662, MsWP.

45. Benedict Arnold and William Brenton to Nicolls, 5 February 1665, CO 1/19, No. 18.

46. Charles II to Rhode Island, 23 April 1664, CO 1/18, No. 57.

47. RIRecs 2:110–111.

48. RIRecs 2:112, 141–142.

49. RIRecs 2:111–119, 127–129; "Cartwright's Report," 14 December 1665, CO 1/19, No. 143.

50. "Cartwright's Report," 14 December 1665, CO 1/19, No. 143; RIRecs 2:99–110. The appeals were complex. Horod Long's complaint about two men who had taken advantage of her was addressed not through helping her reclaim her inheritance but instead fining both her and her former common-law husband. William Dyer ended up having to apologize for his too strong criticism of the Rhode Island government expressed in his appeal to the royal commissioners. For William Harris's appeal regarding land, see Irving Richman, introduction to the Harris Papers, *Collections of the Rhode Island Historical Society* 10 (1902): 14–15.

51. RIRecs 2:106–111, 127–29, 154–166.

52. "Cartwright's Report," 14 December 1665, CO 1/19, No. 143.

53. DCHNY 3:53, 55–56; Gabriel Glickman, "Protestantism, Colonization, and the New England Company in Restoration Politics," *Historical Journal* 59, No. 2 (2016): 369–372, 380; John Eliot et al., *The New Testament of our Lord and Savior Jesus Christ* (Cambridge, MA, 1661), A3r–A3v; John Eliot et al., *The Holy Bible* (Cambridge, MA, 1663), A3v–A4r; Hall, *Ways of Writing*, 169–170.

54. Samuel Gorton, *Simplicities Defence* (London, 1646), A3r; *Journal of John Winthrop*, 383–384n39; Roger Williams to John Winthrop, 8 March 1641, *Correspondence of Roger Williams*, 1:215; MassRecs 4.2.256–257, 261; Gura, *Glimpse of Sion's Glory*, 276–282, 291–301; Pulsipher, *Subjects unto the Same King*, 25–26, 29–32; Cogley, *John Eliot's Mission* , 24; Francis Bremer, *John Winthrop: America's Forgotten Founding Father* (Oxford, 2003), 299–301; Carla Gardina Pestana, "Gorton, Samuel," ODNB; Philip Gura, "Gorton, Samuel," ANB.

55. Roger Williams believed that Miantonomo had a right to give away Pomham's and Socononoco's land because they were subject to him. Providence Plantations to Massachusetts, 12 May 1656, RIRecs 1:342. LaFantasie qualifies this judgment, writing that Williams's "ethnocentric biases made him exaggerate the chief sachems' authority." *Correspondence of Roger Williams*, 2:453–454n6.

56. MassRecs 2.40; *Journal of John Winthrop*, 458–462; Pulsipher, *Subjects unto the Same King*, 26–28; Fisher and Silverman, *Ninigret*, 55; Joshua Micah Marshall, "'A Melancholy People': Anglo-Indian Relations in Early Warwick, Rhode Island, 1642–1675," *NEQ* 68, No. 3 (September 1995): 404–405; Cogley, *John Eliot's Mission*, 27–28, 30–39; Elisha Potter, *Early*

History of Narragansett (Providence, 1835), 33–34. The Massachusett sachem Cutshamekin supported Pomham's and Sococonoco's right to their lands over and against Miantonomo. The role of Benedict Arnold, Pomham and Soconoco's interpreter, and his father, William Arnold, is less clear. For Massachusetts's military and territorial interests in encouraging Arnold and others' submission, see *Journal of John Winthrop*, 413; Cogley, *John Eliot's Mission*, 23–35; and Neal Salisbury, *Manitou and Providence: Indians, Europeans, and the Making of New England, 1500–1643* (Oxford, 1982), 230.

57. *Journal of John Winthrop*, 132, 413.

58. *Journal of John Winthrop*, 476–488; "The humble petition of Samuel Gorton [et al.]," 4 March 1665, Danforth Papers, 68; *Samuel Gorton's Letter to Lord Hyde in Behalf of the Narragansett Sachems* [1662] (Providence, 1930), 10–15; Hazard, ed., *Historical Collections*, 2:10; MassRecs 2.40–41, 44, 51–53, 57; the petition is also in MassRecs 4.2.253–255.

59. *Journal of John Winthrop*, 494–495, 513. This decision to arm Pomham and Sococonoco was not isolated; the Bay would also arm the Nashaway against the Mohawk in 1663. Lisa Brooks, *Our Beloved Kin: A New History of King Philip's War* (New Haven, 2018), 110.

60. Christine DeLucia argues that Miantonomo's "visionary call for multitribal unification" in the 1640s "arguably laid intellectual and social groundwork for the resistances of the 1670s." *Memory Lands: King Philip's War and the Place of Violence in the Northeast* (New Haven, 2018), 127.

61. Samuel Gorton and Randall Howldon [Holden] to Nicolls, 9 November 1667, CO 1/21, No. 142.

62. Gura, *Glimpse of Sion's Glory*, 282–291 (see also 302–303); *Journal of John Winthrop*, 638–640, 671–677, 700–705; Dunn, *Puritans and Yankees*, 48–50. For Gorton's close relationship to English Levellers, see Michelle Burnham, "Samuel Gorton's Leveller Aesthetics and the Economics of Colonial Dissent," *WMQ* 67, No. 3 (July 2010): 433–437, 443–457; for his appeal to Londoners, see Field, *Errands into the Metropolis*, 47–48, 54–62; and for a comparison of Gorton and Williams regarding Native treaties, see Jeffrey Glover, *Paper Sovereigns: Anglo-Native Treaties and the Law of Nations, 1604–1664* (Philadelphia, 2014), 200–217. The 1644 Narragansett petition, signed with the marks of Pessicus, Canonicus, and Mixano, witnessed by Auwashoosse and Tomanick, is printed in *Gorton's Letter to Lord Hyde*, 18–20.

63. Pomham, Petition to the Massachusetts General Court, ca. 1647, MassArch 30.11; MassRecs 3.116, 145; Williams to Winthrop, 10 November 1649, *Correspondence of Roger Williams*, 1:301–303, 305n19. Roger Williams was also involved in the earlier petition.

64. Williams to Massachusetts, 12 May 1656, *Correspondence of Roger Williams*, 2:450. At this point Williams believed the best way forward was for Pomham to agree to remove, adding that Nawwashawsuck had an additional claim (2:451).

65. RIRecs 1:405–406; *Rhode Island Court Records* (Providence, 1920), 1:55; Marshall, "A Melancholy People," 98.

66. For episodes of conflict, as well as increasing numbers of Natives laboring as "servants" in Warwick, see Marshall, "A Melancholy People," 405–417.

67. Samuel Gorton, John Wickes, and Randall Howlden [Holden] to Edward Hutchinson, William Hudson, and Amos Richardson, 24 March 1661, MsCP, fol. 5.

68. Williams to Massachusetts, 5 October 1654, RIRecs 1:292–293, 512–513.

69. Gorton et al. to Massachusetts, 22 August 1661, MassArch II.20 (modernized transcript in *Collections of the Rhode Island Historical Society* 2 (1835): 224–230).

70. *Gorton's Letter to Lord Hyde*, 10–15.

71. Woodward, *Prospero's America*, 288–289.

72. *Gorton's Letter to Lord Hyde*, 10–15; see also RIRecs 1:512. Remarkably, Gorton's earlier printing of the 1644 Narragansetts' submission would acquire "the status of an official treaty." Glover, *Paper Sovereigns*, 223–224.

73. Pulsipher, *Subjects unto the Same King*, 55; Cartwright to Gorton, 26 May 1665, CO 1/19, No. 65.

74. "The humble petition of Samuel Gorton et al.," 68–70; Gura, *Glimpse of Sion's Glory*, 284; MassArch II.17.

75. See, for example, Williams to Massachusetts, 15 November 1655, in *Correspondence of Roger Williams*, 2:443–447.

76. Neal Salisbury, "Indians and Colonists in Southern New England After the Pequot War: An Uneasy Balance," in *Pequots in Southern New England: The Fall and Rise of an American Indian Nation*, ed. Laurence Hauptman and James Wherry (Norman, 1993), 90–92. For regional pressures, and Massachusetts's failure to defend Native allies, see Brooks, *Our Beloved Kin*, 109–111.

77. "Cartwright's Report," 14 December 1665, CO 1/19, No. 143; Declaration of his Majesty's Commissioners to the Narragansett Indians, 20 March 1665, CO 1/19, No. 40; Carr, Cartwright, and Maverick to Sec. Bennet, 27 May 1665, DCHNY 3:97; Order of the King's Commissioners about Narragansett, 29 March 1665, RIRecs 2:59–60; Fisher and Silverman, *Ninigret*, 99–100; Pulsipher, *Subjects unto the Same King*, 30–31.

78. RIRecs 2:93–95; Public Instructions for Connecticut, DCHNY 3:56; Petition of William Billing, and Answer, 21 March 1664, *Collections of the MHS*, Ser. 5, 9 (1885): 67; "Cartwright's Report," 14 December 1665, CO 1/19, No. 143; Dunn, *Puritans and Yankees*, 157–158.

79. Pulsipher, *Subjects unto the Same King*, 215.

80. RIRecs 2:128.

81. MassArch CVI.100; Howard Chapin, ed., *Early Records of the Town of Warwick* (Providence, 1926), 149; RIRecs 2:132.

82. Williams to Carr, *Correspondence of Roger Williams*, 2:551, 553n9; Fisher and Silverman argue based on this letter that Pomham had entered into a tributary relationship with Philip Metacom (*Ninigret*, 101).

83. "Notes relating to America," ca. 1662–1663, CO 1/21, No. 174.

84. Gorton, *Simplicities Defence*, 26.

85. "Cartwright's Answer," *Clarendon Papers*, 99.

86. For another (more sympathetic) view on Maverick and toleration, see Roper, "The Fall of New Netherland," 666–708.

87. Cartwright to Gorton, 26 May 1665, CO 1/19, No. 65.

88. Winthrop to Samuel Wyllys, 14 May 1662, Ms. L1v.1.5, Boston Athenaeum; Woodward, *Prospero's America*, 251–274.

89. ConnRecs 1:433, 435, 437–438.

90. Connecticut to New Haven, March 1664, NHRecs, 532; see also Bremer, *Building a New Jerusalem*, 300.

91. NHRecs, 545; Harris, *Restoration*, 46 ("rakish"); New Haven to Connecticut, 14 December 1664, NHRecs, 552–553. For the inflammatory role of the physician Bray Rossiter and complex negotiations involving the towns of Guilford and Stamford, see Dugre, "New Haven's Sacrifice," 21–30.

92. Carr, Cartwright, and Maverick to Winthrop, 9 March 1665, *Collections of the MHS*, Ser. 5, 9 (1885): 66; Woodward, *Prospero's America*, 279–288; see also Palfrey, *History of New England*, 2:592–594.

93. ConnRecs 1:439–441.

94. Oath dated May 1665. Charles Evans, "Oaths of Allegiance in Colonial New England," *Proceedings of the AAS* 31, No. 2 (October 1921): 423.

95. William Jones, in 1662; he would soon be elected a magistrate. His relationship to the executed regicide John Jones is disputed. Edward E. Atwater, *History of the Colony of New Haven* (New Haven, 1881), 422.

96. ConnRecs 1:15.

97. Nicolls to Winthrop, 23 February 1665, *Collections of the MHS*, Ser. 5, 9 (1885): 64; ConnRecs 1:439–441.

98. ConnRecs 1:439.

99. Woodward, *Prospero's America*, 288.

100. Cartwright to Prence, 3 March 1665 and 8 July 1665, Winslow Family Papers II, MHS.

101. Private Instructions, DCHNY 3:59.

102. Hugh Barbour, *Quakers in Puritan England* (New Haven, 1964), 218; H. Larry Ingle, *First Among Friends: George Fox and the Creation of Quakerism* (Oxford, 1996), 8; Craig Horle, *Quakers and the English Legal System, 1660–1688* (Philadelphia, 1988), 16–18.

103. Denying involvement in plots, Fox proclaimed the Lord would overthrow Charles II's kingdom if he did not stop arresting the righteous (especially Friends). George Fox, *Journal*, ed. Norman Penney (Cambridge, 1911), 1:371, 361–362, 370. See also Richard Greaves, "Shattered Expectations? George Fox, the Quakers, and the Restoration State, 1660–1685," *Albion* 24, No. 2 (Summer 1992): 237–239; Ingle, *First Among Friends*, 189–191; Barbour, *Quakers in Puritan England*, 203, 23; Kate Peters, *Print Culture and the Early Quakers* (Cambridge, 2005), 205–206. On Quaker repudiation of divine-right monarchy, and their subordination of reason to collective spiritual intuition, see Jane Calvert, *Quaker Constitutionalism and the Political Thought of John Dickinson* (Cambridge, 2009), 67–78. Andrew Murphy makes a compelling case, however, for William Penn's embrace of reason alongside the Inner Light. Murphy, *Liberty, Conscience, and Toleration: The Political Thought of William Penn* (Oxford, 2016), 8, 49–52, 125–133. On Burrough's use of reason in his theological argumentation, see Pink Dandelion and Stephen Angell, "Outcasts of Israel: The Apocalyptic Theology of Edward Burrough and Francis Howgill," *Early Quakers and Their Theological Thought* (Cambridge, 2015), 124–125.

104. Coffey, *Persecution and Toleration*, 170.

105. *A Proclamation of Both Houses of Parliament* (London, 1660), 1.

106. Margaret Fell, *A Declaration and an Information* (London, 1660), 4; Elsa Glines, *Undaunted Zeal: The Letters of Margaret Fell* (Richmond, 2003), 277, 282.

107. Fell did articulate sincere affection for the king, warding off possible concerns about feigned love or mixed intentions. Fox, *Journal*, 1:371, 361–362, 370. See also Ingle, *First Among Friends*, 190–192.

108. Rosemary Moore, *The Light in Their Consciences: Early Quakers in Britain, 1646–1666* (University Park, 2000), 178–183, 168–170; Adrian Davies, *The Quakers in English Society, 1655–1725* (Oxford, 2000), 170; Meredith Baldwin Weddle, *Walking in the Way of Peace: Quaker Pacifism in the Seventeenth Century* (Oxford, 2001), chaps. 2–3; Richard Allen, "Restoration Quakerism, 1660–1691," in *Oxford Handbook of Quaker Studies*, ed. Stephen Angell

and Pink Dandelion (Oxford, 2013), 29–46, esp. 30–32. For petitions (including women's petitions) and military involvement in 1659 and the significance of fear of Quakerism to the Restoration itself, see Barry Reay, "The Quakers, 1659, and the Restoration of the Monarchy," *History* 63, No. 208 (June 1978): 193–213; and Catie Gill, *Women in the Seventeenth-Century Quaker Community: A Literary Study of Political Identities, 1650–1700* (Burlington, 2005), chap. 3. For Quakers' general dismissal of petitions and other direct political measures as "placing too much weight on worldly authority," see Peters, *Print Culture*, 210, 227. Peters argues that Quakers' very use of printed suffering narratives established an expectation of "popular political involvement" (212).

109. Edward Burrough, *A Visitation of Love unto the King* (London, 1660), 21, 37; Massachusetts General Court, *Humble Petition and Address . . . unto . . . Charles the Second* (London, 1660), 5–6. Burrough had already engaged in debates with John Bunyan and Richard Baxter. For an extended discussion of why civil disobedience was "based on a strong sense of political obligation," see Calvert, *Quaker Constitutionalism*, 63 and chaps. 1–2. Phyllis Mack argues that "righteous and sober Quakers were, in fact, more obedient citizens than the members of some other radical sects." Mack, *Visionary Women: Ecstatic Prophecy in Seventeenth-Century England* (Berkeley, 1992), 132.

110. Edward Burrough, *A Declaration of the Sad and Great Persecution* (London, 1661), 10. For an analysis of Burrough's writings and both Quaker and puritan efforts to distance themselves from the English civil wars, see Adrian Chastain Weimer, "Quakers, Puritans, and the Problem of Godly Loyalty in the Early Restoration," in *The Worlds of William Penn*, ed. Andrew Murphy and John Smolinski (New Brunswick, 2019), 283–302.

111. Hooton, Ms. D. Portfolio iii.34, Friends Library, London. A section of the manuscript is damaged; see also Emily Manners, *Elizabeth Hooton, First Quaker Woman Preacher* (London, 1914), 36–37 and another account in Ms. D. Portfolio iii.27. Hooton's story is told more fully in Weimer, "Elizabeth Hooton and the Lived Politics of Toleration in Massachusetts Bay." For Hooton's activities in England, see Christine Trevett, *Women and Quakerism in the 17th Century* (York, 1991), 16–22; and Mack, *Visionary Women*, 127–46. For Margaret Fell's political activities, muted during her 1664–1668 imprisonment, see Fell, *A Brief Collection of Remarkable Passages* (London, 1710), 5–6; and Bonnelyn Young Kunze, *Margaret Fell and the Rise of Quakerism* (Stanford, 1994), 131–42. The Quaker Act was formulated in July 1661 and implemented in May 1662. Moore, *Light in Their Consciences*, 182–85.

112. Manners, *Elizabeth Hooton*, 37, 39; Hooton, Ms. D. Portfolio iii.34, 46, 48, 55. See also Elizabeth Hooton, "To the King and both Houses of Parliament," printed at the end of [Thomas Taylor], *To the King* ([London, 1670]), 6–7. For the architectural setting and soundscape, see Kirilka Stavreva, "Prophetic Cries at Whitehall: Gender Dynamics of Early Quaker Women's Injurious Speech," in *Women, Gender and Radical Religion in Early Modern Europe*, ed. Sylvia Brown (Boston, 2007), 35. Other tolerationist movements, including William Penn's in the 1680s, also involved increased attention to the restraint of vice; see Ethan Shagan, *Rule of Moderation: Violence, Religion and the Politics of Restraint in Early Modern England* (Cambridge, 2011), 298–310. Hooton at another point reminded the king of the taxes she and her family had personally paid into the royal coffers; Hooton, Ms. D. Portfolio iii.65. Susanna Calkins argues that Charles II may have issued the royal patent to remind the colonies of his authority. Calkins, "Colonial Whips, Royal Writs and the Quaker Challenge: Elizabeth Hooton's Voyages Through New England in the Seventeenth Century," *Journeys* 5, No. 2 (December 2004): 85.

113. "E[lizabeth] H[ooton] to G[eorge] F[ox] concerning some spirits in New Engl which had run out from the trueth. not pfed to be read," AR Barclay Mss. 153, Library of the Society of Friends, microfilm (London, 1980). "Country" in this context meant "rural areas" or "countryside" (Oxford English Dictionary Online). See also Joseph Besse, *Collection of the Sufferings* (London, 1753), 2:229; Hooton, Ms. D. Portfolio iii.27; and Manners, *Elizabeth Hooton*, 39.

114. Hooton, Ms. D. Portfolio iii.43. For Quakers' broader critiques of puritan lawmaking, see Goodman, *Banished*, 94–100.

115. Hooton, Ms. D. Portfolio iii.61.

116. This anecdote circulated widely, and Hooton may have been its source. Bishop, *New-England Judged*, 1:218n; MassRecs 4.2.149, 184; Bliss, *Revolution and Empire*, 157.

117. Hooton, Ms. D. Portfolio iii.61.

118. Manners, *Elizabeth Hooton*, 4; "Sir Joseph Williamson's Original Notes relating to New England," CO 1/17, No. 115; see also Hooton, Ms. D. Portfolio iii.59.

119. Hooton, Ms. D. Portfolio iii.61.

120. Cartwright to Nicolls, 19 April 1665, DCHNY 3:94.

121. Manners, *Elizabeth Hooton*, 50; see also Hooton, Ms. D. Portfolio iii.62.

122. Besse, *Collection of the Sufferings*, 2:221–223.

123. Bishop, *New-England Judged*, 1:337. These debates took place primarily at Christiansen's appeals trial. Christiansen had come to support William Leddra, soon to face the scaffold.

124. Bishop, *New-England Judged*, 1:337. See also William Sewel, *History of the Rise, Increase, and Progress of the People called Quakers* (London, 1722), 278–280; Besse, *Collection of the Sufferings*, 2:222–223; MassRecs 4.2.20–21.

125. For an earlier version of Christiansen's legal strategy, see Humphrey Norton's 1658 letter to the governor and assistants of Plymouth: Norton, *New-England's Ensigne* (London, 1659), 38, see also 79–80. Whether the court actually read Norton's letter is unknown. Most dialogues with magistrates in the 1650s focused on definitions of wickedness and righteousness. Margaret Fell urged Quakers to discover specific laws used to prosecute them so Quakers could highlight legal confusion and corruption within suffering narratives. Peters, *Print Culture*, 200.

126. Chu, *Neighbors, Friends, or Madmen*, 90, see also 70; Carla Gardina Pestana, "The City upon a Hill Under Siege: The Puritan Perception of the Quaker Threat to Massachusetts Bay, 1656–1661," *NEQ* 56, No. 3 (September 1983): 351; MassRecs 4.2.2–3; MassArch X.274B.

127. MassArch X.273A; Sewel, *History of the Rise*, 279–280; Besse, *Collection of the Sufferings*, 2:222.

128. Bishop, *New-England Judged*, 1:457–459; Hooton, Ms. D. Portfolio iii.27; Manners, *Elizabeth Hooton*, 44. For Quakers and the appeals issue, see Osgood, *American Colonies*, 3:165–166.

129. MassRecs 4.2.233; see also the letter from Carr, Cartwright, and Maverick to nonfreemen in MassRecs 4.2.174. The letter supposedly went to "some in Ipswich & in other places" (4.2.233)

130. Edward Rawson to Sec. Morrice, 6 December 1661, CO 1/15, No. 93.

131. John Wilson, *A Seasonable WATCH-WORD* [1665] (Cambridge, MA, 1677), 8–10; see also Foster, *The Long Argument*, 177.

132. John Higginson to Massachusetts General Court, 1663, Higginson Family Papers, MHS; Higginson, *Cause of God and His People*, 12; Richard Hallowell, *Quaker Invasion of*

Massachusetts (Boston, 1887), 94. For epidemiological language used for dissenters throughout the colonies, see Chris Beneke, *Beyond Toleration: The Religious Origins of American Pluralism* (Oxford, 2006), 26–31; for the fraying of consensus around enforcing a high level of uniformity in religion, and especially capital punishment, see Coffey, *Persecution and Toleration*, 6.

Chapter 8

1. "Declaration of the General Court of Massachusetts," DCHNY 3:95; see also Carr and Maverick to Arlington, 20 November 1665, CO 1/19, No. 132; DCHNY 3:107; *Memorandum by Captain Bre[e]don*, DCHNY 3:271; Thomas Deane to Clarendon, 22 June 1665, *Clarendon Papers*, 68; and Pulsipher, *Subjects unto the Same King*, 61.

2. MassArch CVI.100a–101.

3. MassArch CVI.103a.

4. 1 Kings 12:7, 12 and notes, Geneva Bible (London, 1599); MassArch CVI.103a.

5. MassArch CVI.103.

6. Hubbard, *General History*, 582.

7. MassRecs 4.2.177.

8. Nicolls to Winthrop, 4 May 1665, Winthrop Family Papers, MHS.

9. MassRecs 4.2.177–178.

10. Private Instructions, DCHNY 3:58, 60.

11. William Morrice to Mass., 25 February 1664, DCHNY 3:90–91; De Krey, *London and the Restoration*, 26.

12. Maverick to Nicolls, 5 March 1665, DCHNY 3:93.

13. Cartwright to Nicolls, 4 February 1665, DCHNY 3:87; Bartlett Whiting, *Early American Proverbs and Proverbial Phrases* (Cambridge, MA, 1977), 20.

14. MassRecs 4.2.182.

15. MassRecs 4.2.182; Pulsipher, *Subjects unto the Same King*, 60.

16. MassRecs 4.2.173. Cartwright later said the motion to call people to Boston was Maverick's idea and he had tried to moderate it. "Cartwright's Answer," *Clarendon Papers*, 89–90. William Hubbard thought the General Court's concerns about safety were valid and Cartwright's anger unjustified, especially his "harsh and angry words, not needful here to be inserted" (*General History*, 582).

17. Hull, "Diaries," 3:217.

18. Manners, *Elizabeth Hooton*, 4; Hooton, Ms. D. Portfolio i.135; see also iii.27. The royal commissioners may have tried, unsuccessfully, to release at least one Quaker from prison. Bishop, *New-England Judged*, 1:461. Baptists too, emboldened by the presence of the royal commission, would gather a church in Boston on 28 May 1665. Mostly long-time residents and former members of puritan churches, Baptists did not publicly ally themselves with Nicolls, Carr, Cartwright, or Maverick. Baptists' avoidance of the royal commission may have factored into Bay leaders' generally greater sympathy for Baptists than Quakers (although after the 1668 Baptist debate the court would banish three leaders). William McLoughlin and Martha Davidson, "The Baptist Debate of April 14–15, 1668," *Proceedings of the MHS*, Ser. 3, 76 (1964): 92–93; Carla Gardina Pestana, *Quakers and Baptists in Colonial Massachusetts* (Cambridge, 1991), 44; Weimer, *Martyrs' Mirror*, chap. 4.

19. Hull, "Diaries," 3:216–217.

20. Hubbard, *General History*, 582.

21. "Cartwright's Answer," *Clarendon Papers*, 89–90. At their 18 April 1665 meeting the Massachusetts Council did decide to hire artists to create a map of the Bay and Plymouth, "w[ith] all Convenient speede," but it is not clear they intended it for the royal commission (MassArch CVI.102a). They told the royal commissioners in early May that they were working on it (MassRecs 4.2.187). The court finally supplied a map on 24 May 1665, although it does not seem to have satisfied. It may have been lost when Cartwright was captured (MassRecs 4.2.213–214; MassArch CVI.133; DCHNY 3:106–107). The crown was still trying to get an accurate map from Thomas Temple in 1667. Temple to [Sec. Arlington], 10 December 1667, CO 1/21, No. 155; see also MassArch CCLXXXVII.3–3a. For Cartwright's frustration with Prence for not supplying a map, see Cartwright to Gov. Prence, 8 July 1665, Winslow Family Papers II, MHS, No. 22; for Winthrop's reluctance to provide geographical information, see Woodward, *Prospero's America*, 272–276, 282–299; and for the larger map-making story, see Nathan Braccio, "Map Scarcity in Early Colonial New England," *Early American Studies* 19, No. 3 (Summer 2021): 457–494.

22. MassRecs 4.2.186; Hubbard, *General History*, 583.

23. MassRecs 4.2.184; see also "Cartwright's Report," DCHNY 3:110; "Cartwright's Answer," *Clarendon Papers*, 94.

24. Danforth Papers, 56–57; MassRecs 4.2.184.

25. Mass. General Court to Royal Commissioners, 5 May 1665, in MassRecs 4.2.187; draft in MassArch CVI.112.

26. MassArch CVI.112; Danforth Papers, 60; MassRecs 4.2.187; Royal Commissioners to Mass. General Court, May 1665, Danforth Papers, 61.

27. MassRecs 4.2.149; Bliss, *Revolution and Empire*, 157; Reid, *Maine, Charles II, and Massachusetts*, 73. For the ritual of courtroom apologies, see Kamensky, *Governing the Tongue*, 135–142.

28. MassRecs 4.2.110; Lucas, "Colony or Commonwealth," 97–98. On the regicides, all the court could say was that no other people "attained of high treason" besides Whalley and Goffe had arrived in the colony, that the two men had arrived before news of their arrest warrant, and that Kellond and Kirke had diligently performed their search. MassArch CVI.114; MassRecs 4.2.201–202.

29. MassArch CVI.79 (draft differs from official version); MassRecs 4.2.130.

30. MassRecs 4.2.205.

31. "Cartwright's Answer," *Clarendon Papers*, 88–89.

32. "Cartwright's Report," DCHNY 3:111. As early as 1667 the General Court debated procedures for censuring or ejecting an elected official who proved themselves "vitious in Conversation" or not "orthodox in religion." MassArch XLVIII.81–82.

33. MassRecs 4.2.165, 200.

34. MassArch CVI.117; MassRecs 4.2.200–201; see also 203 on congregants' power to call ministers, as well as practices of arbitration.

35. *Book of the General Lawes and Libertyes*, 26–27.

36. MassArch CVI.117; MassRecs 4.2.200.

37. Richter, *Before the Revolution*, 261.

38. The version of the oath of allegiance presented to the magistrates by the royal commissioners is in Danforth Papers, 64, with several phrases omitted (probably scribal error).

39. MassArch CVI.117; first part same as MassRecs 4.2.200.

40. MassRecs 4.2.200.

41. MassArch CVI.124a; see also 123.

42. *Journal of John Winthrop*, 432.

43. Charles Evans, "Oaths of Allegiance in Colonial New England," *Proceedings of the AAS* 31, No. 2 (October 1921): 395; *Book of the General Lawes*, 84.

44. MassArch CVI.123.1; MassRecs 4.2.200–201. Osgood noted this clause "clearly withdrew from his obligation to the king the entire content of the subject's obligation to Massachusetts" (*American Colonies*, 3:183).

45. MassRecs 4.2.205.

46. Danforth Papers, 77–80.

47. MassArch CVI.132a, 133a; Danforth Papers, 91. See also Bliss, *Revolution and Empire*, 157.

48. Danforth Papers, 88, 91.

49. "Cartwright's Answer," *Clarendon Papers*, 99–100.

50. The practice of appeals, or retrying a "whole cause" in a superior judicature, was a relatively recent practice in English courts; it derived not from the common-law tradition but from the civil law, which was rooted in both Roman and canon law. Mary Sarah Bilder, "Salamanders and Sons of God: The Culture of Appeal in Early New England," in *The Many Legalities of Early America*, ed. Christopher Tomlins and Bruce Mann (Chapel Hill, 2001), 50–77.

51. MassRecs 4.2.25.

52. Committee of Lords and Commons, 25 May 1647, in Joseph H. Smith, *Appeals to the Privy Council from the American Plantations* (New York, 1950), 48n303, see also 45–49; MassRecs 4.1.455; Edward McManus, *Law and Liberty in Early New England* (Amherst, 1993), 77–78; Bilder, "Salamanders," 70–76; Gura, *Glimpse of Sion's Glory*, 296–303.

53. MassRecs 4.2.130.

54. Endicott to Clarendon, 8 November 1664, MsCP, fol. 121.

55. Clarendon to Massachusetts, 15 March 1665, MsCP, fol. 235, printed in Hutchinson, *History*, 1:450–451.

56. Declaration of Massachusetts Council, 6 September 1664, MassArch CVI.81.

57. "Cartwright's Report," DCHNY 3:113.

58. This letter is only in the manuscript version sent to London, not the court record (ed. Shurtleff). A prefatory note reads: "This following, was meant for a conclusion but being disliked, was not given in." CO 1/19, No. 56, fols. 45–46.

59. "A narrative of the case of John Porter, Junior," 30 May 1665, MassRecs 4.2.216–217; "Humble Petition of John Porter Junior," 1 April 1665, CO 1/19, No. 42. For Porter's speech, see Kamensky, *Governing the Tongue*, 105–115.

60. "Humble Petition of John Porter Junior," 1 April 1665, CO 1/19, No. 42.

61. "Cartwright's Answer," *Clarendon Papers*, 93–94; MassRecs 4.2.184; see also Danforth Papers, 56.

62. Kamensky, *Governing the Tongue*, 109.

63. Carr, Cartwright, and Maverick, Statement regarding John Porter Jr., 8 April 1665, CO 1/19, No. 42.

64. MassArch CVI.109; MassRecs 4.2.195.

65. MassRecs 4.2.195.

66. Danforth Papers, 91. Danforth's date of 21 May is probably an error, as the conference took place prior to the formal position statements on the court of appeals.

67. "Cartwright's Answer," *Clarendon Papers*, 97.

68. MassRecs 4.2.196.

69. Quote from Danforth's summary of the conference in Danforth Papers, 91–92.

70. MassRecs 4.2.196–197.

71. Danforth Papers, 91–92.

72. MassRecs 4.2.197; Danforth Papers, 92. Cartwright later explained why he would have judged Deane's case by the law of England: the king had supposedly instructed them "to give such reparations to Tho[mas] Dean as upon the meritts of the cause, & by vertue of the sayd act of parliament he ought to receive." "Cartwright's Answer," *Clarendon Papers*, 97. The language of considering the "merits of the cause" was commonly used by those who supported appeals, linking them with equity and justice. Bilder, "Salamanders and Sons of God," 57.

73. MassRecs 4.2.196–197.

74. Hubbard, *General History*, 583.

75. "Cartwright's Answer," *Clarendon Papers*, 97, 105.

76. MassRecs 4.2.197.

77. In his later hearing before the General Court on 27 May 1665 Deane said "how his majesty came by any complaint wee know not; I made none; but that complaint was made sixe months before I went hence" (MassRecs 4.2.219). For ways the Navigation Acts could actually benefit colonies, see Margaret Ellen Newell, *From Dependency to Independence: Economic Revolution in Colonial New England* (Ithaca, 1998), 78–82.

78. Bailyn, *New England Merchants*, 122–125, 135–137.

79. MassRecs 4.2.218.

80. DCHNY 3:54; MassArch CVI.90; MassRecs 4.2.193.

81. MassRecs 4.2.219, 202.

82. MassArch CVI.114a. Deputies did not consent to the precise wording of this magistrates' draft, but agreed in general.

83. MassArch CVI.116a; MassRecs 4.2.199. Paul Lucas sees the magistrates as most strongly denying the commissioners' right to sit as a court of appeals; in my reading both sides were against it, the deputies most strongly. Overall Lucas's insistence on an intensely oppositional framework obscures the negotiation and consensus building that went on in the court. Lucas, "Colony or Commonwealth," 105–106. Over the issue of sending agents in late 1666, however, clearer alliances formed.

84. MassRecs 4.2.203–204.

85. Lucas, "Colony or Commonwealth," 105; MassRecs 4.2.203–204, 206. Cartwright would later remember colonists' alarm at the royal commissioners' claim that "the King was to expound any passage in their charter; for he who granted knew best what he had granted." "Cartwright's Answer," *Clarendon Papers*, 95–96.

86. In the middle of this conversation the magistrates finally took their qualified oaths. MassRecs 4.2.206–208.

87. MassRecs 4.2.208–209; Gov. Bellingham to Clarendon, 30 May 1665, *Clarendon Papers*, 62; draft in MassArch CVI.136–137.

88. MassRecs 4.2.210. See also Pulsipher, *Subjects unto the Same King*, 61.

89. Hubbard, *General History*, 583.

90. Nadhorth to Sec. Morrice, 26 October 1666, DCHNY 3:140–142.

91. Increase Mather, Diary, 25 May 1665.

92. MassRecs 4.2.210–211. They also asked for their commission, the king's letters, and all papers given to the court to be "printed & published," which the General Court declined to do, although they made copies for themselves and friends in England. MassArch CVI.140a.

93. Greene, *Peripheries and Center*, 36–38.

94. "Cartwright's Answer," *Clarendon Papers*, 98.

95. MassRecs 4.2.21, 212–215. The royal commissioners said it was against the king's will for anyone else to hear the case.

96. Danforth Papers, 96–97.

97. Hull, "Diaries," 3:217.

98. "Cartwright's Answer," *Clarendon Papers*, 97, 99. From the proverb, "I know best where the shoe wringeth [pinches] me." Walter Skeat, *Early English Proverbs* (Oxford, 1910), no. 277. There is some later evidence that the commissioners were chastened on this point. When asked to revisit a case in Rhode Island in 1666, they declined, Nicolls and Carr writing, "we cannot resume a cause into our cognizance which hath passed a Jury and two General Assemblies" without violating the Rhode Island charter, "unlesse we were first convict that they have acted directly contrary to the Lawes of England." Nicolls and Carr to Dyre, ca. 1666, CO 1/20, No. 200.

99. Hubbard, *General History*, 583.

100. MassArch CVI.91, printed in MassRecs 4.2.194; Bilder, *Transatlantic Constitution*, 47–56; Pulsipher, *Subjects unto the Same King*, 62, 93–94.

101. Breedon to Council for Foreign Plantations, 11 March 1661, DCHNY 3:30–40.

102. The king's private instructions said to diligently study the laws made before, during, and after the "late usurping Government" (Cromwell's) and find any laws contrary to the king's "dignity" or to the justice, "lawes and customes of this realme." In the king's mind (or Clarendon's), the colonists had already agreed to revise their laws (DCHNY 3:58).

103. MassRecs 4.2.211.

104. Haskins, *Law and Authority in Early Massachusetts*, 113–140; Dayton, *Women Before the Bar*, 27–34; Hall, *A Reforming People*, chap. 4.

105. Revision item 19, though referring to the colonial law regarding Jesuits, is actually about wars: the point was to make sure the colony made alliances only with England's friends and saw as enemies only England's enemies (Jesuits, unless part of a diplomatic or merchant expedition, or shipwrecked, could still be outlawed). MassRecs 4.2.213; *Book of the General Lawes*, 38. Item 21 also falls into this category; the royal commissioners demanded the law allow the king to impress soldiers.

106. MassRecs 4.2.212–213; *Book of the General Lawes*, 32, 72. On the mint, see Peterson, *City-State of Boston*, 147–169; and Jonathan Barth, "'A Peculiar Stampe of Our Owne': The Massachusetts Mint and the Battle over Sovereignty, 1652–1691" *NEQ* 87, No. 3 (September 2014): 500–504. On reforestation and garden cultivation, see Kate Mulry, *An Empire Transformed: Remolding Bodies and Landscapes in the Restoration Atlantic* (New York, 2021), 166–171, 212.

107. MassRecs 4.1.102–103, 4.2.213; *Book of the General Lawes*, 40–41. Colonists too claimed moral high ground; see John Eliot's 1661 dedication of the Algonquian New Testament to Charles II, in which Eliot put forward the translation as evidence of the colonists' "honest and pious Intentions" toward Native peoples, rebutting reports of "any malevolent Aspect from those that bear evil will to this Sion." Eliot, *New Testament* (Cambridge, MA, 1661), A3v, A4v.

108. Nicolls to Winthrop, 23 February 1665, *Collections of the MHS*, Ser. 5, 9 (1885): 64.

109. "Cartwright's Report," DCHNY 3:110–111.

110. Thomas Breedon and Thomas Temple argued on Maverick's side. Increase Mather, Diary, 19 December 1664.

111. MassRecs 4.2.192.

112. *Book of the General Lawes*, 27–28; MassRecs 4.2.212.

113. MassRecs 4.2.212–213.

114. MassRecs 4.2.212; *Book of the General Lawes*, 27. Twenty years later when royal governor of the Dominion of New England, Edmund Andros, again took away the power to appoint holidays it was arguably the final straw that led to his overthrow.

115. W-W- to William Goffe, 18 December 1661, Mather Papers, 167.

116. Church of England, *The Book of Common-prayer* (London, 1662), Ss7r; Holly Brewer, "Slavery, Sovereignty, and 'Inheritable Blood': Reconsidering John Locke and the Origins of American Slavery," *American Historical Review* 122, No. 4 (October 2017): 1045.

117. "Cartwright's Answer," *Clarendon Papers*, 98 (responding to the account in MassRecs 4.2.211).

118. MassRecs 4.2.211; "Cartwright's Report," DCHNY 3:111.

119. MassRecs 4.2.234–235. This section and the fast day proclamation may have been sent to England with the rest of the court's "improvement" or defense of the May orders and counterorders.

120. MassRecs 4.2.235–236. On Sunday Mitchell echoed this language, calling people "to be fervent in prayer" not "onely as a taske" but with "spiritual fervency." [Jonathan Mitchell], 25 June 1665, First Church Cambridge Sermon Papers, Houghton Library, Harvard University.

121. Pierce, ed., *Records of the First Church in Salem*, 103–104; see also Hull, "Diaries," 3:218; *Records of the First Church of Dorchester*, 47.

122. MassRecs 4.2.232; Bellingham to Morrice, 31 May 1665, CO 1/19, No. 68.

Chapter 9

1. Peterson, *City-State of Boston*, 140.

2. Sehr, *Colony and Commonwealth*, 50.

3. Hannah Farber, "The Rise and Fall of the Province of Lygonia, 1643–1658," *NEQ* 82, No. 3 (2009): 512–513; Peterson, *City-State of Boston*, 142–144. For an alternate reading that assumes high levels of discontent with Massachusetts Bay's authority, see Roper, "The Fall of New Netherland," 691, 698. Portsmouth, Dover, and Exeter had submitted to Massachusetts earlier through the influence of Hugh Peter. David Dewar, "The Mason Patents: Conflict, Controversy, and the Quest for Authority in Colonial New Hampshire," *Constructing Early Modern Empires: Proprietary Ventures in the Atlantic World, 1500–1750*, ed. L. H. Roper and B. Van Ruymbeke (Boston, 2007), 282; Reid, *Maine, Charles II, and Massachusetts*, 86–87.

4. Edward Godfrey to Sec. Nicolas, 15 July 1660 and 7 April 1663, *Collections of the Maine Historical Society* 9 (1887): 356, 359. See also Reid, *Maine, Charles II, and Massachusetts*, 40–44. Godfrey would die in February 1664.

5. "Considerations in order to Establishing his Majesty's Interests in New England," ca. 1662–1663, CO 1/18, No. 46. For Clarendon's authorship, see Palfrey, *History of New England*, 2:578. In this early draft the royal commissioners were supposed to first visit Portsmouth. Clarendon was concerned (rightly) that if they started in Boston, Massachusetts leaders would "Mingle and intermeddle" with their attempts to exert control over the Northeast.

6. Cartwright to Nicolls, 3 June 1665, CO 1/19, No. 72.

7. George Cartwright to Col. Nicolls, 3 June 1665, CO 1/19, No. 72.

8. Maverick to Clarendon, 24 July 1665, *Clarendon Papers*, 71. For the region's economic growth, see Bailyn, *New England Merchants*, 124.

9. Maverick to Clarendon, 24 July 1665, *Clarendon Papers*, 71–72; Hubbard, *General History*, 585. George [Cartwright] to (Sec. Arlington?), 14 December 1665, CO 1/19 No. 143 ("Indian Sachem," "the more northerly"). Carr said the sachem "lives near the great lake from whence flows Merrimack river." For the tension between Abenaki and English assumptions about these kinds of deeds and transactions, see Ian Saxine, *Properties of Empire: Indians, Colonists, and Land Speculators on the New England Frontier* (New York, 2019), 13–34.

10. They also stopped in Newbury. Maverick to Nicolls, 18 June 1665, CO 1/19, No. 74; Bailyn, *New England Merchants*, 122.

11. Osgood, *American Colonies*, 1:376.

12. Maverick to Clarendon, 24 July 1665, *Clarendon Papers*, 71; Royal Commissioners to Massachusetts, 16 July 1665, DCHNY 3:99; Carr, Cartwright, and Maverick to Sec. Bennet, 26 July 1665, DCHNY 3:101; George [Cartwright] to (Sec. Arlington?), 14 December 1665, CO 1/19 No. 143. For Massachusetts Bay's efforts to gather depositions and documents defending the line much further north, see MassArch CVI.133, 154; and Massachusetts, Answer to . . . the petition of Ferdinando Gorges (1665), CO 1/19, Nos. 1–2. The latter document is based partly on a letter to Leverett in London: Hutchinson Papers, 2:37–40.

13. Maverick to Nicolls, 18 June 1665, CO 1/19, No. 74; see also Hubbard, *General History*, 584. For population, see "Estimated Population of American Colonies: 1610 to 1780," Series Z 1–19.

14. Carr and Maverick to Nicolls, 20 November 1665, DCHNY 3:108.

15. MassRecs 4.2.152–153; Maverick to Nicolls, 18 June 1665, CO 1/19, No. 74; Maverick and Carr to Sec. of State, 20 November 1665, DCHNY 3:107–108; see also Cartwright to Nicolls, 3 June 1665, CO 1/19, No. 72.

16. Maverick and Carr to Sec. of State, 20 November 1665, DCHNY 3:106–107; MassArch CVI.142a.

17. MassArch CVI.142; Carr, Cartwright, and Maverick to Sec. Bennet, 26 July 1665, DCHNY 3:101; George [Cartwright] to (Sec. Arlington?), 14 December 1665, CO 1/19 No. 143; Reid, *Maine, Charles II, and Massachusetts*, 86–88.

18. Carr and Maverick to Sec. of State, 20 November 1665, DHCNY 3:106–108; Carr, Cartwright, and Maverick to Sec. Bennet, 26 July 1665, DCHNY 3:101.

19. MassArch CVI.144.

20. MassArch CVI.145, 144a, 146–146a.

21. Maverick to Clarendon, 24 July 1665, *Clarendon Papers*, 73; Joseph Mason to Robert Mason, 16 July 1665, CO 1/19, No. 80.

22. Nicholas Shapleigh to [Robert] Mason, 20 May 1667, CO 1/19 No. 48. See also Dewar, "The Mason Patents," 288. Although some recent scholars see resentment against the Bay, Osgood concluded that in Piscataqua "the royal commissioners were unable to secure a following which possessed strength at all sufficient to overcome the influence of Massachusetts and its reputation for efficient government" (*American Colonies*, 3:188).

23. MassRecs 4.2.266.

24. MassRecs 4.2.266.

25. Sibley, *Biographical Sketches*, 1:367–380; Frank Hackett, ed., *Portsmouth Records* (Portsmouth, 1886), 1:111–112.

26. Owen Stanwood, *Empire Reformed: English America in the Age of the Glorious Revolution* (Philadelphia, 2011), 37–38, 76–77.

27. MaineRecs 1:286; Dover petition, MassRecs 4.2.268.

28. Jeremy Belknap, *History of New-Hampshire* (Dover, 1831), 1:28–29; *Journal of John Winthrop*, 392.

29. Hackett, ed., *Portsmouth Records*, 1:98–99. The 1640 document was copied in between the February and March 1665 records. Robert Mason had supplied the parish silver.

30. Hubbard, *General History*, 584.

31. MassRecs 4.2.266.

32. Joseph Mason to Robert Mason, 16 July 1665, CO 1/19, No. 80; see also Belknap, *History of New-Hampshire*, 1:60.

33. MassRecs 4.2.267–268.

34. The selectmen wrote to Boston again on 13 July with "thankfull hearts" for the Council's "speedy & seasonable Advice." MassArch CVI.147.

35. MassArch CVI.146b, 149; Reid, *Maine, Charles II, and Massachusetts*, 88.

36. Joseph Mason to Robert Mason, 16 July 1665, CO 1/19, No. 80; MassArch CVI.147.

37. MassArch CVI.147, 146b.

38. Carr, Cartwright, and Maverick to Sec. Arlington, 26 July 1665, CO 1/19 No. 82, printed in DCHNY 3:101–102.

39. MassArch CVI.149.

40. Dover selectmen to Massachusetts Council, MassArch CVI.149, printed in Nathaniel Bouton, ed., *Documents and Records Relating to the Province of New-Hampshire* (Concord, 1867), 1:273–274.

41. Deposition of Robert Purrington, in Bouton, ed., *Documents*, 1:287.

42. Portsmouth and Strawberry Bank Petition, CO 1/19, No. 76, printed in John Jenness, *Transcripts of Original Documents in the English Archives, Relating to . . . New Hampshire* (New York, 1876), 48–49, 6.

43. Depositions of Henry Sherburn [Sherborne], Robert Purrington, and John Joanes, in Bouton, ed., *Documents*, 1:286–287; MassArch CVI.149.

44. Undated petition to king included in CO 1/19, No. 82I. Bernard Bailyn argues the royal commissioners' visit "defined mercantile family groups," such as the one responsible for this petition, "whose rivalries dominated local politics for the next half-century" (*New England Merchants*, 124).

45. MassRecs 4.2.267–268.

46. Wells Court petition to King, 18 July 1665, CO 1/19 No. 82II; Maverick to Clarendon, 11 August 1665, *Clarendon Papers*, 78.

47. Carr to [Sec. Morrice], 5 December 1665, CO 1/19, No. 142I-IV, DCHNY 3:109–110.

48. MassArch CVI.151; Richard Godbeer, *Sexual Revolution in Early America* (Baltimore, 2004), 94–95.

49. MassRecs 4.2.249.

50. Dover selectmen to Massachusetts Council, MassArch CVI.149, printed in MaineRecs 1:273–274.

51. Massachusetts Council to Royal Commissioners, prior to 16 July 1665, DCHNY 3:98.

52. Royal Commissioners to Massachusetts, 16 July 1665, DCHNY 3:99–100. They wrote from "Piscataquay River," 16 July 1665. Richard Nicolls, who had gone back to New York, was not a signer.

53. Royal Commissioners to Massachusetts, 16 July 1665, DCHNY 3:99; J. Sears McGee, *The Godly Man in Stuart England: Anglicans, Puritans, and the Two Tables, 1620–1670* (New Haven, 1976), 116–119; Rose, *Godly Kingship in Restoration England*, 136–146.

54. Carr, Cartwright, and Maverick to Sec. Bennet, 26 July 1665, DCHNY 3:101.

55. Reid, *Maine, Charles II, and Massachusetts*, 46–52, 82; Saxine, *Properties of Empire*, 32–33.

56. MaineRecs 1:198–199, 49–50. They gathered 107 signatures, probably a majority of adult Anglo-American males in Kittery, York, and Falmouth, but less than half of Wells's.

57. Gookin to Ferdinando Gorges, 1663, *NEHGR* 13 (1859): 349–350.

58. George Cleeve to Massachusetts magistrates, 24 November 1662, in James Baxter, *George Cleeve of Casco Bay, 1630–1667* (Portland, ME, 1885), 198–199.

59. MaineRecs 2:142; Joseph Felt, *Ecclesiastical History of New England* (Boston, 1862), 2:322; see also MaineRecs 1:195–198; Reid, *Maine, Charles II, and Massachusetts*, 46–49; and Gookin to Gorges, 1663, *NEHGR* 13 (1859): 350. Court record in *The Jordan Memorial*, 72–73; see also MassRecs 4.2.70, 94; and DCHNY 3:111.

60. MassRecs 4.1.426, 434; MaineRecs 2:140; MassArch 10:92–96; Charles Pope, *Pioneers of Maine and New Hampshire* (Boston, 1908), 68.

61. MaineRecs 2:142; Reid, *Maine, Charles II, and Massachusetts*, 49, 52; Kenneth Morrison, *The Embattled Northeast: The Elusive Ideal of Alliance in Abenaki-Euramerican Relations* (Berkeley, 1984), 105–108.

62. MaineRecs 2:151, 137–141. For Massachusetts leaders' language as loosely Filmerian (primarily appealing to authority such as the king or charter) rather than proto-Lockean (relying on consent), see Mary Beth Norton, *Founding Mothers and Fathers: Gendered Power and the Forming of American Society* (New York: Knopf, 1996), 310–311, 321. Recent histories that find a substantial contingent of Maine inhabitants either sympathetic to Massachusetts rule or interested in the security Massachusetts could provide include Charles E. Clark, *Eastern Frontier: The Settlement of Northern New England, 1610–1763* (New York, 1970), see esp. 63–64, 78–79; and Laura Chmielewski, *Spice of Popery: Converging Christianities on an Early American Frontier* (Notre Dame, 2012), 32–33. Pulsipher finds strong groups supporting both the royal intervention and Massachusetts's authority, with cultural tensions related to patterns of settlement between Massachusetts and Maine (*Subjects unto the Same King*, 40–43, 63–64).

63. Charles II to Maine Inhabitants, 11 June 1664, *Hutchinson Papers*, 2:110–112; Cartwright to Nicolls, 30 January 1665, CO 1/19, No. 11; see also MassRecs 4.2.243–245.

64. MassRecs 4.2.236–247; Massachusetts, Answer to . . . the petition of Ferdinando Gorges (1665), CO 1/19, Nos. 1, 2; Pulsipher, *Subjects unto the Same King*, 52–53. For the communication between Gorges's justices and the Massachusetts Council in November 1664, see MassArch III.264–265.

65. MaineRecs 1:213–215; Hubbard, *General History*, 584–585; Reid, *Maine, Charles II, and Massachusetts*, 54–55.

66. Carr, Cartwright, and Maverick to Sec. Bennet, 26 July 1665, DCHNY 3:101. See also Maverick to Clarendon, 24 July 1665, *Clarendon Papers*, 71. For Shapleigh, see Emerson Baker,

The Devil of Great Island: Witchcraft and Conflict in Early New England (New York, 2007), 115–117. Shapleigh would later serve as Nicolls's agent and advocate joining New Hampshire to Maine. Shapleigh to [Robert] Mason, 20 May 1667, CO 1/19 No. 48.

67. MassRecs 4.2.249; Carr, Cartwright, and Maverick to Sec. Arlington, 26 July 1665, CO 1/19 No. 82, printed in DCHNY 3:101–102.

68. Royal Commissioners, Commission for Justices of the Peace in Maine, 23 June 1665, in James Baxter, ed., *Documentary History of the State of Maine* (Portland, 1889), 4:258; MassArch III.265a–266; see also MaineRecs 1:213–214.

69. MaineRecs 1:215–216. Jordan was also named one of two tiebreakers.

70. Maverick to Clarendon, ca. 1661–1663, *Clarendon Papers*, 37–38.

71. Symonds and Danforth to Carr, 4 July 1665, CO 1/19 No. 70; Maverick to Clarendon, 24 July 1665, *Clarendon Papers*, 71; Carr and Maverick to Sec. Arlington, 20 November 1665, CO 1/19, No. 132; DCHNY 3:107.

72. Maverick to Clarendon, 11 August 1665, *Clarendon Papers*, 77–78.

73. Wells Court petition to Charles II, 18 July 1665, CO 1/19 No. 82II.

74. CO 1/19 No. 82.III [18? July 1665] (copied 19 October 1665).

75. Carr to [Sec. Morrice], 5 December 1665, CO 1/19, No. 142I–IV, DCHNY 3:109–110.

76. *Hutchinson Papers*, 2:122–124; see also MassRecs 4.2.249, which mentions threats from the royal commissioners themselves.

77. MassRecs 4.2.278–279. Deputies originated the request for conferences; the magistrates consenting. MassArch CVI.153b.

78. Maverick to Clarendon, 7 November 1665, *Clarendon Papers*, 79–80.

79. Carr and Maverick to Sec. Arlington, 20 November 1665, CO 1/19, No. 131.VI; MassRecs 4.2.276.

80. Francis Champernowne, Edward Rishworth, and Edward Johnson to Carr and Maverick, [October 1665?], CO 1/19, No. 133 (enclosed with the following); Carr and Maverick to Arlington, 20 November 1665, CO 1/19, No. 132; DCHNY 3:108; see also Reid, *Maine, Charles II, and Massachusetts*, 93–95; MassRecs 4.2.267.

81. MassRecs 4.2.269–270; Portsmouth petition copy in MassArch CVI.157; Dover petition in MassRecs 4.2.268; MaineRecs 1:286; Hubbard, *General History*, 586.

82. MassRecs 4.2.273, 267; MaineRecs 1:29; see also Maverick to Clarendon, 7 November 1665, *Clarendon Papers*, 79–80. Carr may have helped orchestrate the bail money: Carr to Sec. of State, 5 December 1665, DCHNY 3:109; Carr and Maverick to Sec. Arlington, 20 November 1665, CO 1/19, No. 131; MassArch CVI.164.

83. Carr and Maverick to Sec. Arlington, 20 November 1665, CO 1/19, Nos. 131I–XIII, printed in DCHNY 3:107–108; Maverick to Clarendon, 7 November 1665, *Clarendon Papers*, 79–80; MassRecs 4.2.292–293, 304–305; MassArch CVI.165; Reid, *Maine, Charles II, and Massachusetts*, 94.

84. Carr assumed the king's judgment was due to people who "maliciously columniated" him at court, slanderers motivated by "reveng." He wrote to Sec. Morrice protesting that the king's "favour" was worth more to him than life itself. Carr to Charles II, 1 August 1665, CO 1/19, No. 87; Carr to [Sec. Morrice], 5 December 1665, CO 1/19, No. 142, printed in DCHNY 3:109–110. In fact, Nicolls had been the one who reported disapprovingly to London of Carr's land grabs and utter dishonesty in the Delaware Bay. Nicolls to Clarendon, 21 November 1664, MsCP, fols. 127–130; Nicolls to [Sec. Arlington], October 1664, CO 1/18, No. 107, printed in DCHNY 3:69–70.

85. RIRecs 2:93–95; Public Instructions for Connecticut, DCHNY 3:56; Fisher and Silverman, *Ninigret*, 58, Pulsipher, *Subjects unto the Same King*, 58–59; Reid, *Maine, Charles II, and Massachusetts*, 70–76.

86. Carr to [Sec. Morrice], 5 December 1665, CO 1/19, No. 142, DCHNY 3:109–110. LaFantasie writes, "Warwick Neck was not included in the territory Carr coveted, but he probably figured that Pomham's removal from the neck would put the Warwick purchasers in his debt, thus manipulating them into supporting his acquisition of lands south of the town" (*Correspondence of Roger Williams*, 2:554n11). See also Dunn, *Puritans and Yankees*, 159–160.

87. Carr to Arlington, 9 April 1666, CO 1/20, No. 43, printed in RIRecs 2:137. Naushwahcowet and Assowawet were also at the meeting, which took place at the home of Richard Smith, an investor in the Atherton Company and a supporter of Pomham's.

88. *Correspondence of Roger Williams*, 1:282n10, 2:552n1; Eliot to Carr, 9 January 1666, enclosure with Carr to Arlington, 9 April 1666, CO 1/20, No. 43I. Carr wrote that Eliot was someone "of whom Pumham ordinarily takes councell," although Richard Cogley has found little evidence of previous meetings between them. Cogley, *John Eliot's Mission*, 187–188.

89. Carr to Arlington, 9 April 1666, CO 1/20, No. 43; Carr to [Sec. Morrice], 5 December 1665, CO 1/19, No. 142, DCHNY 3:109–110. Carr said he spent the winter in "Rhode Island" before going to Warwick; he probably stayed in Providence.

90. Carr to Pomham, 24 February 1666 and Carr to Eliot, 28 February 1666, enclosures with Carr to Arlington, 9 April 1666, CO 1/20, No. 43–43I.

91. Roger Williams to Carr, 1 March 1666, enclosure with CO 1/20, No. 43–43I; Grandjean, *American Passage*, 87–89; Fisher and Silverman, *Ninigret*, 54–55. LaFantasie argues, alternatively, that the "late confederacy" statement was "a gasconade by which Roger Williams hoped to explain his motives for meddling in the Pomham affairs without an invitation" (*Correspondence of Roger Williams*, 2:554n11).

92. Williams to Carr, 1 March 1666.

93. Carr to Arlington, 9 April 1666, CO 1/20, No. 43; Chapin, ed., *Early Records of the Town of Warwick*, 172–173. The Shawomets remained on their land for another decade, until they sided with Philip Metacom in the war and Connecticut soldiers set fire to their village in late 1675. Pomham survived until July 1676; his son was sold as an enslaved laborer. "Pumham," Native Northeast Portal, https://nativenortheastportal.com/bio/bibliography/pumham-1676, accessed 16 August 2021.

94. Chapin, ed., *Early Records of the Town of Warwick*, 172–173. Marshall suggests the "Awashkooke" mentioned, who told the Native Americans to leave peacefully and said Thomas Willet "had taken order with Capt: john green allready about the matter," is Taccomanan, the Coweset sachem's son ("'A Melancholy People,'" 100, 172–173).

95. Chapin, ed., *Early Records of the Town of Warwick*, 172–173. There are further dimensions to the Native story that deserve thorough treatment within much broader indigenous contexts. Philip Metacom had declared himself "subject to the Kinge of England" back in 1662 as part of renegotiating an alliance with Plymouth Colony, a decision that had little to do with Charles II. According to Roger Williams, the royal commissioners heard a land case involving Philip Metacom and the Narragansetts, on which they asked Williams to testify, with inconclusive outcome. By 1671 Philip Metacom was disdaining colonial authority in favor of Charles II's. The royal commissioners also tried to remove Pequots—people who had survived a devastating war in the 1630s—"on the eastern side of Pawkatuck River" in order to "leave the King's Province free" of them. The Massachusett sachem Wampatuck would submit to Charles

II in 1666. PlymRecs 4:25–26; Williams to Massachusetts General Court, 7 May 1668, *Correspondence of Roger Williams*, 2:577–579n4; Pulsipher, *Subjects unto the Same King*, 57–58, 106; Carr, Cartwright, and Maverick to Connecticut, 25 March 1665, *Collections of the MHS*, Ser. 5, 9 (1885): 72; but see also Carr and Nicolls to all his Majesties Subjects, 20 November 1666, Microfilm Reel 1, Elisha Potter Papers, Rhode Island Historical Society, regarding Pequot sachem Herman Garrett's land. See also Craig Yirush, "'Chief Princes and Owners of All': Native American Appeals to the Crown in the Early-Modern British Atlantic," in *Native Claims: Indigenous Law Against Empire*, ed. Saliha Belmessous (Oxford, 2012), 129–151.

96. MassRecs 4.2.257–265; "Cartwright's Report," 14 December 1665, CO 1/19, No. 143.

97. Cartwright to Prence, 3 March 1666, Winslow Family Papers II, MHS.

98. See, for example, letters from Richard Smith to John Winthrop in Daniel Berkeley Updike, *Richard Smith: First English Settler of the Narragansett Country* (Boston, 1937), 80–83; Narragansett Inhabitants to Connecticut, 3 July 1663, Wyllys Papers, *Collections of the Connecticut Historical Society* 21 (1924): 144; Rhode Island to Clarendon, September 1666, printed in RIRecs 2:158; and Osgood, *American Colonies*, 3:179.

99. Maine Justices to Nicolls, 22 November 1665, CO 1/19 No. 134; Commission and instructions by Massachusetts regarding Maine, 20 May 1668, in Baxter, ed., *Documentary History of the State of Maine*, 4:301 (see also 216–224); MassRecs 4.2.372; Hubbard, *General History*, 593–594; John Josselyn, *Two Voyages to New-England* (London, 1675), 151–152; Leverett to Boyle, 10 May 1673, *Correspondence of Robert Boyle*, ed. Michael Hunter, Antonio Clericuzio, and Lawrence Principe (London, 2001), 4:350; Chmielewski, *Spice of Popery*, 32–33; Reid, *Maine, Charles II, and Massachusetts*, 95–97; Saxine, *Properties of Empire*, 36–41.

100. Nicolls to Winthrop, 24 July 1667, DCHNY 3:158; see also Edward Rishworth to Carr, 30 October 1665, CO 1/19, No. 133.

101. DCHNY 3:57–61; "Considerations in order to Establishing his Majesty's Interests in NE."

102. Maverick to Clarendon, 24 July 1665, *Clarendon Papers*, 70.

Chapter 10

1. Bellingham and General Court to Morrice, 31 May 1665, CO 1/19, No. 68l; Bellingham to Boyle, *Correspondence of Robert Boyle*, 2:467–471.

2. "Queries about Religious Matters," in MsWP.

3. Clarendon to Massachusetts, 15 March 1665, MsCP, fol. 235, printed in Hutchinson, *History*, 1:450–451.

4. Bellingham and Court to Clarendon, 30 May 1665, *Clarendon Papers*, 62; draft in MassArch CVI.136–137.

5. Bellingham and General Court to Morrice, 31 May 1665, CO 1/19, No. 68.

6. Bellingham and General Court to Clarendon, 30 May 1665, *Clarendon Papers*, 61–62.

7. Bellingham and General Court to Morrice, 31 May 1665, CO 1/19, No. 68.

8. Bellingham and General Court to Morrice, 31 May 1665, CO 1/19, No. 68.

9. Bellingham and General Court to Morrice, 31 May 1665, CO 1/19, No. 68.

10. Henry Parker, *Observations upon some of his Majesties Late Answers* (London, 1642), 8; Sommerville, "English and Roman Liberty," 207–208; Alan Houston, "Republicanism, the Politics of Necessity, and the Rule of Law," in *A Nation Transformed*, 248; James Hart and Richard Ross, "The Ancient Constitution in the Old World and the New," in *World of John Winthrop: Essays on England and New England, 1588–1649*, ed. Francis Bremer and Lynn Botelho (Charlottesville, 2005), 237–272.

11. [Richard Bellingham, Francis Willoughby, Daniel Gookin, Thomas Danforth, Edward Rawson] to [London supporter], 7 July 1665, MassArch CVI.141. This letter accompanied a report on the negotiations with the royal commissioners.

12. For example, see the political tracts bound together in Mather Library 0682 (AAS), which include *A Collection of Several Speeches, Messages, and Answers of the Kings Majestie, to both Houses of Parliament* (London, 1642), a document that contained petitions, as well as the tract *Touching the Fundamentall Lawes, Or Politique Constitution of this Kingdome, The Kings Negative Voice, and The Power of Parliaments* (London 1643); Increase Mather noted reading *The votes of the Lords & Commons assembled in Parliament touching no farther address to the King* (London, 1647 [1648]). Increase Mather, Diary, March 1664.

13. MassRecs 4.2.221–222, 227–228; on repugnancy and divergence, see Bilder, *Transatlantic Constitution,* 40–46.

14. For the language of "interest," see Mathiowetz, *Appeals to Interest in Seventeenth-Century England*, 61–68; Quentin Skinner, *Visions of Politics* (Cambridge, 2002), 2:163, 177–183, 398–399; Valeri, *Heavenly Merchandize*, 127–134; Thomas Kidd, *The Protestant Interest: New England After Puritanism* (New Haven, 2004); and Katherine Carté, *Religion in the American Revolution: An Imperial History* (Chapel Hill, 2021), chap. 1.

15. Mitchell's 1662 sermon in *Elijah's Mantle* (Boston, 1722), 1–5, MHS copy, corrected according to the manuscript by Thomas Prince; Higginson, *Cause of God and His People*, 17, 12; *Elijah's Mantle* (1722), 7. In the 1663 preface John Wilson and Samuel Whiting, noting plots against the Bay, urged readers to "awake & stand to maintaine this cause" through prayer and action (A2r–A2v). For these sermons' concepts of godly rulership, and the relationship between covenant theology and contractual political theory, see Breen, *Character of a Good Ruler*, 64, 99–102, 282–285; Harry Stout, *The New England Soul: Preaching and Religious Culture in Colonial New England* (Oxford, 1986), 34–36, 70–73; and Miller, *New England Mind*, 1:407–416.

16. MassRecs 4.2.227–230. A copy of the 1602 *Magna Charta* is in Mather Library 0347, AAS.

17. MassRecs 4.2.231–234.

18. MassRecs 4.2.231–234. On arbitrary rule, see Hall, *A Reforming People*, chap. 1.

19. MassRecs 4.2.232–233.

20. MassRecs 4.2.239–240, 252–253; see also 240–251, 265–273.

21. MassRecs 4.2.253–265, drawing on language from the 1629 charter.

22. MassRecs 4.2.231–232, 264–265.

23. [Bellingham et al.] to [London supporter], 7 July 1665, MassArch CVI.141.

24. [Bellingham et al.] to [London supporter], 7 July 1665, MassArch CVI.141.

25. Daniel Gookin's family also had a long-standing leaseholder relationship with Boyle. Boyle to Ashurst, ca. March 1665, *Correspondence of Robert Boyle*, 2:459; Glickman, "Protestantism, Colonization, and the New England Company," 374–375; Woodward, *Prospero's America*, 263–266. For Boyle's later help, however, see John Leverett to Robert Boyle, 10 May 1673, *Correspondence of Robert Boyle*, 4:348.

26. Philip Muth, "The Ashursts: Friends of New England" (PhD diss., Boston University, 1967), 31–39, 54–55; Baxter, *Reliquiae Baxterianae*, 2:108–109, 337.

27. Ashurst to Boyle, 2 November 1665, *Correspondence of Robert Boyle*, 2:573–574.

28. Leverett's narrative is not extant. Davenport to Leverett, 24 June 1665, in *Letters of John Davenport*, ed. Calder, 248–249.

29. Davenport to Leverett, 24 June 1665, in *Letters of John Davenport*, ed. Calder, 248–249.

30. *Journal of John Winthrop*, 140; Winship, *Godly Republicanism*, 202.

31. Davenport to Leverett, 24 June 1665, in *Letters of John Davenport*, ed. Calder, 248–249.

32. Davenport to Leverett, 24 June 1665, in *Letters of John Davenport*, ed. Calder, 249–252; see also Suffolk Files, Case 696.

33. J. G. A. Pocock, *The Machiavellian Moment: Florentine Political Thought and the Atlantic Republican Tradition* (Princeton, 1975), 335–345. For secularizing tendencies, see Bliss, *Revolution and Empire*, 157–158.

34. MassRecs 4.2.274–277.

35. *Records of the First Church of Dorchester*, 48; Pierce, ed., *Records of the First Church in Salem*, 107–108; Hull, "Diaries," 3:156; MassRecs 4.2.279 (a court-proclaimed fast); MassArch X.16.

36. Samuel Danforth, Roxbury Church Records, *NEHGR* 34 (January–April 1880): 165; Hull, "Diaries," 3:220–221.

37. Hubbard, *General History*, 581–586; Hall, *Worlds of Wonder*, 103–114. Some papers may have eventually arrived via a seaman who declared of New England, "the Countrey is up in Rebellion." SP 82/10, fol. 259.

38. Bellingham to [?], 12 August 1666, *Collections of the MHS*, Ser. 4, 7 (1865): 598–599.

39. Maverick to Clarendon, 7 November 1665, *Clarendon Papers*, 80.

40. MassRecs 4.2.280. This providential outlook was rarely coupled with the kind of American exceptionalism appearing in later centuries; colonists were keenly aware of the work of God elsewhere and of divine judgment against themselves. See Adrian Chastain Weimer, "Huguenot Refugees and the Meaning of Charity in Early New England," *Church History* 86, No. 2 (June 2017): 365–397.

41. "Cartwright's Report," 14 December 1665, CO 1/19, No. 143.

42. Clarendon to Nicolls, 13 April 1666, DCHNY 3:116.

43. Olson, *Anglo-American Politics*, 46–47.

44. Charles II to New England, 10 April 1666, CO 1/20, No. 44.

45. Before the letter's belated arrival Corbett had already been released on bond. At the 23 May 1666 General Court he had been fined £20, with £5 for costs, and £100 bond for good behavior. MassRecs 4.2.305.

46. Bishop, *New England Judged* (London, 1703), 2:349; MassRecs 4.2.149, 184.

47. Clarendon to Nicolls, 13 April 1666, DCHNY 3:116.

48. Paul Seaward, "Hyde, Edward, first earl of Clarendon," ODNB.

49. *Records of the First Church of Dorchester*, 51; MassRecs 4.2.280.

50. Nicolls to Massachusetts, 6 July 1666, *Hutchinson Papers*, 2:134.

51. Nicolls to Sec. of State, 24 October 1666, DCHNY 3:136. Nicolls identifies the thief as John Scott, a man who would disrupt political relationships wherever he went.

52. "Humble Peticion of Samuel Mavericke," 30 August 1663, SP 44/13, fol. 356; see also fol. 335.

53. Maverick to Winslow, 11 August 1666, Winslow Family Papers II, MHS; Hull, "Diaries," 3:222.

54. MassArch CVI.98a.

55. Maverick to Winthrop, 29 August 1666, *Collections of the MHS*, Ser. 4, 7 (1865): 313.

56. Bliss, *Revolution and Empire*, 158–159.

57. For example, Mather Library 0682, AAS, probably bound in the 1680s but likely circulating in the colony much earlier. Leverett's regiment fought under Whalley in the siege of Worcester. Bremer, *First Founders*, 149.

58. A. S. P. Woodhouse, ed., *Puritanism and Liberty: Being the Army Debates (1647–9)* (Chicago, 1974), 29. The concern at Putney was also arbitrary rule by the Presbyterian-led parliament. Increase Mather was traveling to Hadley, possibly seeking Goffe and Whalley's advice; he also spoke with a third regicide, John Dixwell, who arrived in 1665. Increase Mather, Diary, May/June 1665; Hall, *Last American Puritan*, 43–45, 54–55, 75; Wilson, "Web of Secrecy," 523–524; Hammer, *Pugnacious Puritans*, 31–36.

59. "Boston Petition" in Danforth Papers, 103; manuscripts in MassArch CVI.106, 167–173. According to Maverick, most Hingham inhabitants also signed a petition, "but their unworthy deputy delivered it not." Maverick to Cartwright, ca. September 1666, *Clarendon Papers*, 127.

60. Scott McDermott, "Body of Liberties: Godly Constitutionalism and the Origin of Written Fundamental Law in Massachusetts, 1634–1666" (PhD diss., Saint Louis University, 2014).

61. Bailyn, *New England Merchants*, 124; Valeri, *Heavenly Merchandize*, 84.

62. Danforth Papers, 100.

63. "Boston Petition" in Danforth Papers, 103–104; MassArch CVI.106, 167–173.

64. William Hubbard, ms. fast day sermon, 3 December 1662, fols. 92–95, notes in Nathaniel Rogers, Sermon notebook, Ipswich Papers, AAS.

65. John Woodbridge's son Benjamin also signed; he would soon take Windsor, Connecticut's pulpit.

66. Parker, "To the High and Mighty Prince Charles the Second."

67. Lucas, "Colony or Commonwealth," 106.

68. "Boston Petition" in Danforth Papers, 104–105.

69. Breedon to Clarendon, 22 October 1666, *Clarendon Papers*, 129–130; see also CO 5/903, fols. 176–178.

70. Royalist treatise, 1666, Charles Lowell Papers, MHS, printed as "The Massachusetts Patent," *Proceedings of the MHS* 46 (1913): 288–289; Jean Bodin, *Six Books of the Common-Wealthe*, trans. Richard Knolles (London, 1606), I.x.155; for the meaning of "absolute" in this context, see Harris, *Restoration*, 57. The 1666 treatise exists in a single copy. J. S. Maloy has found three colonial copies of Bodin's work: "Bodin's Puritan Readers and Radical Democracy in Early New England," *Journal of Intellectual History* (January 2017): 1–26. See also R. H. C., "The Rule of Law in Colonial Massachusetts," *University of Pennsylvania Law Review* 108, No. 7 (May 1960): 1008.

71. "Massachusetts Patent," 287–288, 295–297. The Roman or British concept of *imperium* referred more to the reach of the king's authority than an expanding far-flung territory, although both colonists and royal officials were also grappling with the implications of geographic distance for sovereignty. Armitage, *Ideological Origins of the British Empire*, 29–36.

72. "Massachusetts Patent," 296–297, 302, 286–287, 293. For a version of political casuistry in which "standing upon extream right, may prove extream wrong," see Higginson, *Cause of God and His People*, 20–21.

73. "Massachusetts Patent," 287–88; for additional arguments based on "a cleare purchase of the unconquerd indians right in those parts," see Massachusetts to Morrice, 16 December 1663, MassArch CVI.67; see also Massachusetts to Charles II, 19 October 1664, MassRecs 4.2.129. John Eliot and Daniel Gookin alluded to similar points in a 1662 case: O'Brien, *Dispossession by Degrees*, 40–41. Craig Yirush sees these arguments from purchase as "largely instrumental, invoked to undermine the Crown's claim to property in the Americas"

(*Settlers, Liberty, and Empire*, 76; see also 111). Christopher Tomlins makes the important point that even if colonists had allowed that Indian rulers enjoyed sovereignty, the extent and meaning of that sovereignty were easily minimized, and defining it was assumed to belong to English colonizers (*Freedom Bound*, 154–155, 157). See also Richard Tuck, *Rights of War and Peace: Political Thought and the International Order from Grotius to Kant* (Oxford, 1999), 123–126. Early leaders such as John Winthrop had initially not viewed purchase as necessary, seeing land and authority as the king's to dispense through charters. However, beyond the "fictive realm projected in the charter," which elided the presence of Native peoples, in practice colonists generally tended to recognize Native sovereignty and negotiate purchases. Further, "by treating military arrangements as a matter of diplomacy, the colonial authorities involved were tacitly accepting native independence." In short, "most New Englanders seemed to want it both ways"—crown grants *and* purchases from sachems. Allan Greer, *Property and Dispossession: Natives, Empires and Land in Early Modern North America* (Cambridge, 2018), 206; see also Ken MacMillan, *Sovereignty and Possession in the English New World: The Legal Foundations of Empire, 1576–1640* (Cambridge, 2006), 31–41, 46–48.

74. Thomas Mayhew to John Winthrop, 5 March 1665, *Collections of the MHS*, Ser. 4, 7 (1865): 41–42.

75. Hutchinson, *History*, 1:216–217, summarizing arguments made in 1664–1665 by Massachusetts leaders. For other earlier English versions of this theory of the land's availability because the Native Americans were not *using* it, which were not actually based in Roman law but introduced by humanists such as Thomas More, see Tomlins, *Freedom Bound*, 138, 143–144. For a review of the scholarship on Native farming practices and both colonists' and some modern scholars' tendency to overlook them, see James Merrell, "Second Thoughts on Colonial Historians and American Indians," *WMQ* 69, No. 3 (July 2012): 469–473.

76. Hutchinson, *History*, 1:216–217. Samuel Adams and others made good use of these 1660s discussions about law and subjection in their 1773 debates. There is some (murky) evidence that colonists in the 1660s were reading from an Irish playbook regarding legislative independence, a playbook authored primarily by Catholics but also taken up by Protestants such as William Domville. For example, in 1643 MPs discussed whether "the power of the Parliament in England extended only to that Kingdome," and if the broader authority of parliament's statutes was contingent on being "found agreable to the constitution" of Ireland by its own parliament. *Declaration of the Commons assembled in Parliament* (London, 1643), 33. This tract, along with *True Demands of the Rebels in Ireland* (London, 1642), was owned by the Mathers (Mather Library 0682, AAS). See also Hutchinson, *History*, 1:272–273; and Patrick Kelly, "Sir William Domville: A Disquisition . . . ," *Analecta Hibernica*, No. 40 (2007): 20–21.

77. "Massachusetts Patent," 287–289, 291–295. Both sides also weighed in on whether a colony was a corporation: "Massachusetts Patent," 296–297; Hutchinson, *History*, 1:216–217; see also *Journal of John Winthrop*, 648–679. For the blurred line between them, see Konig, *Law and Society*, 22–26; Philip J. Stern, *The Company-State: Corporate Sovereignty and the Early Modern Foundations of the British Empire in India* (Oxford, 2011); and the forum opened by William Pettigrew, "Corporate Constitutionalism and the Dialogue Between the Global and Local in Seventeenth-Century English History," *Itinerario* 39, no. 3 (2016): 487–525.

78. "Massachusetts Patent," 293 (summarizing the other side's arguments); for Coke, see Daniel Hulsebosch, "The Ancient Constitution and the Expanding Empire: Sir Edward Coke's British Jurisprudence," *Law and History Review* 21 (2003): 455–479; and MacMillan, *Sovereignty and Possession*, 33–34.

79. *Journal of John Winthrop*, 662; Ross, "Career of Puritan Jurisprudence," 232; Bilder, *Transatlantic Constitution*, 55.

80. "Massachusetts Patent," 293–294, 289–290.

81. Clarendon to Nicolls, ca. 1664–1665, MsCP, fol. 141.

82. Hull, "Diaries," 3:222–223. Thomas Danforth, notebook, 1662–1666, MHS. Other ministers present were Richard Mather, Zechariah Symmes, Samuel Whiting, and Thomas Cobbet. The printed Danforth Papers omit the sermon fragments, whose placement immediately prior to the General Court meeting notes suggests the same occasion. The Danforth Papers editors' attribution to Francis Willoughby seems unlikely.

83. Danforth Papers, 98; Higginson, *Cause of God and His People*, 6; Mitchell, *Nehemiah on the Wall*, 31–32.

84. Afterward Danforth copied in full one loyalist petition. Danforth Papers, 99; Hall, *Ways of Writing*, 172. See Hutchinson, *History*, 1:218n for "Mr. Cobbet's letter & MS. papers." See also Sosin, *English America*, 120; Bliss, *Revolution and Empire*, 158–159; Pulsipher, *Subjects unto the Same King*, 68–69.

85. George Bancroft, *History of the United States of America* (Boston, 1850), 1:222.

86. Danforth Papers, 99. Danforth's manuscript of the debate only uses initials. The editors of the printed Danforth Papers misidentified Symonds as "Stoughton" and Denison as "Dudley." Daniel Denison Slade, "Major-General Daniel Denison," *NEHGS* 23, No. 1 (January 1869): 316–320; Daniel Denison, "Autobiography," *NEHGR* 46 (January 1892): 127.

87. Isaac Greenwood, "The Willoughby Family of New England," *NEHGR* 30 (January 1876): 72–74.

88. William Lamont, "Puritanism, Liberty, and Putney," in *The Putney Debates of 1647: The Army, the Levellers, and the English State*, ed. Michael Mendle (Cambridge, 2001), 243–245; Danforth Papers, 99–100.

89. Danforth Papers, 99–100.

90. Danforth Papers, 100. Jurists such as Sir Edward Coke had long worked to impose legal limits on royal prerogative. Many parliamentarians would have argued that legislative power was equally shared by king, lords, and commons, a position that Charles I inadvertently introduced. John Reid, "The Jurisprudence of Liberty: The Ancient Constitution in the Legal Historiography of the Seventeenth and Eighteenth Centuries," in *The Roots of Liberty: Magna Carta, Ancient Constitution, and the Anglo-American Tradition of Rule of Law*, ed. Ellis Sandoz (Columbia, 1993), 251; Corinne Weston and Janelle Greenberg, *Subjects and Sovereigns: The Grand Controversy over Legal Sovereignty in Stuart England* (Cambridge, 1981), 35–51; Pocock, *Machiavellian Moment*, 362–375.

91. Danforth Papers, 100–101.

92. Hutchinson, *History*, 1:218n; see also Miller, *New England Mind*, 1:410. For similar ideas, see Coffey, *Politics, Religion and the British Revolutions*, 176–183.

93. MassRecs 4.2.317; drafts in MassArch CVI.98a, 166; Edward Rawson to Sec. Morrice, October 1666, CO 1/20, No. 162.

94. Danforth Papers, 108–109.

95. Danforth Papers, 100–101. John Pynchon's 11 July 1666 report from "our Indians" of the movement of 1,500 French troops is in MassArch LXVII.170. The manuscript of the vote about Canada is in MassArch CVI.166a. Connecticut to Bellingham, 10 July 1666, *Collections of the MHS* 10, Ser. 3 (1849): 63–64.

96. Peterson, *City-State of Boston*, 148–151.

97. MassRecs 4.2.318; SP 29/191, fol. 3; SP 29/150, fol. 30. For Warren, see John Ehrman, *The Navy in the War of William III, 1689–1697: Its State and Direction* (Cambridge, 2012), 58.

98. Breedon to Clarendon, 22 October 1666, *Clarendon Papers*, 129; Bliss, *Revolution and Empire*, 92.

99. Danforth Papers, 110–111; MassRecs 4.2.318. The General Court had discussed reserving trees for the use of the Royal Navy the previous year in May/June 1665, but the deputies did not consent. MassArch LX.51a–52b.

100. Danforth Papers, 110–111; MassRecs 4.2.318.

101. Danforth, too, may have contributed; as Harvard College's treasurer he was known for helping beleaguered students—English or Native—out of personal funds. General Court order, 20 October 1666, Miscellaneous Bound, MHS; Francis Willoughby et al. to Navy Commissioners, 20 July 1668, CO 1/23, No. 17; MassRecs 4.2.327–329; Samuel Nadhorth to Morrice, 26 October 1666, CO 1/20, No. 155; DCHNY 3:141. In April 1668 the General Court was still asking town selectmen to solicit contributions for the masts (MassRecs 4.2.369–370).

102. Mark A. Peterson, The *Price of Redemption: The Spiritual Economy of Puritan New England* (Stanford, 1997), 30; Valeri, *Heavenly Merchandize*, 83, 85.

103. Hull, Usher, and Scottow, Petition to Mass. General Court, 23 October 1666, MassArch CVI.179; "Commonalty," *OED*.

104. Hull, "Diaries," 3:217.

105. Hull, Usher, Scottow, Petition, MassArch CVI.179; Lucas, "Colony or Commonwealth," 107.

106. Colclough, *Freedom of Speech in Early Stuart England*, 150–153.

107. Kupperman, "Definitions of Liberty on the Eve of Civil War"; Farber, "The Rise and Fall of the Province of Lygonia," 490–513.

108. MassArch CVI.174a–175a; William Sumner Appleton, "The Loyal Petitions of 1666," *Proceedings of the MHS*, Ser. 2, 6 (June 1891): 7. A simple version of the deputies' questions is in *Collections of the MHS*, Ser. 3, 1 (1846): 59–60.

109. MassArch CVI.179.

110. Maverick to Nicolls, 18 June 1665, CO 1/19, No. 74.

111. MassArch CVI.176–177; Appleton, "The Loyal Petitions of 1666," 6–8. Appleton slightly backtracked, saying he had "honor & Respect" even to the 1664 petitioners, although he disagreed with them.

112. When Ipswich and Salem elected Appleton and another leading petitioner, Edmond Batter, as deputies a year or two later other deputies tried to prevent them holding office, citing their role in the 1666 petitions. However, their towns pushed back and the magistrates intervened, saying there had to be a good legal reason to prevent an elected deputy from holding office. MassArch CVI.182–183, 187; Appleton, "The Loyal Petitions of 1666," 8–10; Sydney Perley, *History of Salem* (Salem, 1926), 2:398.

113. Nadhorth to Morrice, 26 October 1666, CO 1/20, No. 155; DCHNY 3:139–142. Observing that "Nadhorth" is an anagram of both surnames, John Gorham Palfrey guessed the author was either Thomas Danforth or William Hathorne (*History*, 2:628n1). Pulsipher thought the author either Thomas Danforth or his brother the minister Samuel Danforth (*Subjects unto the Same King*, 286n86). The writer Nathaniel Hawthorne and his family, descendants of William Hathorne, believed Hathorne to be the sole author. "William Hathorne, ms. letter to [William Morrice]," Berg Collection Mss., New York Public Library.

114. Nadhorth to Morrice, 26 October 1666, DCHNY 3:139–142.

115. 1 Samuel 15; Breedon to Clarendon, 22 October 1666, *Clarendon Papers*, 129; Nicolls, Carr, and Maverick to Bellingham and Court, 3 November 1666, MassArch CVI.180–181, printed in *Hutchinson Papers,* 2:135–137.

116. Nicolls to Morrice, 24 October 1666, DCHNY 3:136. Nicolls in another letter blamed "a Violent faction in the Massachusett" who were responsible for "the contempts" of the king's "messages." Nicolls to John Allyn, 19 September 1666, Wyllys Papers, *Collections of the Connecticut Historical Society* 21 (1924): 163.

117. Carr and Maverick to Clarendon, 10 January 1667, *Clarendon Papers*, 158. After Carr initiated a brawl in a local tavern and defied an arrest warrant (as we saw in the Introduction), he hastily left for England, dying just after the ship landed. Maverick stayed on in New York, continuing to complain about the Bay in increasingly desperate letters.

118. MassRecs 4.2.321–322; *Records of the First Church of Dorchester*, 51–52; Pierce, ed., *Records of the First Church in Salem*, 113; Roxbury Church Records, 165; Hull, "Diaries," 3:221–223.

119. Henry Wheatley, ed., *Diary of Samuel Pepys* (New York, 1893), 2:366. New England masts had enriched the Royal Navy before, but the timing, at a crucial moment in the war effort, was significant.

120. Charles II to Massachusetts [1666], CO 1/20, Nos. 14, 15; Bellingham and Council to Gov. Willoughby of Barbados, 21 August 1667, *Hutchinson Papers,* 2:154–155.

121. Charles II to Massachusetts, ca. 1667–1668, CO 1/23, No. 18.

Chapter 11

1. Berkeley to Nicolls, 20 May 1666, in *Papers of Sir William Berkeley*, ed. Warren M. Billings (Richmond, 2007), 280.

2. Evan Haefeli, *Accidental Pluralism: America and the Religious Politics of English Expansion, 1497–1662* (Chicago, 2021), 305–306; Haskell, *For God, King, and People*, 325; Warren Billings, *A Little Parliament: The Virginia General Assembly in the Seventeenth Century* (Richmond, 2004), 44–45; Brent Tarter, "Bacon's Rebellion, the Grievances of the People, and the Political Culture of Seventeenth-Century Virginia," *Virginia Magazine of History and Biography* 119, No. 1 (2011): 13–36.

3. "Answers to the Inquiries from the Council for Foreign Plantations," 20 June 1671, in *Papers of Sir William Berkeley*, 397.

4. Haskell, *For God, King, and People*, 285–331.

5. Haskell, *For God, King, and People*, 76; Sosin, *English America*, 157–159. A major conflict involved the location of forts and urban investment. Musselwhite, *Urban Dreams, Rural Commonwealth*, 122–129. High taxes aimed at buying out these new Northern Neck proprietors were one factor leading to Bacon's Rebellion. Tarter, "Bacon's Rebellion," 11. Governor Nicolls also protested when Charles II granted New York land to crown favorites. Nicolls to Clarendon, 30 July 1665, *Clarendon Papers*, 75.

6. "Notes, explanatory . . . of the Virginian agents," November 1675, in John Burk, *History of Virginia*, vol. 2 (Petersburg, VA, 1805), appendix: li–liii; 152; David Lovejoy, *The Glorious Revolution in America* (New York, 1972), 125.

7. Tarter, "Bacon's Rebellion," 4.

8. Hulsebosch, *Constituting Empire*, 48–53.

9. Charles II to Modyford, 16 November 1665, CO 1/19, No. 126. Tangier was included in the Company of Royal Adventurers (later the Royal African Company) in 1663; Charles II

would give up Bombay in 1667. Tristan Stein, "Tangier in the Restoration Empire," *Historical Journal* 54, No. 4 (December 2011): 990; Israel, "The Emerging Empire," 428–433; Daniel Richter, *Trade, Land, Power: The Struggle for Eastern North America* (Philadelphia, 2013), 100; Koot, *Empire at the Periphery*, chap. 3; Swingen, *Competing Visions of Empire*, 59–62.

10. Tangier was also exempt from the Navigations Acts. Richard Dunn, *Sugar and Slaves: The Rise of the Planter Class in the West Indes, 1624–1713* (Chapel Hill, 1972), 155–156; Swingen, *Competing Visions of Empire*, 65–74; Sarah Barber, "Power in the English Caribbean: The Proprietorship of Lord Willoughby of Parham," in *Constructing Early Modern Empires: Proprietary Ventures in the Atlantic World, 1500–1750* (Boston, 2007), 210; Nuala Zahedieh, "Modyford, Thomas," ODNB. For the challenges of demilitarizing Jamaica, see Carla Pestana, *English Conquest of Jamaica: Oliver Cromwell's Bid for Empire* (Cambridge, 2017), 223–239.

11. Stanwood, *Empire Reformed*, 25.

12. The first theory has been advanced by Jenny Hale Pulsipher; the second by Daniel Richter. Pulsipher, *Subjects unto the Same King*, 70, 120; Richter, *Trade, Land, Power*, 99–111.

13. J. Williamson to Gov. Leverett, 20 March 1676, SP 44/43, fol. 42; Lovejoy, *Glorious Revolution*, 134.

14. R. N. Toppan, ed., *Edward Randolph* (New York, 1967), 2:232–233, 236, 253; Richard Bushman, *King and People in Provincial Massachusetts* (Chapel Hill, 1985), 99–104; Stanwood, *Empire Reformed*, 26; Michael G. Hall, *Edward Randolph and the American Colonies* (Chapel Hill, 1960), 22–30.

15. MassRecs 5:100; Richard Johnson, "Stoughton, William," ANB; Hall, *Edward Randolph*, 32–52; Peterson, *City-State of Boston*, 156.

16. Hall, *Faithful Shepherd*, 242; Hall, *Edward Randolph*, 55–63; Lovejoy, *Glorious Revolution*, 140–147.

17. "Answer of the Elders," 4 January 1681, CO 1/46, No. 83; Increase Mather, Diary, 17 October 1680. See also John Higginson to Increase Mather, 1681, Mather Papers 280–282, advocating resistance based on the model of Esther.

18. Increase Mather, Diary, 7 January 1681.

19. Daniel Gookin, Petition, 14 February 1681, Thomas Prince Papers, 1661-1743, MHS.

20. Gookin, Petition, 14 February 1681. On the franchise and freedom of worship for high church conformists, also at issue, Gookin basically repeated the arguments of 1665. The charter granted the liberty to determine "freemens Admision," and there was no law against the Church of England, but for the government to positively encourage "that worship" might "offend God; and <bee A> condem[n]ing the doings & sufferings of our selves & fathers that first planted this country."

21. Gookin, Petition, 14 February 1681.

22. Halliday, *Dismembering the Body Politic*, 196–212, 205, 191; Cotton Mather to John Cotton, 28 February 1683, *The Correspondence of John Cotton Junior*, ed. Sheila McIntyre and Len Travers (Boston, 2009), 287; see also MassArch CVI.293. The *quo warranto* against Bermuda was orchestrated by an ambitious individual, Francis Burghill, rather than the crown. Richard Dunn, "The Downfall of the Bermuda Company: A Restoration Farce," *WMQ* 20, No. 4 (October 1963): 487–512.

23. MassRecs 5:307–315, 390; Peterson, *City-State of Boston*, 159.

24. Samuel Nowell to John Richards, 28 March 1683, in *The Glorious Revolution in America: Documents on the Colonial Crisis*, ed. Michael Hall, Lawrence Leder, and Michael Kammen (Chapel Hill, 1964), 22–23.

25. Governor Cranfield to the Lords of Trade and Plantations, 27 March 1683, CO 5/940, fol. 90; "Address from the inhabitants of Massachusetts to the King," received 4 June 1683, CO 1/52, No. 3; MassRecs 5:387–388, possibly responding to the "Petition of Edward Randolph and other loyal inhabitants of Massachusetts to the King," received 28 June 1683, CO 1/52, No. 20; see also MassArch CVI.277–277b, 292.

26. Toppan, ed., *Edward Randolph*, 3:30; MassArch CVI.298.

27. Toppan, ed., *Edward Randolph*, 3:247.

28. "Arguments Against Relinquishing the Charter," *Collections of the MHS*, Ser. 3, 1 (1846): 75–81.

29. Stanwood, *Empire Reformed*, 31–36; Bushman, *King and People*, 100–101; Belknap, *History of New Hampshire*, 1:93–111; Gov. Cranfield to Leoline Jenkins, 20 February 1683, CO 1/51, No. 34.

30. Moodey to Thomas Hinckley, 12 February 1684, *Collections of the MHS*, Ser. 4, 5 (1861): 116–120.

31. Moodey did not actually go to jail but instead was confined to Captain Stileman's house. Moodey to Hinckley, 12 February 1684, *Collections of the MHS*, Ser. 4, 5 (1861): 119.

32. Moodey to Hinckley, 12 February 1684, *Collections of the MHS*, Ser. 4, 5 (1861): 118, 120. For political uses of martyr rhetoric, see Weimer, *Martyrs' Mirror*.

33. Bouton, ed., *Documents and Records*, 1:482–483 (legal papers regarding Moodey's case); Belknap, *History*, 1:110; Stanwood, *Empire Reformed*, 37–39.

34. Stanwood, *Empire Reformed*, 76–77. Stanwood notes that the population was not all of Moodey's ilk; some were curious about high Church of England worship and enjoyed the new maypoles.

35. William Blathwayt to Lord Effingham, 9 December 1684, in *Papers of Francis Howard, Baron Howard of Effingham, 1643–1695*, ed. Warren Billings (Richmond, 1989), 170.

36. MassRecs 5:516; Hall, *Edward Randolph*, 99.

37. Dunn, *Puritans and Yankees*, 236–243. On the land grant issue, Andros assumed the colony, as a corporation, could not create new corporations (the towns).

38. Peterson, *City-State of Boston*, 166–167.

39. Affidavit by John Wise et al., 1687, in Edward Rawson[?], *Revolution in New England Justified*, in William Henry Whitmore, ed., *Andros Tracts* (Boston, 1874), 1:84–85; Stanwood, *Empire Reformed*, 78.

40. Rawson[?], *Revolution in New England Justified*, in *Andros Tracts*, 1:125–126.

41. *Andros Tracts*, 1:88–90. John Palmer, who defended Andros in *An Impartial Account of the State of New England* (London 1690), also argued for dominion based on discovery. The author of *Revolution in New England Justified* (most likely Edward Rawson, possibly Increase Mather) argued this was "not a Christian, but an unchristian Principle," because the Bible says that "the Heathen Nations, and the Sons of Adam, and not the Children of Israel only, have a right to the Earth" (123). They asked Palmer if Christians could also give away non-Christian land in the East and West Indies, violently expelling inhabitants like the Spanish did? Even Balaam's ass could instruct him on this point, having acknowledged her "Infidel" master's "right of Dominion" (*Andros Tracts* 1:124, citing Numbers 22). On this debate, and

the larger legal and imperial context of Andros's policies, see Yirush, *Settlers, Liberty, and Empire*, 64–78.

42. Paige, *History of Cambridge*, 75.

43. The text has "Willow," but see MassArch CXXVIII.300; the mistranscription was noted in Joshua Coffin to William Willis, 14 May 1831, printed in *Willis Records* (London, 1902), 10. *A Narrative of the Miseries of New-England* (1689); reprinted 1775.

44. Toppan, ed., *Edward Randolph*, 3:230.

45. "Puritan Leaders Justify Their Actions," 6 June 1689, in *Glorious Revolution*, ed. Hall, Leder, and Kammen, 49.

46. Danforth to Increase Mather, 30 July 1689, *Hutchinson Papers,* 2:310–311; Danforth to Thomas Hinckly, 20 April 1689, *Collections of the MHS*, Ser. 4, 5 (1861): 191; Stanwood, *Empire Reformed*, 103, 124; for the religious negotiations on the English side, see Scott Sowerby, *Making Toleration: The Repealers and the Glorious Revolution* (Cambridge, 2013).

47. Danforth to Increase Mather, 30 July 1689, *Hutchinson Papers,* 2:311, 313–314. See also Samuel Mather's Account, April 1689, in *Glorious Revolution*, ed. Hall, Leder, and Kammen, 39–40.

48. Danforth to Increase Mather, 30 July 1689, *Hutchinson Papers,* 2:313–314.

49. "Puritan Leaders Justify Their Actions," 48.

50. *Andros Tracts* 1:129–130. These words and citations (from 2 Kings) echo lines from John Cotton's 1651 thanksgiving sermon defending the regicide: "There is a Lawfull & Loyall Conspiracy as well as a Disloyall & wicked Conspiracy." Bremer, "In Defense of Regicide," 118.

51. "Puritan Leaders Justify Their Actions," 48.

52. Cotton Mather, *Eleutheria* (London, 1698), 75–76. These tropes were available to both traditionalists and liberals. See Foster, "Rereading Liberalism," 491–494, 498–499.

53. McConville, *King's Three Faces*, 262, 199–200. For Jonathan Mayhew's more radical efforts around the 100th anniversary of the regicide to counter "the revival of Tory obedience principles by high-church clergy," see J. Patrick Mullin, *Father of Liberty: Jonathan Mayhew and the Principles of the American Revolution* (Lawrence, 2017), chap. 2 (quote on 46).

54. Jeremiah Dummer, *A Defence of the New-England Charters* (London, 1721 [written 1715]), 8–10, 66–80; Stephen Foster and Evan Haefeli, "British North America in the Empire," in *British North America in the Seventeenth and Eighteenth Centuries*, ed. Stephen Foster (Oxford, 2013), 35–36, 60–61; Yirush, *Settlers, Liberty, and Empire*, 83–111; William Pencak, *War, Politics and Revolution in Provincial Massachusetts* (Boston, 1981), 61–80. For newspapers, see for example 24 February–3 March 1766 Supplement to the *Boston-Gazette*; and *Boston Evening-Post*, 4 January 1768, 1, 4. For an assessment of the broader uses of Stuart prerogative to deny parliamentary authority in the 1760s and 1770s, see Eric Nelson, "Patriot Royalism: The Stuart Monarchy in American Political Thought, 1769–75," *WMQ* 68, No. 4 (October 2011): 533–572; and Daniel Hulsebosch, "The Plural Prerogative," *WMQ* 68, No. 4 (October 2011): 583–587.

55. *Elijah's Mantle* (Boston, 1722; rev. ed. 1774).

56. See, for example, Andrew Eliot, *A Sermon Preached before His Excellency Francis Bernard* (Boston, 1765), 42–48; Amos Adams, *A Concise, Historical View of the Perils . . . of New-England* (Boston, 1769), 22–23; Judah Champion, *A Brief View of the Distresses, Hardships and Dangers our Ancestors Encounter'd* (Hartford, 1770); and Samuel Cooke, *A Sermon Preached at Cambridge* (Boston, 1770).

57. *Providence Gazette*, 19 December 1772, 3; *Boston Evening-Post*, 21 December 1772, 3; *Newport Mercury*, 28 December 1772, 3.

58. John Reid, ed., *Briefs of the American Revolution* (New York, 1981), 64–68.

59. Foster and Haefeli, "British North America," 37.

60. James Cooper, *Tenacious of Their Liberties* (Oxford, 1999), 5, 27–45. See also Bremer, *Lay Empowerment and the Development of Puritanism*.

61. Reid, ed., *Briefs of the American Revolution*, 32–33, 126.

62. This is not to link puritanism to modern notions of liberty and democracy or repeat the errors of Whiggish historiography but rather to trace specific textual and intellectual appropriations. For stories passed down, see Winship, *Godly Republicanism*, 41; and Roger Clap, *Memoirs of Captain Roger Clap* (Boston, 1731), 21–22. For civil glosses on Christian liberty in the eighteenth century, see James Byrd, *Sacred Scripture, Sacred War: The Bible and the American Revolution* (Oxford, 2013), 133–136; and Bartholomew Peter Schiavo, "The Dissenter Connection: English Dissenters and Massachusetts Political Culture, 1630–1774" (PhD diss., Brandeis University, 1976), 441. For the use of the stories of Esther and the curse of Meroz, see Byrd, *Sacred Scripture, Sacred War*, chap. 3; Alan Heimert, *Religion and the American Mind, from the Great Awakening to the Revolution* (Cambridge, 1966), 333, 457, 471, 490, 501–509; and Erin Shalev, "Evil Counselors, Corrupt Traitors, and Bad Kings: The Hebrew Bible and Political Critique in Revolutionary America and Beyond," in *Resistance to Tyrants, Obedience to God: Reason, Religion, and Republicanism at the American Founding*, ed. Dustin Gish and Daniel Klinghard (Lanham, 2013), 106–113. In Shalev's words, in the era of the American Revolution the figure of the evil-counselor Haman in the story of Esther became a "popular" vehicle for "protecting the king while severely criticizing his policies" (107).

63. McConville, *King's Three Faces*, 192, 193, 218.

64. Yirush, *Settlers, Liberty, and Empire*, 235; Thomas Ingersoll, *The Loyalist Problem in Revolutionary New England* (Cambridge, 2016), 2–7, 50–51, 64–65; Pauline Maier, *The Old Revolutionaries: Political Lives in the Age of Samuel Adams* (New York, 1980), 19–20, 28–29; McConville, *King's Three Faces*, 268; Alfred Young, "English Plebeian Culture and 18thc American Radicalism," in *The Origins of Anglo-American Radicalism*, ed. Margaret Jacob and James Jacob (Boston, 1984), 197–199. For the significance of "imperial protestantism" and the shared goals and assumptions of transatlantic protestant networks see Carté, *Religion in the American Revolution*, 25; for the strength of New England's historical memory, see Michael Hattem, *Past and Prologue: Politics and Memory in the American Revolution* (New Haven, 2020), 47–79.

Conclusion

1. While people like Jean Bodin used Cicero's *salus populi* to justify giving the king emergency powers, Mitchell's use of the phrase was closer to that of 1640s parliamentarians working to limit royal prerogative. John Higginson also appealed to *salus populi*. Higginson, *Cause of God and His People*, 20–21. For similar use by Samuel Rutherford, see Coffey, *Politics, Religion and the British Revolutions*, 169. See also Skinner, *Visions of Politics*, 2:326; and Sommerville, "English and Roman Liberty," 208.

2. The last sentence was a contemporary proverb, found also in Richard Mather's diary from the 1630s. Mitchell, *Nehemiah on the Wall*, 9, 31–32. Mitchell also drew on the English apocalyptic writer Thomas Brightman to argue that "the Kingdome of God is after a sort visibly seen . . . when God setteth up godly Rulers to govern his people."

3. Mitchell cited Nicholas Bacon's *Mediocria Firma* on this point (29). For natural law principles and the overarching call to moderation in Massachusetts election sermons, see John Buchanan, "Drumfire from the Pulpit: Natural Law in the Colonial Election Sermons of Massachusetts," *American Journal of Legal History* 12, No. 3 (July 1968): 235; A. W. Plumstead, *The Wall and the Garden: Selected Massachusetts Election Sermons, 1670–1775* (Minneapolis, 1968), 5; and Miller, *New England Mind*, 1:428–431. On the Nehemiah theme, see Breen, *Character of a Good Ruler*, 100–103; and Meredith Neuman, "Failures of Consensus: Contesting Election Sermons in Puritan New England," in *Stories of Nation: Fictions, Politics, and the American Experience*, ed. Martin Griffin and Christopher Hebert (Knoxville, 2017), 181–197.

4. Mitchell, *Nehemiah on the Wall*, 22–24, 19–20. Mitchell paraphrased the topic of Cobbet's sermon again on p. 33: "the Lord is with you, while you be with him; as we excellently heard the last year" (33). Harry Stout noted the tendency of second-generation election day preachers to "incorporate key phrases or biblical texts from the founders' sermons into their own." Stout, *The New England Soul*, 71. Winthrop's sermon was not printed in its own time. For the longer history of the uses and misuses of this puritan (and Catholic) trope, see Abram Van Engen, *City on a Hill: A History of American Exceptionalism* (New Haven, 2020).

5. Mitchell, *Nehemiah on the Wall*, 14.

6. For colonists' strong and ongoing monarchical impulses, see McConville, *King's Three Faces*. Craig Yirush adds to McConville's thesis to argue that, while highly monarchical, eighteenth-century "settlers conceived of monarchical authority as connected to the protection of their rights, and thus as contractual and conditional" (*Settlers, Liberty, and Empire*, 22n50).

7. Collinson, "*De Republica Anglorum*," 18 ("prophetic"); Withington, *Politics of Commonwealth*, 243–248 ("self-reflective"); Bozeman, *To Live Ancient Lives*, 159–160. For the centrality of religion to political theory and language in the seventeenth century, see Margo Todd, "Anti-Calvinists and the Republican Threat in Early Stuart Cambridge," in *Puritanism and Its Discontents*, ed. Laura Knoppers (Newark, 2003), 85; Rose, *Godly Kingship in Restoration England*, 3; and Natalie Zemon Davis, "Missed Connections: Religion and Regime," *Journal of Interdisciplinary History* 1, No. 3 (Spring 1971): 392–394. Steve Pincus and Alan Houston argue that post-Restoration "growth in the English state was accompanied by the increasing differentiation of politics and religion," although they seem to place the shift after 1680 and do not deal substantially with New England. Pincus and Houston, introduction to *A Nation Transformed: England After the Restoration*, ed. Alan Houston and Steve Pincus (Cambridge, 2001), 13–14.

8. This is not to argue that public-spiritedness was a uniquely puritan contribution to American political life but rather that the political culture that developed in early New England, one informed by puritanism, embraced a strong and distinct form of it. Todd, *Christian Humanism and the Puritan Social Order*, 28–42 ("selfish passions" quote on 28–29). For the longer influence of this tradition of political activism and sacrifice, see Edmund Morgan, "The Puritan Ethic and the American Revolution," *WMQ* 24, No. 1 (January 1967): 3–20; Sydney Ahlstrom, "The Puritan Ethic and the Spirit of American Democracy," in *Calvinism and the Political Order* (Philadelphia, 1965), 97–106; and Maier, *Old Revolutionaries*, 3–50. For the distinctiveness of New England culture, see John Murrin, "A Roof Without Walls: The Dilemma of American National Identity," in Richard Beeman et al., *Beyond Confederation* (Chapel Hill, 1987), 343–348.

9. My findings on broad-based consensus are in line with recent studies of New England's political economy and religious culture that highlight the unusual cohesion of the population in the later seventeenth century, demonstrating how Boston and its hinterlands rallied together to sustain a singular moral, spiritual, and political economy. The men and women of New England were committed to godly walking, local arbitration of disputes, governmental autonomy, expansionist trade, and freehold landownership. Peterson, *City-State of Boston*, chaps. 2–3; Douglas Winiarski, *Darkness Falls on the Land of Light: Experiencing Religious Awakenings in Eighteenth-Century New England* (Chapel Hill, 2017), part 1. On consensus around economic policy, see Newell, *From Dependency to Independence*, 61–62. For strong older scholarship identifying these alliances, see Wall, *Massachusetts Bay*; Lucas, "Colony or Commonwealth"; Bailyn, *New England Merchants*; Foster, *The Long Argument*, 196–202; and E. Brooks Holifield, "On Toleration in Massachusetts," *Church History* 38, No. 2 (June 1969): 188–200.

10. Mitchell, *Nehemiah on the Wall*, 30–31, 28–29.

11. These were also years when Charles II's power was not yet substantially drained by the Anglo-Dutch wars or by angry disapproval of his lifestyle and policies. In the broader picture, however, there is still disagreement about when centralization of the peripheries by the metropole—an "imperial consciousness" leading to a more coherent or coercive policy—became conceivable, desirable, or possible. MacMillan, "'Bound by Our Regal Office,'" 67–69 (quote on 67); Sosin, *English America*, 2–3, 98; Greene, *Peripheries and Center*, 10–14; Richard Johnson, *Adjustment to Empire: The New England Colonies, 1675–1715* (New Brunswick, 1981), 24; Harris, *Restoration*, 61–66; Armitage, *Ideological Origins of the British Empire*, 6–9.

12. Elizabeth Parkinson, *The Establishment of the Hearth Tax, 1662–66* (Kew, 2008); Maurice Lee, "The Worcester Veterans and the Restoration Regime in Scotland," in *Scotland in the Age of Two Revolutions*, ed. Sharon Adams and Julian Goodare (Woodbridge, 2014), 135–154; Kristen Block and Jenny Shaw, "Subjects Without an Empire: The Irish in the Early Modern Caribbean," *Past & Present*, No. 210 (February 2011): 49–53.

13. Glickman, "Protestantism, Colonization, and the New England Company," 369–370.

14. Thomas Shepard, 3 October 1662 private fast sermon, Octavo 5, Shepard Family Papers, AAS. Nikolas Bowie emphasizes the significance of the charter as a written document, one that could not be changed at the king's whim. Bowie, "Why the Constitution Was Written Down," *Stanford Law Review* 71 (June 2019): 1400; see also John Witte, "How to Govern a City on a Hill: The Early Puritan Contribution to American Constitutionalism," *Emory Law Journal* 39 (1990): 41–64.

15. Royal Commissioners to Massachusetts General Court, 2 May 1665, Danforth Papers, 57.

16. Clap, *Memoirs*, 21–22.

INDEX

ACKNOWLEDGMENTS

The archivists and historians who have shared—or humored—my fascination with seventeenth-century manuscripts and the people who wrote them have added immeasurably to this book. I am especially indebted to Ashley Cataldo, Elizabeth Pope, Molly Hardy, Nan Wolverton, and Thomas Knoles in Worcester, and Daniel Hinchen, Peter Drummey, Elaine Heavey, Anna Cook, Conrad Wright, and Kate Viens in Boston. Their kindness made the American Antiquarian Society and the Massachusetts Historical Society intellectual homes during the months I spent at each place. And their skill and interest led to many manuscripts being uncovered I would not have otherwise found. I am also grateful for assistance, in person and remote, from staff at the British Library, Bodleian Library, National Archives, Connecticut State Library, New York Public Library, John Carter Brown Library, Rhode Island Historical Society, Houghton Library, Phillips Library, Small Special Collections at the University of Virginia, Newberry Library, Huntington Library, Massachusetts Archives, New England Historic Genealogical Society, Boston Athenaeum, Amherst College Archives, and Boston Public Library. Special thanks are also due to the dean, provost, library staff, and History Department at Providence College. There are too many to list but I hope each of my colleagues knows how thankful I am that I get to work alongside them each semester. My chair, Sharon Murphy, has provided stellar advice and advocacy from the beginning. A Committee to Aid Faculty Research Grant from Providence College and two long-term National Endowment for the Humanities (NEH) fellowships made much of this research possible (any views, findings, conclusions, or recommendations expressed in this book do not necessarily reflect those of the NEH).

I had the good fortune to present chapter drafts and receive transformative feedback at the Omohundro Institute/Early Modern Studies Institute Workshop at the Huntington Library, the Washington Early American Seminar, the Pauline Maier Early American History Seminar, and the American

Antiquarian Society. I am grateful to Catherine Brekus, Karen Kupperman, Erik Seeman, Frank Bremer, Holly Brewer, Abram Van Engen, Meredith Neuman, Russell Hillier, Andrew Murphy, Laurel Daen, Walter Woodward, Brendan McConville, James Hrdlicka, Ken MacMillan, and my remarkable AAS Fellows' workshop—Katherine Grandjean, Samantha Harvey, Reeve Houston, Roberto Saba, the late Sarah Schuetze, and Steven Bullock—for chapter comments and source ideas. Our indefatigable workshop leader Peter Onuf read an entire early draft with keen insight for larger contexts and showed us a model of joyful, humane scholarly life.

My Providence-area writing group—Edward Andrews, Charlotte Carrington-Farmer, Linford Fisher, and Owen Stanwood—read many chapter drafts over many gatherings, offering the best concoction of festivity and critique. Stephen Foster, Mark Valeri, David D. Hall, Evan Haefeli, Cornelia Hughes Dayton, Tim Harris, and Mark Peterson read the entire manuscript, offering extraordinary—and gracious—expertise. Sincere appreciation to Eric Bennett and Stacia Pelletier for writing advice, and to Gordon Thompson for cartographic skills. Robert Lockhart at the University of Pennsylvania Press has been a superb editor and wonderful conversation partner. I am also grateful to the University of Pennsylvania Press's expert anonymous readers, and to series editor Daniel Richter, who gave tremendously helpful feedback on the full book manuscript and map, and generously shared his own work-in-progress.

Since graduate school, Heather Curtis's companionship on academic and life journeys has been an inestimable gift. Jennifer Trafton, Caroline Braskamp, Tamara McLaughlin, and Cindy Comiso have been lifting my spirits for more than half my life. In Rhode Island, I am surrounded by smart women with a gift for encouragement—Cara Mitnick, Brenda Santos, Shelli Edgar, Lisa Faille, Michelle Baer, Jen Arden, Tracy Keller, Lindsey Tavares, Jessalyn Link; and Ann Huyck, Margrete Jean-Louis, Melissa Hughes, Kristie Puster, Mary Watkins, and Catherine Ford. To my parents, Bill and Meredith Chastain, my siblings Ryan, Alan, and Karen Chastain, my parents-in-law, Bill and Eathel Weimer, my brilliant husband, Ryan, and our ever-inspiring teenage daughters, Annabel and Briella, my unending thanks for love, humor, and snacks. This book is dedicated to my teacher David D. Hall, with heartfelt gratitude for his intellectual vitality and friendship.

* * *

The editors of the *New England Quarterly* and *Early American Literature* have kindly granted permission to use material from Adrian Chastain Weimer, "The Resistance Petitions of 1664–1665: Confronting the Restoration in Massachusetts Bay," *New England Quarterly* 92, No. 2 (June 2019): 221–262; and Adrian Chastain Weimer, "The 'Contynuance of our Civell and Religious Liberties': Plymouth Colonists' 1665 'Humble Addrese' to the King," *Early American Literature* 56, No. 1 (2021): 219–232.